Gaelic-English
English-Gaelic
DICTIONARY

Gaelic-English
English-Gaelic
DICTIONARY

GEDDES & GROSSET

Published 2006 by Geddes & Grosset,
David Dale House, New Lanark, ML11 9DJ

Gaelic–English dictionary compiled by Dougal Buchanan,
English–Gaelic dictionary compiled by RLS Ltd

Pronunciation system devised by
and © Michael Bauer, 2004

Introduction by Michael Bauer

ISBN 10: 1 84205 591 7
ISBN 13: 978 1 84205 591 5

Printed and bound in Poland

POLSKABOOK

Contents

Abbreviations   7

Introduction   9

   1 Using this Dictionary   9

   2 Spelling System and
      Pronunciation   10

   3 Stress   14

   4 Initial Vowels   15

   5 More on Softening (Lenition)   15

Gaelic–English Dictionary   17

English–Gaelic Dictionary   149

Abbreviations

abbrev	abbreviation	*m/f*	a noun, the gender of which may change according to what it names, its case (often the genitive) or its dialect
adj	adjective		
adv	adverb		
anat	anatomy		
arith	arithmetic		
art	article	*milit*	military term
aux	auxiliary	*mus*	music
coll	colloquial term	*n*	noun
comput	computing	*neg*	negative
conj	conjunction	*npl*	plural noun
corres	correspondence	*occas*	occasionally
derog	derogatory	*orthog*	orthography
esp	especially	*part*	particle
excl	exclamation	*pers*	personal
f	noun (feminine)	*phys*	physical
fam	familiar	*pl*	plural
fig	figurative use	*poet*	poetical term
fin	financial	*poss*	possessive
fml	formal	*pp*	present or past participle
govt	government	*pref*	prefix
gram	grammar	*prep*	preposition
imper	imperative	*pron*	pronoun
interj	interjection	*refl*	reflexive
interr	interrogative	*rel*	relative
law	law term	*relig*	religion
ling	linguistics	*sing*	singular
lit	literature, literary	*usu*	usually
m	noun (masculine)	*v*	verb
math	mathematics	*vulg*	vulgar
med	medical		

Introduction

As a pocket dictionary of Gaelic, this publication is a convenient reference for anyone interested in Gaelic. It covers a broad range of terms and phrases for a wide variety of possible applications in both traditional and modern settings.

Gaelic has many sounds foreign to English and its orthography, though highly efficient and regular, is not immediately accessible to the newcomer. This makes the new Pronunciation Guide used in this dictionary particularly useful as a source of information.

There are various places which offer a variety of Gaelic language and cultural courses, both short term or immersion. For courses and more information on either you are best advised to contact either the Gaelic College in Skye (Sabhal Mòr Ostaig, Teanga IV44 8RQ www.smo.uhi.ac.uk) or Stow College in Glasgow (Stow College, 43 Shamrock St., Glasgow G4 9LD www.stow.ac.uk).

But whatever your aims this dictionary offers an intriguing starting point into one of Europe's most fascinating languages.

1 Using this Dictionary

You must bear in mind that Gaelic is an inflecting language and has a process commonly referred to as lenition whereby the first sound of a word is affected by preceding words or particles. People relatively unfamiliar with the language should bear the following points in mind when using this dictionary:

- Lenition manifests itself in the spelling as an <h> inserted after the first consonant of a word. When searching for a word you will find it under its (unlenited) root form by mentally removing the <h>. In the phrase *mo mhàthair* for example, *mhàthair* will be found under *màthair*.
- After certain particles, <h-> is prefixed to a following word. You will find it under its root form without the <h-> (see the following entry for an example).
- Cases often manifest themselves by changing the sound of a final consonant which is shown in the spelling by inserting an <i> before

the last consonant. Words also can add a final -e. Again, terms are listed in their root forms, so in the phrases *dath mo leabhair* and *balla na h-eaglaise*, *leabhair* and *eaglaise* will be found under *leabhar* and *eaglais* respectively.

Some of the less obvious changes are:

a → oi
a → ui
a → i
ea → ei & i
eò → iùi
eu → èi & eòi
io → i
ìo → i
o → ui
ò → ùi.

2 Spelling System and Pronunciation

Written Gaelic undoubtedly looks daunting at first sight with its profusion of vowels, h's and seemingly silent letters. But it is a very efficient tool for spelling the many sounds of Gaelic and much more regular and easy to learn to read than English. Here are just two very important points to help you on your way:

Like many other languages, Gaelic uses two letter combinations to represent certain sounds. Think of English *sip* and *ship* or *far* and *fear*. The same thing happens in Gaelic in a very regular fashion. The most obvious is the insertion of H after a consonant. This is to show that the consonant has been "softened" or "lenited". Thus **m**, pronounced [m] becomes **mh**, pronounced as [v] and so on. Lenition is extremely common in Gaelic and you will come across it all the time.

In most cases, Gaelic has at least two variants of the same consonant. There are two C's, two D's, three L's and so on. In order to spell that without having to use a profusion of symbols, the medieval Gaelic scribes came up with an ingenious way of indicating the pronunciation of a consonant through its environment. This is akin to what happens to G in English *gone* and *gin* for example – only much more regular. A consonant which is flanked by A O or U vowels may be thought of as "normal" (more commonly referred to as "broad" or **leathann** in Gaelic. However, if it is flanked by E and I vowels their pronunciation changes and it becomes "slender" or **caol**. So in many cases these slenderising vowels are not "pronounced" but have the important function of indicating the consonant quality.

One good set of examples are the words *càrn* (meaning a heap) and *ceàrn* (meaning a corner). The only difference in the pronunciation of these two words is in the first C: *càrn* (because it is followed by a broad vowel) is [kārn] and *ceàrn* (because the C is followed by a slender vowel) is [k'ārn] – but there is no E vowel to be heard as such. That is what most of those silent letters are there for.

Below is a guide to the pronunciation used in this dictionary. The first column contains the symbol used, the second an explanation of the sound or how it is made and the third contains the IPA symbol for the sound in question to help those who are familiar with that system.

[a]	an [a] sound with a clear quality like in Scots or Northern English last: **cas** [kas]	a
[ā]	same as [a] only long: **bà** [bā]	a:
[b]	as P in combinations like **sp**it: **cab** [kab]	ƀ
[ch]	as in Scots lo**ch**, or German Ba**ch**. This sound is made by holding your tongue in a K position and squeezing air through a small gap between your tongue and the roof of your mouth: **ach** [ach]	x
[ch']	as in German i**ch**. This sound is like [ch] only a lot more forward at your hard palate: **eich** [ech']	ç
[d]	as T in combinations like **st**ick but with the tip of your tongue touching the base of your teeth: **ad** [ad]	ḏ
[d']	similar to J in **j**ungle, but voiceless. This means that if you put your hand on your adam's apple you feel no vibration while making this sound. It is like the difference between **p**ad (no voicing) and **b**ad (voicing) in English: **diùid** [d' d']	ḏ
[e]	a clear [e] sound like the first vowel in English m**ai**d or Scots they c**a**me: **eich** [ech']	e
[ē]	like [e] only long: **ceum** [kēm]	e:
[ɛ]	as in English m**e**t: **bean** [bɛn]	ɛ
[ɛ̄]	like [ɛ] only long: **mè** [mɛ̄]	ɛ:

11

[ə]	a "neutral vowel" as in English **an**: cas**a**n [kasən]	ə
[f]	as in English: **af** [af]	f
[g]	as K in combinations like skunk: **g**ad [gad]	g̊
[g']	like [g] only a lot more forward at your hard palate: **g**ed [g'ed]	g̊ʲ
[gh]	to make this sound, start by saying GA. Now say it again, but this time allow some air to flow between your tongue and where your tongue touches the roof of your mouth throughout the GA. Now drop the vowel. It is the right sound when you can hold the [gh] without the vowel for more than 5 seconds: **gh**ad [ghad]	ɣ
[gh']	like [gh] only a lot more forward at your hard palate approximating a Y sound: **dh**i [gh'i]	ʝ
[h]	as in English: **sh**on [hon]	h
[ʰ]	a not fully pronounced [h] sound which occurs before P, T, C in the middle or at the end of words in Gaelic but is never written in the spelling (before slender consonants this is pronounced further forward in the mouth): ma**c** [maʰk]	ʰ/ç
[i]	as in English **see**, but a lot shorter: th**i**g [hig']	i
[ī]	as in English **see**: ch**ì** [ch'ī]	i:
[ɪ]	as in English **bid**: à**l**ainn [āLɪN']	ɪ
[k]	as in English: **c**as [kas]	k
[k']	like [k] only a lot more forward at your hard palate: m**i**c [miʰk']	kʲ
[L]	a "dark L". This sound is made by touching the base of your teeth with the tip of your tongue while lowering the back of your tongue (imagine having a large a piece of candy at the back of your mouth) and then making an L sound: **l**ag [Lag]	ɫ
[L']	a "palatal L". This sound is made by squeezing the back of your tongue against the roof of your mouth and then making an L sound. It occurs in Italian meg**l**io or Spanish caba**ll**o: **l**eag [L'eg]	ʎ

12

[l]	as in English: baile [balɪ]	l
[m]	as in English: mac [maʰk]	m
[N]	a "dark N". This sound is made by touching the base of your teeth with the tip of your tongue while lowering the back of your tongue (imagine having a large a piece of candy at the back of your mouth) and then making an N sound: ann [auN]	ṇ
[N']	a "palatal N". This sound is made by squeezing the back of your tongue against the roof of your mouth and then making an N sound. It occurs in Italian signora or Spanish cañon: nì [N']	ɲ
[n]	as in English: cana [kanə]	n
[ng]	similar English ring: long [Lɔung]	ŋg
[o]	a clear [o] sound like in Scottish English so. It occurs in French agneau and German Ohr: bog [bog]	o
[ō]	like [o] only long: bò [bō]	o:
[o]	a so called "unrounded" [o]. This sound is made by putting your mouth into an [o] position and then spreading your lips <u>without</u> moving your tongue (imagine that you are grinning widely while saying [o]): goid [god']	ɤ
[ō]	same as [o] only long: adhbran [ōbran]	ɤ:
[ə]	as in English malt, but a lot shorter: sona [sɔnə]	ɔ
[ɔ̄]	as in English malt: òg [ɔ̄g]	ɔ:
[p]	as in English: pana [panə]	p
[R]	as in Russian erno. This sound is made by producing a rolled R as in Scottish English barrel or Spanish perro while lowering the back of your tongue (imagine having a large a piece of candy at the back of your mouth): bàrr [bāR]	ʀ
[r]	a "tapped R" as in Spanish pero. This sound is made by rapidly tapping the bony ridge behind your teeth with the tip of your tongue once: caran [karan]	ɾ

[r']	as [r] but with the tip of your tongue touching the base of your teeth: mìr [mīr']	ṛ
[s]	as in English but with slightly less lip rounding: san [sən]	s
[š]	as in English ship, but with slightly spread lips: seo [šɔ]	ʃ
[t]	as in English T but with the tip of your tongue touching the base of your teeth: tana [tanə]	t̯
[t']	similar to English chick, but with slightly spread lips: teas [t'es]	t̯ʲ
[u]	as in English you, but a lot shorter: uga [ugə]	u
[ū]	as in English you: cù [kū]	u:
[ɯ]	a so called "unrounded" [u]. This sound is made by putting your mouth into an [u] position and then spreading your lips <u>without</u> moving your tongue (imagine that you are grinning widely while saying [u]). It occurs in Japanese tsuru: uiseag [ɯšag]	ɯ
[ɯ̄]	as [u] only long: aom [ɯ̄m]	ɯː
[v]	as in English veal: bho [vo]	v
[y]	as in English year. This sound is never written in the spelling but occurs after certain slender B P F M sounds: beò [bjɔ̄]	j
[.]	an audible "breaking" of a long vowel into two syllables. These sounds are is best thought of as two separate vowels coming together, somewhat similar to combinations like raw oil in English: ogha [o.ə]	.

3 Stress

In Gaelic, stress generally falls onto the first syllable of a word. In those instances where this is not the case the stressed syllable has been marked in italic print in the phonetic transcription. This mostly happens with certain adverbs and compound nouns e.g. *an-seo* [ənšɔ]

4   Initial Vowels

In Gaelic, words that begin with a vowel have what is called "soft onset" which means that it is not preceeded by a glottal stop (as in the Cockney pronunciation of butter as *bu'er*). Instead they are preceeded by a glide, a bit like a very faint y sound. In some instances this is very audible (for example in word beginning with *eò-* or *iu-*), but generally very weak.

5   More on Softening (Lenition)

It can be very confusing when you are trying to look up a word because softening changes the first sound of a word. Since it is so common in Gaelic, here is a list of how softening changes the spelling and the pronunciation of a sound. Remember that the broadness/slenderness of a consonant depends on the vowels around it. So the spelling inserts H after the consonant and there are two possible pronunciations (broad vs slender).

Spelling	Pronunciation Broad Consonants	Spelling	Pronunciation Slender Consonants
b > bh	[b] > [v]	b > bh	[bj] > [vj]
c > ch	[k] > [ch]	c > ch	[k'] > [ch']
d > dh	[d] > [gh]	d > dh	[d'] > [gh']
f > fh	[f] > silent	f > fh	[f] > silent
g > gh	[g] > [gh]	g > gh	[g'] > [gh']
l > l	[L] > [L]	l > l	[L'] > [l]
m > mh	[m] > [v]	m > mh	[m] > [vj]
n > n	[N] > [n]	n > n	[N'] > [n]
p > ph	[p] > [f]	p > ph	[pj] > [fj]
r > r	[R] > [r]	r > r	[R] > [r]
s > sh	[s] > [h]	s > sh	[š] > [hj]
t > th	[t] > [h]	t > th	[t'] > [hj]

Although softening may seem a rather strange concept at first, it is very common in many languages, even English. It often occurs when a consonant gets stuck between two vowels and "softens" to a weaker consonant or disappears – hence the term Leniton. Think of the German word *Mutter* and the English *mother*, where the T in the middle has weakened to a TH.

There is one difference with Gaelic and the other Celtic languages. Historically this softening does not only happen in the middle of words, but also at the beginning. The reason this is not always obvious today is because in many cases the vowel that caused softening in the first place has been lost. For example, *an fhois* is lenited because thousands of years ago *an* used to be *sinda* – which ended in a vowel and therefore softened the F in *fois*. So it all makes sense in a way.

Gaelic–English Dictionary

A

a [ə] *prep* to. • *rel pron* that. • *poss pron* his/her.

a'[1] [ə] *art* the; of the.

a'[2] *see* **ag**. [ə]

ab [ab] *m* abbot.

abachadh [abəchəgh] *m* ripening.

abaich [abıch'] *adj* mature, ripe. • *v* mature, ripen.

abaichead [abıch'əd] *m* maturity, ripeness.

abaid [abıd'] *f* abbey.

abair [abır'] *v* say.

abair amadan! [abır' amadan] *excl* what a fool!

abairt [abıršd'] *f* phrase, expression.

àbhacas [āvəʰkəs] *m* mirth, ridicule.

àbhachd [āvəchg] *f* humour.

àbhachdach [āvəchgəch] *adj* amusing.

abhag [afag] *f* terrier.

abhainn [avıN'] *f* river.

àbhaist [āvīsd'] *f* custom, habit.

àbhaisteach [āvīsd'əch] *adj* usual.

a-bhàn [əvān] *adv* down.

a-bhon-dè [əvōN'd'ē] *adv* day before yesterday.

a-bhon-raoir [əvōNRoir'] *adv* night before last.

a-bhon-uiridh [əvōNur'ı] *adv* year before last.

a-bhos [əvōs] *adv* over here, hither.

ablach [abLəch] *m* carcase.

abstol [absdəL] *m* apostle.

aca [aʰkə] *prep pron* at them. • *poss pron* their.

acadamh [aʰkədəv] *m* academy.

acaid [aʰkıd'] *f* stabbing pain.

acainn [aʰkıN'] *f* apparatus; tools.

acainneach [aʰkıN'əch] *adj* equipped.

acair [aʰkır'] *f* anchor.

acaire [aʰkır'ə] *f* acre.

acarsaid [aʰkırsəd'] *f* harbour, mooring.

ach [ach] *conj* but.

achadh [achəgh] *m* field.

ach a-mhàin [ach avān] *prep* except, apart from.

a-chaoidh [əchoiy] *adv* always, for ever.

achd [achg] *f* (*politics*) act.

a-chèana [əch'ēnə] *adv* already.

a chèile [ə ch'ēli] *pron* each other.

a chiall! [ə ch'iaL] *excl* good heavens!

a chionn [əch'ūN] *prep* because of.

a chionn is gu [əch'ūN sgə] *conj* because.

achlais [achLıš] *f* armpit.

achlasan [achLasan] *m* armful.

achmhasan [achvəsən] *m* reprimand.

a-chum [əchūm] *prep* for.

a-chum is gu [əchūm sgə] *conj* in order that.

17

a' cnàmh na cìre [ə krāv nə k'īr'ɪ] chewing the cud; mulling things over.

acraich [aʰkrɪch'] v anchor, moor.

acras [aʰkrəs] m hunger.

acrasach [aʰkrəsəch] adj hungry.

actair [agdɛr'] m actor.

a' cur [ə kur] part snowing.

ad [ad] f hat.

adag [adag] f haddock.

adha [a.ə] m liver.

a dh'aindheoin [əghaN'ən] prep in spite of.

a dh'aithghearr [əghach'aR] adv soon.

adhaltraiche [o.əLtrɪch'ə] m adulterer.

adhaltranas [o.əLtrənəs] m adultery.

a dh'aon ghnothach [əghūnə ghro.əch] adv expressly, deliberately.

a dh'aon rùn [əghūnə Rūn] adv expressly, deliberately.

adhar [a.ər] m air, sky.

adharc [o.ərk] f horn.

adharcach [o.ərkəch] adj horned.

a dh'easbhaidh [əgh'ɛsvɪ] adv lacking, needed.

a dh'fhad [əghad] adv long, in length.

a dh'ionnsaigh [əgh'ūNsɪch'] prep to, towards; against.

a dhìth [əgh'ī] adv lacking, required; in short supply.

adhartach [o.əršdəch] adj progressive.

adhartas [o.əršdəs] m progress.

adhbhar [ōvər] m cause, reason.

adhbhar-gàire [ōvərgār'ɪ] m laughing stock.

adhbrann [ōbrəN] f ankle.

a dheòin no a dh'aindeoin [əgh'ōN' nə əghaN'ən] adv willy-nilly.

a dh' fhad [əghad] adv long, in length.

aoradh [ūrəgh] m worship.

a' dol bàs [ə dɔL bās] part dying out.

Afraga [afrəgə] m Africa.

Afraganach [afrəgənəch] m/adj African.

ag, a' [əg] [ə] part introducing pres part.

agad [agəd] prep pron at you (sing)
• poss pron your (sing).

agaibh [agɪv] prep pron at you (pl)
• poss pron your (pl).

againn [agɪN'] prep pron at us. • poss pron our.

agallamh [agəLəv] m interview; conversation.

agam [agəm] prep pron at me. • poss pron my.

ag eudach rithe [əg ēdəch r'i.ə] jealous about her.

àgh [ōgh] m joy; good fortune.

agh [ogh] f heifer.

aghaidh [ō.ɪy] f face; nerve, cheek.

aghaidh-choimheach [ō.ɪcho.ɪch'] f mask.

aghann [oghəN] f frying pan.

a ghaoil! [ə ghūl] excl love! dear!

àghmhor [ōghvər] adj pleasant; joyful.

a ghràidh! [ə ghrāy] excl dear! love!

agus [agəs] conj and.

a h-uile càil [ə hulɪ kāl] everything.

a h-uile duine [ə hulɪ duN'ə] everyone, everybody.

a h-uile sian [ə hulɪ šiən] f everything.

aibidil [abɪd'ɪl] *f* alphabet.

aibidealach [abɪd'əLəch] *adj* alphabetical.

aice [ɛʰk'ı] *prep pron* at her. • *poss
pron* her.

àicheadh [āch'əgh] *m* denial.

àicheadh [āch'əgh] *v* deny.

aideachadh [ad'əchəgh] *m* confession.

aidich [ad'ıch'] *v* confess, own up.

aifrionn [afr'əN] *m* Mass.

aig [ɛg'] *prep* at; in the possession
of.

aig a' cheann thall [ɛg' ə ch'auN
hauL] *adv* in the end, eventually.

aig àmannan [ɛg' auməNən] *adv* at
times.

aig an taigh [ɛg' ən toy] *adv* at
home.

aig baile [ɛg' balı] *adv* at home.

aige [ɛg'ı] *prep pron* at him. • *poss
pron* his.

àigeach [āig'əch] *m* stallion.

aighearach [agh'ərəch] *adj* cheerful, merry.

aighearachd [agh'ərəchg] *f* cheerfulness.

aigne [eg'nı] *f* spirit; mind.

aig Sealbh tha brath! [ɛg' šaLav ha
bra] *excl* Heaven knows!

ailbhinn [alivıN'] *f* flint.

àile [ālı] *m* air, atmosphere.

àileach [āləch] *adj* airy.

aileag [alag] *f* (*with art*) **an aileag** [ə
Nalag] hiccups.

àill [āL'] *f* desire, will.

àillleag [āL'ag] *f* jewel.

àillidh [āL'ı] *adj* shining; beautiful.

aillse [aL'šı] *f* cancer.

aillseag [aL'šag] *f* caterpillar.

ailtire [alt'ır'ə] *m* architect.

ailtireachd [alt'ır'əchg] *f* architecture.

Aimeireaga [amer'əgə] *f* America.

Aimeireaganach [amer'əgənəch]
m/adj American.

aimhreit [air'ıt'] *f* disorder, trouble.

aimhreiteach [air'ıt'əch] *adj* quarrelsome.

aimsir [ɛmɛšır'] *f* weather.

aimsireil [ɛmɛšır'ɛl] *adj* temporal;
climatic.

ain- [aN'] *prefix* un-.

aindheoin [aN'ən] *f* reluctance.

aindheonach [aN'ənəch] *adj* reluctant.

aineach [aN'əch] *adj* (*gram*) imperative.

aineolach air [aN'əLəch ɛr'] *adj* unfamiliar with.

aineolas [aN'əLəs] *m* ignorance.

aingeal [aing'aL] *m* angel.

ainm [ɛnɛm] *m* name.

ainmeachadh [ɛnɛməchəgh] *m*
naming; mentioning.

ainmear [ɛnɛmɛr] *m* noun.

ainmeil [ɛnɛmɛl] *adj* famous.

ainmhidh [ɛnɛvı] *m* animal.

ainmich [ɛnɛmıch'] *v* name; mention.

ainmneach [ɛnɛmN'əch] *adj* (*gram*)
nominative.

ainneamh [aN'ıv] *adj* scarce, rare.

ainneart [aN'əršd] *m* violence.

aintighearn [aN't'ı.ərn] *m* tyrant,
oppressor.

air [ɛr'] *prep* on; about. • *prep pron*
on him, on it (*m*).

air adhart [ɛr' o.əršd] *adv* forwards,
onwards.

air a dheagh dhòigh [ɛr'ə gh'o
ghōy] on good form; chuffed.

air aghaidh [ɛr' ō.ɪy] *adv* forward(s).

air ais [ɛr' ɛš] *adv* back; ago.

air allaban [ɛr' aLəban] *adv* wandering.

air alt is gu [ɛr' aLt sgə] *conj* so that.

air an dùthaich [ɛr' ən dū.ɪch'] *adv* in the country.

air an spot [ɛr' ən sboʰt] *adv* on the spot.

air a phronnadh [ɛr' ə froNəgh] *adv* drunk.

air ball [ɛr' bauL] *adv* immediately.

air banais [ɛr' baniš] *adv* at a wedding.

air beulaibh [ɛr' biaLɪv] *prep* in front of.

air bhàinidh [ɛr' vāN'ɪ] *adv* mad with rage.

air bhog [ɛr' vog] *adv* afloat.

air bhoile [ɛr' volɪ] *adv* furious, raging.

air bith [ɛr' bih] *adv* any at all.

air bòrd [ɛr' bōrd] *adv* aboard, on board.

air chall [ɛr' chauL] *adv* lost.

airchealladh [ɛr'ch'əLəgh] *m* sacrilege.

air chois [ɛr' choš] *adv* up and about.

air choreigin [ɛr' chɔreg'ɪn] *adj* some or other.

air chor is gu [ɛr' chɔr sgə] *conj* so that.

air chrith [ɛr' ch'r'ih] *adv* shaking, shivering.

air chuthach [ɛr' chu.əch] *adv* mad; furious.

air chothrom a [ɛr' chorəm] *conj* able to, fit to.

air corra-biod [ɛr' kɔRəbīd] *adv* on tiptoe.

air cùl [ɛr' kūL] *prep* behind.

air cùlaibh [ɛr' kūLɪv] *prep* behind.

air cumha is gu [ɛr' ku.ə sgə] *conj* on condition that.

àird [ārd'] *f* point, promontory.

air dàir [ɛr' dār'] *adv* on heat, rutting.

àirde [ārd'ɪ] *f* height; (*mus*) pitch.

aire [ar'ɪ] *f* attention.

air deireadh [ɛr' d'era'əgh] *adv* last.

air dheireadh [ɛr' gh'er'əgh] *adv* lagging behind.

air dhòigh is gu [ɛr' ghōy sgə] *conj* so that; in order that.

air dòigh [ɛr' dōy] *adv* in good order.

air do shocair! [ɛr' də hɔʰkɛr'] *excl* steady on! go easy!

air dreach [ɛr' drɛch] *adv* looking like.

air eagal gu [ɛr' egal gə] *conj* lest; for fear that.

àireamh [ār'əv] *f* number.

àireamhair [ār'əvɛr'] *m* calculator.

àireamh fòn [ār'əv fōn] *f* phone number.

air èiginn [ɛr' ēg'iN'] *adv* hardly, barely; with difficulty.

air fad [ɛr' fad] *adv* entirely, completely; all.

air falbh [ɛr' falav] *adv* away, gone.

air feadh [ɛr' fyogh] *prep* throughout, all over.

air fleòdradh [ɛr' flōdrəgh] *adv* floating.

air flod [ɛr' flɔd] *adv* floating, afloat.

airgead [ɛr'ɛg'əd] *m* money; silver.

airgeadach [ɛr'ɛg'ədəch] *adj* well-off, monied.

airgead-pòcaid [ɛr'ɛg'əd pōʰkɪd'] *m* pocket-money.

airgead pronn [ɛr'ɛg'əd prəuN] *m* small change.

airgead ullamh [ɛr'ɛg'əd uLəv] *m* ready money, cash.

air iasad [ɛr' iəsəd] *adv* on loan.

airidh [ar'ɪ] *adj* worthy, deserving.

àiridh [ār'ɪ] *f* shieling.

air iomrall [ɛr' imərəL] *adv* wandering; astray, erring.

air iteig [ɛr' iʰt'ɛg'] *adv* flying, on the wing.

air leth [ɛr' L'eh] *adv* apart; exceptional.

air leth-mhisg [ɛr' L'evišg'] *adv* tipsy.

air leth-shùil [ɛr' L'ehūl] *adv* one-eyed.

air mo aigne [ɛr' meg'nɪ] *adv* on my mind.

air mo aire [ɛr' mar'ɪ] *adv* on my mind.

air mhisg [ɛr' višg'] *adv* drunk.

air mhodh eile [ɛr' vɔgh elɪ] *adv* otherwise, alternatively.

air mo chùram [ɛr' mə chūrəm] *adv* on my mind; under my responsibility.

air mo sgàth [ɛr' mə sgā] *adv* for my sake.

àirneis [ārN'ɪš] *f* furniture.

àirneis-chogaidh [ārN'ɪšchɔgɪ] *m* munitions.

air neo [ɛR N'ɔ] *conj* or else, otherwise.

air sgàth [ɛr' sgā] *prep* on account of, because.

air sgàth is gu [ɛr' sgā sgə] *conj* because.

airson [ɛRsɔn] *prep* for; in favour of. • *conj* in order to.

airson a rèic [ɛRsɔn ə rēʰk'] *adv* sale, for.

air snàmh [ɛr' sNāv] *adj* inundated, flooded.

air stailc [ɛr' sdalk'] *adv* on strike.

air thoiseach air [ɛr' hɔšəch ɛr'] *prep* ahead of.

airtnealach [aršN'əLəch] *adj* sad, weary.

air thuaiream [ɛr' huər'əm] *adv* at random.

air uairean [ɛr' uər'ən] *adv* at times.

air uaireann [ɛr' uər'əN] *adv* occasionally.

air urras [ɛr' uRəs] *adv* on bail.

aiseag [ašəg] *f* ferry.

aiseal [ašaL] *f* axle.

aisean [ašan] *m* rib.

aiseirigh [ašer'ɪ] *f* resurrection; resurgence.

Aisia [ēšə] *f* (*with art*) **an Aisia** [ə N'ēšə] Asia.

Aisianach [ēšənəch] *m/adj* Asian.

aisling [ašling'] *f* dream; vision.

aiste[1] [ašt'ɪ] *f* essay.

aiste[2] [ašt'ɪ] *prep pron* out of her, out of it (*f*).

àite [āʰt'ɪ] *m* place.

àiteach [āʰt'ach] *m* cultivation.

àiteachas [āʰt'əchəs] *m* agriculture.

àite-coise [āʰt'ɪkɔšɪ] *m* pedestrian crossing.

aiteal [aʰt'aL] *m* glimpse.

aiteamh [aʰt'əv] *m* thaw.

àite-còmhnaidh [āʰt'ɪkɔnɪ] *m* dwelling place.

àite-fuirich [āʰt'ɪfur'ɪch'] *m* dwelling place.

àiteigin [āʰt'eg'ɪn] *m* some place or other.

àite-suidhe [āʰt'ɪsui.ɪ] *m* seat, sitting place.

aithghearr [ach'aR] *adj* short; quick; abrupt.

aithghearrachd [ach'aRəchg] *f* short cut. • *adv* **an aithghearrachd** [ən ach'aRəchg] swiftly, sharpish.

aithne [aN'ɪ] *f* acquaintance.

aithnich [aN'ɪch'] *v* know, recognise.

aithreachail [ar'əchal] *adj* repentant.

aithreachas [ar'əchəs] *m* repentance.

aithris [ar'ɪš] *v* recite. • *m* report.

àltich [āʰt'ɪch'] *v* cultivate.

aitreabh [aʰt'r'r'əv] *m* building; dwelling.

àl [āL] *m* litter, young.

àlainn [āLɪN'] *adj* lovely; fine.

a laoigh! [ə Loy] *excl* my love! my dear!

Alba [aLabə] *f* Scotland.

Albais [aLabɪš] *f* Scots language.

Albannach [aLabəNəch] *m/adj* Scotsman, Scot; Scottish.

alcol [aLkɔL] *m* alcohol.

allaban [aLəban] *m* wandering.

allaidh [aLɪ] *adj* wild.

allt [auLt] *m* stream, burn.

alt [aLt] *m* joint; method; (*gram*) article.

altachadh [aLtəchəgh] *m* (*prayer*) grace.

altair [aLtɪr'] *f* altar.

altraim [aLtrəm] *v* foster; nurse.

am[1] *poss* [əm] *poss pron* their.

am[2] [əm] *art* the.

àm [aum] *m* time. • *adv* **aig amannan** [ɛg' aməNən] at times. • **an t-àm a dh'fhalbh** [ən taum ə ghaLav] the past.

a-mach [əmach] *adv* out (*motion*).

a-mach air a' bhus [əmach ɛr' ə vus] *adv* overflowing.

a-mach à seo! [əmach a šə] *excl* get out!

amadan [amadan] *m* (male) fool, silly man.

amaideach [amad'əch] *adj* foolish, silly.

amaideas [amad'əs] *m* foolishness.

a-màireach [əmār'əch] *adv* tomorrow.

amais [amɪš] *v* aim; hit upon.

amaiseach [amɪšəch] *adj* accurate.

amalach [aməLəch] *adj* complicated.

amar [amər] *m* basin; pool.

amar-ionnlaid [aməríūNLɪd'] *m* wash basin.

amar-snàmh [amərsNāv] *m* swimming pool.

am bitheantas [əm bihəntəs] *adv* usually, normally.

am bliadhna [əm bliənə] *adv* this year.

am broinn [əm broiN'] *prep* inside, within.

am bròn [əm brōn] *adv* in mourning.

am feasd [əm fesd] *adv* ever; for ever.

amh [af] *adj* raw; unripe.

amhaich [avɪch'] *f* neck; throat.

a-mhàin [əvāN'] *adv* only.

àmhainn [āvɪN'] *f* oven.

amharas [avərəs] *m* suspicion.

amharasach [avərəsəch] *adj* suspicious, distrustful.

amharc [au.ərk] *m* sight.

am measg [əm mesg] *prep* among.

a-muigh [əmuy] *adv* outside (*location*).

an¹ [ən] *art* the; of the.

an² [ən] *poss pron* their.

an³ [ən] *prep* in.

an-abaich [anabıch'] *adj* unripe; premature.

anabarrach [anabaRəch] *adj/adv* extreme(ly).

an aghaidh [ən ō.iy] *prep* against.

anail [anal] *f* breath.

an ainm an àigh! [ən ɛnɛm ə Nāy] *excl* in Heaven's name!

anainn [anıN'] *f* eaves.

an àite [ən āʰt'ı] *prep* instead of.

a-nall [əNāL] *adv* over here, hither (*motion*).

anam [anam] *m* soul.

ana-mhiann [ana viəN] *m* lust.

an àrd [ən ārd] *adv* up (*motion*).

anart [anəršt] *m* linen.

anart bàis [anəršd bāš] *m* shroud.

an-asgaidh [ənasgı] *adv* free of charge.

an ath bhliadhna [ən ah vliaNə] *adv* next year.

an ath dhoras [ən ah ghorəs] *m* next door.

an ath oidhche [ən ah oi.ch'ı] *adv* tomorrow night.

an ceann [ən k'auN] *prep* (*of time*) in, after.

an ceann a chèile [ən k'auN əch'ēlı] *adv* one after the other, in succession.

an ceartuair [ən k'aršdər'] *adv* just now, presently.

an clàr a aodainn [ən kLār ūdıN'] *adv* full in the face.

an coimeas ri [ən kɔməs r'i] *prep* compared to.

an coinneimh [ən koN'ıv] *prep* towards.

an cois [ən kɔš] *adv* near; accompanying.

an comhair [ən ko.ır'] *prep* in the direction of.

an comhair a chinn [ən ko.ır' ə ch'iN'] *adv* head first.

an comhair a thoisich [ən ko.ır' ə hošıch'] *adv* frontwards.

an-còmhnaidh [ənkōnı] *adv* always, constantly.

an crochadh [ən krɔchəgh] *adv* hanging.

an crochadh air [ən krɔchəgh ɛr'] *prep* depending on.

an cumantas [ən kuməndəs] *adv* commonly, normally.

an dà chuid [ən dā chud'] *pron* both.

an dà latha [ən dā La.a] *m* changed days.

an dàn [ən dān] *adv* destined, ordained.

an dara cuid a no b [ən darə kud' ɛı nɔ bī] either a or b.

an-dè [ənd'ē] *adv* yesterday.

an dèideadh [ən d'ēd'əgh] toothache.

an dèidh [ənd'ē] *prep* after.

an dèidh sin? [ənd'ē šin] *adv* so?

an-diugh [ənd'u] *adv* today.

an dòlas! [ən dōLəs] *excl* woe is me!

an-dràsta [əndrāsdə] *adv* just now.

an-dràsta fhèin [əndrāsdə hēn] *adv* this instant.

an droch-shùil [ən drɔch hūl] *f* the evil eye.

an ear [əN'ɛr] *adv* eastern.

an-earar [əN'ɛrər] *adv* day after tomorrow.

an eisimeil [ən ešımɛl] *adv* dependent (on).

anfhann [anauN] *adj* infirm.

an-fhoiseil [anošɛl] *adj* restless, uneasy.

an impis [ən ĩmpıš] *conj* about to.

an-iochdmhor [an iəchgvər] *adj* merciless, pitiless.

an iomadh-chomhairle [ən iuməghcho.ırlə] in a quandary.

an ìre mhath [ən īr'ı va] *adv* quite, fairly; just about.

an làthair [ən Lā.ır'] *adv* present.

a-nìos [ənıəs] *adv* up (*up from below towards speaker*).

a-nise [əníšı] *adv* now.

an là roimhe [ən La.a Rɔi.ı] *adv* the other day.

an lùib [ən Luib] *prep* involved in/with.

anmoch [anaməch] *adj* late.

ann¹ [auN] *adv* there.

ann² [auN] *prep pron* in him; in it (*m*).

annad [aNəd] *prep pron* in you (*sing*).

annaibh [aNıv] *prep pron* in you (*pl*).

annainn [aNıN'] *prep pron* in us.

annam [aNəm] *prep pron* in me.

ann an [auN ən] *prep* in.

ann an cabhag [auN ən kafag] *adv* in a hurry.

ann an dà-rìreabh [auN ən darīr'əv] *adv* serious, in earnest.

ann an droch staid [auN ən drəch sdad'] *adv* in a bad way.

annas [aNəs] *m* rarity; novelty.

annasach [aNəsəch] *adj* novel; odd.

anns a' bhad [auNs ə vad] *adv* immediately.

anns a' chiad dol-a-mach [auNs ə ch'iad dɔLəmach] in the first instance.

anns an [auNs ən] *prep* in the.

anns an dealachadh [auNs ən d'ɛLəchəgh] *adv* on parting.

annta [auNtə] *prep pron* in them.

a-nochd [əNɔchg] *adv* tonight.

an-raoir [əRūr'] *adv* last night.

an sàs [ən sās] *adv* captured; involved.

an-seo [ənšɔ] *adv* here (*location*).

an-sheo [anə hyɔ] *adv* here (*location*).

an-shin [anə hin] *adv* there (*location*).

an-shiud [anə hid] *adv* there, yonder (*location*).

anshocrach [anahɔʰkrəch] *adj* uneasy.

an-sin [ənšín] *adv* there (*location*).

an-siud [ənšid] *adv* there, yonder (*location*).

an taca ri [ən taʰkə r'i] *prep* compared to, alongside.

an taic ri [ən taiʰk' r'i] *prep* leaning on/against; in comparison with.

an taobh a-muigh [ən tūv əmuy] *m* outside (*location*).

an taobh an ear [ən tūv əN'ɛr] *m* the east.

an taobh an iar [ən tūv əN'iər] *m* the west.

an taobh a-staigh [ən tūv əsdoy] *m* inside.

an taobh sear [ən tūv šɛr] *m* the east.

an taobh siar [ən tūv šiər] *m* the west.

an t-Eilean Sgitheanach [ən t'elansgī.ənəch] *m* (the Isle of) Skye.

an tòir air [ən tōr' ɛr'] *prep* in pursuit of; looking for.

an toiseach [ən tɔšəch] *adv* at first.

an uair a [ə Nuər'ə] *conj* when.

an uairsin [ə Nuər'šin] *adv* then, next.

a-nuas [ənuəs] *adv* down (*down from above towards speaker*).

an-uiridh [ənur'ı] *adv* last year.

a-null [əNūL] *adv* thither; over (*motion*).

a-null thairis [əNūL har'ıš] *adv* abroad, overseas (*motion*).

an urra ri [ən uRə r'ı] *prep* responsible for; in charge of.

aocoltach [ūkɔLtəch] *adj* dissimilar.

aodach [ūdəch] *m* cloth; clothes.

aodach-leapa [ūdəch L'ɛʰpə] *m* bedclothes.

aodach oidhche [ūdəch oi.ch'ı] *m* nightclothes.

aodann [ūdəN] *m* face; hillface.

aodionach [ūd'ənəch] *adj* leaky.

aoibhneach [oivN'əch] *adj* glad.

aoigh [ui] *m* guest; resident.

aoigheachd [ui.chg] *f* hospitality.

aoigheil [ui.ɛl] *adj* generous; hospitable.

aoir [ūr'] *f* satire.

aois [ūš] *f* age.

aol [ūL] *m* lime.

aon [ūn] *adj* one.

aonach [ūnəch] *m* moor, moorland.

aonad [ūnəd] *m* unit.

aona deug [ūnə d'iag] *adj* eleventh.

aonadh [ūnəgh] *m* union.

aonadh-cèaird [ūnəgh k'ārd'] *m* trade union.

aonaich [ūnıch'] *v* unite, combine.

aonaran [ūnəran] *m* hermit; loner.

aonaranach [ūnəranəch] *adj* lonely; desolate.

aon chuid a no b [ūn chud' eı nə bī] either a or b.

aon deug [ūn d'iag] *n* eleven.

aon fhillte [ūn iL't'ı] *adj* uncomplicated.

aon inntinneach [ūn iN'd'ıN'əch] *adj* unanimous.

aonta [ūndə] *m* agreement.

aontaich [ūndıch'] *v* agree.

aosta [ūsdə] *adj* old, aged.

aotrom [ūtrəm] *adj* light; trivial.

aotromaich [ūtrəmıch'] *v* lighten; alleviate.

aotroman [ūtrəman] *m* bladder.

aparan [aʰparan] *m* apron.

ar (n-) [ar] *poss pron* our.

àr [ār] *m* slaughter.

àra [ārə] *f* kidney.

àrach [ārəch] *m* rearing, upbringing.

àrachas [ārəchəs] *m* insurance.

àradh [ārəgh] *m* ladder.

àraich [ārıch'] *v* raise, bring up.

àraid [ārıd'] *adj* particular; peculiar.

àraidh [ārı] *adj* particular; exceptional.

ar-a-mach [arəmach] *m* rebellion, rising.

aran [aran] *m* bread.

ar-aon [ərūn] *adv* both.

arbhar [ara.ər] *m* corn.

àrc [ārk] *f* cork.

Arcach [arkəch] *adj/n* Orcadian.

Arcaibh [arkıv] *m* Orkney.

àrdachadh [ārdəchəgh] *m* promotion; rise.

àrdaich [ārdıch'] *v* raise; increase.

àrdan [ārdan] *m* pride, arrogance.
àrdanach [ārdanəch] *adj* proud, arrogant.
àrd-doras [ārd dɔrəs] *m* lintel.
àrd-easbaig [ārd esbɪg'] *m* archbishop.
àrd-ìre [ārd īr'ɪ] *adj* (*education, etc*) higher, high-level.
àrd mo chlaiginn [ārd mə chLag'ɪN'] *adv* at the top of my voice.
àrd-ollamh [ārdɔLəv] *m* professor.
àrdsgoil [ārdsgɔl] *f* secondary school.
àrd-ùrlar [ārdūrLər] *m* stage, platform.
àrd-urram [ārduRəm] *m* honour, distinction; reverence.
a-rèir [ərēr'] *prep* according to.
a-rèir choltais [ərēr' chɔLtɪš] *adv* seemingly, apparently.
a-rèist [ərēšd'] *adv* in that case.
argamaid [argəmɪd'] *f* argument.
a-riamh [əriəv] *adv* ever.
a-rithist [əri.ɪšd'] *adv* again.
ar leam [ar ləm] *v* I consider.
arm [aram] *m* army.
armachd [araməchg] *f* armour.
armaich [aramɪch'] *v* arm.
arm-lann [aramLəN] *f* armoury.
arsa [arsə] *v* say, says, said.
àrsaidh [ārsɪ] *adj* ancient.
àrsaidheachd [ārsɪ.əchg] *f* archaeology.
àrsair [ārsɛr'] *m* archaeologist.
às [as] *prep* out of, from. • *prep pron* out of him, out of it (*m*).
às a' cheud [as ə ch'iad] *adv* percent.
às a' chumantas [as ə chuməntəs] *adv* out of the ordinary.
asad [asəd] *prep pron* out of you (*sing*).

asaibh [asɪv] *prep pron* out of you (*pl*).
asaid anabaich [asɪd' anabɪch'] *f* miscarriage.
asainn [asɪN'] *prep pron* out of us.
asal [asaL] *f* ass; donkey.
asam [asəm] *prep pron* out of me.
às an amharc [as ən au.ərk] *adv* out of sight.
às an làthair [as ən Lā.ɪr'] *adv* out of sight.
às aonais [as ūnɪš] *prep* without.
as bith cò [əs bi kō] *prep* whoever.
as bith cuine [əs bi kuN'ɪ] *adv* whenever.
as bith dè [əs bi d'ē] *prep* whatever.
às d' aonais [as tūnɪš] without you.
às eugmhais [as ēgɪš] *prep* without.
à sealladh [a šaLəgh] *adv* out of sight.
asgaidh [asgɪ] *f* present, gift.
a shiorraidh! [ə hiəRɪ] *excl* for Heaven's sake!
às leth [as L'e] *prep* on behalf of.
às mo chiall [as mə ch'iaL] *adv* out of my mind.
às mo rian [as mə riən] *adv* out of my mind.
asta [asdə] *prep pron* out of them.
a-staigh [əsdogh'] *adv* in, inside (*location*).
astar [asdər] *m* distance; speed.
a-steach [əsd'ach] *adv* in, inside (*motion*).
a-steach do [əsd'ach dɔ] *prep* into.
as t-fhoghar [əs tovər] *adv* in Autumn.
Astràilia [asdrālia] *f* Australia.
Astràilianach [asdrālianəch] *m/adj* Australian.
as ùr [as ūr] *adv* afresh; anew.

at [aʰt] v swell, puff up. • m swelling.
ataireachd [aʰtər'əchg] f (of sea) swell, surge.
ath [ah] adj next.
àth¹ [āh] f kiln.
àth² [āh] m ford.
ath- [ah] prefix re-.
athair [ahır'] m father; progenitor.
athair-cèile [ahır'kēlı] m father-in-law.
athaireil [ahır'ɛl] adj fatherly.
athaiseach [ahišəch] adj dilatory.
ath-aithris [a har'ıš] v repeat.
a thaobh [ə hūv] prep concerning.
atharrachadh [ahRəchəgh] m change, alteration.
atharraich [ahəRıch'] v change, alter.
atharrais [ahəRıš] v imitate, mimic.
ath-bheòthachadh [ah vyɔ̄.əchəgh] m renaissance.

ath-bheòthaich [ah vyɔ̄.ıch'] v revive.
ath-chruthaich [ah chruhıch'] v recreate.
ath-dhìol [ah gh'iəL] v repay.
ath-leasachadh [ah lesəchəgh] m redevelopment; (with art) **an t-Ath-leasachadh** [ən tah lesəchəgh] the Reformation.
ath-leasaich [ah lesıch'] v redevelop.
ath-nuadhachadh [ah nuəchəgh] m renewal.
ath-nuadhaich [ah nuə.ıch'] v renew.
athraichean [ar'ich'ən] mpl forefathers.
ath-sgrìobh [ah sgrīv] v rewrite.
ath-sgrùdadh [ah sgrūdəgh] m revision.
a thuilleadh air [ə huiL'əgh] prep in addition to.

B

b' àbhaist dhomh [bāvĭšd' ghɔ] v I used to.
bac [baʰk] v prevent; obstruct.
bacach [baʰkəch] adj lame. • m lame person.
bacadh [baʰkəgh] m prevention; obstacle.
bacan [baʰkan] m hobble.
bachall [bachəL] m crozier.
bachlach [bachLəch] adj curly.
bachlag [bachLag] f curl, ringlet.
bachlaich [bachLich'] v curl.
bad [bad] m place; clump.
badan [badan] m thicket.
baga [bagə] m bag; hand-bag.
bagaid [bagıd'] f bunch; cluster.

bagair [bagır'] v threaten.
bagairt [bagıršd'] f threat.
bàgh [bāgh] m bay, cove.
bagradh [bagrəgh] m threat.
bàidh [bāy] f affection; favour.
bàidheil [bāyɛl] adj kindly.
baidhsagal [baisəgəL] m bicycle.
baile [balı] m township, village. • adv **aig baile** [eg' balı] at home.
bailead [baləd] m ballad.
baile beag [balı beg] m village, small town.
baile mòr [balı mōr] m town, city.
baile-margaid [balımaragıd'] m market town.
baile-puirt [balıpuršd'] m sea port.

bàillidh [bāL'ı] *m* bailiff; baillie.
b' àill leam? [baL'əm] *adv* pardon?
bàine [bāN'ı] *adj* whiter, whitest.
bàinead [bāN'əd] *f* whiteness.
bainne [baN'ı] *m* milk.
bainne lom [baN'ı Loum] *m* skimmed milk.
bàirdse [bārd'šı] *f* barge.
bàirlinn [bārlıN'] *f (law)* summons.
bàirneach [bārN'əch] *f* barnacle, limpet.
baist [bašd'] *v* baptise, christen.
Baisteach [bašd'əch] *adj/m* Baptist.
baisteadh [bašd'əgh] *m* baptism.
bàl [bāL] *m (dance)* ball.
balach [baLəch] *m* boy, lad.
balachan [baLəchan] *m* wee boy.
balbh [baLəv] *adj* dumb; speechless.
balbhan [baLavan] *m* dumb person.
balg [baLag] *m* abdomen; blister.
balgair [baLagɛr'] *m* fox; rogue.
balgam [baLagam] *m* sip; swig.
balgan [baLagan] *m* mushroom; toadstool.
balgan-buachair [baLagambuəchır'] *m* edible mushroom.
ball [bauL] *m* organ; member.
balla [baLə] *m* wall.
bàlla [bāLə] *m* ball.
ball-acainn [bauLaʰkıN'] *m* tool.
ballach [baLəch] *adj* speckled, spotted.
ball-airm [bauler'em] *m* weapon.
ball-àirneis [bauLārnıš] *m* piece of furniture.
ballan [baLan] *m* tub.
ball-aodaich [bauLūdıch'] *m* garment.
ball-basgaid [bauLbasgıd'] *m* basketball.

ball-bodhaig [bauLbo.ıg'] *m* bodily organ.
ball-coise [bauLkošı] *m* football.
ball-dòbhrain [bauLdōrɛN'] *m (on skin)* mole.
ball-maise [bauLmaši] *m* ornament.
ball pàrlamaid, BP [bauLpārLəmıd'] *m* member of Parliament, MP.
ballrachd [bauLrəchg] *f* membership.
ball-seirce [bauLšer'k'ı] *m* beauty spot.
ball-stèidhe [bauLšt'ē.ı] *m* baseball.
bàn [bān] *adj* blonde; white; blank; fallow.
bana bhuidseach [bana vud'šəch] *f* witch.
bana charaid [bana charıd'] *f* female friend or relative; *(corres)* **A Bhana-charaid** [ə vana charıd'] Dear Madam.
bana chliamhainn [bana ch'liəvɛN'] *f* daughter-in-law.
ban adhaltraiche [ban ōəLtrıch'ə] *f* adulteress.
bànag [bānag] *f* sea trout.
bana ghaisgeach [bana ghašg'əch] *f* heroine.
banail [banal] *adj* womanly, feminine.
banais [banıš] *f* wedding.
Ban Albannach [ban aLabəNəch] *f* Scotswoman.
banaltram [banaLtrəm] *f* nurse.
bana mhaighistir-sgoile [bana vaišd'ır' sgolı] *f* school-mistress.
bana phrionnsá [bana friuNsə] *f* princess.
banarach [banarəch] *f* milkmaid, dairymaid.
banca [bankə] *m* bank.

bancair [bankɛr'] *m* banker.

bancaireachd [bankır'əchg] *f* banking.

bàn-dhearg [bāngh'ɛrag] *adj* light red.

ban dia [ban d'ia] *f* goddess.

ban diùc [ban d'ūʰk] *f* duchess.

bàn-ghorm [bānghərəm] *adj* pale blue.

ban ìompaire [ban īmpər'ə] *f* empress.

ban leòmhann [ban L'ɔ̄.əN] *f* lioness.

bann [bauN] *m* strip; bandage.

banntach [bauNdəch] *m* hinge.

banntrach [bauNdrəch] *f* widow(er).

ban ogha [ban o.ə] *f* grand-daughter.

bànrigh [bānri] *f* queen.

ban rùnaire [ban rūnər'ə] *f* (female) secretary.

baoghalta [bö.əLtə] *adj* stupid.

baoghaltachd [bö.əLtachg] *f* stupidity.

baoit [böʰt'] *f* (fishing) fly, bait.

baoiteag [böʰt'ag] *f* (fishing) fly, bait.

baoth [böh] *adj* foolish, simple.

bàr [bār] *m* (hotel, etc) bar.

barail [baral] *f* opinion.

baraille [barıL'ı] *m* barrel.

bàrd [bāRd] *m* poet, bard.

bàrdachd [bāRdachg] *f* poetry.

bàrr [bāR] *m* top; cream; crop.

Barrach [baRəch] *m/adj* Barra person, from Barra.

barrachd [baRəchg] *f* surplus; more.
 • *prep* **barrachd air** [baRəchg ɛr'] more than. • *adv* **a bharrachd** extra, in addition, **a bharrachd air sin** [ə vaRəchg ɛr' šin] moreover.

barragach [baRagəch] *adj* creamy.

Barraigh [baRay] *m* Barra.

barrall [baRəL] *m* shoelace.

barrantas [baRantəs] *m* pledge, guarantee.

bàrr na teangaidh [bāR nə t'ɛngı] *m* tip of the tongue.

bas [bas] *f* palm.

bàs [bās] *m* death.

bàsaich [bāsıch'] *v* die.

bas-bhualadh [bas vuəLəgh] *m* applause.

basgaid [basgıd'] *f* basket.

bàsmhor [bāsvər] *adj* mortal; deadly.

bàsmhorachd [bāsvərəchg] *f* mortality.

bata [baʰtə] *m* stick.

bàta [bāʰtə] *m* boat.

bata-coiseachd [baʰtəkošəchg] *m* walking stick.

bàta-aisig [bāʰtašıg'] *m* ferry.

bàta-ràmh [bāʰtəRāv] *m* rowing boat.

bàta-sàbhalaidh [bāʰtəsāvəLı] *m* lifeboat.

bàta-siùil [bāʰtəšūl] *m* sailing boat.

bàta-smùide [bāʰtəsmūd'ı] *m* steamer.

bàta-teasairginn [bāʰtət'ɛsır'g'ıN'] *m* lifeboat.

bàth [bā] *v* drown; muffle.

bàthach [bāhəch] *f* byre, cow-shed.

bathais [bahıš] *f* forehead; impudence.

bathar [bahər] *m* goods, merchandise.

bàthte [bāʰt'ı] *adj* drowned.

bàta-iasgaich [bāʰtıəsgıch'] *fishing* boat.

beach [byach] *m* bee; wasp.

beachd [byachg] *m* idea; opinion.
beachdail [byachgal] *adj* abstract.
beachd-smaoinich,
  [byachgsmūnıch'] *v* meditate.
beachlann [byachLəN] *m* beehive.
beag [beg] little by little.
beagan [began] *adv* a bit, slightly.
  • *m* a little; few.
beag-nàrach [beg nārəch] *adj*
  shameless.
bealach [byaLəch] *m* pass, col; detour.
bealaidh [byaLı] *m* broom.
Bealltainn [byauLtıN'] *f* May Day,
  Beltane.
bean[1] [bɛn] *f* wife.
bean[2] [bɛn] *v* touch, meddle with.
bean- [bɛn] *prefix* woman-, female.
bean an taighe [bɛnəntɛhı] **bean-
  taighe** [bɛntɛhı] *f* housewife;
  landlady.
bean-bainnse [bɛnbaıN'šı] *f* bride.
bean-eiridinn [bɛner'ıd'ıN'] *f* nurse.
bean-ghlùine [bɛnghLūN'ı] *f* midwife.
beannachadh [byaNəchəgh] *m* be-
  atification; greeting.
beannachd [byaNəchg] *f* blessing;
  regards.
beannachd leibh! [byaNəchg loiv]
  excl goodbye!
beannaich [byaNıch'] *v* bless.
beannaich do [byaNıch' də] *v* greet.
beannaichte [byaNıch't'ə] *adj*
  blessed.
bean phòsda [bɛn fɔ̄sdə] *f* married
  woman, Mrs.
bean ri [bɛn r'ı] *v* brush against.
bean-shìthe [bɛnhī.ı] *f* fairy woman.
bean-taighe *see* **bean an taighe**.
  [bɛn tɛhı]

bean-teagaisg [bɛn t'ɛgıšg'] *f* (female) teacher.
bean uasal [bɛnuəsəL] *f* noblewom-
  an; (*fml*) **a Bhean uasal!** [ə
  vɛnuəsəl] *excl* Madam! (*corres,
  fml*) Dear Madam.
beàrn [byārn] *f* gap; notch.
beàrnan-brìde [byārnanbr'īd'ı] *f*
  dandelion.
Beàrnarach [byārnərəch] *m* Bern-
  eray person.
Beàrnaraigh [byārnəray] *f* Bern-
  eray.
beàrr [byāR] *v* shave; shear.
bearradair [byaRədɛr'] *m* barber.
beart [byaRšd] *f* machine.
beartach [byaRšdəch] *adj* rich,
  wealthy.
beartas [byaRšdəs] *m* riches,
  wealth.
beart-fhighe [byaRšdí.ı] *f* loom.
beatha [bɛhə] *f* life.
beathach [bɛhəch] *m* animal.
beathach-mara [bɛhəchmarə] *m*
  sea-creature.
beathaich [bɛhıch'] *v* feed; maintain.
beatha-eachdraidh [bɛhɛchdrı] *f*
  biography.
beic [beʰk'] *f* curtsey.
Beilg [belig'] *f* (*with art*) **a' Bheilg** [ə
  velig'] Belgium.
Beilgeach [belig'əch] *m/adj* Bel-
  gian.
being [being'] *f* bench.
beinn [beiN'] *f* ben, mountain.
Beinn Nibheis [beiN'íviš] *f* Ben Ne-
  vis.
beinn-teine [beiN't'ɛnı] *f* volcano.
beir [ber'] *v* irreg bear; give birth
  to.

beir air [bɛr' ɛr'] v seize; overtake.

beir air làimh air [bɛr' ɛr' lāiv ɛr'] v shake hands with.

beirm [ber'im] f yeast.

beò [byɔ] adj alive, living.

beò-ghlacadh [byō ghLaʰkəgh] m obsession.

beòshlaint [byōLand'] f livelihood.

beothaich [byō.ıch'] v revive; liven up.

beothail [byō.al] adj lively, active.

beothalachd [byō.əLəchg] f vivacity.

beuc [biaʰk] m roar, bellow. • v roar, bellow.

beud [bēd] m harm, loss.

beul [biaL] m mouth.

beul a bhith [biaL ə vi] adv about to be.

beul-aithris [biaLahr'ıš] f oral tradition.

beulchar [biaLchər] adj plausible, smooth-talking.

beul ìochdair [biaL īachgɛr'] m lower lip.

beul-oideachas [biaLod'achəs] f lore.

beul ri [biaL r'i] prep nearly.

beul uachdair [biaL uachgɛr'] m upper lip.

beum [bēm] m stroke; blow.

beum-grèine [bēmgrēnı] m sunstroke.

Beurla [byōRLə] f (often with art) a' **Bheurla** [ə vyōRLə] English.

beusach [bēsəch] adj modest; well-behaved.

beus-eòlas [bēsyōLəs] m ethics.

bha [vā] past tense of v **bith**

bhàrr [vāR] ~ [far] prep off, down from.

bha spòrs agam [va sbōrs agəm] v I enjoyed myself/had fun.

Bhèineas [vēnəs] f Venus.

bheir [ver'] future tense of v **thoir**

bho see **o**.

bhòt [vɔʰt] v vote.

bhuaibh see **uaibh**

bhuainn see **uainn**

bhuaipe see **uaipe**

bhuaithe see **uaithe**

bhuam see **uam**

bhuapa see **uapa**

bhuat see **uat**

bhur see **ur**

biadh [biəgh] m food; meal.

biadhlann [biəLəN] m refectory, canteen.

bian [bian] m fur, hide.

biast [biəsd] f beast.

biastail [biəsdal] adj bestial.

biath [biəh] v feed; fodder.

bìd[1] [bīd'] v bite.

bìd[2] [bīd'] m chirp.

bideag [bīd'ag] f fragment, crumb.

bidse [bid'šı] f bitch. • excl a **bhidse!** [ə vid'šı] sod it!

bile[1] [bilı] f lip, rim.

bile[2] [bilı] m (politics) bill.

bileag [bilag] f petal; (commerce) bill.

binid [binıd'] f rennet.

binn[1] [bīN'] adj sweet.

binn[2] [bīN'] f judgement; sentence.

binnean [biN'an] m peak.

binneas [biN'əs] m sweetness.

bìoball [bībəL] m bible.

bìoballach [bībəLəch] adj biblical.

biodach [bidəch] adj tiny; trifling.

biodag [bidag] f dirk, dagger.

bìog [biəg] f chirp. • v cheep, chirp.

biolar [byɔLər] *f* cress.

biona [binə] *f* bin.

biona-stùir [binə sdūr'] *f* dustbin.

bior [bir] *m* point; prickle.

biorach [birəch] *adj* sharp, pointed.

bioran [biran] *m* a pointed stick.

biorra-crùidein [biRəkrūd'ɛN'] *m* kingfisher.

bior-ròstaidh [biRōsdɪ] *m* (*cooking*) spit.

biotais [biʰtɪš] *m* beet.

bìrlinn [bīrlɪN'] *f* galley, birlinn.

bith[1] [bih] *f* existence, being. • *v* be.

bìth[2] [bīh] *f* tar, pitch.

bith- [bi] *prefix* ever-.

bith bheò [bih vyō] *adj* ever-living, immortal.

bith bhuan [bih vuən] *adj* eternal, everlasting.

bitheanta [bihəndə] *adj* frequent, common.

bitheantas [bihəndəs] *m* frequency.

bith-eòlas [bih yōLəs] *m* biology.

bithis [bi.ɪš] *f* screw.

bithiseach [bi.ɪšəch] *adj* spiral.

blais [bLaš] *v* taste.

blàr [bLār] *m* plain; battle(field).

blas [bLas] *m* flavour; accent.

blasad [bLasəd] *m* taste.

blasad bìdh [bLasəd bī] *m* bite to eat.

blasaich [bLasɪch'] *v* flavour.

blasmhor [bLasvər] *adj* full of flavour.

blasta [bLasdə] *adj* tasty.

blàth[1] [bLā] *m* bloom, blossom.

blàth[2] [bLā] *adj* warm; affectionate.

blàthaich [bLā.ɪch'] *v* warm.

blàth-chridheach [bLā ch'r'ī.əch] *adj* warm-hearted.

blàths [bLās] *m* warmth.

bleideag [bled'ag] *f* flake.

bleith [bleh] *v* grind, pulverise.

bleoghainn [blɔ.ɪN'] *v* milk.

bliadhna [bliənə] *f* year.

bliadhnach [bliənəch] *adj* yearling.

bliadhnail [bliənal] *adj* annual, yearly.

bliadhna-leum [bliənəlēm] *f* leap year.

bliadhna ùr [bliənə ūr] *f* new year.

blian [blian] *v* sunbathe.

bloigh [bLɔy] *f* half.

bloighd [bLɔid] *f* fragment, splinter.

bloinigean-gàraidh [bLɔN'ɪg'angāri] *m* spinach.

blonag [bLɔnag] *f* lard.

bò [bō] *f* cow.

bò-bhainne [bōvaN'ɪ] *f* milk cow.

bobhla [bouLə] *m* bowl.

boc [bɔʰk] *m* billy goat; roebuck.

bòc [bɔʰk] *v* swell, bloat.

bòcan [bōʰkan] *m* apparition; bogyman.

boc-earba [bɔkɛrabə] *m* roe-buck.

bochd [bɔchg] *adj* poor; unfortunate; poorly.

bochdainn [bɔchgɪN'] *f* poverty; misfortune.

bogsa [bɔgsə] *m* box.

bogsa ciùil [bɔgsə k'ūl] *m* accordion.

bogsa fòn [bɔgsə fōn] *m* phonebox.

bocsair [bɔʰksɛr'] *m* boxer.

bogsa litrichean [bogsə Liʰt'r'ɪch'ən] *m* letterbox.

bod [bɔd] *m* penis.

Bòd [bōd] *m* Bute.

bodach [bɔdəch] *m* old man, old guy.

Bodach na Nollaig [bɔdəch nə NɔLɛg'] *m* Santa Claus.

bodach-ròcais [bɔdəchRɔ̄ʰkɪš] *m* scarecrow.

bodach-sneachda [bɔdəchšN'ɛchgə] *m* snowman.

bodhaig [bo.ɪg'] *f* body.

bodhair [bo.ɪr'] *v* deafen.

bodhar [bo.ər] *adj* deaf. • *m* deaf person.

bòdhran [bō.ran] *m* bodhran.

bodraig [bɔdrɪg'] *v* bother, trouble.

bog[1] [bɔg] *adj* soft; tender. • *v* soak, steep.

bog[2] [bɔg] *v* bob, dip.

bogadaich [bɔgədɪch'] *f* bouncing, bobbing.

bogaich [bɔgɪch'] *v* soften.

bog fliuch [bɔg fluch] *adj* soaking wet.

bogha [bo.ə] *m* bow; curve.

bogha-frois [bo.əfrɔš] *m* rainbow.

boglach [bɔgLəch] *f* bog.

bòid [bōd'] *f* oath; swearing.

Bòideach [bōd'əch] *m/adj* from Bute.

bòidhchead [bōich'əd] *f* beauty.

bòidheach [bōi.əch] *adj* pretty, beautiful.

boile [bɔlɪ] *f* madness; frenzy.

boillsg [bɔL'šg'] *m* flash; gleam. • *v* flash; glitter, shine.

boillsgeach [bɔLšg'əch] *adj* gleaming; glittering.

boinne [bɔN'ɪ] *f* drop.

boinneag [bɔN'ag] *f* droplet.

boireann [bɔr'əN] *adj* female, feminine.

boireannach [bɔr'əNəch] *m* woman, female.

boireannaich [bɔr'əNɪch'] *mpl* womenfolk.

boireannta [bɔr'əNdə] *adj* effeminate.

boiseag [bɔšag] *f* slap; palmful.

boladh [bɔLəgh] *m* smell.

bò-laoigh [bōLuy] *f* in-calf cow.

bolgan [bɔLɔgan] *m* bulb.

boltrach [bɔLtrəch] *m* smell; perfume.

boma [bɔmə] *m* bomb.

bonaid [bɔnɪd'] *f* bonnet, cap.

bonaid bhiorach [bɔnɪd' virəch] *f* Glengarry (bonnet).

bonn [bouN] *m* base; coin.

bonnach [bɔNəch] *m* bannock; scone.

bonnach uighe [bɔNəch ui.ɪ] *m* omelette.

bonn airgid [bouN ɛr'ɛg'ɪd'] *m* coin; silver medal.

bonn còmhraidh [bouN kōrɪ] *m* chat.

bonn cuimhne [bouN kuiN'ɪ] *m* medal.

bonn-dubh [bouNdu] *m* heel.

borb [bɔrɔb] *adj* wild, barbarous.

borbair [bɔrɔbɛr'] *m* barber.

bòrd [bōrd] *m* board; table.

bòrd-ceadachaidh [bōrdk'edəchɪ] *m* licensing board.

bòrd-dàmais [bōrdāmɪš] *m* draught board.

bòrd-dubh [bōrdu] *m* blackboard.

bòrd-geal [bōrdgّaL] *m* whiteboard.

bòrd-iarnaigidh [bōrdiərnɪg'ɪ] *m* ironing board.

bòrd-sgrìobhaidh [bōrdsgrīvɪ] *m* desk.

bòrd slàinte [bōrdsLāN'd'ɪ] *m* health board.

bòstail [bōsdal] *adj* boastful.

botal [bɔʰtəL] *m* bottle.

botal teth [bɔʰtəL t'e] *m* hotwater bottle.

bòtann [bɔ̄ʰtəN] *m* boot, wellie.

bothan [bɔhan] *m* cottage; she-been.

bothan àiridh [bɔhan ār'ı] *m* sheiling bothy.

bracaist [braʰkıšd'] *f* breakfast.

brach [brach] *v* ferment; (*boil, etc*) gather.

brachadh [brachəgh] *m* fermentation; pus.

bradan [bradan] *m* salmon.

brag [brag] *m* bang.

bragail [bragal] *adj* boastful.

braich [braich'] *f* malt.

braid [brad'] *f* theft, thieving.

bràigh[1] [brāy] *m* upper part; upland.

bràigh[2] [brāy] *m* captive; hostage.

bràighdeanas [brāid'ənəs] *m* captivity.

braidhm [broim] *m* fart.

braisead [brašad] *f* impetuosity.

bràiste [brāšd'ı] *f* brooch.

bràmair [brāmır'] *m* girlfriend.

branndaidh [brauNdı] *f* brandy.

braoisg [brūšg'] *f* grin; grimace.

braoisgeil [brūšg'ɛl] *adj* grinning.

braon [brūn] *v* drizzle. • *m* drop;.

bras [bras] *adj* hasty; bold.

brat [braʰt] *m* cover; mat; cloak.

bratach [braʰtəch] *m* banner, flag.

brath[1] [brah] *v* betray; inform on.

brath[2] [brah] *m* knowledge; advantage.

bràth [brāch] *m* judgement; **gu bràth tuilleadh** [gə brāch tuL'əgh] *adv* (*with neg v*) never again.

brathadair [brahədɛr'] *m* betrayer.

brathadh [brahəgh] *m* betrayal.

bràthair [brāhır'] *m* brother.

bràthair-athar [brāhır'ahar] *m* uncle.

bràthair-cèile [brāhır'k'ēlı] *m* brother-in-law.

bràthair-màthar [brāhır'māhar] *m* uncle.

brat-leapa [braʰtL'ɛʰpə] *m* bedcover, coverlet.

brat-ùrlair [braʰtūrLır'] *m* carpet.

breab [br'eb] *v* kick. • *m* kick.

breabadair [br'ebədɛr'] *m* weaver; daddy-long-legs.

breac[1] [br'ɛʰk] *adj* speckled, variegated.

breac[2] [br'ɛʰk] *m* trout.

breacadh-seunain [br'ɛʰkəghšianɛN'] *m* freckles.

breacag [br'ɛʰkag] *f* bannock.

breacan [br'ɛʰkan] *m* plaid, tartan cloth.

breacanach [br'ɛʰkanəch] *adj* tartan.

breac bhallach [br'ɛʰk vaLəch] *adj* freckled.

breac-òtraich [br'ɛʰkɔ̄ʰtrıch] *f* (*with art*) **a' bhreac-òtraich** [ə vr'ɛʰkɔ̄ʰtrıch] chicken pox.

buinneach [buN'əch] *f* (*with art*) **a' bhuinneach** [ə vuN'əch] diarrhoea.

brèagha [br'ia.ə] *adj* fine, lovely.

Breatannach [br'eʰtəNəch] *m/adj* Briton; British.

breice [br'eʰk'ı] *f* brick.

breicire [br'eʰk'ır'ə] *m* bricklayer.

brèid [br'ēd'] *m* kerchief; patch.

brèid shoithichean [br'ēd' ho.ıch'ən] *m* dishcloth.

brèige [br'ēg'ı] *adj* deceitful; artificial.

breisleach [br'ešləch] *m* confusion; delirium.

breislich [br'ešlıch'] *v* talk irrationally.

breith[1] [br'e] *f* birth.

breith[2] [br'e] *f* decision; sentence.

breith anabaich [br'e anabıch'] *f* abortion.

breithnich [br'enıch'] *v* judge; assess.

breug [br'iag] *f* lie.

breugach [br'iagəch] *adj* lying.

breugaire [br'iagər'ə] *m* liar.

breug-riochd [br'iag riəchg] *m* disguise.

breun [br'ēn] *adj* putrid, corrupt.

briathar [br'iəhər] *m* term.

briathran [br'iəhrən] *mpl* statements, words.

briathran teicneolach [br'iəhrən teʰk'N'ɔLəch] *mpl* technical terms.

brìb [br'īb] *v* bribe. • *f* bribe.

brìgh [br'ī] *f* meaning; essence; energy.

brìghmhor [br'īvər] *adj* pithy; energetic.

briogais [br'igıš] *f* trousers, breeches.

briosgaid [br'isgıd'] *f* biscuit.

bris [br'iš] *v* break, smash.

briseadh [br'išəgh] *m* break, fracture.

briseadh-cridhe [br'išəghkrī.ı] *m* heartbreak.

briseadh-dùil [br'išəghdūl] *m* disappointment.

briseadh-latha [br'išəghLa.a] *m* daybreak.

brisg [br'išg'] *adj* crisp; brittle.

briste [br'išd'ı] *adj* broken, smashed.

britheamh [br'ihəv] *m* judge.

broc [broʰk] *m* badger.

brochan [brochan] *m* porridge.

brod [brɔd] *v* drive on; encourage. • *m* goad, prod.

bròg [brōg] *f* shoe, boot.

broilleach [brɔL'əch] *m* bosom, chest.

broinn [brɔiN'] *f* interior.

bròn [brōn] *m* sadness, sorrow.

brònach [brōnəch] *adj* sad, sorrowful.

brosnachadh [brɔsnəchəgh] *m* encouragement.

brosnachail [brɔsnəchal] *adj* encouraging.

brosnaich [brɔsnıch'] *v* encourage; arouse.

brot [brɔʰt] *m* soup, broth.

broth [brɔh] *m* rash.

brù [brū] *f* womb; belly; bulge.

bruach [bruəch] *f* (*river, etc*) bank.

bruadair [bruədır'] *v* dream.

bruadar [bruədər] *m* dream.

brùchd [brūchg] *v* burst out; belch. • *m* belch.

brù-dhearg [brūgh'ɛrag] *m* robin.

bruich [brich'] *v* cook; boil. • *adj* cooked; boiled.

bruicheil [brich'ɛl] *adj* sultry.

brùid [brūd'] *m* brute; beast.

brùidealachd [brūd'əLəchg] *f* brutality.

brùideil [brūd'ēl] *adj* brutal.

bruidhinn [bri.ıN'] *v* talk, speak. • *f* talk, talking.

bruidhinn ri [bri.ıN' r'i] *v* talk to.

bruidhneach [briN'əch] *adj* talkative, chatty.

bruis [bruš] *f* brush.

bruis-aodaich [bruš ūdıch'] *f* clothes brush.

bruis-fhiaclan [bruš iəʰkLən] *f* toothbrush.

bruisig [brušıg'] *v* brush.

brùite [brūʰt'ı] *adj* bruised; oppressed.

brùth [brūh] *v* bruise; shove.

bruthach [bru.əch] *m* bank, slope.

bruthainneach [bru.ıN'əch] *adj* sultry.

bu, b' [bə] *v* was, were; would be.

buachaille [buəchəL'ı] *m* cowherd.

buachailleachd [buəchəL'əchg] *f* cattle herding.

buachaillich [buəchəLıch] *v* herd cattle.

buachar [buəchər] *m* cowdung.

buadh [buəgh] *f* quality, virtue.

buadhair [buəghɛr'] *m* adjective.

buadhmhor [buəvər] *adj* effective; successful.

buaic [buəʰk'] *f* wick.

buaidh [buəy] *f* victory; success; influence.

buail [buəl] *v* hit.

buail a-steach [buəl əšd'ach] *v* call in, drop in.

buail bas [buəl bas] *v* applaud.

buaile [buəlı] *f* sheepfold.

buailteach [buəlt'əch] *adj* liable, apt to.

buain [buəN'] *f* reaping, harvest(ing).

buair [buər'] *v* upset; tempt.

buaireadh [buər'əgh] *m* temptation.

buaireas [buər'əs] *m* anxiety; confusion.

buaireasach [buər'əsəch] *adj* troublesome.

bualadh [buəLəgh] *m* blow.

buan [buən] *adj* lasting, durable.

buannachd [buəNəchg] *f* profit, advantage.

buannaich [buəNıch] *v* win.

buar [buər] *m* herd.

bucaid [buʰkıd'] *f* bucket.

bucas [buʰkəs] *m* box.

bu chiatach orm [bə ch'iəʰtəch ərəm] *v* I should.

bu chòir dhomh [bə chōr' ghə] *v* I ought, I should.

bugair [bugır'] *m* bugar.

buideal [bud'aL] *m* bottle.

buidhe [bui.ı] *adj* yellow; lucky.

buidheach [bui.əch] *adj* thankful, grateful.

buidheachas [bui.əchəs] *m* gratitude.

buidheagan [bui.agan] *f* yolk.

buidheann [bui.əN] *m* group; firm.

buidheann-cluich [bui.əNkLuch'] *m* playgroup.

buidheann-obrach [bui.əNəbrəch] *m* working party.

buidheann-òigridh [bui.əNɔ̃ig'r'ı] *m* youth club/group.

buidheann-strì [bui.əNsdr'ĩ] *m* pressure group.

buidhe-ruadh [bui.ı ruəgh] *adj* auburn.

buidhinn [bui.ıN'] *v* win.

buidhre [buir'ı] *f* deafness.

buidseach [bud'šəch] *m* wizard.

bùidsear [būd'šɛr] *m* butcher.

buige [buig'ı] *f* softness; moistness.

buil [bul] *f* consequence; conclusion.

buileach [buləch] *adv* completely, quite.

buileann [buləN] *f* loaf.

builgean [bulig'an] *f* bubble.

builgeanach [bulig'anəch] *adj* bubbly.

builich air [bulıch' ɛr'] *v* bestow upon.

buill a' chuirp [buL' ə chuir'p] *mpl* parts of the body.

buille [buL'ı] *f* blow; emphasis; (*mus*) beat.

buille cridhe [buL'ı krī.ı] *f* heartbeat.

buill-ghineamhain [buL'gh'inəvɛN'] *mpl* genitals.

buin do [buN' də] *v* belong to; be related to.

buinnig [buN'ıg'] *v* win.

buin ri [buN' r'i] *v* interfere with.

buinteanas [buN'd'ənəs] *m* links, relationship.

buirbe [bur'ibı] *f* barbarity, wildness.

bumailear [bumalɛr] *m* oaf; no-user.

bun [bun] *m* base, bottom, foot.

bunait [bunat'] *f* foundation, fundamentals.

bunaiteach [bunat'əch] *adj* stable; fundamental(ist).

bunasach [bunəsəch] *adj* radical.

bun-dealain [bun d'alɛN'] *m* power point.

bun-os-cionn [bunɔsk'ūN] *adv* upside down.

bun-sgoil [bunsgɔl] *f* primary school.

buntàta [buntā^htə] *m* potato(es).

buntàta pronn [buntā^htə prɔuN] *m* mashed potato(es).

bùrach [būrəch] *m* mess, guddle.

bùrn [būrn] *m* water (*Lewis dialect*).

burraidh [buRı] *m* fool, blockhead.

bus[1] [bəs] *m* bus.

bus[2] [bus] *m* mouth; grimace, pout.

bùth [bū] *f* shop.

bùth-chungaidh [bū chungı] *f* pharmacist's.

bùth-èisg [bū ēšg'] *f* fish shop.

C

cab [kab] *f* gob.

cabach [kabəch] *adj* talkative.

cabadaich [kabədıch'] *f* chatter.

cabaireachd [kabır'əchg] *f* chatter.

càball [kābəL] *m* cable.

cabar [kabər] *m* rafter, pole; caber.

cabar droma [kabər drɔmə] *m* ridge pole.

cabar fèidh [kabər fēy] *m* deer's antlers.

cabhag [kafag] *f* haste.

cabhagach [kafagəch] *adj* hurried, hasty.

cabhlach [kauLəch] *m* fleet.

cabhsair [kausɛr'] *m* pavement, causeway.

cabstair [kabsdɛr'] *m* horse's bit.

cac [ka^hk] *v* defecate. • *m* excrement.

càch [kāch] *pron* other people, the others.

càch a chèile [kāch ə ch'ēlı] *pron* each other.

cadal [kadəL] *m* sleep.

cadalach [kadəLəch] *adj* sleepy.

cafaidh [kafı] *f* café.

cagailt [kagılt'] *f* hearth, fireside.

cagainn [kagıN'] *v* chew.

cagair [kagır'] *v* whisper.

cagar [kagər] *m* whisper; secret.

caibe [kaibı] *m* spade; mattock.

caibeal [kaibəL] *m* chapel.

caibideal [kabıd'ɛl] *m* chapter.

caibideal a h-aon [kabɪd'ɛl əhūn] chapter one.

caidil [kad'ɪl] *v* sleep.

caidil gu math! [kad'ɪl gə ma] *excl* sleep well!

càil¹ [kāl] *f* desire; appetite.

càil² [kāl] *m* thing.

cailc [kalk'] *f* chalk.

caileag [kalag] *f* girl, lassie.

caill [kaɪL'] *v* lose; miss.

caill do rian [kaɪL' də rían] *v* go out of your mind.

cailleach [kaL'əch] *f* old woman; wifie; hag.

cailleach dhubh [kaL'əch ghu] *f* nun.

cailleach-oidhche [kaL'əchoí.ch'ɪ] *f* owl.

caill mùn [kaɪL' mūn] *v* wet oneself.

caillte [kaɪL'tɪ] *adj* lost.

caillteach [kaɪL't'əch] *adj* ruinous.

càil sam bith [kāl səm bi] *m* anything at all.

càin¹ [kāN'] *v* scold.

càin² [kāN'] *f* duty, levy.

cainb [kanib] *f* hemp.

caineal [kanaL] *m* cinnamon.

cainnt [kaɪN'd'] *f* speech, language.

caiptean [kabd'ɛn] *m* captain, skipper.

càir [kār'] *v* repair.

càirdeach do [kārd'əch də] related to.

càirdean [kārd'ən] *mpl* friends; relations.

càirdeas [kārd'əs] *m* friendship; kinship.

càirdeas fola [kārd'əs fɔLə] *m* blood relationship.

càirdeil [kārd'ɛl] *adj* friendly.

càirdineal [kārd'ɪnaL] *m* cardinal.

càireas [kār'əs] *m* (*in mouth*) gum(s).

cairgein [karig'ɛN'] *m* carrageen.

cairt¹ [karšt'] *v* tan (leather); muck out.

cairt² [karšt'] *f* card; chart.

cairt³ [karšt'] *f* cart.

cairt-bhòrd [karšd'vōrd] *m* cardboard.

cairt-chluiche [karšd'chLuch'ɪ] *f* playing card.

cairteal [karšd'aL] *m* quarter.

cairteal na h-uarach [karšd'aL nə huərəch] *m* quarter hour.

cairt-iùil [karšd'iūl] *f* navigation chart.

cairt-Nollaig [karšd'nɔLɛg'] *f* Xmas card.

cairt-phuist [karšd'fušt'] *f* postcard.

càise [kāšɪ] *m* cheese.

caise [kašɪ] *f* abruptness; impetuosity.

caisg [kašg'] *v* abate; prevent.

Càisg [kāšg'] *f* (*with art*) **a' Chàisg** [ə chāšg'] Easter.

caismeachd [kašməchg] *f* alarm; march.

caisteal [kašdaL] *m* castle.

càite? [kāt'ɪ] *interrog adv* where?

caith [kah] *v* wear; spend; consume; waste.

caitheamh [kahəv] *m* (*with art*) **a' chaitheamh** [ə chahəv] tuberculosis.

caithte [kaʰt'ɪ] *adj* worn-out; consumed.

caithteach [kaʰt'əch] *adj* wasteful.

Caitligeach [kaʰtlɪgəch] *m/adj* Catholic.

càl [kāL] *m* cabbage, kale.

cala [kaLə] *m* harbour.

càl-colaig [kāL kɔLɛg'] *m* cauli-flower.

calg [kaLag] *m* prickle.

calg-dhìreach [kaLaggh'īr'əch] *adv* completely.

calg-dhìreach an aghaidh [kaLaggh'īr'əch ən ō.ɪ] *adv* dead against.

call [kauL] *m* loss; waste.

calla [kaLə] *adj* tame, domesticated.

callaich [kaLɪch'] *v* tame, domesticate.

callaid [kaLɪd'] *f* fence; hedge.

calltainn [kauLtɪN'] *m* hazel.

calma [kaLamə] *adj* stout; sturdy.

calman [kaLaman] *m* dove, pigeon.

calpa[1] [kaLapə] *m* (*leg*) calf.

calpa[2] [kaLpə] *m* (*fin*) capital.

cam [kaum] *adj* bent, curved.

camachasach [kama chasəch] *adj* bow-legged.

camag [kamag] *f* curl, ringlet; bracket.

camagach [kamagəch] *adj* curled, curly.

caman [kaman] *m* shinty stick.

camanachd [kamanəchg] *f* shinty.

camara [kamara] *m* camera.

camas [kaməs] *m* bay.

càmhal [kā.əL] *m* camel.

camhanaich [kavanɪch'] *f* dawn, twilight.

campa [kampə] *m* camp.

campaich [kampɪch'] *v* camp.

can [kan] *v* say.

cana [kanə] *m* tin, can.

canabhas [kanavəs] *m* canvas.

canach [kanəch] *m* bog cotton.

can air [kan ɛr'] *v* say for.

cànan [kānan] *m* language, tongue.

cànanach [kānanəch] *adj* linguistic.

canastair [kanəsdɛr'] *m* tin, can, canister.

Canadach [kanadəch] *m/adj* Canadian.

can ri [kan r'i] *v* call.

caochail [kūchal] *v* change, alter; die.

caochladh [kūchLəgh] *m* change, alteration.

caochlaideach [kūchLɪd'əch] *adj* changeable, fickle.

caog [kūg] *v* blink; wink.

caogad [kūgad] *m* fifty.

caoidh [kūy] *v* lament, weep; mourn.

caol [kūL] *adj* narrow; thin. • *m* strait, kyle.

caolan [kūLan] *m* gut, intestine.

caol an droma [kūL ən drɔmə] *m* small of the back.

caol an dùirn [kūL ən dūrN'] *m* wrist.

caolas [kūLəs] *m* strait, kyle(s).

Caolas Bòideach [kūLəs bōd'əch] *m* Kyles of Bute.

caol na coise [kūL nə kɔši] *m* ankle.

caol-shràid [kūLrād'] *f* vennel, alley.

caon [kūn] *adj* wily.

caomh [kūv] *adj* dear, beloved.

caomhain [kūvɛN'] *v* save, economise.

caora [kūrə] *f* sheep, ewe.

caorann [kūrəN] *f* rowan.

car[1] [kar] *m* turn; stroll; trick. • *as adv* a bit, somewhat.

car[2] [kar] *prep* during, for.

càr [kār] *f* car.

carabhaidh [karavɪ] *m* boyfriend.

carach [karəch] *adj* wily; unreliable.

carachd [karəchg] *f* wrestling.

caractar [karaktər] *m* (*play, etc*) character.

càradh [kārəgh] *m* repair; state, condition.

caraich [karɪch] *v* move.

càraich [kārɪch] *v* repair.

caraiche [karɪch'ə] *m* wrestler.

caraid[1] [karɪd'] *m* friend, relative; (*corres*) **A Charaid** [ə charɪd'] Dear Sir; **A Chàirdean** [ə chārd'ən] Dear Sirs.

càraid[2] [kārɪd'] *f* pair; twins.

càraid phòsda [kārɪd' fɔsdə] *f* married couple.

car a' mhuiltein [kar ə vult'ɛN'] *m* somersault.

caran [karan] *adv* a bit, slightly.

carbad [karabəd] *m* vehicle; carriage; craft.

carbad-eiridinn [karabəder'ɪd'ɪN'] *m* ambulance.

cargu [kargu] *m* cargo.

càrn [kārn] *v* pile up; accumulate.
• *m* heap; cairn; hill.

càrnaid [kārnɪd] *f* carnation.

càrnan [kārnan] *m* cockroach.

càrn-cuimhne [kārnkuiN'ı] *m* monument.

càrr [kārn] *f* dandruff.

carragh [kaRəgh] *m* rock; stone pillar.

carraig [kaRɛg'] *f* rock.

carson? [karson] *interrog adv* why?

carson a chiall? [kəRson ə ch'iaL] *excl* why on earth?

cartadh [karšdəgh] *m* mucking out.

carthannas [karhəNəs] *m* kindness; charity.

cas[1] [kas] *f* foot; leg; handle.

cas[2] [kas] *adj* steep; impetuous;.

càs [kās] *m* difficulty, predicament.

casad [kasəd] *m* cough.

casadaich [kasədɪch'] *v* cough.

casa-gobhlach air [kasagoLəch ɛr'] *prep* astride.

casaid [kasɪd'] *f* complaint; accusation.

cas-chrom [kaschrəum] *f* footplough.

casgadh [kasgəgh] *m* prevention.

casgair [kasgɛr'] *v* slay, massacre.

casgairt [kasgɪršd'] *f* slaughter, butchery.

casgan [kasgan] *m* brake.

casg-gineamhainn [kasginəvɪN'] *m* contraception; contraceptive.

cas-lom [kasLəum] *adj* barefoot, barelegged.

cas-ruisgte [kasrŭšg't'ı] *adj* barefoot, barelegged.

cas toisich [kas tošɪch'] *f* foreleg.

cat [kaht] *m* cat.

cat fiadhaich [kaht fiə.ich'] *m* wildcat.

cath [kah] *m* battle; warfare.

càth [kāh] *f* chaff.

cathadh [kahəgh] *m* snowdrift.

cathag [kahag] *f* jackdaw.

cathair [kahɪr'] *f* chair; city.

cathair-chuibhle [kahɪr'chuĭlı] *f* wheelchair.

cathair-eaglais [kahɪr'ɛgLɪš] *f* cathedral.

cath-bhuidheann [kahvui.əN] *f* batallion.

cead [k'ed] *m* permission; permit, licence.

ceadach [k'edəch] *adj* tolerant.

ceadachail [k'edəchal] *adj* permissive.

ceadaich [k'edɪch'] *v* permit, allow.

ceadaichte [k'edɪch't'ı] *adj* allowed.

cairt-shiubhail [karšt'*híu*.al] *m* passport.

cead dràibhidh [k'ed drãivɪ] *m* driving licence.

cead telebhisein [k'ed televišɛN'] *m* television licence.

ceàird [k'ãrd] *f* trade, craft.

cealg [k'aLag] *f* deceit; hypocrisy.

cealgach [k'aLagəch] *adj* deceitful; hypocritical.

cealgair [k'aLagɛr'] *m* deceiver, cheat; hypocrite.

cealla [k'aLə] *f* (*biol*) cell.

ceanalta [k'anəLtə] *adj* pretty, comely.

ceangail [k'ɛ.al] *v* tie; join.

ceangal [k'ɛ.əL] *m* connection; bond.

ceann [k'auN] *m* head; end.

ceannach [k'aNəch], **ceannachd** [k'aNəchg] *m* purchase, buying, shopping.

ceannaich [k'aNɪch'] *v* buy.

ceannaich air dhàil [k'aNɪch' ɛr' ghãl] *v* buy on credit.

ceannaiche [k'aNɪch'ə] *m* purchaser; merchant.

ceannard [k'aNərd] *m* leader; chief.

ceann-cinnidh [k'auN k'iN'ɪ] *m* clan chief.

ceann daoraich [k'auN dūrɪch'] *m* hangover.

ceann-feadhna [k'auN fyoghnə] *m* clan chief.

ceann goirt [k'auN gɔršd'] *m* sore head, headache.

ceann-làidir [k'auN Lãd'ɪr'] *adj* headstrong.

ceann-pholan [k'auN fəLan] *m* tadpole.

ceann-rùisgte [k'auN Rūšg't'ɪ] *adj* bareheaded.

ceannsaich [k'auNsɪch'] *v* conquer; control; tame.

ceannsal [k'auNsəL] *m* authority.

ceannsalach [k'auNsəLəch] *adj* authoritative.

ceann-simid [k'auN šimɪd'] *m* tadpole.

ceann-suidhe [k'auN sui.ɪ] *m* president.

ceann-uidhe [k'auN ui.ɪ] *m* destination.

ceap[1] [k'ɛʰp] *m* block; lump.

ceap[2] [k'ɛʰp] *m* cap.

ceapach [k'ɛʰpəch] *m* (garden) plot, bed.

ceapaire [k'ɛʰpər'ə] *m* sandwich.

cearb [k'ɛrab] *f* rag; defect.

cearbach [k'ɛrabəch] *adj* clumsy; ragged.

cearc [k'ɛrk] *f* hen.

cearcall [k'ɛrkəL] *m* circle, ring.

cèard [k'ẽrd] *m* tinker, smith.

cèardach [k'ẽrdəch] *f* smithy.

cèard-airgid [k'ẽrd ɛr'ɛg'id'] *m* silversmith.

cèard-umha [k'ẽrd u.ə] *m* coppersmith.

ceàrn [k'ãrn] *m* corner; district.

ceàrnach [k'ãrnəch] *adj* square.

ceàrnag [k'ãrnag] *f* square.

ceàrr [k'ãR] *adj* wrong; left.

ceàrraiche [k'ãRɪch'ə] *m* gambler.

ceart [k'aršt] *adj* correct; just; same.

ceartachadh [k'aršdəchəgh] *m* correction; marking.

ceartaich [k'aršdɪch'] *v* correct; put right.

ceartas [k'aršdəs] *m* justice.

ceart gu leòr [k'aršd gə L'ōr] *adv* right enough; okay!

ceart-mheadhan [k'aršd vian] *m* dead centre.

ceart-uilinn [k'aršd ulıN'] *f* right angle.

ceasnachadh [k'esnəchəgh] *m* questioning; questionnaire.

ceasnaich [k'esnıch'] *v* question; interrogate.

ceathach [k'ehəch] *m* fog; vapour.

ceathrad [k'erəd] *m* forty.

ceathramh [k'erəv] *adj* fourth. • *m* quarter.

ceathrar [k'erər] *m* foursome.

cèic [k'ēʰk'] *f* cake.

cèidse [k'ēd'šı] *f* cage.

ceil (air) [k'el ɛr'] *v* hide, conceal (from).

cèile [k'ēlı] *m* spouse; counterpart.

cèilidh [k'ēlı] *m* visit; ceilidh.

ceileir [k'elır'] *v* sing sweetly, warble.

ceilp [k'elp] *f* kelp.

Ceilteach [k'elt'əch] *m/adj* Celt; Celtic.

ceimig [k'emıg'] *f* chemical substance.

ceimigeachd [k'emıgəchg] *f* chemistry.

ceimigear [k'emıgɛr] *m* chemist.

cèin [k'ēn] *adj* foreign; faraway.

cèir [k'ēr'] *f* wax.

cèir-chluaise [k'ēr'chLuəšı] *f* ear wax.

cèis [k'ēš] *f* frame; envelope.

cèiseag [k'ēšag] *f* cassette.

ceist [k'ešd'] *f* question; problem; point.

ceisteachan [k'ešd'əchən] *m* questionnaire.

ceistear [k'ešd'ɛr] *m* questioner; question master.

Cèitean [k'ēʰt'an] *m* (*with art*) an **Cèitean** [ən k'ēʰt'an] May.

ceithir [k'ehır'] *m/adj* four.

ceò [k'ō] *m* mist; haze; smoke.

ceòl [k'ōL] *m* music.

ceòladair [k'ōLədər'] *m* musician.

ceòl beag [k'ōLbeg] *m* light music for the pipes.

ceòlmhor [k'ōLvər] *adj* musical; melodious.

ceòl mòr [k'ōLmōr] *m* classical pipe music, pibroch.

ceòthach [k'ōhəch] *adj* misty.

ceud [k'iəd] *m* hundred.

ceudameatair [k'iədəmɛtɛr'] *m* centimetre.

ceudamh [k'iədəv] *adj* hundredth.

ceud mìle fàilte! [k'iəd mīlı fālt'ı] *excl* a hundred thousand welcomes!

ceudna [k'iadnə] *adj* same.

ceud taing! [k'iəd taing'] *excl* many thanks! thanks a lot!

ceum [k'ēm] *m* step; pace; degree.

ceum air cheum [k'ēm ɛr' ch'ēm] *adv* step by step.

ceumnachadh [k'ēmnəchəgh] *m* graduation.

ceumnaich [k'ēmnıch'] *v* graduate.

ceumnaiche [k'ēmnıch'ə] *m* graduate.

ceus[1] [k'ēs] *v* crucify.

ceus[2] [k'ēs] *m* suitcase.

ceusadh {k'ēsəgh] *m* crucifixion.

cha, chan [cha] [chan] *part negating the clause or sentence.*

cha bheir mi hò-rò-gheallaidh air . . . [cha vɛr' mi hō rō gh'aLı ɛr'] I don't give a toss for . . .

cha b' urrainn dhomh gun . . . [cha buRıN' ghə gən] I couldn't help.

chaidh [chay] *past tense of v* **rach.**

chaidh agam air [chay agəm ɛr'] *v* I managed it.

cha mhòr [cha vōr] *adv* nearly.

cha mhòr nach [cha vōr nach] *conj* almost.

chan *see* **cha.** [chan]

chan fhada thuige! [chan ad huig'ı] it won't be long!

chan iongnadh e! [chaN' iənəch ɛ] no wonder!

cha leig thu leas . . . [cha L'eg' u les] *v* you don't need to.

chì [ch'ī] *future tense of v* **faic.**

cho [chə] *adv* so, as.

cho luath is . . . [chə Luəs] *conj* as soon as . . .

cho math sin [chə ma šin] *adv* that good, as good as that.

chuala [chuəLə] *past tense of v* **cluinn.**

chuca *see* **thuca.**

chugad *see* **thugad.**

chugaibh *see* **thugaibh.**

chugainn *see* **thugainn.**

chugam *see* **thugam.**

chuice *see* **thuice.**

chuige *see* **thuige.**

chun [chun] *prep* to, towards, up to.

chun an-seo [chun ə šə] *adv* up to now, so far.

chunnaic [chuNık'] *past tense of v* **faic.**

ciad [k'iad] *adj (with art)* **a' chiad** [ə ch'iad] the first.

ciad-fhuasgladh [k'iaduəsgləgh] *m* first aid.

ciall [k'iaL] *f* sense(s); meaning.

ciallach [k'iaLəch] *adj* sensible.

ciallaich [k'iaLıch] *v* mean.

ciamar? [k'imər] *interrog adv* how?

cia mheud? [k'e viad] *interrog adv* how many? how much?

cian [k'ian] *adj* distant; long. • *m* distance; remoteness.

cianail [k'ianal] *adj* sad.

cianalach [k'ianaləch] *adj* homesick.

cianalas [k'ianaLəs] *m* sadness.

ciar [k'iər] *adj* dark; swarthy; dun.

ciatach [k'iətəch] *adj* pleasant; attractive.

cidhe [k'ı.ı] *m* quay.

cidsin [k'id'šın] *m* kitchen.

cileagram [k'iləgram] *m* kilogram.

cilemeatair [k'iləmɛʰtɛr'] *m* kilometre.

cill [k'īL'] *f* cell; church; kirkyard.

cineal [k'inaL] *m* race; species.

cinn [k'īN'] *v* grow; multiply.

cinneadail [k'iN'ədal] *adj* clannish.

cinneadh [k'iN'əgh] *m* clan; people; surname.

cinneas [k'iN'əs] *m* growth.

cinne-daonna [k'iN'ı dūNə] *m (with art)* **an cinne-daonna** [ən k'iN'ı dūNə] mankind.

cinnt [k'īN'd'] *f* certainty.

cinnteach [k'īN'd'əch] *adj* certain; confident.

ciobair [k'ībɛr'] *m* shepherd.

cìoch [k'īəch] *f* breast.

ciochag [k'īəchag] *f* valve.

ciomach [k'iməch] *m* prisoner; detainee.

cion [k'in] *m* lack; desire.

cionta [k'ində] *m* guilt; guilty action.

ciontach [k'indəch] *adj* guilty. • *m* guilty person; offender.

ciontaich [k'indɪch'] *v* commit an offence.

ciora [k'irə] *f* pet sheep.

ciorram [k'iRəm] *m* disability, handicap.

ciorramach [k'iRəməch] *adj* disabled, handicapped. • *m* disabled person; (*pl with art*) **na ciorramaich** [nə k'iRəmɪch'] the disabled.

ciotach [k'iʰtəch] *adj* left-handed.

cipean [k'iʰpan] *m* stake; tether post.

cìr [k'īr'] *v* comb. • *f* comb; cud.

cìrean [k'īr'an] *m* (*of hen, etc*) comb, crest.

cìr-mheala [k'īr'vyaLə] *f* honeycomb.

cìs [k'īš] *f* tax; taxation.

cìs-chusbainn [k'īščhusbɪN'] *f* customs duty.

cìs-chinn [k'īšch'iN'] *f* poll tax.

cìs-oighreachd [k'īšoír'əchg] *f* inheritance tax.

ciste [k'išt'ɪ] *f* (*furniture*) chest.

ciste-chàir [k'išt'ɪchār'] *f* car boot.

ciste-laighe [k'išt'ɪLai.ɪ] *f* coffin.

ciste-urrais [k'išt'uRɪš] *f* trust fund.

ciùb [k'ūb] *m* cube.

ciùbach [k'ūbəch] *adj* cubic.

ciùbhran [k'ūran] *m* drizzle, shower.

ciudha [k'u.ə] *f* queue.

ciùin [k'ūN'] *adj* gentle; quiet; calm.

ciùineas [k'ūN'əs] *m* calm, calmness.

ciùinich [k'ūN'ɪch'] *v* quieten, calm down.

ciùraig [k'ūrɪg'] *v* (*bacon, etc*) cure.

ciùrr [k'ūR] *v* hurt; torture.

ciùrrte [k'ūRt'ɪ] *adj* hurt, injured.

clabar-snàimh [kLabər sNāiv] *m* flipper.

cill-mhanach [k'īL'vanəch] *m* cloister.

clach [kLach] *v* stone. • *f* stone; (*fam*) testicle.

clachach [kLachəch] *adj* stony.

clachair [kLachɛr'] *m* (stone-)mason.

clachan [kLachan] *m* village; kirktown; kirkyard.

clach-bhalg [kLachvaLag] *f* (*toy, etc*) rattle.

clach-chuimhneachan [kLachchuiN'əchan] *f* memorial, monument.

clach-ghràin [kLachghrāN'] *f* granite.

clach-mheallain [kLachvyaLɛN'] *f* hailstone.

clach na sùla [kLach nə sūLə] *f* eyeball.

clach uasal [kLach uəsəL] *f* precious stone.

cladach [kLadəch] *m* shore, beach.

cladh [kLogh] *m* kirkyard, cemetery.

cladhaich [kLo.ɪch'] *v* dig.

cladhaire [kLo.ər'ə] *m* coward.

cladhaireach [kLo.ər'əch] *adj* cowardly.

clag [kLag] *m* bell.

clagarsaich [kLagərsɪch'] *f* clinking; rattling.

clag-rabhaidh [kLagRavɪ] *m* alarm bell.

claidheamh [kLai.əv] *m* sword.

claidheamhair [kLai.əvɛr'] *m* swordsman.

claidheamh caol [kLai.əv kūL] *m* rapier.

claigeann [kLag'əN] *m* skull.

clàimhean [kLāivan] *m* latch.

clais [kLaš] *f* ditch; furrow.

claisneachd [kLašnəchg] *f* hearing.

clamhan [kLavan] *m* buzzard.

clann [kLauN] *f* children; clan.

clann-nighean [kLauN'i.an] *f* (*collective*) girls.

claoidh [kLuy] *v* exhaust; vex.

claoidhte [kLuit'ɪ] *adj* exhausted.

claon [kLūn] *v* incline; go astray; pervert. • *adj* awry; oblique; perverse.

claonadh [kLūnəgh] *m* slant, slope; squint; perversion.

clàr [kLār] *m* board; table; record.

clàraich [kLārɪch'] *v* record.

clàr-amais [kLāramɪš] *m* index.

clàr-aodainn [kLārūdɪN'] *m* brow, forehead.

clàr-dùthcha [kLārdúchə] *m* map.

clàr-fhiacail [kLāríəʰkɪl] *f* incisor.

clàr-gnothaich [kLārgrɔ.ɪch'] *m* agenda.

clàr-innsidh [kLāríšɪ] *m* table of contents.

clàr-oideachais [kLārod'əchɪš] *m* curriculum.

clàrsach [kLārsəch] *f* harp; Celtic harp, clarsach.

clàrsair [kLārsɛr'] *m* harper.

clàr-tìde [kLārt'íd'ɪ] *m* timetable.

clas [kLas] *m* class.

clasaigeach [kLasɪgəch] *adj* classical.

cleachd [klachg] *v* use; accustom.

cleachdadh [klachgəgh] *m* habit; practice.

cleachte ri [klachtɪ r'i] *adj* accustomed to, used to.

cleas [kles] *m* feat; trick.

cleasachd [klesəchg] *f* conjuring; juggling.

cleasaiche [klesɪchə] *m* actor; comic; conjurer.

cleas-chluich [kleschLuich'] *f* comic film/play.

clèir [klēr'] *f* clergy; Presbytery.

clèireach [klēr'əch] *m* clergyman; clerk. • *m/adj* Presbyterian.

clèireachail [klēr'əchal] *adj* clerical.

cleòc [klɔʰk] *m* cloak.

clì [klī] *adj* left.

cliabh [kliav] *m* pannier; creel; (*anat*) chest.

cliamhainn [klia.ɪN'] *m* son-in-law.

cliath [kliah] *v* (*agric*) harrow. • *f* grate, bars; harrow.

cliathach [kliahəch] *f* side, flank.

cliath-theine [kliahenɪ] *f* fire grate.

cliath-uinneig [kliauN'ɛg'] *f* window bars.

clìomaid [klīmɪd'] *f* climate.

clis [kliš] *adj* nimble.

cliseachd [klišəchg] *f* nimbleness, agility.

clisg [klišg'] *v* start, jump; startle.

clisgeach [klišg'əch] *adj* jumpy, on edge; timid.

clisgeadh [klišg'əgh] *f* start, fright.

clisgear [klišg'ɛr] *m* exclamation.

clisg-phuing [klišg'fuing'] *f* exclamation mark.

cliù [klū] *m* fame; reputation.

cliùiteach [klūʰt'əch] *adj* famous, celebrated.

cliùthaich [klū.ɪch'] *v* praise.

clò¹ [kLɔ̄] *m* cloth; tweed.

clò² [kLɔ̄] *m* print; printing press.

clòbha [kLɔ̄və] *f* clove.

clobha [kLou.ə] *m* tongs.

clòbhar [kLɔ̄bər] *m* clover.

clobhsa [kLɔusə] *m* (*in tenement, etc*) close.

clò-bhuail [kLɔ̃vuəl] v print.

clò-bhuailte [kLɔ̃vuəlt'ı] adj printed.

clò-bhualadair [kLɔ̃vuəLədɛr'] m printer(s).

clò-bhualadh [kLɔ̃vuəLəgh] m printing; publication.

clò-chadal [kLɔ̃chadaL] m doze, dozing.

clochar [kLɔchər] f convent.

clogaid [kLɔgıd'] f helmet.

clòimh [kLɔ̃y] f wool.

clòimhteachan [kLɔ̃it'əchan] m eiderdown.

Clò Mòr na Hearadh [kLɔ̃mɔ̃r nə herəgh] m Harris Tweed.

closach [kLɔsəch] f carcase.

clòsaid [kLɔ̃sıd'] f closet.

clò-sgrìobh [kLɔ̃sgrīv] v type.

clò-sgrìobhadair [kLɔ̃sgrīvədɛr'] m typewriter.

clò-sgrìobhadh [kLɔ̃sgrīvəgh] m typing; typescript.

clò-sgrìobhaiche [kLɔ̃sgrīvıch'ə] m typist.

cluain [kLuaN'] f meadow, pasture.

cluaineas [kLuaN'əs] m retirement.

cluaran [kLuəran] m thistle.

cluas [kLuəs] f ear; handle.

cluasag [kLuəsag] f pillow.

cluas-fhàinne [kLuəsāN'ı] f earring.

club [kLub] m club.

clùd [kLūd] m rag; cloth.

cluich [kLuch'] m play; game. • v play.

cluich-bùird [kLuch'būrd'] m board game.

cluicheadair [kluch'ədɛr'] m player; actor.

cluinn [kLuiN'] v hear.

cnag [krag] v crunch; bang, knock. • f bang, knock.

cnag-aodaich [kragūdıch'] f clothes peg.

cnag-dealain [kragd'ɛLɛN'] f electric plug.

cnag na cùise [krag nə kūšı] f the crux of the matter.

cnàimh [krāiv] m bone.

cnàimh an droma [krāiv ən drəmə] m the spine, the backbone.

cnàimheach [krāivəch] m skeleton.

cnàimhseag [krāivšag] f acne; blackhead.

cnàimh-slinnein [krāivšliN'ɛN'] f shoulder-blade.

cnàimh-uga [krāivugə] m collarbone.

cnàmh [krāv] v chew; digest.

cnàmhach [krāvəch] adj bony.

cnàmh a' chìr [krāv ə ch'ı̄r'] v chew the cud.

cnap [krahp] m block; lump, knob.

cnapach [krahpəch] adj lumpy, nobbly.

cnap-starra [krahp sdaRə] m stumbling block.

cnatan [krahtan] m (often with art) cold, tha an cnatan orm [ha ən krahtan ɔrəm]I have a cold; an cnatan mòr [ən krahtan mɔ̃r] m influenza.

cnead [kr'ed] m groan.

cnèadaich [kr'iadıch'] v caress; stroke.

cneutag [kr'iahtag] f small ball, puck.

cnò [krɔ̃] f nut.

cnoc [krɔhk] m hill.

cnocach [krɔhkəch] adj hilly.

cnocan [krɔhkan] m hillock.

cnò-challtainn [krɔ̃chauLtıN'] m hazelnut.

cnò-Fhrangach [krōrangəch] *m* walnut.

cnò-thalmhainn [krōhaLavıN'] *m* peanut.

cnuas [kruəs] *v* chew; ponder.

cnuimh-thalmhainn [kruivhaLavıN'] *f* earthworm.

co- [kə] *prefix* co-.

cò? [kō] *interrog pron* who? which?

cò aca [kō aʰkə] *conj* whether.

co-aimsireil [kə.ɛmɛšırɛl] *adj* contemporary.

cò air bith? [kō ɛr' bi] *interrog pron* whoever?

co-dhalta [kəghaLtə] *m* foster brother/sister

cò am fear? [kō əm fɛr] which one?

co-aoiseach [kə.ūšəch] *m/adj* contemporary.

co-aontaich [kə.ūntıch'] *v* agree.

cò às? [kō as] *adv* where from?

cobhair [kə.ır'] *f* help; relief.

cobhair orm! [kə.ır' ərəm] *excl* help! help me!

cobhar [kə.ər] *m* foam.

co-bhuail [kəvuəl] *v* collide.

còc [kōʰk] *m (fuel)* coke.

còcaire [kōʰkər'ə] *m* cook, chef.

còcaireachd [kōʰkər'əchg] *f* cookery.

cochall [kəchəL] *m* husk; hood.

co-cheangail [kəch'e.al] *v* tie together; connect.

co-cheangailte [kəch'e.alt'ı] *adj* linked together.

co-chomann [kəchoməN] *m* commune; co-operative.

co-chòrd [kə chōrd] *v* agree mutually.

co-chothrom [kə chəRəm] *m* balance, equilibrium.

co-chruinnich [kə chruiN'ıch'] *v* assemble.

co-chruinneachadh [kəchruiN'əchəgh] *m* assembly; collection.

còco [kōʰkə] *m* cocoa.

co-dhèanta [kə gh'iantə] *adj* put together.

co-dhiù [kogh'ū] *conj* whether.

co-dhiù [kogh'ū] *adv* anyway; at least.

co-dhlùthaich [kə ghLū.ıch'] *v* condense.

co-dhùin [kədhūN'] *v* conclude; end.

co-dhùnadh [kəghūnəgh] *m* conclusion; end.

co-èigneachadh [kə.ēg'r'əchəgh] *m* compulsion.

co-èignich [kə.ēg'r'ıch'] *v* compel.

cofaidh [kəfı] *m* coffee.

co-fharpais [kə.arpıš] *f* competition.

co-fharpaiseach [kə.arpıšəch] *m* competitor.

co-fhlaitheas [kə.Laihəs] *m* commonwealth.

co-fhreagair [kə.regır'] *v* match; correspond.

co-fhulangach [kə.uLəngəch] *adj* sympathetic.

co-fhulangas [kə.uLəngəs] *m* sympathy.

cofhurtachd [kə.uršdəchg] *f* consolation; comfort.

cofhurtaich [kə.uršdıch'] *v* comfort, console.

cofhurtail [kə.uršdal] *adj* comfortable.

cò fon ghrèin . . . ? [kō fon ghrēn] who on earth . . . ?

cogadh [kəgəgh] *m* war; warfare.

cogais [kɔgɪš] *f* conscience.
co-ghin [kɔgh'in] *v* mate, copulate.
co-ghineadh [kɔgh'inəgh] *m* mating, copulation.
co-ghnìomhair [kɔghriəvɛr'] *m* adverb.
coibhneas [koiN'əs] *m* kindness, kindliness.
coibhneil [koiN'ɛl] *adj* kind, kindly.
coidse [kɔd'ši] *f* coach.
còig [kōg'] *m/adj* five.
còigeamh [kōg'əv] *adj* fifth.
còignear [kōg'N'ɛr] *m* fivesome.
coigreach [koig'r'əch] *m* foreigner; stranger.
coileach [koL'əch] *m* (*fowl*) cock.
coileach-gaoithe [koL'əchgui.ɪ] *m* weathercock.
coilean [kɔlən] *v* accomplish; complete.
coileanta [kɔləndə] *adj* completed; perfect.
coilear [kɔlɛr] *m* collar.
coille [koL'ɪ] *f* wood.
coilleag [koL'ag] *f* cockle.
coillear [koL'ɛr] *m* forestry worker; woodcutter.
coille mhòr [koL'ɪ vōr] *f* forest.
coimeas [koiməs] *f* comparison; like(s) of. • *v* compare, liken.
coimeasach [koiməsəch] *adj* comparable.
coimh- [kə] *prefix* co-.
coimheach [kɔi.əch] *adj* foreign; unfamiliar. • *m* foreigner; stranger.
coimhead [kɔi.əd] *v* watch; look.
coimhead air [kɔi.əd ɛr'] *v* look at.
coimhead ri [kɔi.əd r'i] *v* expect.
coimhearsnach [kɔi.əršnəch] *m* neighbour.

coimhearsnachd [kɔi.əršnəchg] *f* neighbourhood.
coimheatailt [kɔvɛtalt'] *f* alloy.
coimhlion [kɔlən] *v* accomplish; complete.
coimisean [kɔmɪšan] *m* commission.
coimpiutair [kɔmpyuʰtɛr'] *m* computer.
coineanach [koN'anəch] *m* rabbit.
còinneach [kōN'əch] *f* moss.
coinneal [koN'aL] *f* candle.
coinneamh [koN'əv] *f* meeting.
coinnich [koN'ɪch'] *v* congregate.
coinnich ri [koN'ɪch'] *v* meet.
coinnleir [koiN'L'ɛr'] *m* candlestick.
co-ionnan [kɔ.iuNan] *adj* identical, the same.
còir [kōr'] *f* obligation; right; justice. • *adj* decent; worthy; kindly.
coirbte [koribt'ɪ] *adj* corrupt.
coirce [kɔrk'ɪ] *m* oats.
coire[1] [kor'ɪ] *f* wrong; blame.
coire[2] [kɔr'ɪ] *m* kettle; cauldron; corrie.
coireach [kor'əch] *adj* guilty; responsible. • *m* guilty person; offender.
coirich [kor'ɪch'] *v* blame.
còir-shlighe [kōr'li.ɪ] *f* right of way.
coiseachd [kɔšəchg] *f* walking.
coisich [kɔšich'] *v* walk.
coisiche [kɔšɪchə] *m* walker, pedestrian.
coisinn [kɔšiN'] *v* win; earn.
còisir [kōšir'] *f* choir.
coisrig [kɔšr'ɪg'] *v* consecrate; devote.
coitcheann [kəʰt'əN] *adj* common, communal; general, universal.
coithional [kohɛnaL] *adj* congregation.

coitich [kɔʰt'ıch'] v urge.

co-labhairt [kɔLavıršt'] f conference.

cola-breith [kɔLa br'eh] m birthday.

cola-deug [kɔLa d'ag] m fortnight.

colaiste [kɔLəšd'ı] f college.

colann [kɔLəN] f body.

colbh [kɔLəv] m column.

Colla [kɔLə] m Coll.

Collach [kɔLəch] m/adj from Coll.

collaidh [kɔLı] adj sensual, carnal.

coltach [kɔLtəch] adj likely.

coltach ri [kɔLtəch r'i] prep like.

coltaich ri [kɔLtəch r'i] v compare to.

coltas [kɔLəs] m appearance.

com [koum] m bosom, chest area.

coma [komə] adj indifferent; unconcerned.

coma co-dhiubh [komə kogh'ū] adj quite indifferent.

comain [komeN'] f obligation.

coma leat! [komə laʰt] excl never mind! don't worry!

comanachadh [komanəchəgh] m Communion.

comanaich [komanıch'] v take Communion.

comanaiche [komanıch'ı] m communicant.

comann [komaN] m association; club, society.

comann eachdraidh [komaN ɛchdrı] m history society.

comar [komər] f confluence.

comas [komas] m ability; faculty.

comasach [komasəch] adj able.

comasach air [komasəch ɛr'] capable of.

comas inntinn [komas īN'tıN'] m mental ability.

comataidh [komətı] f committee.

combaist [koumbıšd'] f compass.

comh- [kɔ] prefix co-.

comhachag [ko.əchag] f barn-owl.

comhair [ko.ır'] f direction.

comhairle [kɔ.ərlı] f advice; council.

comhairleach [kɔ.ərləch] m adviser.

comhairlich [kɔ.ərlıch'] v advise.

comhairliche [kɔ.ərlıch'ə] m councillor.

comharrachadh [kɔhəRachəgh] m marking, correction.

comharradh [kɔhəRəgh] m mark; sign; symbol.

comharradh-ceiste [kɔhəRəghk'ešd'ı] m question mark.

comharradh-rathaid [kɔhəRəghRa.ıd'] m road sign.

comharradh-stiùiridh [kɔhəRəghsd'ūr'ı] m landmark.

comharraich [kɔhəRıch'] v mark, correct.

comhart [kɔ.əršd] m (of dog) bark.

comhartaich [kɔ.əršdıch'] v (of dog) bark.

còmhdach [kōdəch] m cover, covering.

còmhdaich [kōdıch'] v cover.

còmhdaichte [kōdıch't'ə] adj covered.

còmhdhail [kō.al] f congress, conference.

co-mheasgaich [kɔvısgıch'] v intermix, mix; amalgate; mingle.

cò mheud? [kō viad] interrog adv how much? how many?

còmhla¹ [kōLə] adv together.

còmhla² [kōLə] m/f door.

còmhlan [kōLan] m band; company.

còmhlan-ciùil [kōLank'ūl] *m* (*mus*) band, group.

còmhla ri [kōLə r'i] *prep* with, along with.

còmhnaich [kōnɪch'] *v* live, dwell.

còmhnaidh [kōnɪ] *f* dwelling.

còmhnard [kōnard] *adj* level; smooth. • *m* plain; level ground.

còmhradh [kōradh] *m* conversation, talk.

còmhradh beag [kōragh beg] *m* chat.

còmhrag [kōrag] *f* combat; conflict.

còmhrag dithis [kōrag d'i.ɪš] *f* duel.

còmhraiteach [kōrat'əch] *adj* talkative, chatty.

còmhstri [kōsdri] *f* strife; competition.

com-pàirtich [kompāršdɪch'] *v* take part.

companach [kompanəch] *m* companion; pal.

companaidh [kompanɪ] *f* firm, company.

companas [kompanəs] *m* companionship.

comraich [komrɪch'] *f* sanctuary.

còn [kōn] *m* cone.

conaire [konər'ə] *f* rosary.

conaltrach [konaltrəch] *adj* social; sociable.

conaltradh [konaltrəgh] *m* conversation; company.

conasg [konəsg] *m* gorse, whins.

constabal [konsdəbaL] *m* constable.

connadh [koNəgh] *m* fuel.

connlach [kouNLəch] *f* straw.

connrag [kouNrag] *f* consonant.

connsachail [kouNsəchal] *adj* quarrelsome; argumentative.

connsaich [kouNsɪch] *v* argue, quarrel.

connspaid [kouNsbɪd'] *f* dispute; controversy; wrangling.

connspaideach [kouNsbɪd'əch] *adj* disputatious; controversial.

conntraigh [kouNtray] *f* neap tide.

consal [konsaL] *m* consul.

consan [konsan] *m* consonant.

co-obrachadh [ko.obrəchəgh] *m* co-operation; co-operative.

co-obraich [ko.obrɪch'] *v* co-operate.

co-ogha [ko.o.ə] *m* cousin.

co-oibriche [ko.obr'ɪch'ə] *m* fellow worker.

cop [koʰp] *m* foam, froth.

copach [koʰpəch] *adj* frothy, foaming.

copag [koʰpag] *f* dock, docken.

cupan [kuʰpan] *m* cup.

copar [koʰpər] *m* copper.

co-phòitear [kofɔʰt'ɛr] *m* drinking companion.

cor [kor] *m* state, condition.

còraichean daonna [kōrɪch'ən dūNə] *fpl* human rights.

corcair [korkɛr'] *adj* purple.

corcais [korkɪš] *f* cork.

còrd[1] [kōrd] *v* agree.

còrd[2] [kōrd] *m* cord.

còrdadh [kōrdəgh] *m* agreement, understanding.

còrd ri [kōrd r'i] *v* please.

còrn [kōrn] *m* drinking horn; corn.

Còrn [kōrn] *f* (*with art*) a' **Chòrn** [ə chōrn] Cornwall.

Còrnach [kōrnəch] *m*/*adj* Cornishman; Cornish.

corp [korp] *m* body; corpse.

corpailear [korpalɛr] *m* corporal.

corp-làidir [kɔrpLăd'ır'] *adj* able-bodied.

corporra [kɔrpəRə] *adj* bodily, corporal.

còrr [kɔR] *adj (number)* odd. • *m (with art)* **an còrr** [ən kɔR] the rest, everything else; anything else.

corra [kɔRə] *adj* odd, occasional.

corrag [kɔRag] *f* finger.

corra-ghritheach [kɔRəghri.əch] *f* heron.

corran [kɔRan] *m* sickle.

còrr is [kɔR is] *prep* more than.

còs [kɔs] *m* hollow.

còsach [kɔsəch] *adj* hollow.

co-shamhlachd [kɔhauLəchg] *f* parable.

cosg [kɔsg] *v* cost; spend; waste. • *m* cost; waste.

cosgail [kɔsgal] *adj* costly.

cosgais [kɔsgɪš] *f* cost.

cosgaisean siubhail [kɔsgɪšən šu.al] *fpl* travel costs.

co-sheirm [kɔherim] *f* harmony.

co-shìnte [kɔhīnt'ı] *adj* parallel.

cosnadh [kɔsnəgh] *m* earning; employment; work.

costa [kɔsdə] *m* coast.

còta [kɔʰtə] *m* coat.

còta-bàn [kɔʰtəbān] *m* petticoat.

còta-leapa [kɔʰtəL'εʰpə] *m* dressing gown, housecoat.

còta-mòr [kɔʰtəmōr] *m* overcoat.

cotan [kɔʰtan] *m* cotton.

cothrom [kɔRəm] *adj (number)* even. • *m* chance, opportunity; balance.

cothromach [kɔRəməch] *adj* fair; decent.

cothromaich [kɔRəmıch'] *v* weigh; balance.

cothrom na Fèinne [kɔRəm nə fēN'ı] *m* fair chance.

co-thuit [kɔhuʰt'] *v* coincide.

co-thuiteamas [kɔhuʰt'əməs] *m* coincidence.

cràbhach [krāvəch] *adj* devout, pious.

cràdh [krāgh] *m* pain; anguish.

craiceann [kraʰk'əN] *m* skin.

cràidh [krāy] *v* pain; torment.

cràidhteach [krāit'əch] *adj* grievous, painful.

cràin [krāN'] *f* sow.

crann [krauN] *m* mast; plough; crane; bolt; *(with art)* **an Crann** [ən krauN] the Saltire, St Andrew's Cross; **an Crann-Ceusaidh** [ən krauNk'ēsı] Christ's Cross.

crannag [kraNag] *f* pulpit; milk churn; crannog.

crannchur [krauNchər] *m* drawing lots; fate.

crann-fìona [krauNfiənə] *m* vine.

crann-sgaoilidh [krauNsgūlı] *m* transmitter; TV mast.

crann-sneachda [krauNsN'εchgə] *m* snowplough.

crann-tarsainn [krauNtarsıN'] *m* crossbar.

craobh [krūv] *f* tree.

craol [krūL], *less common* **craobh-sgaoil** [krūvsgūl] *v* diffuse; broadcast.

craoladh [krūLəgh] *m* broadcasting.

craos [krūs] *m* maw; gluttony.

craosach [krūsəch] *adj* gluttonous.

craosaire [krūsər'ə] *m* glutton.

crasg [krasg] *f* crutch (for walking).

crosgan [krɔsgan] *m* starfish.

crath [krah] v shake, tremble; brandish.

creach [kr'ɛch] v plunder; ruin. • f ruination; plunder.

creachann [kr'ɛchəN] m scallop.

crèadh [kr'ɛ̄] f clay.

crèadhadair [kr'ɛ̄.ədɛr'] m potter.

crèadhadaireachd [kr'ɛ̄.ədɛr'əchg] f pottery.

creag [kr'eg] f crag; hill.

creagach [kr'egəch] adj craggy.

creamh [kr'ɛv] m leek.

creapan [kr'ɛʰpan] m stool.

creathail [kr'ɛhal] f cradle.

creid [kr'ed'] v believe; think, consider.

creideamh [kr'ed'əv] m belief; trust; religion.

creideas [kr'ed'əs] m trust.

crèim [kr'ɛ̄m] v nibble.

crèis [kr'ɛ̄s] f grease.

crèiseach [kr'ɛ̄səch] adj greasy.

creithleag [kr'ɛlag] f cleg, horsefly.

creud [kr'ɛ̄d] f creed.

creutair [kr'ɛ̄ʰtɛr'] m creature.

creutair bochd [kr'ɛ̄ʰtɛr' bochg] m poor soul.

criathar [kr'iəhər] m sieve, riddle.

criathraich [kr'iəhrɪch'] v sieve, riddle.

crìdhe [kr'ī.ɪ] m heart; courage.

crìdhealas [kr'ī.əLəs] m heartiness; conviviality.

crìdheil [kr'ī.ɛl] adj hearty; jovial.

crìoch [kr'iəch] f end; boundary.

Crìochan [kr'iəchən] fpl (with art) **na Crìochan** [nə kr'iəchən] the Borders.

crìochnach [kr'iəchnəch] adj finite.

crìochnaich [kr'iəchnɪch'] v finish.

crìochnaichte [kr'iəchnɪch't'e] adj finished.

criomag [kr'imag] f bit; crumb; (pl) **criomagan** [kr'imagən] bits and pieces, odds and ends.

crìon [kr'iən] v wither; dry up. • adj tiny; petty; withered.

crìoplach [kr'iʰpLəch] m cripple.

crios [kr'is] m belt.

Crìosdachd [kr'iəsdəchg] f Christendom.

Crìosdaidh [kr'iəsdɪ] m Christian.

Crìosdaidheachd [kr'iəsdɪ.əchg] f Christianity.

Crìosdail [kr'iəsdal] adj Christian.

Crìosdalachd [kr'iəsdaləchg] f Christian-ness.

criostal [kr'isdaL] m crystal.

crith [kr'i] v tremble, shiver. • f trembling, shivering.

critheanach [kr'ihənəch] adj shaky; scary.

crith-thalmhainn [kr'ihaLavɪN'] f earthquake.

crò [krɔ̄] m cattle pen, fold.

croch [krɔch] v hang.

crochadair [krɔchədɛr'] m hangman; hanger.

crochadh [krɔchəgh] m hanging.

crochte [krɔcht'ɪ] adj hung; hanged.

crodh [kro] m cattle, livestock.

crodh-bainne [krobaN'ɪ] m dairy cows.

crodh-dàra [krodārə] m breeding cattle.

crò-dhearg [krɔ̄gh'ɛrag] adj crimson.

cròg [krɔ̄g] f paw; fist.

cròic [krɔ̄iʰk'] f antler.

croich [kroich'] f gallows. • excl X **na croiche!** [nə kroich'ɪ] damned X! bloody X!

crois [krɔ̄s] f cross; crucifix.

crois rathaid [krɔš] *f* crossroads.

croit[1] [krɔɪʰt'] *f* croft.

croit[2] [krɔʰt'] *f* (*on back*) hump.

croitear [krɔʰt'ɛr] *m* crofter.

croitse [krɔʰt'ʃɪ] *f* (*for walking*) crutch.

crom [krɔum] *v* bend, incline; descend, climb down. • *adj* bent, crooked; curved.

cromag [kromag] *f* hook; comma; cromag, crook.

cromagan turrach [kromagən tuRəch] *fpl* inverted commas.

crom air [krɔum ɛr'] *v* set to.

cromchasach [krɔumchasəch] *adj* bandy-legged.

cron [krɔn] *m* harm; fault.

cronaich [krɔnɪch'] *v* chide, scold.

cronail [krɔnal] *adj* harmful, hurtful.

crònan [krɔnan] *m* humming; murmuring; buzzing; (*stags*) belling.

crò snàthaid [krɔ sNãhɪd'] *m* eye of needle.

crosta [krɔsdə] *adj* cross; naughty.

crotach [krɔʰtəch] *adj* humpbacked.

crotal [krɔʰtaL] *m* lichen.

cruach [kruəch] *v* heap, stack. • *f* heap; rick.

cruachann [kruəchəN] *f* hip.

cruadal [kruədaL] *m* hardship; hardihood.

cruadalach [kruədaLəch] *adj* difficult; hardy.

cruadhaich [kruəi.ɪch'] *v* harden; solidify.

cruaidh [kruəy] *f* steel. • *adj* hard; harsh; hardy.

cruaidh-chàs [kruəichãs] *m* emergency; tight corner.

cruaidh-chrìdheach [kruəich'r'ĩ.əch] *adj* hard-hearted.

cruan [kruən] *m* enamel.

cruas [kruəs] *m* hardness; harshness; toughness.

crùb [krūb] *v* crouch; cringe; crawl.

crùbach [krūbəch] *adj* lame. • *m* lame person.

crùbag [krūbag] *f* crab.

crùban [krūban] *m* crouch, squat.

crùdh [krū] *v* (*horse*) shoe.

crudha [kru.ə] *m* horseshoe.

cruinn [kruiN'] *adj* round; accurate; assembled.

cruinne [kruiN'ɪ] *f* sphere, globe; (*with art*) **a' chruinne** [ə chruiN'ɪ] the earth, the globe.

cruinneachadh [kruiN'əchəgh] *m* gathering, assembly; collection.

cruinne-cè [kruiN'ɪk'ē] *f* (*with art*) **a' chruinne-cè** [ə chruiN'ɪk'ē] the world.

cruinn-eòlas [kruiN' yōLəs] *m* geography.

cruinnich [kruiN'ɪch'] *v* gather, assemble; (*fruit, etc*) pick.

cruinn-leum [kruiN'lēm] *m* standing jump.

crùisgean [krūšg'an] *m* oil lamp, cruisie.

cruit-chòrda [kruʰt'chōrdə] *f* harpsichord.

cruitheachd [krui.əchg] *f* creation; (*with art*) **a' Chruitheachd** [ə chrui.əchg] the world; the universe, Creation.

cruithear [krui.ɛr] *m* creator; (*with art*) **an Cruithear** [ən krui.ɛr] God, the Creator.

Cruithneach [kruiN'əch] *m/adj* Pict; Pictish.

cruithneachd [kruiN'əchg] f wheat.

crùn [krūn] v crown. • m crown.

crùnadh [krūnəgh] m crowning, coronation.

cruth [kruh] m shape; figure; appearance.

cruthaich [kruhıch'] v create.

cù [kū] m dog.

cuach [kuəch] f bowl, quaich.

cuagach [kuəgəch] adj bent; limping.

cuaille [kuəL'ı] m club, cudgel.

cuairt [kuəršt'] f circuit; stroll; trip.

cuan [kuan] m sea, ocean; **an Cuan Sgìth** [ən kuan sgī] the Little Minch; **an Cuan Siar** [ən kuan šiər] the Atlantic Ocean.

cuaraidh [kuarı] m quarry.

cuaran [kuəran] m sandal.

cuartaich [kuərštıch'] v surround; enclose.

cùbaid [kūbıd'] f pulpit.

cubhaidh [kuvı] adj fitting.

cùbhraidh [kūrı] adj sweet, fragrant.

cucair [kuʰkɛr'] f cooker.

cù-chaorach [kūchūrəch] m sheepdog.

cùdainn [kūdıN'] f large tub.

cudrom [kudrəm] m weight; importance; stress.

cudromach [kudrəməch] adj weighty, important.

cugallach [kugəLəch] adj unsteady; dodgy; unreliable.

cuibhle [kuilı] f wheel.

cuibhle-stiùiridh [kuilısd'ūr'ı] f steering wheel.

cuibhreach [kuirəch] m chain.

cuibhreann [kuirəN] m portion; allowance.

cuibhreann-ciorraim [kuirəNk'iRəm] m disability allowance.

cuibhrich [kuir'ıch] v chain.

cuibhrig [kuir'ıg'] f quilt, coverlet.

cuid [kud'] f share; part. • pron some.

cuid-aodaich [kud'ūdıch'] f clothes, clothing.

cuideachadh [kud'əchəgh] m help.

cuideachail [kud'əchal] adj helpful.

cuideachd[1] [kud'əchg] f company; companions.

cuideachd[2] [kud'əchg] adv too, also.

cuideachdail [kud'əchgal] adj sociable, fond of company.

cuideigin [kud'eg'ın] f someone, somebody.

cuide ri [kud'ı r'ı] prep with, along with.

cuidhteag [kuiʰt'ag] f whiting.

cuidhteas [kuiʰt'əs] m receipt; riddance.

cuidich [kud'ıch'] v help, assist.

cuid oidhche [kud' oi.ch'ı] f night's lodging.

cùil [kūl] f corner, nook.

cuilbheart [kulivɛršt] f trick; stratagem.

cuilc [kulk] f reed; cane.

cùil-chumhang [kūlchu.əng] f tight corner, fix.

cuilc Innseanach [kulk īšəNəch] f bamboo.

cuileag [kulag] f fly, house-fly.

cuilean [kulan] m puppy; cub.

cuimhne [kuiN'ı] f memory; remembrance.

cuimhneachan [kuiN'əchan] m memorial; memorandum.

cuimhneachan-cogaidh [kuiN'əchankɔgı] m war memorial.

cuimhnich [kuiN'ıch'] *v* remember.

cuimir [kuimır'] *adj* succinct; neat; shapely.

Cuimreach [kumr'əch] *m/adj* Welshman; Welsh.

Cuimrigh [kumr'ı] *f (with art)* **a' Chuimrigh** [ə chumr'ı] Wales.

cuimsich [kuimšıch'] *v* aim.

cuine? [kuN'ı] *interrog adv* when?

cuing [kuing'] *f* yoke; *(with art)* **a' chuing** [ə chuing'] *f* asthma.

cuinneag [kuiN'ag] *f* bucket; milking pail.

cuinnean [kuiN'an] *m* nostril.

cuip [kuiʰp] *v* whip. • *f* whip.

cuir [kur'] *v* put; send; *(seed, etc)* sow, plant.

cuir a dh'iarraidh [kur' əghiəRı] *v* send for.

cuir air [kur' ɛr'] *v* light, turn/switch on; put on, don.

cuir air an spàrr [kur' ɛr' ən spāR] *v* save; stow away.

cuir air an teine [kur' ɛr' ən t'enı] *v* light the fire.

cuir air ath latha [kur' ɛr' ən ah La.a] *v* defer, put off.

cuir air bhonn [kur' ɛr' vouN] *v* found, set up.

cuir air chois [kur' ɛr' chɔš] *v* found, set up.

cuir air dòigh [kur' ɛr' dōy] *v* organise; put right.

cuir air earalas [kur' ɛr' ɛraLəs] *v* forewarn, alert.

cuir air flod [kur' ɛr' fləd] *v* float; launch.

cuir air leth [kur' ɛr' L'eh] *v* put aside; save.

cuir air meidh [kur' ɛr' mey] *v* balance.

cuir air mheomhair [kur' ɛr' vyɔ.ır'] *v* commit to memory.

cuir air snàmh [kur' ɛr' sNāv] *v* inundate, flood.

cuir aithne air [kur' aN'ı ɛr'] *v* get to know.

cuir a-mach [kur' ə mach] *v* bring up, vomit.

cuir am bogadh [kur' əm bogagh] *v* steep.

cuir am breislich [kur' əm brešlıch'] *v* confuse, mix up.

cuir am fad [kur' əm fad] *v* lengthen, make longer.

cuir an cèill [kur' ən k'ēL] *v* express, put into words.

cuir an clò [kur' ən kLō] *v* print; publish.

cuir an cràdh [kur' ən krāgh] *v* torture.

cuir an eanchainn à [kur' əN' ɛnachıN' a] *v* brain.

cuir an geall gu [kur' ən g'yauL gə] *v* bet that.

cuir an òrdugh [kur' ən ōrdu] *v* put in order.

cuir an sàs [kur' ən sās] *v* capture; arrest.

cuir an suarachas [kur' ən suərəchəs] *v* belittle, disparage.

cuir an tairgse [kur' ən tɛrig'ši] *v* make available.

cuir an teagamh [kur' ən t'ɛgəv] *v* cast doubt upon.

cuir às an teine [kur' as ən t'enı] *v* put the fire out.

cuir às do [kur' as dɔ] *v* abolish; kill.

cuir às mo leth ... [kur' as mə le] *v* accuse me of. ...

cuir bacadh air [kur' baʰkəgh ɛr'] *v* obstruct; prevent.

cuir bun-os-cionn [kur' bunɔsk'ūN] *v* upend, overturn.

cuir bus air [kur' bus ɛr'] *v* grimace, pout.

cuir cabhag air [kur' kafag ɛr'] *v* rush, hurry.

cuir car de [kur' kar d'e] *v* move.

cuir ceart [kur' k'aršd] *v* correct, put right.

cuir cèilidh air [kur' k'ēlɪ ɛr'] *v* go to see, visit.

cuir cleas air [kur' kles ɛr'] *v* play a trick/joke on.

cuir clisgeadh air [kur' klišg'əgh ɛr'] *v* startle.

cuir coire air [kur' kor'ɪ ɛr'] *v* blame, lay blame on.

cuir cruinn [kur' kruiN'] *v* toss coin.

cuir crìoch air [kur' krīch ɛr'] *v* complete, finish.

cuir dàil air [kur' dāl ɛr'] *v* delay.

cuir dath air [kur' dah ɛr'] *v* colour.

cuir dheth [kur' gh'eh] *v* turn/switch off; doff, take off; talk away, jabber on.

cuir do thaic orm/rium [kur' də haiʰk' ɔrɔm/r'ium] *v* lean on me; depend on me.

cuir dragh air [kur' drogh ɛr'] *v* worry; bother, trouble.

cuireadh [kur'əgh] *m* invitation.

cuir eagal air [kur' egal ɛr'] *v* frighten.

cuir earbsa ann an [kur' ɛrabsə auN ən] *v* put trust in, rely on.

cuir eòlas air [kur' yōLəs ɛr'] *v* get to know.

cuir fàilte air [kur' fālt'ɪ ɛr'] *v* welcome.

cuir fios do [kur' fis dɔ] *v* let know, inform.

cuir fodha [kur' fo.ə] *v* sink, scuttle.

cuir fon choill [kur' fɔn choL'] *v* outlaw.

cuir geall [kur' gyauL] *v* place a bet.

cuir gruaim [kur' gruaim] *v* frown, scowl.

cuir gu feum [kur' gə fēm] *v* use, utilise.

cuir impidh air [kur' īmpɪ ɛr'] *v* persuade, urge.

cuir iongantas air [kur' iəndəs ɛr'] *v* amaze, astound.

cuir luach air [kur' Luach ɛr'] *v* value; evaluate.

cuirm [kurim] *f* feast, banquet.

cuir ma sgaoil [kur' mə sgūl] *v* set free.

cuirm-bhainnse [kurim*vai*N'ši] *f* wedding reception.

cuirm-chnuic [kurim*chruk*'] *f* picnic.

cuirmeach [kurimǝch] *adj* festive.

cuir meal do naidheachd air [kur' myaL də nɛ.əchg ɛr'] *v* congratulate.

cuir mo chùl ri [kur' mə chūL r'i] *v* turn my back on.

cuir mùig air [kur' mūig' ɛr'] *v* frown, scowl.

cuir oillt air [kur' oiL't' ɛr'] *v* terrify; horrify.

cuir rian air [kur' Rian ɛr'] *v* put in order, organise.

cuir romham [kur' Rɔ.əm] *v* make up my mind, resolve (to).

cuir smùid [kur' smūd'] *v* smoke, emit smoke.

cuir seachad [kur' šachǝd] *v* pass, spend.

cuir sneachd [kur' šN'ɛchg] *v* snow.

cuir stad air [kur' sdad ɛr'] *v* put a stop/end to.

cùirt [kūršd'] *f* court.

cùirtean [kūršd'an] *m* curtain.

cùirteil [kūršd'ɛl] *adj* courteous; courtly.

cuir thairis [kur' har'ıš] *v* overflow.

cuir thar a chèile [kur' har əch'ēlı] *v* set at loggerheads.

cuir timcheall [kur' t'imich'əL] *v* send/pass round.

cùirt-lagha [kūršt'Loghə] *f* law court.

cuir urram air [kur' uRəm ɛr'] *v* honour.

cùis [kūš] *f* matter, business; (*pl*) **cùisean** [kūšən] things, matters.

cùis-bheachd [kūšvyachg] *f* abstraction, abstract idea.

cùisear [kūšɛr] *m* (*gram*) subject.

cùis-ghràin [kūšghrāN'] *f* abomination.

cùis-lagha [kūšLoghə] *f* lawsuit.

cuisle [kušlı] *f* vein; pipe.

cuislean [kušlən] *m* flute.

cuisle-chinn [kušlıch'iN'] *f* aorta.

cuisle-chiùil [kušlıch'ūl] *f* flute.

cuisle-mhòr [kušlıvōr] *f* artery.

cùl [kūL] *m* nape; hair of head; back.

cùlaibh [kūLıv] *m* back part. • *adv* **cùlaibh air beulaibh** [kūLıv ɛr' biaLıv] back to front; vice versa.

culaidh [kuLı] *f* garment; suit of clothes; butt, object.

culaidh-choimheach [kuLıchəi.əch] *f* fancy dress.

culaidh-fharmaid [kuLıaramıd'] *f* object of envy.

cularan [kuLəran] *m* cucumber.

cùl-chàin [kūLchāN'] *v* slander.

cùl-chàineadh [kūLchāN'əgh] *m* slander, backbiting.

cullach [kuLəch] *m* boar.

cùl-mhùtaire [kūLvū^htər'ə] *m* smuggler.

cùl-mhùtaireachd [kūLvū^htər'əchg] *f* smuggling.

cùl na h-amhaich [kūL nə havıch'] *f* the back of the neck.

cùl na làimhe [kūL nə Lāivı] *m* the back of the hand.

cultar [kuLtər] *m* culture.

cum [kum] *v* shape, form.

cùm [kūm] *v* keep.

cumadh [kuməgh] *m* shape, form.

cùm air [kūm ɛr'] *v* continue, go on.
  • *excl* **cùm ort!** [kūm ɔršt] keep at it! on you go!

cùm air ais [kūm ɛr' ɛš] *v* hold back, delay.

cùm a-mach [kūm əmach] *v* assert, claim.

cuman [kuman] *m* bucket; milking pail.

cumanta [kumandə] *adj* common, ordinary.

cumantas [kumandəs] *m* usualness, normality.

cùm às an làthair [kūm as ən Lāhır'] *v* keep away; keep out of sight.

cùm caismeachd ri [kūm kašməchg r'i] *v* keep time to.

cùm faire [kūm far'ı] *v* keep watch/guard.

cumha[1] [ku.ə] *f* lament, elegy.

cumha[2] [ku.ə] *m* stipulation, condition.

cumhach [ku.əch] *adj* conditional.

cumhachd [ku.əchg] *m* power; might; (electric) power.

cumhachdach [ku.əchgəch] *adj* powerful; mighty.

cumhachd tuinne [ku.əchg tuiN'ı] *m* wave power.

cumhang [ku.əng] *adj* narrow.

cùmhnant [kūnənd] *m* covenant; contract.

cùm ris! [kūm r'iš] *excl* stick at it! keep it up!

cùm smachd air [kūm smachg ɛr'] *v* keep control of.

cùm suas [kūm suəs] *v* maintain, support.

cùm sùil air [kūm sūl ɛr'] *v* keep an eye on.

cùm taic ri [kūm taiʰk' r'i] *v* support.

cùm taobh ri [kūm tūv r'i] *v* side with, favour.

cunbhalach [kunuvaLəch] *adj* even, regular; steady.

cungaidh [kungɪ] *f* materials; ingredients.

cungaidh-leighis [kungɪ le.ɪš] *f* medicine, drug.

cunnart [kuNəršd] *m* danger, risk.

cunnartach [kuNəršdəch] *adj* dangerous, risky.

cùnnradh [kūNrəgh] *m* contract; deal.

cùnnt [kūNd] *v* count.

cùnntas [kūNdəs] *m* counting; (*finance*) account; narration; score.

cùnntasachd [kūNdəsəchg] *f* accountancy.

cùnntasair [kūNdəsɛr'] *m* accountant.

cuntair [kundɪr'] *m* (*shop, etc*) counter.

cupa [kuʰpə] *m* cup.

cuplachadh [kuʰpLəchəgh] *m* copulation, mating.

cuplaich [kuʰpLɪch'] *v* couple, copulate.

cùpon [kūpən] *m* coupon, voucher.

cur [kur] *m* placing; sending.

currach [kuRəch] *f* coracle.

canù [kanū] *f* canoe.

curaidh [kurɪ] *m* hero.

cùram [kūrəm] *m* care; responsibility.

cùramach [kūrəməch] *adj* careful; prone to worry.

cur na mara [kur nə marə] *m* seasickness.

curran [kuRan] *m* carrot.

curracag [kuRəʰkag] *f* lapwing.

cùrsa [kūrsə] *m* course.

cur-seachad [kuršachəd] *m* hobby, pastime.

cùrtair [kuršdɪr'] *m* curtain.

cus [kus] *m* excess, too much.

cusbainn [kusbɪN'] *f* (*tax*) customs.

cusp [kusp] *f* chilblain.

cuspair [kuspɛr'] *m* subject, topic; (*gram*) object.

cut [kuʰt] *v* gut.

cutair [kuʰtɛr'] *m* fish-gutter.

cuthach [ku.əch] *m* madness; rage.

cuthag [ku.ag] *f* cuckoo.

D

dà [dā] *n/adj* two.

dachaigh [dachı] *f* home.

dà chànanach [dā chānanəch] *adj* bilingual.

dad [dad] *f* thing, anything.

dadaidh [dadı] *m* dad, daddy.

dadam [dadəm] *m* atom; tiny piece.

dà dheug [dā riag] *adj* twelve.

dad ort! [dad ɔršt] *excl* never mind! don't worry!

dag [dag] *m* pistol.

dail [dal] *f* meadow; dale.

dàil [dāl] *f* delay.

dàimh [dāiv] *f* relationship, ties.

dàimheach [dāivəch] *adj* relative.

daingeann [daing'əN] *adj* firm, solid.

daingneach [daing'anəch] *f* fort; stronghold.

daingnich [daing'anıch'] *v* fortify; consolidate; confirm.

dàir [dār'] *m* rutting, heat.

dall [dauL] *v* blind. • *adj* blind. • *m* blind man.

dàmais [dāmıš] *f* draughts.

damh [dav] *m* stag.

dàmhair [dāvır'] *f* rutting; (*with art*) **an Dàmhair** [ən dāvır'] October.

damhan-allaidh [davanaLı] *m* spider.

dàn[1] [dān] *m* fate, destiny.

dàn[2] [dān] *m* poem; song.

dàna [dānə] *adj* daring; impudent; arrogant.

dànachd [dānəchg] *f* poetry, verse.

danns [dauNs] *v* dance.

dannsa [dauNsə] *m* dance.

dannsadh [dauNsəgh] *m* dancing.

dannsair [dauNsɛr'] *m* dancer.

dàn spioradail [dān spirədal] *m* hymn.

daoimean [dūman] *m* diamond.

daoine [dūN'ı] *mpl* people; kinsfolk.

daoine mòra [dūN'ı mōrə] *mpl* big shots, bigwigs.

daoine-sìth [dūN'ıšĭ] *mpl* fairyfolk.

daolag [dūLag] *f* beetle.

daolag-bhreac [dūLagvrɛʰk] *f* ladybird.

daonna [dūNə] *adj* human.

daonnan [dūNan] *adv* always, constantly.

daor [dūr] *adj* dear, expensive.

daorach [dūrəch] *f* drunkenness; spree.

daorachail [dūrəchal] *adj* intoxicating.

daorsa [darsə] *f* captivity.

darach [darəch] *m* oak.

dàrna deug [dārnə d'iag] *adj* twelfth.

dàrna [dārnə] *adj* second.

dà-sheaghach [dā hoghəch] *adj* ambiguous.

dàta [dāʰtə] *m* data.

dath [da] *v* colour; dye. • *m* colour; dye.

dath-bhacadh [da vaʰkəgh] *m* colour bar.

dath-dhall [da ghauL] *adj* colourblind.

dathte [daht'ı] *adj* coloured; dyed.

dà uair [dā uər'] *adv* twice.

de [d'e] *prep* of; from; made of.

dè [d'ē] *pron* what, what?

doirbh [doriv] *adj* hard, difficult.

deachd [d'achg] *v* dictate.

deachdadh [d'achgəgh] *m* dictation.

deachdaire [d'achgər'ə] *m* dictator.

deagh [d'ō] *adj* good. • *adv* well.

deagh bheusan [d'ō vēsən] *f* morals.

deagh chrìdheach [d'ō ch'ī.əch] *adj* good-hearted.

deagh thoil [d'ō həl] *f* good will.

dealachadh [d'ɛLəchəgh] *m* parting.

dealachadh-pòsaidh [d'ɛLəchəghpōsɪ] *m* divorce.

dealaich [d'ɛLɪch'] *v* part; separate; (*elec*) insulate.

dealan [d'ɛLan] *m* electricity.

dealanach [d'ɛLanəch] *m* lightning.

dealanaich [d'ɛLanɪch'] *v* electrify.

dealanair [d'ɛLanɛr'] *m* electrician.

dealan-dè [d'ɛLan d'ē] *m* butterfly.

dealasach [d'ɛLəsəch] *adj* eager, zealous.

dealbh [d'ɛLav] *m* picture; painting; shape. • *v* picture; design; construct.

dealbh-chluich [d'ɛLavchLuch] *m* play.

dealbh-chumadh [d'ɛLavchuməgh] *m* diagram.

dealbh-èibhinn [d'ɛLavēvɪN'] *m* cartoon.

dealg [d'ɛLag] *f* prickle, thorn; pin.

deàlrach [d'āLrəch] *adj* shining, shiny.

deàlraich [d'āLrɪch'] *v* shine, flash, glitter.

dealt [d'ɛLt] *m* dew.

dè am fonn? [d'ēm fouN] (*fam*) how are you?

deamhais [d'e.ɪš] *m* shears.

deamhan [d'ɛ.an] *m* demon.

dèan [d'ian] *v* do; make.

dèan a' chùis [d'ian ə chūš] *v* suffice, do the job/trick.

dèan a' chùis air [d'ian ə chūš ɛr'] *v* manage; defeat.

dèanadach [d'ianədəch] *adj* industrious, active.

dèan aoradh [d'ian ūrəgh] *v* worship.

dèan altachadh [d'ian aLtəchəgh] *v* say grace.

dèan an gnothach [d'ian ən gro.əch] *v* be just the job, do the trick.

dèan bàidh do [d'ian bāy də] *v* do a favour for.

dèan beic [d'ian beʰk'] *v* curtsey.

dèan braoisg [d'ian brūšg'] *v* grin; grimace.

dèan breug [d'ian briag] *v* lie, tell a lie.

dèan bruadar [d'ian bruədər] *v* dream.

dèan cabhag [d'ian kafag] *v* hurry, make haste.

dèan cadal [d'ian kadəL] *v* sleep.

dèan casad [d'ian kasəd] *v* cough.

dèan casaid air [d'ian kasɪd' ɛr'] *v* accuse; make a complaint against.

dèan cnead [d'ian kred] *v* groan.

dèan coimeas eadar [d'ian kɔiməs edər] *v* compare.

dèan còmhradh [d'ian kōrəgh] *v* talk, converse.

dèan cron air [d'ian krɔn ɛr'] *v* harm, injure.

dèan crùban [d'ian krūban] *v* crouch, squat.

dè an dòigh? [d'ē ən dōy] (*fam*) how're you doing?.

dèan dragh [d'ian drogh] *v* worry oneself.

dèan dragh do [d'ian drogh də] *v* cause worry to.

dèan dùrdail [d'ian dūrdal] *v* coo.

dèan faire [d'ian far'ı] *v* be on guard.

dèan faite-gàire [d'ian faʰt'ıgār'ı] *v* smile.

dèan fanaid air [d'ian fanıd' ɛr'] *v* mock, ridicule.

dèan fead [d'ian fed] *v* whistle.

dèan feum [d'ian fēm] *v* come in handy.

dèan feum do [d'ian fēm də] *v* do good to; be useful to.

dèan foill air [d'ian foiL' ɛr'] *v* cheat.

dèan gàirdeachas [d'ian gārd'əchəs] *v* rejoice.

dèan gàire [d'ian gār'ı] *v* laugh.

dèan gràgail [d'ian grāgal] *v* caw, croak.

dèan imrich [d'ian imir'ıch'] *v* move house.

dèan iolach [d'ian iLəch] *v* shout.

dèan iomradh air [d'ian imərəgh ɛr'] *v* mention.

dèan malairt [d'ian maLəršt'] *v* trade, do business.

dèan mèirle [d'ian mērlı] *v* steal.

dèan miodal (do) [d'ian midal də] *v* flatter, fawn (on).

dèan mo dhicheall [d'ian mə gh'īch'əL] *v* do my utmost.

dèan mùn [d'ian mūn] *v* urinate.

deanntag [d'auNdag] *f* nettle.

dèan oilbheum (do) [d'ian ɔlvēm də] *v* give offence (to).

dè rud? [d'ē rud] (*fam*) what?

dèan sèisd air [d'ian šēšd' ɛr'] *v* besiege.

dèan sgairt [d'ian sgaršd'] *v* yell.

dèan sodal do [d'ian sodal də] *v* fawn on, butter up.

dèan sreothart [d'ian sdrɔhəršd] *v* sneeze.

dèan stad [d'ian sdad] *v* stop, call a halt.

dèan sùgradh [d'ian sūgrəgh] *v* make merry, sport.

dèan suidhe! [d'ian sui.ı] *excl* sit down! take a seat!

dèan sùil bheag ri [d'ian sūl veg r'i] *v* wink at.

dèan suiridhe ri [d'ian sur'ı.ə r'i] *v* court.

dèan tàir air [d'ian tār' ɛr'] *v* despise, disparage.

dèan tarcais air [d'ian tarkıš ɛr'] *v* despise.

dèan ulfhart [d'ian uLəršt] *v* howl.

dèan ùrnaigh ri [d'ian ūrnı] *v* pray to.

dearbh [d'ɛrav] *adj* same. • *v* prove; test.

dearbhadh [d'ɛravəgh] *m* proof; test, trial.

dearc [d'ɛrk] *f* berry.

dearcag [d'ɛrkag] *f* little berry.

dearg [d'ɛrag] *adj* red; (*fam*) utter, complete.

deargann [d'ɛragəN] *f* flea.

deargaich [d'ɛragıch'] *v* redden.

dearmad [d'ɛraməd] *m* neglect, negligence; omission.

dearmadach [d'ɛramədəch] *adj* negligent; neglectful.

dearmaid [d'ɛramɪd'] v omit, neglect (to do something).

deàrrsaich [d'āRsɪch'] v shine.

deas [d'es] f south. • adj south; right(-hand); ready; finished; active.

deasachadh [d'esəchəgh] m preparation; editing.

deasaich [d'esɪch'] v prepare; edit.

deasaich biadh [d'esɪch' bɪəgh] v cook.

deasaichear [d'esɪch'ɛr] m editor.

deasbad [d'esbəd] m discussion, debate.

deasg [d'esg] m desk.

deas-ghnàth [d'es ghrā] m ceremony.

dè a tha a dhith air? [d'ē ha ə gh'ī ɛr'] what does he require?

dè tha dol? [d'ē ha dɔL] excl (fam) what's doing?

dè tha thu ris? [d'ē ha u r'iš] excl what are you up to?

de chois [d'e chɔš] adv on foot.

dè do bheachd? [d'ē də vyachg] what do you think?

dè do chor? [d'ē də chōr] excl (fam) how're you doing?

dè fon ghrèin? [d'ē fɔn ghr'ēn] excl what on earth?

deich [d'ech'] n/adj ten.

deichead [d'ech'əd] m decade.

deicheamh [d'ech'əv] adj tenth.

deichnear [d'eich'nɛr] m ten (people).

dèideadh [d'ēd'ədh] m (with art) an dèideadh [ən d'ēd'əgh] toothache.

dèideag [d'ēd'ag] f pebble; toy.

dèidheil air [d'ē.ɛl ɛr'] adj fond of, keen on.

deigh [dey] f ice.

dèile [d'ēlɪ] f board, plank.

dèilig ri [d'ēlɪg' r'i] v deal with, handle.

deimhinne [d'evɪN'ə] adj sure, certain.

dèine [d'ēnɪ] f eagerness; fervour.

dèirc [d'ɛrk'] f charity, alms.

dèirceach [d'ɛrk'əch] m beggar. • adj charitable.

deireadh [d'erədh] m end.

deireannach [d'erəNəch] adj last, final.

deisciobal [d'ešg'əbaL] m disciple.

deise [d'eši] f suit of (clothes).

deiseil [d'ešɛl] adj ready; finished; clockwise; sunwise; handy.

dè na tha e? [dē nə ha ɛ] how much is it?

deò [d'ō] f (with art) an deò [ən d'ō] the breath of life.

deoch [d'och] f drink; booze.

deoch-làidir [d'ochLād'ɪr'] f alcohol; alcoholic drink.

deoch an dorais [d'och ən dɔriš] f parting drink.

deoch-slàinte [d'ochsLāN'd'ɪ] f (drink) toast.

deoghail [d'o.al] v suck; absorb.

deòin [d'ōN'] f consent; willingness.

deònach [d'ōnəch] adj willing.

deònach air [d'ōnəch ɛr'] prepared to.

dè a tha a' dol? [d'ē ha ə dɔL] what's going on?

deuchainn [d'iachɪN'] f examination, test; trying time.

deuchainn-lann [d'iachɪNLəN] m laboratory.

deudach [d'ēdəch] adj dental.

deug [diag] suffix -teen.

deugaire [diagər'ə] m teenager.

deur [d'iar] m tear, teardrop.

dh'[gh], dha [gha] *(for* **do)** *prep* to (before vowels and *fh*).

dhà [ghā] *prep pron* to him; for him; to it; for it *(m)*.

dhachaigh [ghachı] *adv* home(wards).

dhaibh [ghaiv] *prep pron* to them; for them.

dheth[1] [gh'eh] *adv* off.

dheth[2] [gh'eh] *prep pron* of him; off him; of it; off it *(m)*.

dhi [gh'ī] *prep pron* of her; off her; of it; off it *(f)*.

dhibh [gh'iv] *prep pron* of you; off you *(pl)*.

dhinn [gh'iN'] *prep pron* of us; off us.

dhìom [gh'iəm] *prep pron* of me; off me.

dhìot [gh'iəʰt] *prep pron* of you; off you *(sing)*.

dhith [gh'ih] *prep pron* to her; for her; to it; for it *(f)*.

dhiubh [gh'u] *prep pron* of them; off them.

dhomh [ghə] *prep pron* to me; for me.

dhuibh [ghuiv] *prep pron* to you; for you *(pl)*.

dhuine! dhuine! [ghuN'ı ghuN'ı] *excl* oh dear! oh dear!

dhuinn [ghuiN'] *prep pron* to us; for us.

dhut [ghuʰt] *prep pron* to you; for you *(sing)*.

dia [diə] *m* god.

diabhal [d'iəvəL] *m* devil.

diabhlaidh [d'iəvLı] *adj* devilish, fiendish.

diadhachd [d'iəghəchg] *f* godhead; godliness; theology.

diadhaidh [d'iəghı] *adj* pious, godly.

diollaid [d'iəLıd'] *f* saddle.

dian [d'iən] *adj* eager; fierce; intense.

dian-ruith [d'iənruih] *f* headlong rush.

DiarDaoin [d'ıəršdūN'] *m* Thursday.

dias [d'iəs] *f* ear of corn.

dibhearsan [d'ivɛršan] *m* fun; entertainment.

dìblidh [d'ībli] *adj* abject.

dicheall [d'īch'əL] *m* diligence, application.

dicheallach [d'īch'əLəch] *adj* diligent; hardworking.

di-cheannaich [d'īch'aNıch'] *v* behead.

DiCiadain [d'ık'iədɛN'] *m* Wednesday.

DiDòmhnaich [d'ıdōnıch'] *m* Sunday.

dìg [d'īg'] *f* ditch.

DihAoine [d'ıhūN'ı] *m* Friday.

dìle [d'īlı] *f* heavy rain; flood.

dìleab [d'īləb] *f* legacy.

dìleas [d'īləs] *adj* faithful, trusty.

dìle bhàthte [d'īlı vāʰt'ı] *f* downpour.

DiLuain [d'ıLuəN'] *m* Monday.

DiMàirt [d'ımāršt'] *m* Tuesday.

dìmeas [d'īmɛs] *m* disrespect; contempt.

dinn [d'īN'] *v* stuff, cram.

dinnear [d'īN'ɛr] *f* dinner.

diobair [d'ībır'] *v* desert, abandon.

dìobhair [d'īvır'] *v* vomit, sick up.

diochuimhne [d'iəchənı] *f* forgetfulness; oblivion.

diochuimhneach [d'iəchənəch] *adj* forgetful.

diochuimhnich [d'iəchənıch'] *v* forget.

diofar [d'ifər] *f* difference; importance.

diofarach [d'ifərəch] *adj* different.

diogail [d'igal] *v* tickle.

diogalach [d'igaLəch] *adj* ticklish.

dìoghail [d'ī.al] *v* repay; take revenge.

dìoghaltas [d'Ī.aLtəs] *m* revenge.

dealas [d'aLəs] *m* zeal; enthusiasm.

dìolain [d'iəLɛN'] *adj* bastard, illegitimate.

diomb [d'umb] *m* indignation; displeasure.

diombach [d'umbəch] *adj* out of sorts; indignant.

dìombuan [d'iəmbuən] *adj* transient, fleeting.

dìomhain [d'iəvɛN'] *adj* vain; idle.

dìomhair [d'iəvɛr'] *adj* secret.

dìomhanas [d'iəvənəs] *m* vanity, futility.

dìon [d'iən] *v* protect, shelter. • *m* protection, shelter.

dìonach [d'iənəch] *adj* sheltering; safe; wind and watertight.

dìorrasach [d'iəRəsəch] *adj* keen; tenacious.

dìosail [diəsal] *m* diesel.

dìosgail [d'iəsgal] *f* creaking; crunching.

dìosgan [d'iəsgan] *m* grating; squeaking.

diosgo [disgə] *m* disco.

dìreach [d'īr'əch] *adj* straight; upright; just.

dìreach! [d'ir'əch] *excl* quite!, just so!, exactly!

dìreadh [d'īr'əgh] *m* ascent; climbing.

dìrich[1] [d'īr'ich'] *v* straighten.

dìrich[2] [d'īr'ich'] *v* climb.

DiSathairne [d'ɪsahərnɪ] *m* Saturday.

dìsne [d'īšnɪ] *m* dice.

dìt [d'ī̄t'] *v* condemn, sentence.

dìteadh [d'ī̄t'əgh] *m* condemnation; sentence.

dìth [d'ī] *m* lack, want.

dìthean [d'īhan] *m* flower.

dithis [d'i.ɪš] *f* two, twosome, pair.

dìthreabh [d'īrəv] *f* desert, wilderness.

diùc [d'ū̄k] *m* duke.

diùid [d'ūd'] *adj* shy, timid.

diùlt [d'ūLt] *v* refuse; disown.

diù nan . . . [d'ū nən/nəN/nəN'] the worst of . . .

Diùra [d'ūrə] *f* Jura.

Diùrach [d'ūrəch] *m/adj* from Jura.

dleasdanas [dlesdənəs] *m* duty.

dlighe [dli.ɪ] *f* right, due.

dligheach [dli.əch] *adj* rightful, legitimate.

dlùth [dLū] *adj* near; dense.

dlùthaich [dLū.ich'] *v* draw near, approach.

dlùths [dLūs] *m* density.

do[1], **d'** [də] [d] *poss pron* your (*sing*).

do[2], **a** [də] [ə] *prep* to; into; for.

do- [də] *prefix* un-, in-, im-.

dòbhran [dōran] *m* otter.

dòchas [dōchəs] *m* hope.

do-dhèanta [dəgh'iantə] *adj* impossible.

dòigh [dɔy] *m* way, manner; condition.

dòigh-beatha [dɔi bɛhə] *m* lifestyle, way of life.

dòighean [dɔi.ən] *mpl* customs; manners.

dòigheil [dɔi.ɛl] *adj* proper; in good order.

doille [doL'ı] *f* blindness.

doilleir [doL'ər'] *adj* dark; gloomy.

doilleirich [doL'ər'ıch'] *v* darken; obscure.

doimhne [doiN'ı] *f* (*with art*) **an doimhne** [ən doiN'ı] the deep.

doimhneachd [doiN'əchg] *f* depth.

doimhnich [doiN'ıch'] *v* deepen.

doinnean [doiN'an] *f* storm, tempest.

doirbh [dor'iv] *adj* hard, difficult.

doire [dor'ı] *f* grove, thicket, copse.

dòirt [dõršd'] *v* pour; shed; flow.

do-labhairt [dɔLavəršd'] *adj* unspeakable.

dolar [dɔLər] *m* dollar.

dol-a-mach [dɔLəmach] *m* behaviour, conduct.

dòlas [dõLəs] *m* grief.

dol-às [dɔL as] *m* way out, escape.

dol fodha na grèine [dɔL fɔ.ə nə grẽnı] *m* sunset.

dòmhail [dõ.al] *adj* crowded; dense.

domhainn [dɔ.ıN'] *adj* deep; profound.

domhan [dɔ.an] *m* (*with art*) **an Domhan** [ən dɔ.an] the Universe.

dona [dɔnə] *adj* bad; naughty.

donas [dɔnəs] *m* badness, evil; (*with art*) **an Donas** [ən dɔnəs] the Devil.

donn [douN] *adj* brown; brown-haired.

donnal [dɔNəL] *m* howl.

donnalaich [dɔNəLıch'] *f* howling.

doras [dɔrəs] *m* door.

dorcha [dɔrəchə] *adj* dark.

dorchadas [dɔrəchədəs] *m* darkness.

dòrlach [dõrLəch] *m* fistful, handful.

dòrn [dõrn] *m* fist.

dòrtadh-fala [dõrštəghfaLə] *m* bloodshed.

dos [dɔs] *m* bagpipe drone.

dotair [dɔʰtɛr'] *m* doctor.

doth [dɔh] *v* singe, scorch.

drabasdach [drabəsdəch] *adj* obscene.

dràbhail [drãbhal] *adj* grotty.

drabhair [dra.ɛr'] *m* drawer.

dràc [drãʰk] *m* drake.

dragh [drogh] *m* trouble, bother; worry.

draghail [droghal] *adj* worrying; annoying.

dràibh [drãiv] *v* (*car, etc*) drive.

dràibhear [drãivɛr] *m* driver.

drama [dramə] *m* dram.

dràma [drãmə] *m* drama.

dranndan [drauNdan] *m* snarl(ing), growl(ing).

draoidh [druy] *m* druid; magician.

draoidheachd [drui.əchg] *f* wizardry, magic.

draoidheil [drui.ɛl] *adj* magic, magical.

draosda [drũsdə] *adj* smutty, lewd.

draosdachd [drũsdəchg] *f* smut, lewdness.

drathais [dra.ıš] *fpl* underpants; pants, knickers.

dreach [dr'ɛch] *m* appearance, aspect; complexion.

dreallag [dr'ɛLag] *f* (child's) swing.

drèana [dr'ẽnə] *f* drain, drainage ditch.

dreasa [dr'ɛsə] *f* dress.

dreasair [dr'ɛsɛr'] *m* dresser.

dreathan-donn [dr'ɛhandouN] *m* wren.

dreuchd [dr'iachg] *f* occupation, profession.

dreuchdail [dr'iachgal] *adj* professional.

driamlach [dr'iəmLəch] *f* fishing line.

drile [dr'ilı] *f* drill, auger.

drioftair [dr'iftɛr'] *m* (*fishing*) drifter.

drip [dr'iʰp] *f* bustle, state of being busy.

dripeil [dr'iʰpɛl] *adj* busy.

dris [dr'iš] *f* bramble; brier.

drithleann [dr'iləN] *m* sparkle, flash.

driùchd [dr'iūchg] *f* dew.

dròbh [drōv] *m* cattle drove.

dròbhair [drōvɛr'] *m* cattle-drover.

droch [drɔch] *adj* bad.

drochaid [drɔchıd'] *f* bridge.

droch bheart [drɔch vyaršd] *f* vice; evil deed.

droch bheus [drɔch vēs] *f* bad manners.

droch chainnt [drɔch chaiN'd'] *f* bad language, swearing.

droch chòrdadh [drɔch chōrdəgh] *m* disagreement, bad terms.

droch ionnsaigh [drɔch iūN'sı] *f* physical assault.

droch isean [drɔch išan] *m* brat, naughty child.

droch nàdarrach [drɔch nādəRəch] *adj* ill-natured, ill-tempered.

droga [drɔgə] *f* drug; *pl* **drogaichean** [drɔgıch'ən] (*illegal, etc*) drugs.

drùdhag [drū.ag] *f* drop; sip.

druid [drid'] *f* starling.

drùidh [drūy] *v* soak, penetrate (to skin).

drùidh air [drūy] *v* affect, make an impression on.

druim [druim] *m* back; ridge.

drùis [drūš] *f* lust, lechery.

drùiseach [drūšəch] *adj* lustful, lecherous.

druma [drumə] *f* drum.

duais [duəš] *f* wages; reward; award.

dual¹ [duəL] *m* character; birthright.

dual² [duəL] *m* curl, lock; plait.

dualaich [duəLıch'] *v* curl; twist, plait.

dualchainnt [duəLchaiN'd'] *f* dialect.

dualchas [duəLchəs] *m.* hereditary character.

dualtach [duəLtəch] *adj* inherent, natural; **dualtach a bhith** [duəLtəch ə vi] inclined to be.

duan [duan] *m* poem, song.

duanag [duanag] *f* song, ditty.

dùbailte [dūbəlt'ı] *adj* double; dual.

dubh [duh] *v* blacken. • *m* black; ink. • *adj* black; dark-haired.

dubhach [du.əch] *adj* gloomy; in a bad mood.

dubhadh [du.əgh] *m* eclipse.

dubhag [du.ag] *f* kidney.

dubhaigeann [du.aig'əN] *m* abyss, the deep.

dubhan [du.an] *m* hook.

dubhar [du.ər] *m* shade.

dubh às [duh as] *v* erase; blot out.

dubh-dhonn [dughəuN] *adj* dark brown.

dubh-ghorm [dughɔrəm] *adj* dark blue.

Dùbhlachd [dūLəchg] *f* (*with art*) **an Dùbhlachd** [ən dūLəchg] December.

dùbhlan [dūLan] *m* challenge.

dubh-nòta [du nōʰtə] *m* (*mus*) crotchet.

dùblaich [dūbLıch'] v double.
dùdag [dūdag] f bugle.
dubh-thràth [durā] m dusk.
dùil[1] [dūl] f hope; expectation.
dùil[2] [dūl] f created being; element.
duileasg [duləsg] m dulse.
duilgheadas [dulgh'ədəs] m difficulty; problem.
duilgheadasan sòisealta [dulgh'ədəsən sōsəLtə] mpl social problems.
duilich [dulıch'] adj hard, difficult; unfortunate. • excl **tha mi duilich!** [ha mi dulıch'] I'm sorry!
duilleach [duL'əch] m foliage.
duilleachan [duL'əchan] m leaflet.
duilleag [duL'ag] f leaf; page, sheet.
dùin [dūN'] v shut, close.
duine [duN'ı] m man; person; human being; husband. • pron someone; **duine sam bith** [duN'ı səm bi] anyone at all.
duinealas [duN'əLəs] m manliness; decisiveness.
duine cloinne [duN'ıkloN'ı] m child.
duineil [duN'ɛl] adj manly; decisive; mannish.
duine lag-chùiseach [duN'ı Lag chūšəch] m stick-in-the-mud.
duine-uasal [duN'uəsəL] m gentleman; nobleman.

dùinte [dūN'd'ı] adj closed, shut; introvert.
dùisg [dūšg'] v wake, awaken.
Duitseach [duht'šəch] m/adj Dutch person; Dutch.
dùn [dūn] m hill fort, fortress; conical hill.
dùnan [dūnan] m small hill; dung heap.
dùr [dūr] adj stubborn; dour.
dùrachd [dūrəchg] f seriousness; sincerity; greeting.
dùrachdach [dūrəchgəch] adj serious, earnest.
dùraig [dūrıg'] v dare.
durcan [durkan] m pine cone, fir cone.
dùrdail [dūrdal] f cooing.
dùsal [dūsəL] m slumber, snooze.
dusan [dusan] m dozen.
dùsgadh [dūsgəgh] m awakening.
duslach [dusLəch] m dust.
dustach [dusdəch] adj dusty.
dustair [dusdɛr] m duster.
dùthaich [dū.ıch'] f country; homeland; countryside.
dùthchas [dūchəs] m cultural inheritance.
dùthchasach [dūchəsəch] adj native, indigenous.

E

e [ɛ] pron he; him; it (m).
eabar [ɛbər] m mud, mire.
Eabhra [ɛvrə] f Hebrew (language).
Eabhrach [ɛvrəch] m/adj Hebrew.
eacarsaich [ɛhkərsıch'] f exercise.
each [ɛch] m horse.

each-aibhne [ɛchaivN'ı] m hippopotamus.
eachdraiche [ɛchdrıch'ə] m historian.
eachdraidh [ɛchdrı] f history.
eachdraidheil [ɛchdrı.ɛl] adj historical.

each-oibre [ɛchoibr'ɪ] *m* workhorse.

each-uisge [ɛchušg'ɪ] *m* water-horse, kelpie.

eaconamachd [ɛkɔnəməchg] *f* economics.

eaconamaidh [ɛkɔnəmɪ] *m* economy.

eaconamair [ɛkɔnəmɪr'] *m* economist.

Eadailt [edalt'] *f (with art)* **an Eadailt** [ə N'edalt'] Italy.

Eadailteach [edalt'əch] *m/adj* Italian.

eadar [edər] *prep* between; among; both.

eadaraibh [edərɪv] *prep pron* between you; among you.

eadarainn [edərɪN'] *prep pron* between us; among us.

eadar dà bharail [edər dā varal] *adv* undecided; between two stools.

eadar-dhealachadh [edərgh'aLəchəgh] *m* difference; distinction.

eadar-dhealaich [edərgh'aLɪch'] *v* differentiate; distinguish.

eadar-dhealaichte [edərgh'aLɪcht'ə] *adj* different; distinct, separate.

eadar-nàiseanta [edərnāšəndə] *adj* international.

eadar-sholas [edərhɔLəs] *m* twilight.

eadar-theangachadh [edərhɛngəchəgh] *m* translation.

eadar-theangaich [edərhɛngɪch'] *v* translate.

eadhon [eghən] *adv* even.

eadradh [edrəgh] *m* milking.

eag [eg] *f* nick, notch.

eagal [egaL] *m* fear, fright; **eagal mo bheatha** [egaL mə vɛhə] the fright of my life.

eagalach [egaLəch] *adj* prone to fear; terrible, dreadful. • *adv* terribly, dreadfully.

eaglais [egLɪš] *f* church; *(with art)* **an Eaglais Shaor** [ə N'egLɪš hūr] the Free Church; **Eaglais na h-Alba** [egLɪš nə haLabə] the Church of Scotland.

eala [ɛLə] *f* swan.

èalaidh [iaLɪ] *v* creep; sneak away.

ealain [ɛLɛN'] *f* art; **Comhairle Ealain na h-Alba** [kɔ.ərlɪ ɛLɛN' nə haLabə] the Scottish Arts Council.

ealanta [ɛLandə] *adj* artistic.

ealantair [ɛLaNdɛr'] *m* artist.

eallach [ɛLach] *m* load, burden.

ealta [ɛLtə] *f (birds)* flock.

ealtainn [ɛLtɪN'] *f* razor.

eanchainn [ɛnachɪN'] *f* brain.

eanraich [ɛnarɪch'] *f* soup, broth.

ear [ɛr] *f* east.

ear air [ɛr ɛr'] *prep* east of.

earalachadh [ɛraLəchəgh] *m* exhortation.

earalaich [ɛraLɪch'] *v* exhort; caution.

Earranta, Earr. [ɛRəntə] *adj (company)* Limited, Ltd.

earb[1] [ɛrab] *v* trust.

earb[2] [ɛrab] *f* roe-deer.

earb à [ɛrab a] *v* trust in.

earball [ɛrabəL] *m* tail.

earbsa [ɛrabsə] *f* trust; confidence; reliance.

earbsach [ɛrabsəch] *adj* trusting; trustworthy.

eàrlas [iarləs] *m (financial)* deposit.

earrach [ɛRəch] *m* spring; **as t-earrach** [əs t'ɛrəch] in spring.

earrann [ɛRəN] *f* part, section; piece.

eas [es] *m* waterfall.

eas- [es] prefix in-, dis-, un-.

coileach-fiodha [kɔləchfyoghə] m pheasant.

easaonta [esũntə] f disagreement; dissent.

easbaig [esbɪg'] m bishop.

Easbaigeach [esbɪg'ach] m/adj Episcopalian. • adj episcopal.

easbhaidh [esvī] f lack, want, need.

easbhaidheach [esvi.əch] adj needy; needful, lacking.

eascaraid [eskarɪd'] m foe.

èasgaidh [iasgɪ] adj active; willing; **èasgaidh a dhèanamh** [iasgɪ ə gh'ianəv] willing/keen to do it.

easgann [esgaN] f eel.

eas-ùmhail [esū.al] adj disobedient, insubordinate.

eas-urramach [esuRəməch] adj dishonourable.

eathar [ɛhər] m rowing boat.

eatorra [ɛhtəRə] prep pron between them; among them.

èibhinn [ēvɪN'] adj funny, amusing.

èibhleag [ēvlag] f ember.

èideadh [ēd'əgh] m dress, garb; uniform.

eidheann [e.əN] f ivy.

èifeachdach [ēfəchgəch] adj effective; efficient.

eigh [ey] f ice.

eugh [ēv] v shout, call. • f shout, cry.

eighe [e.ə] f (tool) file.

-eigin su [eg'ɪn] ffix some-.

èiginn [ēg'ɪN'] f difficulty; trouble; need; violence.

Eilbheis [elevɪš] f (with art) **an Eilbheis** [ə N'elevɪš] Switzerland.

Eilbheiseach n/ [elevɪšəch] adj Swiss.

èildear [ēld'ɛr] m church elder.

eile [elɪ] adj other; another.

eilean [elan] m island.

eileanach [elanəch] m islander.

Eilean a' Cheò [elanəch'ō] m (nickname) Skye.

Eilean Ì [elanī] m Iona.

Eilean Luing [elanLuing'] m Luing.

Eilean Ruma [elanrumə] m (the Isle of) Rum.

eilid [elɪd'] f hind.

eilthireach [elɪrəch] m foreigner; exile.

einnsean [ēN'šan] m engine.

einnsean-smàlaidh [ēN'šansmāLɪ] m fire engine.

Èipheit [ēfɪt'] f (with art) **an Eipheit** [ə N'ēfɪt'] Egypt.

Èipheiteach [ēfɪt'əch] m/adj Egyptian.

eireachdail [erachgal] adj elegant; handsome.

eireag [erag] f pullet.

Èireannach [ēr'əNach] m/adj Irishman; Irish.

Èirinn [ēr'ɪN'] f Ireland.

èirich [ēr'ɪch'] v rise, get up; rebel.

èirich do [ēr'ɪch' dɔ] v happen to, befall, become of.

eiridinn [er'ɪd'ɪN'] m nursing.

eiridnich [er'ɪd'nɪch'] v nurse, tend.

èirig [ēr'ɪg'] f ransom.

èirigh na grèine [ēr'ɪ nə grēnɪ] f sunrise.

eirmseach [er'ɪmšəch] adj witty.

èist (ri) [ēšd' r'ɪ] v listen (to).

eisimealachd [ešɪmɛLəchg] f dependence.

eisimeileach [ešɪmɛLəch] adj dependent.

eisimpleir [ešɪmplər'] m example.

eist! [ešd'] excl hush! be quiet!

eitean [eʰt'an] m kernel; core.

eòlach [yɔ̄L'ch] *adj* knowledgeable; acquainted.

eòlach air [yɔ̄Ləch] *adv* familiar with.

eòlaiche [yɔ̄Lɪch'ə] *m* expert.

eòlas¹ [yɔ̄Ləs] *m* knowledge; acquaintance.

eòlas² [yɔ̄:Ləs] *m* science.

eòlas-leighis [yɔ̄Ləs L'e.ɪš] *m* (*science of*) medicine.

eòrna [yɔ̄rnə] *m* barley.

Eòrpa [yɔ̄rpə] *f* Europe; (*with art*) **an Roinn Eòrpa** [ən RəiN'ɔ̄rpə *m* Europe.

Eòrpach [yɔ̄rpəch] *m/adj* European.

esan [ɛsən] *pron* (*emphatic form of* **e**) he; him.

eu- [ē] prefix un-, dis-, -less.

euchd [ēchg] *m* feat; achievement.

eucoir [ēkɔr'] *f* crime.

eucoireach [ēkɔr'əch] *m* criminal.

eu-coltach [ēkɔLtəch] *adj* dissimilar; unlikely.

eud [ēd] *m* jealousy; zeal.

eudach [ēdəch] *adj* jealous; zealous.

eudail [ēdal] *f* treasure; **mo eudail!** [mēdal] my dear!

eu-dòchas [ēdɔ̄chəs] *m* hopelessness.

eun [ian] *m* bird, fowl.

eunan-àir [iananär'] *m* bird of prey.

eun-eòlas [ianyɔ̄Ləs] *m* ornithology.

eun-mara [ianmarə] *m* seabird.

eun-uisge [ianušg'ɪ] *m* waterfowl.

euslaint [ēsland'] *f* illness, ill-health.

euslainteach [ēsland'əch] *adj* ill, unhealthy. • *m* invalid; patient.

F

fàbhar [fāvər] *m* favour.

fabhra [faurə] *m* eyelid.

facal [faʰkəl] *m* word; saying.

fa chomhair [fa chou.ɪr'] *prep* opposite; in front of.

faclach [faʰkLəch] *adj* wordy, verbose.

faclair [faʰkLɛr'] *m* dictionary.

faclaireachd [faʰkLɛr'əchg] *f* lexicology; lexicography.

fad [fad] *m* length; the whole, all the.

fada [fadə] *adj* long; tall. • *adv* far, much.

fada air falbh [fad ɛr' faLav] *adv* faraway, distant.

fadachd [fadachg] *f* longing; nostalgia; impatience; boredom.

fadalach [fadaLəch] *adj* late; tedious; long drawn out.

fada nas fheàrr [fadə nə šāR] much/far better.

fad an latha [fad ən La.ə] *adv* all day, the whole day.

fada 'nur comain [fadə nər komɛN'] much obliged to you.

fad às [fad as] *adj* remote, distant; (*person*) withdrawn.

fàd mònach [fād mɔnəch] *m* a single peat.

fad na h-oidhche [fad nə hoi.ch'ɪ] *adv* all night.

fad na h-ùine [fad nə hūN'ɪ] *adv* all the time, constantly.

fad-shaoghalach [fadhū.əLəch] *adv* long-lived.

fad-shaoghalachd [fadhū.əLəchg] *f* longevity.

fàg [fāg] *v* leave; abandon.

faic [fɛʰk'] *v* see.

faiceall [fɛʰk'əL] *f* care, caution.

faiceallach [fɛʰk'əLəch] *adj* careful, cautious.

faiche [faich'ɪ] *f* meadow, grass park.

faicsinneach [fɛʰk'šɪN'əch] *adj* visible; conspicuous.

faide [fad'ɪ] *f* length.

fàidh [fāy] *m* prophet, seer.

fàidheadaireachd [fāi.ədɛr'əchg] *f* prophecy.

faigh [faich'] *v* get, obtain; find.

faigh air ... [faich' ɛr'] *v* get to ..., manage to ...

faigh air adhart [faich' ɛr' o.əršd] *v* get on, progress.

faigh a-mach [faich' əmach] *v* find out, discover.

faigh bàs [faich' bās] *v* die, get killed.

faigh cron do [faich' krɔn dɔ] *v* blame.

faigh cuidhteas de [faich' kuiʰt'əs d'e] *v* get rid/shot of.

faigh do sheise [faich' də heši] *v* meet your match.

faighean [fai.an] *m* vagina.

faigh faire air [faich' far'ɪ ɛr'] *v* spot, catch sight of.

faigh lorg air [faich' Lɔrəg ɛr'] *v* track down, locate.

faigh muin [faich' muN'] *v* have sex, copulate.

faighneach [faiN'əch] *adj* inquisitive, enquiring.

faighnich [faiN'ɪch'] *v* ask, enquire.

faigh seachad air [faich' šachəd ɛr'] *v* get over.

faigh seòl air [faich' šɔL ɛr'] *v* contrive to, manege to.

failc [falk'] *v* bathe.

faileas [falas] *m* shadow; reflection.

faileasach [falasəch] *adj* shadowy.

faillean [faL'an] *m* eardrum.

fàillig [fāL'ɪg'] *v* fail.

fàillinn [fāL'ɪN'] *f* failing, fault; blemish; failure.

falman [faLaman] *m* kneecap.

fail-mhuc [falvuʰk] *f* pigsty.

fàilte [fālt'ɪ] *f* welcome.• *excl* **fàilte oirbh!** [fālt' or'iv] welcome to you! you're welcome!

fàilteach [fālt'əch] *adj* welcoming; hospitable.

fàilteachail [fālt'əchal] *adj* welcoming; hospitable.

fàiltich [fālt'ɪch'] *v* welcome.

fang [fang] *f* sheepfold, fank.

fàinne [fāN'ɪ] *f* (*finger*) ring.

fàinne-phòsaidh [fāN'ɪfɔsɪ] *f* wedding ring.

fàinne-sholais [fāN'ɪhɔLɪš] *f* halo.

faire [far'ɪ] *f* guard; watch.

fàire [fār'ɪ] *f* horizon, skyline.

faireachdainn [farəchgɪN'] *f* sensation; emotion, feeling.

fàireag [fār'ag] *f* gland.

fairich [far'ɪch'] *v* feel; smell.

fairtlich air [faršd'Lɪch' ɛr'] *v* get the better of, defeat; baffle.

faisg [fašg'] *adj* near, close.

fàisg [fāšg'ɪ] *v* squeeze; wring.

faisge [fašg'ɪ] *f* nearness, closeness.

fàisneachd [fāšN'əchg] *f* prophecy.

faite-gàire [faʰt'ɪgār'ɪ] *f* smile.

faitheam [fɛhəm] *m* hem.

faitich [faʰt'ɪch'] *v* smile.

fàl [fāL] *m* hedge; verge.

falach [faLəch] *m* hiding, conceal-
ment.

falachd [faLəchg] *f* feud.

falach-fead [faLəch fed] *m* hide-
and-seek.

falaich [faLɪch'] *v* hide.

falaichte [faLɪch't'ɪ] *adj* hidden,
concealed.

falamh [faLəv] *adj* empty.

falamhachd [faLəvəchg] *f* empti-
ness; void.

falbh [faLav] *v* leave, go away.

falbh a dh'iarraidh [faLav ə gh'iəRɪ]
v go to fetch/get.

falbh air dèirc [faLav ɛr' d'ɛrk'] *v*
beg.

fa leth [fa leh] *adv* separate; apart.

fallainn [faLɪN'] *adj* sound, healthy;
wholesome; able-bodied.

fallas [faLəs] *m* sweat; **tha fallas
orm** [ha faLəs ɔrəm] I'm sweating.

fallasach [faLəsəch] *adj* sweaty.

fallsa [fauLsə] *adj* false, deceitful.

falmadair [faLamədər'] *m* helm.

falmhachd *see* **falamhachd.**
[faLəvəchg]

falmhaich [faLəvich'] *v* empty.

falt [faLt] *m* (*of head*) hair.

famh [fav] *f* (*animal*) mole.

fàmhair [fāvɪr'] *m* giant.

fan [fan] *v* wait; stay.

fanaid [fanɪd'] *f* mockery, ridicule.

fan aig [fan ɛg'] *v* lodge with.

fan air [fan ɛr'] *v* wait for.

fànas [fānəs] *m* space; void.

fainear dhomh [faN'ɛr ghɔ] *adv* on
my mind, in my thoughts.

fann [fauN] *adj* weak, faint.

fannaich [faNɪch'] *v* weaken.

fanntaig [fauNdɪg'] *v* faint, swoon.

faobhar [fūvər] *m* (*of blade*) edge.

faobharaich [fūvərɪch'] *v* sharpen.

faochadh [fūchəgh] *m* relief, respite.

faochag [fūchag] *f* whelk, winkle.

faod [fūd] *v* can, may, might.

faoighe [fui.ɪ] *f* begging, cadging.

faoileag [fūlag] *f* seagull.

faoilidh [fūlɪ] *adj* hospitable; generous; frank.

Faoilteach [fūlt'əch] *m* (*with art*) **am
Faoilteach** [əm fūlt'əch] January.

faoin [fūN'] *adj* silly, foolish; empty-
headed; futile.

faoineas [fūN'əs] *m* silliness, vacui-
ty; futility.

faoinsgeul [fūN'sg'iaL] *m* myth,
legend.

faoisid [fūšɪd'] *f* confession.

faoisidich [fūšɪd'ich'] *v* confess.

faothachadh [fū.əchəgh] *m same as*
faochadh.

faothaich [fū.ich'] *v* relieve, alleviate.

far [far] *prep* from, down from.

far a [farə] *conj* where.

faradh [farəgh] *m* (*rail, etc*) fare.

fàradh [fārəgh] *m* ladder.

far-ainm [farɛnɛm] *m* nickname.

faram [faram] *m* loud noise.

faramach [faraməch] *adj* loud,
noisy.

farchluais [farachLuəš] *f* eavesdrop-
ping.

fàrdach [fārdəch] *f* house; dwelling,
lodging.

farmad [faraməd] *m* envy.

farpais [farpɪš] *m* competition.

farpaiseach [farpɪšəch] *m* competitor.

farranaich [faRanɪch'] *v* tease.

farsaing [farsɪng'] *adj* wide, broad.

farsaingeachd [farsɪng'əchg] *f* width, breadth; area.

farspag [farspag] *f* black-backed gull.

fàs[1] [fās] *v* grow; become.

fàs[2] [fās] *adj* waste, uncultivated; barren.

fàsach [fāsəch] *m* desert, wilderness; deserted place.

fàsaich [fāsɪch'] *v* empty; depopulate.

fàsail [fāsail] *adj* desolate.

fasan [fasan] *m* fashion.

fasanta [fasantə] *adj* fashionable.

fasgach [fasgəch] *adj* sheltered; sheltering.

fasgadh [fasgəgh] *m* shelter, protection.

fasgain [fasgɛN'] *v* winnow.

fa sgaoil [fa sgūl] *adv* free, at liberty.

fastaich [fasdɪch] *v* hire, employ.

fastaidhear [fasdɪ.ɛr] *m* employer.

fàth [fāh] *m* cause; reason; opportunity.

fathann [fahəN] *m* rumour.

feabhas [fyɔ.əs] *m* improvement; excellence.

feachd [fɛchg] *f* army.

fead [fed] *v* whistle. • *f* (*noise*) whistle.

feadag [fedag] *f* (*instrument*) whistle; plover.

feadaireachd [fedɪr'əchg] *f* whistling; playing a whistle.

feadan [fedan] *m* chanter; pipe, tube, spout.

feadhainn [fyɔ.ɪN'] *f* some; (*with art*) **an fheadhainn** [ə N'ɔ.ɪN'] those, the ones.

feagal [fegal] *m* fear, fright (*dialectal form*).

feàirrde [fyāRd'ɪ] *adj* better.

fealladh [fyaLəgh] *m* foul; foul play.

fealla-dhà [fyaLə ghā] *f* joke, jest.

feall-falach [fyauLfaLach] *m* ambush.

feallsanach [fyauLsanəch] *m* philosopher.

feallsanachd [fyauLsanəchg] *f* philosophy.

feamainn [fɛmɪN'] *f* seaweed. • *v* manure (*usu with seaweed*).

feannag [fyaNag] *f* crow; ridge; lazybed.

feannag ghlas [fyaNag ghLas] *f* hooded crow.

feansa [fɛnsə] *f* fence.

fear [fɛr] *m* man; one.

fearail [fɛral] *adj* manly.

fearalachd [fɛraLəchg] *f* manliness.

fear-allabain [fɛaraLəbɛN'] *m* wanderer.

fearann [fɛrəN] *m* ground, land.

fear-bainnse [fɛrbaiN'ši] *m* bridegroom.

fear-brèige [fɛrbrēg'ɪ] *m* puppet.

fear-cinnidh [fɛrk'iN'i] *m* clansman, fellow clansman.

fearg [fɛrag] *f* anger.

feargach [fɛragəch] *adj* angry.

feàrna [fyārnə] *f* alder.

feàrr [fyāR] *adj* better; best.

fear seach fear [fɛr šach fɛr] in turn; one by one.

feart [fyaršt] *f* attention, heed; quality, characteristic.

feasgar [fesgər] *m* afternoon; evening. • *adv* in the afternoon/evening, p.m.

fèath [fia] *m* (*weather*) calm.

fèichear [fēch'ɛr] *m* debtor.

fèileadh beag [fēləgh beg] *m* kilt.

fèill [fēL'] *f* feast, festival, fair; sale, market.

Fèill Brìde [fēL'brīd'ı] *f* (with art) an **Fhèill Brìde** [aN' ēL'brīd'ı] Candlemas.

fèin[1] [fēn], **fhèin** [hēn] *refl pron* self; own.

fèin[2] [fēn] *m* (with art) **am fèin** [əm fēn] the ego, the self.

fèin-eachdraidh [fēnɛchdrı] *f* autobiography.

fèinealachd [fēnəLəchg] *f* selfishness.

fèineil [fēnɛl] *adj* selfish.

fèin-mholadh [fēnvɔLəgh] *m* conceit.

fèin-riaghladh [fēnriəLəgh] *m* selfgovernment.

fèin-spèis [fēnsbēš] *f* conceit, selfregard.

fèis [fēš] *f* festival.

fèist [fēšd'] *f* feast, banquet.

feith [feh] *v* wait; stay.

fèith[1] [fē] *f* muscle; sinew; vein.

fèith[2] [fē] *f* bog, marsh.

feòil [fyōl] *f* meat; flesh.

feòladair [fyōLədər'] *m* butcher.

feòil-muice [fyōlmuıʰk'ı] *f* pork.

feòrag [fyōrag] *f* squirrel.

feòraich [fyōrıch'] *v* ask, enquire.

feuch [fiach] *v* try, attempt; try out, test.

feuch deuchainn [fiach d'iachıN'] *v* sit an exam.

feum [fēm] *v* must, have to; need.
• *m* need; use, usefulness, good.

feumach [fēməch] *adj* needy, in need.

feumail [fēmal] *adj* useful, handy; necessary.

feur [fiar] *m* grass; hay.

feurach [fiarəch] *adj* grassy.

feuraich [fiarıch'] *v* graze.

feusag [fiasag] *f* beard.

feusgan [fiasgan] *m* mussel.

fhad 's a [adsə] *conj* while, as long as.

fhathast [ha.asd] *adv* yet; still.

fhèin[1] [hēn] *refl pron* same as **fèin**[1].

fhèin[2] [hēn] *adv* even.

fhuair [huər'] *past tense of v* **faigh**

fiabhras [fiəvrəs] *m* fever.

fiacail [fiaʰkal] *f* tooth; *pl* **fiaclan fuadain** [fiaʰklən fuadɛN'] false teeth, dentures.

fiach[1] [fiach] *adj* worth, worthwhile; of value.

fiach[2] [fiach] *m* value, worth; debt.

fiach[3] see **feuch**. [fiach]

fiach! [fiach] *excl* lo! behold!

fiachail [fiachal] *adj* worthy, respectable; valuable.

fiaclach [fiaʰkLəch] *adj* toothed, toothy; dental.

fiaclaire [fiaʰkLər'ə] *m* dentist.

fiaclan fuadain see **fiacail**.

fiadh [fiagh] *m* deer.

fiadhaich [fia.ıch'] *adj* wild; angry, furious.

fial [fiaL] *adj* generous; hospitable; tolerant.

fiamh [fiə] *adj* hue, tint; complexion; expression; fear.

fiamh-ghàire [fiəghār'ı] *m* smile.

fianais [fiənıš] *f* evidence, testimony.

fianaiseach [fiənıšəch] *m* witness.

fiar [fiər] *adj* bent; slanting; squinting; cunning.

fiar [fiər] *v* bend, curve; slant; squint.

fiaradh [fiərəgh] *m* slant; squint.

fiar-shùilleach [fiərhūləch] *adj* squint-eyed.

fichead [fich'əd] *m* twenty, a score.

ficheadamh [fich'ədəv] *adj* twentieth.

fideag [fid'ag] *f* (*instrument*) whistle.

fidheall [fi.əL] *f* fiddle, violin.

fidhlear [fīlɛr] *m* fiddler, violinist.

fidir [fid'ɪr'] *v* appreciate, comprehend.

fige [fig'ɪ] *f* fig.

figear [fig'ɛr] *m* (*numerical*) figure.

figh [fī] *v* weave; knit.

fighe [fi.ɪ] *f* weaving; knitting.

figheachan [fi.əchan] *m* pigtail, pony-tail.

figheadair [fi.ədər'] *m* weaver; knitter.

fighte [fīt'ɪ] *adj* woven; knitted.

fileanta [filandə] *adj* eloquent, articulate; fluent.

fileantach [filandəch] *m* native speaker; fluent speaker.

filidh [fīlɪ] *m* poet.

fill [fīL'] *v* fold; pleat; plait.

filleadh [fiL'əgh] *m* fold; pleat; plait.

fillte [fīL't'ɪ] *adj* folded; pleated; plaited.

film [filim] *m* film.

fine [finɪ] *f* clan; tribe.

fiodh [fyogh] *m* wood, timber.

fiolan-gòbhlach [fyuLangōLəch] *m* earwig.

fion [fiən] *m* wine.

fionan [fiənan] *m* vine.

fion-dearc [fiənd'ɛrk] *f* grape.

fion-geur [fiən giar] *m* vinegar.

fionn[1] [fyūN] *v* flay.

fionn[2] [fyūN] *adj* white.

fionnach [fyuNəch] *adj* hairy; rough, shaggy.

fionnadh [fyuNgh] *m* (*animal*) hair.

fionnaireachd [fyuNɪr'əchg] *f* coolness.

fionnan-feòir [fyuNanfyōr'] *m* grasshopper.

fionnar [fyuNər] *adj* cool, fresh; cold, off-hand.

fionnaraich [fyuNərɪch'] *v* cool; refrigerate.

fionnsgeul [fyūNsgiaL] *m* legend.

fìor[1] [fiər] *adj* real; genuine.

fìor[2] [fiər] *adv* very.

fìor-uisge [fiərušg'ɪ] *m* pure water.

fios [fis] *m* knowledge; information; word, message, news.

fiosaiche [fisɪch'ə] *m* prophet, seer; fortune teller.

fiosrach [fisrəch] *adj* well-informed.

fiosrachadh [fisrəchəgh] *m* information.

Fir Chlis [fir' ch'liš] *mpl* (*with art*) **na Fir Chlis** [nə fir' chl'iš] the Northern Lights, Aurora Borealis.

fireann [fir'əN] *adj* masculine, male.

fireannach [fir'əNəch] *m* man; male.

fireannach [fir'əNəch] *adj* truthful.

fireanta [fir'əndə] *adj* same as **fireann**.

fìrinn [fīr'ɪN'] *f* truth.

fitheach [fi.əch] *m* raven.

fiù [fyū] *m* worth, value. • *adj* worth.

fiùdalach [fyūdaLəch] *adj* feudal.

fiù 's [fyūs] *adv* even.

flanainn [fLanɪN'] *f* flannel.

flath [flah] *m* king, prince; ruler.

fleadh [flɛgh] *m* feast, banquet.

fleasgach [flesgəch] *m* youth, stripling; bachelor.

fleisg [flešg'] *f* (*elec*) flex.

fleòdradh [flɔ̄drəgh] *m* floating; buoyancy.

fliuch [fluch] *v* wet. • *adj* wet.

flùr[1] [fLūr] *m* flower.

flùr[2] [flūr] *m* flour.

flùranach [flūrənəch] *adj* flowery.

fo [fɔ] *prep* under, beneath, below; affected by.

fo-aodach [fɔ ūdəch] *m* underwear.

fo bhlàth [fɔ vLā] *adv* in bloom.

fo bh ròn [fɔ vrɔ̄n] *adv* sad, sorrowful.

fo chasaid [fɔ chasɪd'] *adv* accused.

fo chomain [fɔ chomɛN'] *adv* obliged.

fo chùram [fɔ chūrəm] *adv* anxious; preoccupied.

fòd [fɔd] *f* (single) peat; sod; clod of earth.

fodar [fɔdər] *m* fodder.

fodha [fɔ.ə] *prep pron* under him, under it (*m*).

fodhad [fɔ.əd] *prep pron* under you (*sing*).

fodhaibh [fɔ.ɪv] *prep pron* under you (*pl*).

fodhainn [fɔ.ɪN'] *prep pron* under us.

fodham [fɔ.əm] *prep pron* under me.

fo-dhearg [fɔgh'ɛrag] *adj* infra-red.

fo dhìmeas [fɔ gh'īmes] *adv* despised.

fodhpa [fɔʰpə] *prep pron* under them.

fo eagal [fɔ egaL] *adv* afraid.

fo fhiachaibh [fɔ iachɪv] *adv* obliged, under an obligation.

fògair [fɔgɪr'] *v* banish, exile; drive out.

foghain [fɔ.ɛN'] *v* suffice, do, be enough. • *excl* **fòghnaidh sin!** [fōnɪ šin] that will do!

foghar [fɔ.ər] *m* autumn; harvest.

fo gheasaibh [fɔ gh'esɪv] *adv* spellbound, enchanted.

foghlaim [fōLɪm] *v* educate.

foghlaimte [fōLɪmt'ɪ] *adj* educated, learned.

foghlam [fōLəm] *m* education; scholarship.

fòghnadh [fōnəgh] *m* sufficiency.

fòthannan [fōhəNan] *m* thistle.

fo ghruaim [fɔ ghruəim] *adv* gloomy; grumpy, in ill-humour.

fògrach [fōgrəch] *m* exile; fugitive; refugee.

fògradh [fōgrəgh] *m* exile, banishment.

fòid *see* **fòd**. [fɔd']

foidhpe [foiʰpɪ] *prep pron* under her, under it (*f*).

foighidinn [foid'ɪN'] *f* patience.

foighdinneach [foid'ɪN'əch] *adj* patient.

foileag [fɔlag] *f* pancake.

foill [foiL'] *f* deceit; fraud, deception; cheating.

foilleil [foiL'ɛl] *adj* deceitful; fraudulent.

foillsich [foiL'šɪch] *v* publish.

foillsichear [foiL'šɪch'ɛr] *m* publisher.

fo imcheist [fɔ imich'ešd'] *adv* anxious; perplexed.

fo iomagain [fɔ imagɛN'] *adv* anxious; troubled.

fo iongnadh [fɔ iūnəgh] *adv* amazed; abashed.

foinne [foiN'ı] *m* wart.

foirfe [furfı] *adj* perfect; full-grown.

foirfeach [furfəch] *m* (church) elder.

foirmeil [forimɛl] *adj* formal.

fòirneart [fɔrN'ɛršd] *m* violence, force; oppression.

fois [fɔš] *f* rest, ease, leisure; peace.

fo-lèine [fɔ lēnı] *f* vest.

follais [fɔLıš] *f* evidentness, obviousness; clarity; openness.

follaiseach [fɔLıšəch] *adj* evident, clear; public.

fo-mhothachail [fɔ vɔ.əchal] *adj* subconscious.

fo mhulad [fɔ vulad] *adv* sad.

fòn [fɔn] *v* telephone. • *f* telephone.

fònaig [fɔnıg'] *v* telephone.

fo nàire [fɔ nār'ı] *adv* ashamed.

fonn [fouN] *m* tune; mood, state of mind.

fonnmhor [fouNvər] *adj* tuneful, melodious.

for [fɔr] *m* attention; notice; concern.

fo-rathad [fɔ ra.ad] *m* underpass.

forc [fɔrk] *f* fork.

forladh [fɔrLəgh] *m* (army, etc) leave.

forsair [fɔrsɛr'] *m* forester, forestry worker.

fortan [fɔršdan] *m* fortune; luck. • *excl* **fortan leat!** [fɔršdan laʰt] good luck!

for-thalla [fɔrhaLə] *m* foyer.

fosgail [fosgal] *v* open.

fosgailte [fosgalt'ı] *adj* open, opened; frank.

fosgladh [fosgLəgh] *m* opening, gap; opportunity.

fo smachd [fɔ smachg] *adj* under subjection.

fo smalan [fɔ smaLan] *adv* gloomy, melancholy.

fo-thiotalan [fɔhiʰt'əLən] *mpl* subtitles.

fo uallach [fɔ uəLəch] *adv* under stress.

fradharc *see* **radharc**

Fraingis [frang'ıš] *m* (with art) **an Fhraingis** [ən Rang'ıš] French (language).

Frangach [frangəch] *m/adj* Frenchman; French.

fraoch [früch] *m* heather, heath, ling.

fraoidhneas [frūN'əs] *m* fringe.

fras [fras] *v* rain lightly, shower. • *f* shower; seed.

frasair [frasɛr'] *m* (bathroom) shower.

freagair [fr'egır'] *v* answer, reply; suit.

freagairt [fr'egıršd] *f* answer, reply.

freagarrach [fr'egəRəch] *adj* suitable.

frèam [fr'ɛm] *m* frame, framework.

freasdail [fr'esdal] *v* serve, wait on.

freiceadan [fr'eʰk'ədan] *m* watch; guard; (with art) **am Freiceadan Dubh** [əm fr'eʰk'ədan du] the Black Watch.

freiceadan-oirthire [fr'eʰk'ədanər'ir'ə] *m* coastguard.

freumh [fr'ēv] *m* root.

frìde [fr'īd'ı] *f* corpuscle; insect.

frioghan [fr'ighan] *m* bristle.

frionasach [fr'ınasəch] *adj* worried; upset; vexing, niggling.

frith [fr'īh] *f* moorland; deer forest.

frith-ainm [fr'ihɛnɛm] *m* nickname.

frithealadh [fr'ihəLəgh] *m* attendance, service.

frithearra [fr'ihəRə] *adj* touchy; peevish.

fritheil [fr'ihɛl] *v* serve, wait on.

frith-rathad [fr'ira.ad] *m* footpath; track.

froca [frɔʰkə] *m* frock.

fuachd [fuachg] *f* cold, coldness; (*with art*) **am fuachd** [əm fuachg] a/the cold.

fuadach [fuədəch] *m* banishment; driving away; *pl* (*with art*) **na Fuadaichean** [nə fuədɪch'ən] (*hist*) the Highland Clearances.

fuadachadh [fuədəchəgh] *m* same *as* **fuadach**.

fuadaich [fuədɪch'] *v* banish; drive away.

fuadain [fuədɛN'] *adj* artificial, false.

fuadan [fuədan] *m* wandering; exile.

fuaigh [fuəy] *v* sew; stitch; seam.

fuaigheal [fuəgh'al] *m* sewing; stitching; seaming.

fuaigheil [fuəgh'ɛl] *v* sew; stitch.

fuaighte [fuəit'ɪ] *adj* sewn; stitched.

fuaim [fuəɪm] *f* noise; sound.

fuaimneach [fuəɪmnəch] *adj* noisy.

fuaimneachadh [fuəɪmnəchəgh] *m* pronunciation.

fuaimnich [fuəɪmnɪch'] *v* pronounce.

fuaimreag [fuəɪmrag] *f* vowel.

fuaim-thonn [fuəɪmhɔuN] *m* sound wave.

fual [fuəL] *m* urine.

fuar [fuər] *adj* cold.

fuaradair [fuərədər'] *m* refrigerator, fridge.

fuaraich [fuərɪch'] *v* cool, chill.

fuaraidh [fuərɪ] *adj* (*lit and fig*) cool, chilly.

fuaran [fuəran] *m* spring, well.

fuasgail [fuəsgal] *v* release; untie; disentangle; solve.

fuasgladh [fuəsgLəgh] *m* solution; absolution.

fuath [fuəh] *f* hatred, loathing.

fuathach [fuəhəch] *adj* hateful, detestable.

fuathaich [fuəhɪch'] *v* hate, loathe, detest.

fùdar [fūdər] *m* powder.

fùdaraich [fūdərɪch'] *v* powder.

fuidheall [fui.əL] *m* relic; remainder.

fuighleach [fuiləch] *m* rubbish, refuse.

fuil [ful] *f* blood.

fuiling [fulɪŋ'] *v* suffer; bear, put up with.

fuil-mìos [fulmiəs] *f* menstruation, period.

fuilteach [fult'əch] *adj* bloody, gory.

fuiltean [fult'an] *m* (*single*) hair.

fuin [fuN'] *v* bake; knead.

fuineadair [fuN'ədər'] *m* baker.

fuirich [fur'ɪch'] *v* stay; live, dwell; wait; **fuirich aig X** [fur'ɪch' ɛg'] lodge with X. • *excl* **fuirich ort!** [fur'ɪch' ɔršt] hang on! wait a minute! **fuirich orm . . .** [fur'ɪch' ɔrəm] let me see now . . .

fùirneis [fūrN'ɛš] *f* furnace.

fulang [fuləng] *m* suffering; endurance, hardiness.

fulangach [fuləngəch] *adj* hardy; long-suffering; passive.

fulmair [fuLumɛr'] *m* fulmar.

furachail [furachal] *adj* watchful; observant; **furachail air** [furachal ɛr'] on the watch for.

furan [furan] *m* welcome, hospitality.

furasda [furəsdə] *adj* easy.

furm [furum] *m* form, bench.

furtachd [furšdəchg] *f* relief; consolation, solace.

furtaich [furšdɪch'] *v* console, comfort.

G

gabh [gav] ~ [go] *v* take; capture; perform.

gàbhadh [gāvəgh] *m* danger, peril.

gabh a' ghrian [gav ə ghrian] *v* sunbathe.

gàbhaidh [gāvɪ] *adj* dangerous, perilous.

gabhail [gahal] *f* lease; course; reception, welcome.

gabh air [gav ɛr'] *v* make for.

gabh air do shocair [gav ɛr' də həʰkɪr'] *v* take things easily.

gabh air mhàl [gav ɛr' vāL] *v* rent.

gabhaltach [gavaLtəch] *adj* infectious.

gabhaltas [gavaLtəs] *m* tenancy; rented holding.

gabh an cùram [gav ən kūrəm] be converted, become devout.

gabh beachd [gav byachg] *v* form an opinion.

gabh brath air [gav brah ɛr'] *v* take advantage of.

gabh cead (de) [gav ked d'e] *v* take one's leave (of).

gabh cuairt [gav kuəršt'] *v* take a stroll; take a trip.

gabh do anail! [gav tanal] take a rest/breather!

gabh eagal [gav egal] *v* become afraid, take fright.

gabh fois [gav foš] *v* take a rest/break.

gabh gnothach ri [gav gro.əch r'i] *v* interfere with/in; get involved in.

gabh grèim air [gav grēm ɛr'] *v* take hold of, seize.

gabh iongantas [gav iūntəs] *v* be amazed.

gabh mo leisgeul! [gav mɔ lešg'ial] *excl* excuse me!

gabh mo thaobh [gav mɔ hūv] *v* take my side.

gabh nàire [gav nār'ɪ] *v* be/feel ashamed.

gabh os làimh [gav os Lāiv] *v* undertake, take on.

gabh pàirt [gav pāršt'] *v* participate.

gabh ri [gav r'i] *v* accept.

gabh seilbh air [gav šɛliv ɛr'] *v* take possession of.

gabh smùid [gav smūd'] *v* (*fam*) get drunk.

gabh socair [gav sɔʰkɪr'] *v* take one's ease.

gabh suim [gav suim] *v* care.

gabh truas de [gav truəs d'e] *v* take pity on.

gabh ùidh ann an [gav ūy auN ən] *v* take an interest in.

gach [gach] *adj* each, every.

gach aon [gach ūn] *adj* every single.

gach uile [gach ulı] *adj* each and every.

gad [gad] *m* supple stick, switch.

gadaiche [gadıch'ə] *m* thief.

gagach [gagach] *adj* stammering, stuttering.

Gàidheal [gē.aL] *m* Gael; Highlander; Gaelic speaker.

Gàidhealach [gē.əLəch] *adj* Highland.

Gàidhealtachd [gē.əLtəchg] *f* (*with art*) **a' Ghàidhealtachd** [gē.əLtəchg] the Highlands.

Gàidhlig [gālıg'] *f* (*also with art*) **Gàidhlig/a' Ghàidhlig** [ə ghālıg'] Gaelic (language).

gail [gal] *v* weep, cry.

gailbheach [galvəch] *adj* stormy.

gaileiridh [galər'ı] *m* art gallery.

gailleann [gaL'əN] *f* storm, tempest.

gainmheach [gɛnavəch] *f* sand.

gainne [gaN'ı] *f* scarcity.

gainnead [gaN'əd] *m* scarcity.

gàir [gār'] *v* laugh.

gàir [gār'] *m* cry; outcry.

gairbhe [gar'ıvı] *f* roughness; wildness.

gairbhead [gar'ıvəd] *m* roughness; wildness.

gàirdeachas [gārd'əchəs] *m* joy; rejoicing.

gàirdean [gārd'an] *m* arm.

gàireachdainn [gār'əchgıN'] *f* laughing, laughter.

gairleag [garlag] *m* garlic.

gairm [gor'im] *v* cry; call; crow. • *f* cry; call; cock-crow.

gairm-chogaidh [gor'imchəgı] *f* war-cry.

gairmeach [gor'iməch] *adj* (*gram*) vocative.

gàirnealair [gārN'aLɛr'] *m* gardener.

gàirnealaireachd [gārN'aLər'əchg] *f* gardening.

gaiseadh a' bhuntàta [gašəgh ə vuntā^htə] *m* potato blight.

gaisge [gašg'ı] *f* bravery, heroism.

gaisgeach [gašg'əch] *m* hero; champion.

gaisgeil [gašgɛl] *adj* brave, heroic.

gal [gaL] *m* crying, weeping.

galan [gaLan] *m* gallon.

galar [gaLar] *m* disease.

Gall [gauL] *m* Lowlander; non-Gael.

galla [gaLə] *f* bitch.

gallan [gaLan] *m* standing stone.

Gallda [gauLdə] *adj* Lowland.

Galldachd [gauLdəchg] *f* (*with art*) **a' Ghalldachd** [ə ghauLdəchg] the Lowlands.

gàmag [gāmag] *f* octave.

gamhainn [gavıN'] *m* stirk.

gamhlas [gauLəs] *m* malice, ill-will.

gamhlasach [gauLəsəch] *adj* malevolent, spiteful.

gann [gauN] *adj* scarce, scant, rare.

gaoid [gūd'] *f* blemish, defect.

gaoir [gūr'] *f* (*of anguish*) cry.

gaoisid [gūšıd'] *f* animal hair; horsehair.

gaol [gūL] *m* love. • *excl* **a ghaoil!** [ə ghūl] darling! (my) love!

gaolach [gūLəch] *adj* loving; beloved.

gaoth [gū] *f* wind; (*with art*) **a' ghaoth** [ə ghū] wind, flatulence.

gaothach [gū.əch] *adj* windy; flatulent.

gàradh see **gàrradh** [gārəgh]

garbh [garav] *adj* rough; harsh; coarse. • *adv (fam)* very, terribly.

garg [garag] *adj* fierce; unruly.

gàrradh [gāRəgh] *m* wall, stone wall; garden.

gartan [garšdan] *m* garter.

gas [gas] *f* stalk; shoot. • *m* gas.

gasda [gasdə] *adj* handsome; splendid; *(fam)* great.

gath [ga] *m* barb; sting; spear; beam.

gath-grèine [gagrēnɪ] *f* sunbeam.

ge [ge] *conj* though.

gèadh [giagh] *m* goose.

geal [gyaL] *adj* white. • *m* white part of anything.

gealach [gyaLəch] *f* moon.

gealach an abachaidh [gyaLəch ən abachɪ] *f* harvest moon.

gealagan [gyaLagan] *m* egg white.

gealaich [gyaLɪch] *v* whiten.

gealbhonn [gyaLvəuN] *m* sparrow.

geall [gyauL] *v* promise, pledge. • *m* bet, wager; promise.

gealladh [gyaLəgh] *m* promise.

gealladh-pòsaidh [gyaLəghpōsɪ] *m* engagement, betrothal.

gealltanach [gyauLtənəch] *adj* promising.

gealtach [gyauLtəch] *adj* cowardly; fearful.

gealtaire [gyauLtərʼə] *m* coward.

geama [gɛmə] *m* game, match.

geamair [gɛmɛrʼ] *m* gamekeeper.

geamhradh [gyaurəgh] *m* winter.

gean [gʼɛn] *m* mood, frame of mind.

geanmnachd [gʼɛnamnəchg] *f* chastity.

geanmnaidh [gʼɛnamnɪ] *adj* chaste.

geansaidh [gʼɛnsɪ] *m* jersey, jumper.

gèar [gʼiar] *f (engine)* gear.

gearain [gʼɛrɛNʼ] *v* complain, grumble.

gearan [gʼɛran] *m* complaining; complaint.

gearanach [gʼɛranəch] *adj* complaining, querulous.

gearastan [gʼɛrasdən] *m* garrison; *(with art)* **An Gearastan** [ən gʼɛrasdən] Fort William.

Gearmailt [gʼɛramaltʼ] *f (with art)* **a' Ghearmailt** [ə ghʼɛramalt'] Germany.

Gearmailteach [gʼɛramaltʼəch] *m/adj* German.

Gearmailteis [gʼɛramaltʼɪš] *f (with art)* **a' Ghearmailtis** [əghʼɛramaltʼɪš] German (language).

gèarr[1] [gʼāR] *v* cut; castrate. • *adj* short.

gèarr[2] [gʼāR] *f* hare.

gearradh [gʼaRəgh] *m* cut; *pl* **gearraidhean** [gʼaRɪ.ən] *(financial)* cuts.

Gearran [gʼaRan] *m (with art)* **an Gearran** [ən gʼaRan] February.

gearran [gʼaRan] *m* gelding; pony, garron.

geàrr-shealladh [gʼāRhyaLəgh] *m* short-sightedness.

geas [gʼes] *f* enchantment, spell.

geata [gɛʰtə] *m* gate.

ge b'e cò [ge bɛ kō] *pron* whoever.

ged a [gedə] *conj* though, although.

gèile [gēlɪ] *m* gale.

gèill [gēLʼ] *v* yield, surrender.

geimheal [gʼevaL] *m* fetter, shackle.

geimhlich [gʼevlɪchʼ] *v* fetter, shackle.

geinn [gʼēNʼ] *m* chunk; wedge.

geir [gʼerʼ] *f* suet; fat.

gèire [gēr'ı] *f* sharpness; bitterness.

geòcach [g'ɔʰkəch] *adj* greedy, gluttonous.

geòcaire [g'ɔʰkər'ə] *m* glutton.

geòcaireachd [g'ɔʰkər'əchg] *f* greed, gluttony.

geodha [g'ɔ.ə] *m* cove, narrow bay.

geòla [g'ɔ̄Lə] *f* yawl, small boat.

geòlas [g'ɔ̄Ləs] *m* geology.

ge-tà [getā] *adv* though.

geug [g'iag] *f* branch.

geum [g'ēm] *m* bellow; bellowing; lowing. • *v* bellow; low.

geur [g'iar] *adj* sharp; bitter; sarcastic.

geuraich [g'iarıch'] *v* sharpen.

geur-chùiseach [g'iar chūsəch] *adj* smart, shrewd.

gheibh [gh'ev] *future tense of v* **faigh**.

giall [g'iəL] *f* jaw.

Giblean [g'iblan] *m (with art)* **an Giblean** [ən g'iblan] April.

Giblinn see **Giblean**.

gidheadh [g'i.əgh] *adv* nevertheless.

gilb [g'ilib] *f* chisel.

gile [g'ilı] *f* whiteness.

gilead [g'iləd] *m* whiteness.

gille [g'iLı] *m* boy, lad; young man.

gille-brìghde [g'iLıbrīd'ı] *m* oystercatcher.

gin¹ [g'in] *v* beget; conceive; breed.

gin² [g'in] *pron* any; *(with neg v)* none.

gineal [g'inal] *progeny*; race.

ginealach [g'inaLəch] *m* generation.

gineamhainn [g'inəvıN'] *m* conception; breeding.

ginideach [g'inid'əch] *adj (gram)* genitive.

giodar [g'idər] *m* sewage.

giodhar [g'i.ər] *m (engine)* gear.

giomach [g'iməch] *m* lobster.

gioma-goc [g'imə gɔʰk] *m* piggyback.

gionach [g'inəch] *adj* keen, ambitious; greedy.

gionaiche [g'inıch'ə] *f* greed: ambition.

giorrachadh [g'iRəchəgh] *m* shortening; curtailment; abbreviation.

giorrad [g'iRəd] *m* shortness.

giorraich [g'iRıch'] *v* shorten; abbreviate; curtail.

giosg [g'iəsg] *v* gnash.

giùlain [g'ūLεN'] *v* carry.

giùlan [g'ūLan] *m* carrying; carriage; behaviour.

giùran [g'ūran] *m (of fish)* gill.

giuthas [g'u.əs] *m (wood and tree)* pine, fir tree.

glac¹ [gLaʰk] *f* small valley; hollow; palm of hand.

glac² [gLaʰk] *v* catch, trap; grasp; apprehend.

glacte [gLaʰkt'ı] *adj* captured, trapped.

glagadaich [gLagədıch'] *f* clattering; rattling.

glaine [gLanı] *f* cleanliness.

glainne [gLaN'ı] *f* glass.

glainneachan [gLaN'əchən] *fpl* glasses, spectacles.

glais [gLaš] *v* lock.

glaiste [gLašd'ı] *adj* locked.

glam [gLam] *v* gobble, devour.

glan [gLan] *v* clean, cleanse. • *adj* clean; *(fam)* fine, grand.

glaodh¹ [gLūgh] *v* call, shout, yell. • *m* call, shout, yell.

glaodh² [gLū] *v* glue. • *m* glue.

glaodhan [gLū.an] *m* paste; pulp.

glas[1] [gLas] *f* lock.

glas[2] [gLas] *adj* grey; green.

glas-làmh [gLasLàv] *f* handcuff.

glasraich [gLasrɪch'] *f* vegetable(s), greens.

glè [glē] *adv* very.

gleac [glɛʰk] *v* struggle; wrestle. • *m* struggle; wrestling.

gleacadair [glɛʰkədər'] *m* wrestler.

gleadhar [glɛ.ər] *m* uproar.

gleadhraich [glɛrɪch'] *f* clamour, din.

gleann [glɛuN] *m* glen, valley.

glèidh [glē] *v* keep; save; conserve.

glèidhteachas [glēt'achəs] *m* conservation.

Glèidhteachas Nàdair [glēt'achəs Nàdɪr'] *m* Nature Conservancy.

glè mhath [glē va] *adv/adj* very good; very well.

gleoc [glɔʰk] *m* clock.

gleus [glēs] *v* get ready; put in trim; adjust; (*mus*) tune. • *m* condition, trim; mood; (*mus*) tuning.

gleusda [glēsdə] *adj* ready; handy; in good trim; in good humour; (*mus*) tuned.

glic [gliʰk'] *adj* wise; clever; sensible.

gliog [glig] *m* (*sound*) drip, dripping.

gliongartaich [glingəršdɪch'] *m* clinking, jingling.

gloc [gLɔʰk] *v* cackle.

glocail [gLɔʰkal] *f* cackle, cackling.

gloinne [gLɔN'ɪ] *f* glass.

gloinneachan [gLɔN'əchən] *fpl* glasses, spectacles.

glòir [gLɔr'] *m* glory; fame.

glòirich [gLɔr'ɪch'] *v* glorify.

glòir-mhiann [glōr'vian] *m* ambition.

glòrmhor [glōrvər] *adj* glorious.

gluais [gLuəš] *v* move; touch, affect.

gluasad [gLuəsəd] *m* movement; gait; emotional arousal.

gluasadach [gLuəsədəch] *adj* capable of moving.

glug [gLug] *m* gurgling; gulping.

glugan [gLugan] *m* gurgling.

glug caoinidh [gLug kūN'ɪ] *m* sob.

glumag [gLumag] *f* pool (*in burn, etc*); puddle.

glùn [gLūn] *m* knee.

gnàth, gnàthas [grā] [grā.əs] *m* custom; habit.

gnàthach [grāhəch] *adj* customary, normal.

gnàthaich [grāhɪch'] *v* use; accustom; behave towards, treat.

gnè [gr'ɛ] *f* kind; species; gender.

gnìomh [gr'iəv] *m* act, action.

gnìomhach [gr'iəvəch] *adj* active; enterprising; hardworking.

gnìomhachas [gr'iəvəchəs] *m* industry; business; industriousness.

gnìomhaiche [gr'iəvɪch'ə] *m* executive.

gnìomhair [gr'iəvɛr'] *m* verb.

gnog [grog] *v* knock; nod.

gnothach [grɔ.əch] *m* business; matter, affair; errand.

gnù [grū] *adj* surly, sullen.

gnùis [grūš] *f* face; complexion; expression.

gob [gob] *m* beak, bill; (*fam*) gob; point.

gobach [gobəch] *adj* prattling, chattering.

gobaireachd [gobɪr'achg] *f* prattle, prattling.

gobha [go.ə] *m* blacksmith.

gobhal [go.al] *m* fork; (*anat*) crotch.

gobhal-gleusaidh [go.alglēsɪ] *m* tuning fork.

gobhar [go.ər] *f* goat.

gobhlach [gōl̪əch] *adj* forked.

gobhlag[1] [gōlag] *f* pitch-fork, hayfork.

gobhlag[2] [gōl̪ag] *f* earwig.

gobhlan-gaoithe [gōlangū.ɪ] *m* swallow.

goc [gɔʰk] *m* tap; stopcock.

gogail [gogal] *f* cackling; clucking.

goid [god'] *v* steal, thieve. • *f* stealing, thieving.

goil [gol] *v* boil; seethe.

goile [golɪ] *f* stomach.

goileach [goləch] *adj* boiling.

goileam [goləm] *m* prattle, tittle-tattle.

goireas [gor'əs] *m* resource, facility; (*pl*) **goireasan** [gor'əsən] public conveniences.

goireasach [gor'əsəch] *adj* handy, convenient.

goireasan see **goireas.**

goirid [gor'ɪd'] *adj* short; brief.

goirt [gɔršd'] *adj* painful, sore; sour; bitter; severe.

goirtich [gɔršd'ɪch'] *v* hurt.

goistidh [gošd'ɪ] *m* godfather; sponsor; gossip.

gòrach [gōrəch] *adj* stupid; foolish, daft.

gòraiche [gōrɪch'ə] *f* stupidity; foolishness.

gorm [gorəm] *adj* blue; green.

goṛt [gɔršd] *f* famine; starvation.

gràbhail [grāval] *v* engrave.

grad [grad] *adj* sudden; alert; agile.

gràdh [grā] *m* love. • *excl* **a ghràidh!** [ə ghrāy] love! dear!

gràdhach [grā.əch] *adj* loving, affectionate.

gràf [grāf] *m* graph.

gràg [grāg] *m* croak, caw.

gràgail [grāgal] *f* croaking, cawing.

gràin [grāN'] *f* hatred; loathing, disgust; **tha gràin agam air** [ha grāN' agəm ɛr'] I hate him/it.

gràineag [grāN'ag] *f* hedgehog.

gràineil [grāN'ɛl] *adj* hateful, abominable, loathsome.

gràinne [grāN'ɪ] *f* (*single*) grain (*of corn*).

gràinnean [grāN'an] *m* grain (*of sugar, etc*).

gràisg [grāšg'] *f* (*derog*) crowd; mob.

gràisgeil [grāšgɛl] *adj* uncouth, yobbish.

grama [gramə] *m* gram(me).

gramail [gramal] *adj* persistent.

gràmar [grāmər] *m* grammar.

gràmarach [grāmərəch] *adj* grammatical.

gràn [grān] *m* cereal; (*coll*) grain.

granaidh [granɪ] *f* granny.

grannda [grauNdə] *adj* ugly.

gràpa [grāʰpə] *m* (*agricultural*) fork.

gràs [grās] *m* grace; graciousness.

gràsmhor [grāsvər] *adj* gracious.

greadhnach [gr'ɛnəch] *adj* gorgeous; magnificent.

greallach [gr'aLəch] *f* entrails, innards.

greannach [gr'aNəch] *adj* ill-tempered.

greannmhor [gr'auNvər] *adj* cheerful, joyful.

greas [gr'es] v hurry, urge on.
• excl **greas ort!** [gr'es ɔršd] hurry
up!

grèata [gr'ɛʰtə] m grate; grating.

greideal [gr'ed'al] f griddle.

Grèig [gr'ēg'] f (with art) **a' Ghrèig**
[ə ghr'ēg'] Greece.

greigh [gr'ey] f herd; flock; (of
horses) stud.

greigheach [gr'ei.əch] adj gregarious.

grèim [gr'ēm] m grip, grasp, hold;
(med) stitch.

grèim bidh [gr'ēm bī] m bite to eat.

grèim-cluaise [gr'ēmkLuəši] m ear-
ache.

greimeil [gr'emɛl] adj resolute.

greimich ri/air [gr'emıch' r'i/ɛr'] v
seize, grasp.

greimire [gr'emır'ə] m (table) fork.

greis [gr'eš] f while, time.

grèis [gr'ēš] f needlework, embroidery (i.e. the activity, see **obair-
ghrèise** [obır'ghr'ēšı]).

greiseag [gr'ešag] f short while.

Greugach [gr'ēgach] m/adj Greek
person; Greek.

Greugais [gr'ēgıš] f (with art) **a'
Ghreugais** [ə ghr'ēgıš] Greek
(language).

greusaiche [gr'iasıch'ə] m shoemaker, cobbler.

grian [gr'ian] f sun.

grinn [gr'iN'] adj elegant, fine; neat;
accurate.

grinneal [gr'iN'aL] m gravel; (of sea,
etc) bottom.

grinneas [gr'iN'əs] m elegance;
fineness; neatness.

grìogag [gr'īgag] f bead.

Grioglachan [gr'igLachan] m (with

art) **an Grioglachan** [ən gr'igLachan]
the Pleiades.

Griomasach [gr'iməsəch] m/adj
Grimsay person, from Grimsay.

Griomasaigh [gr'iməsı] m Grimsay.

grìos [gr'iəs] m (cookery) grill.

grìosaich [griəsıch'] v (food) grill.

griùlach [gr'ūLəch] f (with art) **a'
ghriùlach** [ə ghr'ūLəch] measles.

grod [grɔd] v rot, putrefy. • adj rotten, rotted, putrid.

grodach [grɔdəch] adj grotty.

grodach-coimhead [grɔdəch kɔi.əd]
adj (fam) grotty-looking.

grodadh [grɔdəgh] m rot, putrefaction.

gròiseid [grōšɛd'] f gooseberry.

gròsair [grōsɛr'] m grocer.

gruag [gruəg] f (head of) hair.

gruagach [gruəgəch] f maid, girl,
young woman.

gruagaire [gruəgər'ə] m hairdress-
er.

gruag-bhrèige [gruəgvr'ēg'ı] f wig.

gruaidh [gruəy] f cheek.

gruaim [gruəım] f gloom, melancholy; scowl; sulkiness; grumpi-
ness.

gruamach [gruəməch] adj gloomy;
morose; sulking; grumpy.

grùdair [grūdɛr'] m brewer.

grùdaireachd [grūdɛr'əchg] f brew-
ing.

grùid [grūd'] f lees, dregs, grounds;
sediment.

grunn [grūN] m crowd; many, lots
of.

grunnd [grūNd] m base; sea-bed.

grùnsgal [grūnsgəL] m growl,
growling.

gruth [gruh] m curd(s); crowdie.

grùthan [grūhan] *m* (*usu animal*) liver.

gu¹ [gə] *prefix introducing an adverb.*

gu² see gus.

guailleachan [guaL'əchan] *m* shawl.

gual [guaL] *m* coal.

gualan [guaLan] *m* carbon.

gualann [guaLəN] *f* shoulder. *f* shoulder.

gual-fiodha [guaLfyoghə] *m* charcoal.

guanach [gruənəch] *adj* giddy, scatter-brained; coquettish.

guanag [guənag] *f* scatter-brained girl; coquettish girl.

gu bochd [gə bəchg] *adv* poorly.

gu bràth [gə brāch] *adv* ever; for ever.

gu bràth tuilleadh [gə brāch tuL'əgh] *adv* (*with neg v*) nevermore.

gu buileach [gə buləch] *adv* entirely.

gucag [guʰkag] *f* (*botany*) bud; bubble.

gucag-uighe [guʰkagui.ɪ] *f* egg-cup.

gu 'chùl [gə chūL] *adv* through and through.

gu dè? [gud'ē] *pron* (*for emphasis*) what?, whatever?.

gu dearbh [gə d'ɛrav] *adv* indeed; definitely.

gu dearbh fhèin [gə d'ɛrav hēn] *adv* extremely.

gu diofair [gə d'ifər] *adv* of importance.

gu dubh dona [gə du dənə] *adv* absolutely terribly.

guga [gugə] *m* young gannet, young solan goose.

gu grad [gə grad] *adv* suddenly; shortly.

gu h-aon sgeulach [gə hūn sg'iaLəch] *adv* unanimously.

gu h-àraid[gə hār'ɪd'], gu h-àraidh [gə hār'ɪ] *adv* especially, particularly.

gu h-iomlan [gə hiəmLan] *adv* fully, absolutely.

guidh [guy] *v* beg, beseech; pray.

guidhe [gui.ɪ] *f* plea, entreaty; prayer.

guilbneach [gulibnəch] *m* curlew.

guin [guN'] *v* sting. • *m* sting.

guineach [guN'əch] *adj* sharp; acerbic; wounding.

guir [gur'] *v* hatch.

guirean [gur'an] *m* pimple, spot.

gu lèir [gə L'ēr'] *adv* entire, entirely.

gu leòr [gə L'ōr] *adv* enough, plenty.

. . . gu leth [gə L'e] *adv* . . . and a half.

gum see gun.

gu mì-fhortanach [gə mī ɔršdanəch] *adv* unfortunately.

gu minig [gə minɪg'] *adv* often.

gun¹ [gum] [gun] *conj* that.

gun² [gən] *prep* without.

gùn [gūn] *m* gown.

gun bhuannachd [gən vuəNəchg] *adv* fruitless.

gun chadal [gən chadaL] *adv* sleepless.

gun chaomhnadh [gən chūvnəgh] *adv* unsparingly.

gun chiall [gən ch'iaL] *adv* senseless; meaningless.

gun chùnntas [gən chūNdəs] *adv* countless, innumerable.

gun dòchas [gən dōchəs] *adv* hopeless.

gun fheum [gəN' ēm] *adv* useless.

gun fhios do X [gəN' is də] without X's knowledge.

gun fhios nach [gəN' is nach] *conj* lest, in case.

gun fhiù [gəN' ū] *adv* worthless.

gun ghluasad [gən ghLuəsəd] *adv* still, motionless.

gun luach [gən Luəch] *adj* worthless.

gun mheang [gən vɛng] *adj* flawless.

gunna [guNə] *m* gun.

gunnair [guNɛr'] *m* gunner.

gun nàire [gən Nār'ɪ] *adv* shameless.

gun obair [gən obɪr'] *adv* unemployed.

gùn-oidhche [gūnoich'ɪ] *m* nightgown.

gun sgillinn ruadh [gən sg'iLɪN' ruəgh] *adv* (stony) broke.

gun smior [gən smir] *adj* spineless, wet.

gun teagamh [gən t'ɛgəv] *adv* doubtless, without a doubt.

gun tomhas [gən to.əs] *adj* incalculable, immeasurable.

gun uiread is [gən ur'əd ɪs] *adv* without so much as.

gurraban [guRəban] *m* crouch, crouching position.

gu ruige [gu Rig'ɪ] *prep* up to, as far as; until.

gu ruige an-seo [gu Rig'ɪ ənšə] *adv* this far; so far, up to now.

gus, gu [gus] [gu] *conj* to, in order to. • *prep* to, towards, up to; until.

gu bhith . . . [gu vi] about to (be) . . .; **gu bhith a' falbh** [gu vi ə faLav] about to leave.

gu sealladh orm! [gu šaLəgh ərəm] *excl* my goodness!

gu sealladh sealbh oirnn! [gu šaLəgh šeLav ərN'] *excl* Heaven preserve us!

gu sìorraidh [gu šiəRɪ] *adv* for ever.

gu sìorraidh bràth [gu šiəRɪ brāch] *adv* for ever and ever.

gu sònraichte [gu sōnrɪch't'ə] *adv* especially, particularly.

guth [guh] *m* voice; news, word; mention; **gun guth air X** [gən ghuh ɛr'] not to mention X.

gu tur [gu tur] *adv* completely, totally, entirely.

H

halò [halō] *excl* hello/hullo.

heactair [hɛktɛr'] *m* hectare.

Hearach [hɛrach] *m/adj* Harris person, from Harris.

Hearadh [hɛrəgh] *f (with art)* **na Hearadh** [nə hɛrəgh] Harris.

heileacoptair [hɛləkᵒʰptɛr'] *m* helicopter.

hidrigin [hidrɪg'ɪn] *m* hydrogen.

Hiort [hiršd] *f* St Kilda.

Hiortach [hiršdəch] *m/adj* St Kildan.

hò-rò gheallaidh [hō rō gh'aLɪ] *m* party, knees-up, hoolie.

I

i [ī] *pron* she, her, it (*f*).

iad [iəd] *pron* they, them.

iadsan [iədsən] *pron* (*emphatic*) they, them.

iall [iəL] *f* thong; dog's leash; strap; strop.

iall bròige [iəL brōg'ı] *f* shoe-lace.

ialtag [iəLtag] *f* (*creature*) bat.

iar [iər] *f* west.

iar-[1] [iər] *prefix* under-, deputy-; **iar-stiùiriche** [iər sd'ūr'ıch'ə] *m* deputy director.

iar-[2] [iər] *prefix* post-; **iar-cheumaiche** [iər ch'ēmnıch'ə] *m* postgraduate.

iar air [iər ɛr'] *prep* west of.

iarann [iərəN] *m* iron.

iargalta [iərgəLtə] *adj* churlish, surly.

iarla [iərLə] *m* earl.

iarmad [iərməd] *m* remnant.

iarmailt [iərmalt'] *f* (*with art*) **an iarmailt** [ə N'iərmalt'] the firmament, the heavens.

iarnaich [iərnıch'] *v* iron.

iar-ogha [iər o.ə] *m* great-grand-child.

iarr [iəR] *v* want; ask for; invite.

iarrtas [iəRtəs] *m* request; demand; (*job, etc*) application.

iasad [iəsəd] *m* borrowing; loan.

iasg [iasg] *m* fish.

iasgach [iasgəch] *m* (*deep-sea, etc*) fishing; angling.

iasgaich [iasgıch'] *v* fish.

iasgair [iasgɛr'] *m* fisherman; angler.

iadh [iəgh] *v* surround; enclose.

idir [id'ır'] *adv usu with neg* (not) at all.

ifhrinn [ir'ıN'] *f* hell.

ifhrinneach [ir'ıN'əch] *adj* hellish, infernal.

Ìle [īlı] *f* Islay.

Ìleach [īləch] *m/adj* Islay person, from Islay.

ìm [īm] *m* butter.

imcheist [imich'ešd'] *f* anxiety, perplexity, dilemma. • *adv* **ann an imcheist** [auN ən imich'ešd'] in a dilemma, perplexed.

imcheisteach [imich'ešd'əch] *adj* worried; worrying.

imich [imich'] *v* depart, go.

imleag [imilag] *f* navel.

imlich [imilıch'] *v* lick, lap. • *f* lick; licking.

impidh [īmpı] *m* persuasion, urging.

impidheach [īmpı.əch] *adj* persuasive.

impireil [īmpır'ɛl] *adj* imperial.

impireileas [īmpır'ɛləs] *f* imperialism.

imrich [imir'ıch'] *v* move house. • *f* moving house, flitting.

inbhe [inivı] *f* rank; level; adulthood.

inbheach [inivəch] *adj* adult. • *m* adult, grown-up.

inbheil [inivɛl] *adj* high-ranking.

inbhir [iN'ır'] *m* confluence; (*of watercourse*) mouth.

inc [ink] *m* ink.

ìne [iN'ı] f toenail, fingernail; claw, talon.

inneal [iN'aL] m machine; implement.

innealach [iN'aLəch] adj mechanical.

inneal-ciùil [iN'aLk'ül] m musical instrument.

inneal-clàir [iN'aLkLār'] m record-player.

inneal-nighe [iN'aLN'i.ı] m washing machine.

inneal-smàlaidh [iN'aLsmāLı] m fire extinguisher.

innean [iN'an] m anvil.

innear [iN'ɛr] f dung, manure.

innidh [iN'ı] f bowels; intestines.

innis¹ [iš] v tell, inform; (story, etc) recount.

innis² [iniš] f island; haugh, inch.

innis breug [iš br'iag] v lie, tell a lie.

Innis Tìle [iN'ıš t'īlı] m Iceland.

innleachd [iN'L'əchg] f device; inventiveness; intelligence; artfulness; stratagem.

innleachdach [iN'L'əchgəch] adj inventive; resourceful; intelligent; cunning.

innleadair [iN'L'ədər] m engineer, mechanic.

innleadair-dealain [iN'L'ədərd'ɛLɛN'] m electrical engineer.

innleadaireachd [iN'L'ər'əchg] f engineering.

innleadair-thogalach [iN'L'əhogaLəch] m civil engineer.

innlich [iN'L'ıch'] v invent, devise; plot.

Innseachan [išəchən] mpl (with art) **na h-Innseachan** [nə hīšəchən] India; the Indies.

Innseanach [išənəch] m/adj Indian.

innte [iN'd'ı] prep pron in her, in it (f).

inntinn [iN'd'ıN'] f mind, intellect.

inntinneach [iN'd'ıN'əch] adj interesting; mental, intellectual.

inntrig [iN'd'r'ıg'] v (building, etc) enter.

ìobair [iəbır'] v (relig) sacrifice, offer up.

ìobairt [iəbıršd'] f (relig) sacrifice, offering.

ìoc [iəʰk] v pay. • m payment.

ìochd [iəchg] f compassion, mercy.

ìochdar [iəchgər] m bottom, base.

ìochdarach [iəchgərəch] adj lower; inferior, subordinate.

ìochdaran [iəchgəran] m inferior, subordinate; subject.

ìochdaranachd [iəchgəranəchg] f inferiority.

ìochdmhor [iəchgvər] adj compassionate, merciful.

ìocshlaint [iəʰkLaN'd'] f medicine, remedy.

ìodhal [iəghəL] m idol.

ìodhlann [iəLəN] f stack-yard.

ìolach [iLəch] f shout.

ìolaire [iLər'ə] f eagle.

ìolaire bhuidhe [iLər'ə vui.ı] f golden eagle.

ìolra [iLrə] m/adj (gram) plural.

ìoma- [imə] prefix multi-.

ìomadach [imədəch] adj many (a).

ìomadach uair [imədəch uər'] adv often, many a time.

ìomadh [iməgh] adj adv many (a).

ìoma-fhillte [imīL't'ı] adj complex, complicated; manifold.

ìomagain [iməgɛN'] f anxiety, worry.

ìomagaineach [iməgɛN'əch] adj anxious; worrying.

iomain [iumɛN'] v drive on (*esp livestock*); propel; play shinty. • f shinty.

iomair [iumɪr'] v (*boat*) row.

iomair an aon ràmh [iumɪr' ən ūn rāv] co-operate, pull together.

iomall [iuməL] m edge, periphery; limit; verge; rim.

iomall a' bhaile [iuməL ə vali] m suburbs.

iomallach [iuməLəch] adj remote, isolated; marginal.

iomchaidh [iməch'ɪ] adj suitable; decent, proper.

iomchair [imchər'] v carry, transport.

iomhaigh [iəvay] f image; likeness; idol.

iomlaid [iumLɪd'] f exchange, barter; (*money*) change.

iomlan [iumLan] adj complete, full, absolute.

iomnaidh [iumnɪ] f solicitude.

iompachadh [iumpəchəgh] m conversion.

iompachan [iumpəchan] m convert, neophyte.

iompaich [iumpɪch'] v persuade; (*relig*) convert.

iompaire [īmpɪr'ə] m emperor.

iompaireachd [īmpɪr'əchg] f empire.

iomradh [imrəgh] m mention; report.

iomraiteach [imraʰt'əch] adj celebrated; notorious.

iomrall [imrəL] m mistake; going astray.

iomrallach [imrəLəch] adj mistaken, erroneous.

iomramh [imrəv] m rowing.

ion- [in] *prefix indicating* able to, worthy of.

ionad [inəd] m place, spot; centre.

ionadail [inədal] adj local.

ionad-cosnaidh [inədkəsnɪ] m job centre.

ionad-latha [inədLa.a] m day centre.

ionad-margaid[inədmarag'ɪd'],
ionad-margaidh [inədmarag'ɪ] m marketplace.

ionad-obrach [inədobrəch] m job centre.

ionad-slàinte [inədsLāN'd'ɪ] m health centre.

ionad-stiùiridh [inədšd'ūr'ɪ] m management centre.

ionaltraich [inəLtrɪch'] v graze.

ionaltradh [inəLtrəgh] m grazing, pasture.

ionann [inəN] adj alike, identical.

ion-dhèanta [ingh'iantə] adj feasible, possible.

iongantach [iəndəch] adj strange; surprising; marvellous.

iongantas [iəndəs] m surprise, amazement; phenomenon, amazing thing.

iongna *see* **ìne**

iongnadh [iənəgh] m amazement.

ion-ithe [in ich'ɪ] adj eatable, edible.

ionmhainn [inɪvɪN'] adj dear, beloved.

ionmhas [inɪvəs] m treasure; finance.

ionmhasair [inɪvəsɛr'] m treasurer.

ionmholta [invoLtə] adj praiseworthy.

ionnan *see* **ionann**

ionndrainn [iuNdrɪN'] v miss, long for.

ionnlad [iuNLəd] *m* washing, ablutions.

ionnlaid [iuNLɪd'] *v* wash, bathe.

ionnsachadh [iuNsəchəgh] *m* learning.

ionnsaich [iuNsɪch'] *v* learn, study.

ionnsaichte [iuNsɪch't'ɪ] *adj* educated; trained.

ionnsaigh [iuNsɪ] *f* attack, assault; attempt.

ionnstramaid [iuNsdrəmɪd'] *f* instrument.

ionracas [inrəʰkəs] *m* honesty; justice; righteousness.

ionraic [inrrʰk'] *adj* honest; just; righteous.

iorgail [irgɪl] *f* tumult.

iorgaileach [irgɪləch] *adj* tumultuous.

ioronas [iərənəs] *m* irony.

ioronta [iərəndə] *adj* ironic.

Ìosa [iəsə] *m* Jesus.

ìosal *see* **ìseal**

Ioslamach [isLəməch] *adj* Islamic.

ìotmhor [iəʰtvər] *adj* (*land, etc*) parched; very thirsty.

ìre [īr'ɪ] *f* degree, level; stage.

iriseal [ir'ɪšəL] *adj* low, lowly; humble.

irisleachd [ir'ɪšLəchg] *f* humility; lowliness.

irislich [ir'ɪšlɪch'] *v* humble; humiliate.

iris [ir'ɪš] *f* magazine, periodical.

is[1] [is] *v* am, is, are.

is[2] [ɪs] (*for* agus) *conj* and.

is beag orm X [is beg ərɔm] *v* I don't like X.

isbean [išban] *m* sausage.

is toil leam X [stɔləm] *v* I like X.

is caomh leam [skūləm] *v* I like X (Lewis dialect).

is ciar leam X [sk'iər ləm] *v* I take a dim view of X.

is cubhaidh dhomh [skuvɪ ghə] *v* it befits me.

is dòcha! [sdōchə] maybe!

is dòcha gun [sdōchə gun] *conj* perhaps.

is duilich leam [sdulɪch' ləm] *v* I find it hard to.

is duilich sin! [sdulɪch' šin] *excl* that's a shame!

ise [iši] *pron* (*emphatic*) she, her.

ìseal [īšəl], **ìosal** [iəsəL] *adj* low; lowly; humble; (*voice, etc*) quiet.

isean [išan] *m* chick; baby animal.

islich [īšlɪch'] *v* become lower; demote.

isneach [išnəch] *f* rifle.

Iosrael [isra.ɛl] *f* Israel.

Iosraelach [isra.ɛləch] *m*/*adj* Israeli, Israelite.

ist! [išd'] *excl* hush! be quiet!

ite [iʰt'ɪ] *f* feather; plumage; fin.

iteach [iʰt'əch] *adj* feathered.

iteachan [iʰt'əchan] *m* bobbin, spool.

iteag [iʰt'ag] *f* small feather; flying, flight.

iteagach [iʰt'agəch] *adj* feathered.

itealaich [iʰt'aLɪch'] *v* fly.

itealan [iʰt'aLan] *m* aeroplane, aircraft.

itealag [iʰt'aLag] *f* kite.

ith [ich'] *v* eat.

iubhar [iu.ər] *m* yew.

iuchair [iuchɪr'] *f* key; **iuchair-ghnìomha** [iuchɪr'ghr'iəvə] *f* (*IT*) function key.

Iuchar [iuchər] *m* (*with art*) **an t-Iuchar** [ən t'iuchər] July.

Iùdhach [iū.əch] *m*/*adj* Jew; Jewish.

iùil-tharraing [iūlhaRɪng'] *f* magnetism.

iùil-tharraingeach [iūlhaRɪng'əch] *adj* magnetic.

L

là *see* **latha** *except for holidays*

labhair [Lavɪr'] *v* speak, talk.

labhairt [Lavɪršd'] *f* speech, speaking.

lach [Lach] *f* (*bird*) duck.

lachdann [LachgəN] *adj* dun, tawny; khaki; swarthy.

ladar [Ladər] *m* ladle, scoop.

ladarna [Ladərnə] *adj* bold; shameless.

ladhar [Lo.ɪr] *m* hoof.

lag¹ [Lag] *adj* weak, feeble.

lag² [Lag] *m* hollow; pit.

lagaich [Lagɪch'] *v* weaken.

lag-chùiseach [Lag chūšəch] *adj* unenterprising.

lagh [logh] *m* law.

laghach [Lo.əch] *adj* nice; kind.

laghail [Loghal] *adj* lawful, legal.

laghairt [Lo.ɪršd] *f* lizard.

Laideann [Lad'əN] *f* Latin (language).

Laidinneach [Lad'ɪN'əch] *adj* Latin.

làidir [Lād'ɪr'] *adj* strong; potent.

laigh [Lay] *v* lie (down); (*plane, etc*) land; subside.

laighe [Lai.ɪ] *f* recumbent position.

laighe na grèine [Lai.ɪ nə gr'ēnɪ] *f* sunset.

laigse [Lag'šɪ] *f* weakness; infirmity; faint.

làimhsich [Laišich'] *v* touch, handle; wield.

lainnir [LaN'ɪr'] *f* glint, sparkle; radiance.

lainnireach [LaN'ɪr'əch] *adj* sparkling; radiant.

làir [Lār'] *f* mare.

làithean-saora [Lai.ənsūrə] *mpl* holidays.

làitheil [lai.ɛl] *adj* dàily; everyday.

là-luain [La.ə LuaN'] *m* doomsday.

làmh [Lāv] *f* hand; handle.

làmhainn [LāvɪN'] *f* glove.

làmh an uachdair [Lāv ən uachgɪr'] *m* the upper hand.

làmh-lèigh [Lāvley] *m* surgeon.

làmh-sgrìobhadh [Lāvsgr'īvəgh] *m* handwriting; manuscript.

làmhthuagh [Lāvhuə] *f* hatchet, chopper.

lampa [Laumbə] *m* lamp.

làn [Lān] *adj* full. • *adv* fully. • *m* one's fill.

Là na Sàbaid [La.ə nə sābɪd'] *m* Sunday, the Sabbath.

làn beòil [Lān byōl] *m* mouthful.

làn chinnteach [Lān ch'īN'd'əch] *adj* completely certain; convinced.

làn chumhachd [Lān chu.əchg] *m* absolute power.

làn chumhachdach [Lān chu.əchgəch] *adj* all-powerful.

làn dùirn [Lān dūrN'] *m* handful, fistful.

làn fhada [Lān adə] *adj/adv* full-length.

langa [Langə] *f* (*fish*) ling.

langanaich [Langanɪch'] *v* (*animals*) bellow; low.

langasaid [Langəsıd'] *f* sofa, couch.

làn-mara [Lānmarə] *m* high tide.

làn mo bhroinn de. [Lān mə bhrəiN' d'e] *m* (*fam*) my bellyful of.

lann [LauN] *f* blade; (*fish*) scale; enclosure; repository.

lanntair [LauNder'] *m* lantern.

làn spàine [Lān sbāN'ı] *m* spoonful.

laoch [Lūch] *m* hero; warrior.

laochan [Lūchan] *m* wee boy, wee hero.

laogh [Lūgh] *m* calf.

laoidh [Lūy] *f* poem; hymn.

laoigh-fheòil [Lūi.yōl] *f* veal.

làr [Lār] *m* ground, floor.

làrach [Lārəch] *f* trace, mark; ruin; site.

làrna-mhàireach [Lārnəvār'əch] *m* the morrow, the next day.

las [Las] *v* set alight; blaze; (*fig*) light up.

lasadair [Lasədər'] *m* match (*for striking*).

lasaich [Lasıch'] *v* loosen; soothe.

lasair [Lasɛr'] *f* flame(s); flash.

lasgan [Lasgan] *m* outburst; (*of anger, etc*) fit.

lasrach [Lasrəch] *adj* flaming; blazing.

lastaig [Lasdıg'] *f/adj* elastic.

latha [La.ə] *m* day.

latha a' bhràtha [La.ə vrāhə] *m* judgement day.

latha-breith [La.ə br'e] *m* birthday.

latha-fèille [La.əfēL'ı] *m* holiday, feastday.

làthair [Lāhır'] *f* presence; sight, view.

latha no latheigin [La.ə nɔ La.eg'ın] *adv* some day or other, one fine day.

latha-trasg [La.ətrasg] *m* fast day.

latheigin [La.eg'ın] *m* some day.

le [le] (*before art* **leis** [leš]) *prep* with; by; belonging to.

leabaidh [L'ebı] *f* bed.

leabhar [L'ɔ.ər] *m* book.

leabharlann [L'ɔ.ərLəN] *f* library.

leabhar-latha [L'ɔ.ərLa.ə] *m* diary, journal.

leabhran [L'ɔ.ran] *m* booklet; brochure.

leac [L'ɛʰk] *f* (*rock*) slab, ledge.

leacag [L'ɛʰkag] *f* tile.

leac teallaich [L'ɛʰk t'ɛLıch'] *f* hearthstone.

leac uaighe [L'ɛʰk uə.ı] *f* gravestone.

leac ùrlair [L'ɛʰk ūrLır'] *f* paving stone.

leag [L'eg] *v* fell; demolish; (*carpet, etc*) lay; (*window, etc*) lower.

leag càin air [L'eg kāN' ɛr'] *v* tax, subject to taxation.

leag gu làr [L'eg gə Lār] *v* raze (*to ground*).

leagh [L'ɔ] *v* melt, thaw; dissolve.

leam [ləm] *prep pron* with/by me.

leamhaich [L'ɛvıch'] *v* exasperate; plague.

leamhach [L'ɛvəch] *adj* insipid.

leamhan [L'ɛvan] *m* elm.

lean [L'ɛn] *v* follow; continue; understand. • *excl* **lean ort!** [L'ɛn ōršt] keep going! . . . **a leanas** [ə lɛnəs] the following . . .

leanabail [L'ɛnabal] *adj* childish, silly; infantile.

leanaban [L'ɛnaban] *m* baby; small child.

leanabh [L'ɛnav] *m* baby; infant; child.

leanailteach [L'εnalt'əch] *adj* continuous, incessant.

leann [L'ūN] *m* beer, ale.

leannan [L'εNan] *m* lover; sweetheart, boyfriend, girlfriend.

leannanachd [L'εNanəchg] *f* courting, courtship.

leannra [L'auNrə] *m* sauce.

leantainneach [L'εndıN'əch] *adj* continuous; persevering; lasting.

leas [Les] *m* benefit, advantage; improvement; **cha leig thu leas . . .** [cha L'eg' u les] you don't need to . . .

leasachadh [L'esəchəgh] *m* improvement; development.

leasaich [L'esıch'] *v* improve; develop.

leasan [L'esan] *m* lesson.

leat [laʰt] *prep pron* with/by you (*sing*).

leatha [le.ə] *prep pron* with/by her, with/by it (*f*).

leathad [L'εhad] *m* slope, hillside.

leathann [L'εhaN] *adj* broad, wide.

leathar [L'εhar] *m* leather.

le chèile [le ch'ēlı] *adv* together; both.

le deagh dhùrachd [le d'ō ghūrəchg] (*corres*) with compliments.

le dùrachd [le dūrəchg] (*corres*) yours sincerely.

le foill [le foiL'] *adv* fraudulently.

leibh [leiv] *prep pron* with/by you (*pl*).

leig [L'eg'] *v* let, allow; leave to; let out, utter; (*weapon*) fire.

leig air [L'eg' εr'] *v* pretend; give away.

leig air dhearmad [L'eg' εr' dh'εraməd] *v* neglect.

leig anail [L'eg' anal] *v* take a breather.

leig às [L'eg' as] *v* let off/out.

leig braidhm [L'eg' broim] *v* fart.

leig brùchd [L'eg' brūchg] *v* belch.

leig cnead [L'eg' kred] *v* groan.

leig de [L'eg' d'e] *v* give up, cease.

leig fead [L'eg' fed] *v* whistle.

leigheas [L'e.əs] *m* cure, remedy.

leighis [L'e.ıš] *v* cure, heal.

leig le [L'eg' le] *v* leave alone, let be.

leig leas *see* **leas**.

leig ma sgaoil [L'eg' mə sgūl] *v* let loose.

leig 'na theine [L'eg' nə henı] *v* set on fire.

leig osna [L'eg' ɔsnə] *v* heave/breathe a sigh.

leig seachad [L'eg' šεchəd] *v* give up, relinquish.

lèine [L'ēnı] *f* shirt.

leinn [leiN'] *prep pron* with/by us.

lèir [L'ēr'] *adj* visible; evident; **is lèir dhomh (gu)** [ıs L'ēr' ghɔ gu] (*ml*) it's clear to me (that).

lèirmheas [L'ēr'vəs] *m* (*book, etc*) review.

lèirsinn [L'ēr'šıN'] *f* sight; perceptiveness.

lèirsinneach [L'ēr'šıN'əch] *adj* visible; perceptive.

leis[1] [L'eš] *f* thigh.

leis[2] [leš] *prep pron* with/by him, with/by it (*m*).

leis a' bhruthaich [leš ə vru.ıch'] *adv* with the slope.

leis an t-sruth [leš ən truh] *adv* downstream.

leis a sin, leis sin [leš ə šin] [leš šin] *adv* whereupon, at that.

leisg [L'ešg'] *adj* lazy; reluctant. • *f* laziness.

le gach deagh dhùrachd [le gach d'ō ghūrəchg] (*corres*) with best wishes.

leisge [L'ešg'ı] *f* laziness.

leisgear [L'ešg'ər] *m* lazy person, lazybones.

leisgeul [L'ešg'iaL] *m* excuse; pretext.

leis sin *see* **leis a sin**.

leiteis [L'eʰt'ıš] *f* lettuce.

leitheach [L'ehəch] *adv* half, semi-.

leitheach slighe [L'ehəch šli.ı] *adv* halfway.

leithid (de) [L'ehıd'] *f* the like(s) (of); **a leithid de . . .** [ə lehıd' d'e] such a . . .

leitir [L'eʰtır'] *f* slope, hillside.

Leòdhasach [L'ō.əsəch] *m*/*adj* Lewisman; from Lewis.

leòmhann [L'ɔ.əN] *m* lion.

leòinteach [L'ɔN'd'əch] *m* casualty, victim; *pl* (*with art*) **na leòintich** [nə L'ɔN'd'ıch'] the injured; the wounded.

leòman [L'ɔman] *m* moth.

leòn [L'ɔn] *v* wound; hurt; injure. • *m* wound; hurt; injury.

leònte [L'ɔnd'ı] *adj* wounded; hurt; injured.

leòr [L'ɔr] *f* enough, sufficiency; **mo leòr de . . .** [mɔ lɔr d'e] my fill of . . .

leotha [lɔ.ə] *prep pron* with/by them.

le sùrd [le sūrd] *adv* with a will.

leth [L'e]
[šia gu L'e] *m* half; side; **sia gu leth** six and a half; **leth-** one of a pair.

leth-asal [L'e.asaL] *f* mule.

lethbhreac [L'evrɛʰk] *m* (*book, etc*) copy, reproduction; match.

lethcheann [L'ech'auN] *m* cheek; side of head.

leth-cheud [L'ech'iad] *m* fifty.

leth-chuid [L'echud'] *f* half.

leth-fhuar [L'e.uər] *adj* lukewarm.

leth uair [L'e huər'] *f* half an hour.

leth-shean [L'ehɛn] *adj* middle-aged.

le tuiteamas [le tuʰt'əməs] *adv* by accident, by chance.

leud [L'iad] *m* breadth, width.

leudaich [L'iadıch'] *v* widen; extend.

leudaichte [L'iadıch't'ə] *adj* widened; flattened.

leug [L'iag] *f* jewel.

leugh [L'ēv] *v* read.

leum [L'ēm] *v* jump, leap; (*nose*) bleed. • *m* jump, leap.

leum-sròine [L'ēmsdrɔN'ı] *m* nosebleed.

leum-uisge [L'ēmušg'ı] *m* waterfall.

le ur cead [ler k'ed] by your leave.

leus [L'ias] *m* light; ray of light; torch; blister.

Lia-Fàil [L'iə fāl] *f* (*with art*) **an Lia-Fàil** [ən L'iə fāl] the Stone of Destiny.

liagh [L'iə] *f* ladle, scoop.

liath [L'iə] *v* make or become grey. • *adj* grey.

liath-reòthadh [L'iərɔ.əgh] *m* frost, hoar frost.

lìbhrig [L'īvrıg'] *v* (*goods, etc*) deliver.

lide [L'id'ı] *m* syllable.

lighiche [L'i.ıch'ə] *m* doctor, physician.

lili [lili] *f* lily.

lìnig [L'īnɪg'] v line.

linn [L'ïN'] m age, period; generation; century; (pl with art) na **Linntean Dorcha** [nə L'ïN'tən dərɔchə] the Dark Ages.

linne [L'iN'ɪ] f pool; waterfall.

liomaid [L'imɪd'] f lemon.

lìomh [L'iəv] v polish, shine. • f polish, gloss.

lìomharra [L'iəvəRə] adj polished, glossy.

lìon¹ [L'iən] v fill; (tide) come in.

lìon² [L'iən] m net; web.• m flax, lint.

lìon damhain-allaidh [L'iən davɛN'aLɪ] m cobweb.

lìonmhor [L'iənvər] adj numerous; abundant.

lionn [L'ūN] m liquid.

lionn-tàthaidh [L'ūNtāhɪ] m concrete, cement.

lionsa [L'insə] f lens.

liopard [L'ipərd] m leopard.

lios [L'is] m garden; enclosure.

Liosach [L'isəch] m/adj Lismore person, from Lismore.

liosda [L'isdə] adj boring.

Lios Mòr [L'is mōr] m Lismore.

liosta [L'isdə] f list.

liotair [L'iʰtɛr'] m litre.

lip [L'iʰp] f lip.

lite [L'iʰt'ɪ] f porridge.

litir [L'iʰt'ɪr'] f letter.

litreachadh [L'iʰtr'əchəgh] m spelling.

litreachas [L'iʰtr'əchəas] m literature.

litrich [L'iʰtr'ɪch'] v spell.

liùdhag [L'ū.ag] f doll.

liut [L'uʰt] f knack.

lobh [Lo] v rot, decay.

lobhadh [Lo.əgh] m rot, putrefaction.

lobhar [Lo.ər] m leper.

lobhta [Loftə] m flat; storey; loft.

locar [Lɔʰkər] m (tool) plane.

lòcast [Lɔʰkəsd] m locust.

loch [Lɔch] m loch, lake.

lochan [Lɔchan] m small loch, pond.

lochd [Lɔchg] m fault; harm.

lochdach [Lɔchgəch] adj harmful.

Lochlann [LɔchLəN] f Scandinavia.

Lochlannach [LɔchLəNəch] m/adj Norseman; Norse; Scandinavian; Viking.

lòchran [Lōchran] m lamp, lantern.

lof [Lɔf] m loaf.

loidhne [Lɔinɪ] f line.

loingeas [Lɔing'əs] m shipping; fleet.

lòinidh [LōN'ɪ] f (with art) an lòinidh [ən LōN'ɪ] rheumatism.

loisg [Lɔšg'] v burn; (gun) fire.

loisgte [Lɔšg't'ɪ] adj burnt.

lòistear [Lōšdɛr] m lodger.

lòistinn [Lōšd'ɪN'] m lodging(s), digs; accommodation.

lom [Lɔum] v strip; shave; shear; mow. • adj bare; bleak; thin.

lomadair [Lɔmədər'] m shearer.

loma làn [Lɔmə Lān] adj full to the brim.

lomnochd [Lɔumnəchg] adj naked.

lòn¹ [Lōn] m food, provisions.

lòn² [Lōn] m pool; puddle; meadow.

lònaid [Lōnɪd'] f lane.

lon-dubh [Lɔndu] m blackbird.

long [Lɔung] f ship.

long-bhriseadh [Lɔungvr'išəgh] m shipwreck.

long-chogaidh [Lɔungchɔgɪ] *f* warship, battleship.

long-fhànais [lɔungānɪš] *f* spaceship.

lorg [Lɔrɔg] *v* find; track down, trace. • *f* vestige; footprint; track.

los [Lɔs] *m* purpose, intention. • *conj* **los gu, los gun** [Lɔs gu/gun] in order that.

lòsan [Lɔ̄san] *m* pane.

losgadh-bràghad [Lɔsgəghbrā.əd] *m* heartburn.

losgann [LɔsgəN] *m* frog.

lot[1] [Lɔʰt] *f* croft; piece of land.

lot[2] [Lɔʰt] *v* wound. • *m* wound.

loth [Lɔ] *f* filly.

luach [Luəch] *m* worth, value.

luachachadh [Luəchəchəgh] *m* valuation.

luachaich [Luəchɪch'] *v* evaluate, value.

luachair [Luəchɛr] *f* rushes.

luachmhor [Luəchvər] *adj* valuable, precious.

luadhadh [Luədəgh] *m* (*cloth*) waulking, fulling.

luaidh[1] [Luay] *v* praise. • *m* praise; beloved person. • *excl* **a luaidh!** [ə Luay] my love! (my) darling!

luaidh[2] [Luay] *v* (*cloth*) waulk. full.

luaisg [Luašg'] *v* rock, sway, toss.

luaithre [Luar'ɪ], **luath** [Luə] *f* ash(es).

luaths [Luəs] *m* speed; agility.

luath[1] [Luə] *adj* fast, quick.

luath[2] [Luə] *f* same as **luaithre**

luathaich [Luəhɪch'] *v* accelerate; hurry on.

luaths [Luəs] *m* same as **luas**.

luath-thrèan [Luərēnə] *f* express (train).

lùb [Lūb] *v* bend; bow. • *f* bend; loop.

lùbach [Lūbəch] *adj* bending; winding; flexible.

lùb a' ghlùin [Lūb ə ghLūN'] *v* kneel, pray.

luch [Luch] *f* mouse.

lùchairt [Lūchɪršd'] *f* palace.

luchd[1] [Luchg] *m* cargo.

luchd[2] [Luchg] *m* people.

luchdaich [Luchgɪch'] *v* load.

luchd-càraidh [Luchkāri] *m* repairers.

luchd-ciùil [Luchk'ūl] *m* musicians.

luchd-eòlais [Luchg'ɔ̄Lɪš] *m* acquaintances.

luchd-frithealaidh [LuchgfrihəLɪ] *m* attendants.

luchdmhor [Luchgvər] *adj* capacious.

luchd-obrach [Luchgobrəch] *m* workers; workforce.

luchd-siubhail [Luchgšu.al] *m* (*coll*) travellers.

luchd-stiùiridh [Luchgšd'ūr'ɪ] *m* managers, management.

luchd-turais [Luchgturɪš] *m* (*coll*) tourists.

luchraban [Luchraban] *m* dwarf, midget.

lùdag [Lūdag] *f* little finger; hinge.

lugha [Lughə] *comp adj* smaller, smallest.

lùghdachadh [Lūdəchəgh] *m* reduction; abatement.

lùghdaich [Lūdɪch'] *v* lessen; shrink; abate.

Lugsamburg [Lugsəmburg] *m* Luxembourg.

Lugsamburgach [Lugsəmburgəch] *m/adj* Luxembourger, from Luxembourg.

luibh [Luiv] *f* herb; plant; weed.

luibh-eòlas [Luivyɔ̄Ləs] *m* botany.

luibhre [Luir'ı] *f* leprosy.

luideach [Lud'əch] *adj* shabby, scruffy.

luideag [Lud'ag] *f* rag.

luidhear [Lui.ɛr] *m* funnel, chimney.

Luinn [LuiN'] *f* Luing.

Luinneach [LuiN'əch] *m/adj* Luing person, from Luing.

luinneag [LuiN'ag] *f* song, ditty.

Lùnasdal [LūnəsdaL] *m* (*with art*) **an Lùnasdal** [ən LūnəsdaL] August;

Latha Lùnasdail [La.ə Lūnəsdal] Lammas Day.

lurach [Lurəch] *adj* pretty; nice; beloved.

lurgann [LurugəN] *f* shin.

lus [Lus] *m* herb; plant; weed.

lus na meala [Lus nə myaLə] *m* honeysuckle.

lùth [Lū], **lùths** [Lūs] *m* power of movement; energy.

lùthmhor [Lūvər] *adj* strong; agile; energetic.

lùths *m same as* **lùth**.

M

ma [ma] *conj* if.

màb [māb] *v* revile, vilify.

mac [maʰk] *m* son; **mac bràthar** [maʰk brāhar], **mac piuthar** [maʰk pyu.ar] *m* nephew.

mac an aba [maʰkənabə] *m* ring finger.

mac an donais! [maʰk ən dɔnɪš] *excl* damn it!

mac an duine [maʰk ən duN'ı] *m* humanity, humankind.

macanta [maʰkandə] *adj* meek, submissive.

machair [machɛr'] *f* machair; plain; (*with art*) **a' Mhachair Ghallda** [ə vachɛr' ghauLdə] the Lowlands.

machlag [machlag] *f* womb, uterus.

mac-meanmna [makmɛnamnə] *m* imagination.

mac-meanmnach [makmɛnamnəch] *adj* imaginary; imaginative.

mac na bracha [maʰk nə brachə] *m* malt whisky.

mac-samhail [maʰksau.al] *m* equal,

match; likeness.

mac-talla [maʰktaLə] *m* echo.

madadh-allaidh [madəghaLı] *m* wolf.

madadh ruadh [madəgh ruəgh] *m* fox.

madainn [madıN'] *f* morning. • *adv* **sa' mhadainn** [sə vadıN'] a.m.

ma dh'fhaoidte [ma ghūt'ı] *adv/conj* maybe, perhaps.

mag (air) [mag ɛr'] *v* mock, make fun (of).

màg [māg] *f* paw.

magadh [magəgh] *m* mockery.

magail [magal] *adj* mocking, jeering.

magairle [magırlə] *m* testicle.

maghar [ma.ər] *m* fly, bait.

maide [mad'ı] *m* wood, timber; stick; **maide-droma** [mad'ıdromə] *m* ridge pole, roof-tree.

maide poite [mad'ı pɔʰtı] *m* spirtle.

maidse [mad'šı] *m* match (*for striking*).

màidsear [mādšɛr] *m* (*rank*) major.

maighdeann [moid'əN] *f* maiden; virgin; spinster. (*address*) **a Mhaighdeann X!** [ə void'əN] Miss X!

maighdeannas [moid'əNəs] *m* maidenhood, virginity.

maighdeann-mhara [moid'əNvarə] *f* mermaid.

maigheach [mai.əch] *m* hare.

maighstir [maišd'ır'] *m* master; (*address*) **a Mhaighstir X!** [ə vaišd'ır'] Mister X!

maighstir-sgoile [maišd'ır'sgɔlı] *m* schoolmaster.

màileid [mālıd'] *f* suitcase; briefcase; bag.

màileid-droma [mālıd'dromə] *f* rucksack.

màileid-làimhe [mālıd'Laivı] *f* handbag.

maille [maL'ı] *f* slowness; delay.

maille ri [maL'ı r'i] *prep* with, along with.

maillich [maL'ıch'] *v* delay; procrastinate.

mair [mar'] *v* last, continue; **mair beò** [mar' byō] live, survive.

maireann [mar'əN] *adj* living; enduring; **X nach maireann** [nach mar'əN] the late X.

maireannach [mar'əNəch] *adj* eternal; durable; long-lived.

màirnealach [mārN'aLəch] *adj* dilatory; boring.

mairtfheoil [maršd'ōl] *f* beef.

maise [maši] *f* beauty.

maiseach [mašəch] *adj* beautiful.

maisich [mašıch'] *v* beautify; decorate; (*face*) make up.

màithreil *see* **màthaireil**

màl [māL] *m* rent.

mala [maLə] *f* brow; eyebrow.

malairt [maLıršd'] *f* trade, business; barter.

malairtich [maLıršdıch'] *v* trade; barter.

màlda [māLdə] *adj* coy, bashful.

mall [mauL] *adj* slow, tardy.

mallachd [maLəchg] *f* curse.

mallaich [maLıch'] *v* curse.

mallaichte [maLıch'tə] *adj* cursed, damned.

mamaidh [mamı] *f* Mummy.

manach [manəch] *m* monk.

manachainn [manachıN'] *f* monastery.

manadh [manəgh] *m* omen.

manaidsear [manıd'šɛr] *m* manager.

Manainneach [manıN'əch] *m/adj* Manxman; Manx.

mang [mang] *f* fawn.

maodal [mūdəL] *f* paunch.

maoidh [muy] *v* threaten.

maoil [mūl] *f* forehead, brow.

Maoil [mūl] *f* (*with art*) **a' Mhaoil** [ə vūl] the Minch.

maoile [mūlı] *f* baldness.

maoin [mūN'] *f* wealth; goods, chattels.

maol [mūL] *m* cape, promontory; rounded hill. • *adj* blunt; bald.

maorach [mūrəch] *m* shellfish.

maor-eaglais [mūreglıš] *m* church officer.

maor-obrach [mūrobrəch] *m* foreman, gaffer.

maoth [mū] *adj* soft; tender-hearted.

maothaich [mū.ıch'] *v* soften.

mapa [mahpə] *m* map.

mar [mar] *prep* as; like. • *conj* **mar a** [mar ə]as, how; **mar gun** [mar gun] as if, as though.

mar a bheatha [mar ə vɛhə] *adv* for dear life.

marag [marag] *f* pudding.

maraiche [marɪch'ə] *m* sailor, seafarer.

mar an ceudna [mar ən k'iadnə] *adv* likewise, too.

marbh [marav] *v* kill. • *adj* dead.

marbhaiche [maravɪch'ə] *m* killer; murderer.

marbhan [maravan] *m* corpse.

marbhrann [maravraN] *m* elegy.

marbhtach [maravtəch] *adj* deadly, fatal.

mar bu chòir [mar bə chōr'] *adv* fittingly.

marcachadh [markəchəgh] *m* riding; horsemanship.

marcaich [markɪch'] *v* ride.

marcaiche [markɪch'ə] *m* rider, horseman.

margaid [maragɪd'] *m* market.

mar eisimpleir [mar ešɪmplɛr'] (*abbrev* **m.e.**) *adv* for example.

margadh [maragəgh] *m* market; **am Margadh Coitcheann** [əm maragəgh kɔʰt'əN] the Common Market.

margarain [maragərɛN'] *m* margarine.

màrmor [mārmər] *m* marble.

maille ri [maL'ɪ r'i] *prep* with, along with.

màrsail [mārsal] *f* march; marching.

mar sin [mar šin] *adv* so.

mar sin leat/leibh! [mar šin laʰt/ leiv] *excl* goodbye!

Màrt [māršt] *m* Mars; (*with art*) **am Màrt** [əm māršt] March.

mart [maršt] *m* beef animal.

màs [mās] *m* buttock; (*fam*) arse, bum.

mas e do thoil e [mašə də hɔlɛ] *adv* please.

mas e ur toil e [mašə ər tɔlɛ] *adv* (*polite*) please.

mas fhìor [maš iər] *adv* kidding, pretending.

maslach [masLəch] *adj* disgraceful, shameful.

masladh [masLəgh] *m* disgrace, shame.

maslaich [masLɪch'] *v* disgrace, put to shame.

ma-tà [matā], **ma-thà** [mahā] *adv* then, in that case.

matamataig [maʰtamatɪg'] *m* mathematics.

math [ma] *m* good. • *adj* good.

ma-tha *see* **ma-tà**

mathachadh [mahəchəgh] *m* manure; fertilizer.

mathaich [mahɪch'] *v* manure; enrich.

màthair [māhɪr'] *f* mother.

màthair-chèile [māhɪr'*ch'*ēlɪ] *f* mother-in-law.

màthaireil [māhɪr'ɛl] *adj* motherly, maternal.

màthair-uisge [māhɪr'ušg'ɪ] *m* fountainhead.

mathan [mahan] *m* (brown) bear.

mathanas [mahanəs] *m* forgiveness, pardon.

mathan bàn [mahan bān] *m* polar bear.

mathas [mahəs] *m* goodness.

math dhà-rìreadh! [ma gharīr'ə] *excl* excellent!

math do [ma dɔ] *v* forgive.

ma thogras tu [ma hogrəs du] if you like.

math thu-fhèin! [ma u hēn] *excl* well done! good for you!

meadhan [mi.an] *m* middle, centre; medium, mechanism; waist; average; *pl* **na meadhanan** [nə mi.anən] (*press, etc*) the media.

meadhanach [mi.anəch] *adj* middling, so-so; average.

meadhan-aois [mi.an ūš] *f* middle age.

meadhan-aoiseil [mi.an ūšɛl] *adj* medieval.

meadhan-chearcail [mi.an ch'ɛrkal] *m* equator.

meadhan-latha [mi.an La.ə] *m* midday, noon.

meadhan-oidhche [mi.an oi.ch'ı] *m* midnight.

Meadhan-thìreach [mi.an hīr'əch] *adj* Mediterranean.

meal [mɛL] *v* enjoy. • *excl* **meal do/ ur naidheachd!** [mɛL də/ər Nɛ.achg] congratulations!

meal-bhucan [mɛlvuʰkan] *m* melon.

meall[1] [myauL] *v* deceive; cheat; entice.

meall[2] [myauL] *m* lump; lumpy hill.

meallach [mɛLəch] *adj* beguiling, bewitching.

mealladh [mɛLəgh] *m* deceit, deception; enticement.

meall an sgòrnain [myauL ən sgōrnɛN'] *m* Adam's apple.

meallta [myauLtə] *adj* deceived; cheated.

mealltach [myauLtəch] *adj* deceitful; cheating; deceptive.

mealltair [myauLtɛr'] *m* deceiver; cheat.

meall-uisge [myauLušg'ı] *m* heavy shower.

mean [mɛn] *adj* little, tiny; **mean air mhean** [mɛn er' vɛn] little by little.

mèanan [mianan] *m* yawn.

mèananaich [miananıch'] *f* yawning.

meanbh [mɛnav] *adj* tiny, minute.

meanbh-chuileag [mɛnavchulag] *f* midge.

meang [mɛng] *f* fault, flaw; abnormality.

meangach [mɛngəch] *adj* abnormal.

meangan [mɛngan], **meanglan** [mɛngLan] *m* branch, bough.

meann [mɛuN] *m* (*goat*) kid.

mearachadh [mɛrəchagh] *m* aberration.

mearachd [mɛrəchg] *f* mistake, error.

mearachdach [mɛrəchgəch] *adj* wrong, erroneous.

mèaran [mēran] *m* yawn.

mèaranaich [mēranıch'] *f* yawning.

mèarrsaidh [mēRsı] *m* march, marching.

meas[1] [mes] *m* valuation; respect, esteem; **is mise le meas** [ıs mišı le mes] (*corres*) yours sincerely. • *v* estimate; evaluate; esteem; think.

meas[2] [mes] *m* fruit.

measach [mesəch] *adj* fruity.

measail [mesal] *adj* respected; respectable; valued.

measail (air) [mesal ɛr'] *adj* fond (of).

measarra [mesəRə] *adj* moderate; temperate.

measarrachd [mesəRəchg] *f* moderation; abstinence.

meas-chraobh [meschrūv] *f* fruit tree.

measgaich [mesgɪch'] *v* mix, mingle.

measgaichear [mesgɪch'ɛr] *m* mixer.

meata [mɛʰtə] *adj* faint-hearted; feeble.

meatailt [mɛʰtalt'] *f* metal.

meatair [mɛʰtɛr'] *m* metre.

meatrach [mɛʰtrəch] *adj* metric.

meidh [mey] *f* scales; equilibrium.

meil [mel] *v* mill, grind.

meileabhaid [meləvɪd'] *f* velvet.

meilich [mɛlich'] *v* chill; numb.

mèilich [mēlich'] *f* bleat, bleating; baa, baaing.

mèinn[1] [mēN'] *f* temperament; appearance.

mèinn[2] [mēN'] *f* mine; ore.

mèinneach [mēN'əch] *adj* mineral.

mèinneadair [mēN'ədər'] *m* miner.

mèinnear [mēN'ɛr] *m* mineral.

mèinnearachd [mēN'ərəchg] *f* mining; mineralogy.

mèinne-ghuail *see* **mèinn-ghuail**.

mèinneil [mēN'ɛl] *adj* mineral.

mèinn-eòlas [mēN'ōLəs] *m* mineralogy.

mèinn-ghuail [mēN'ghuɛl] *f* coal-mine.

meirg [mɛr'ig'] *v* rust. • *f* rust.

meirg-dhìonach [mɛr'ig'dh'iənəch] *adj* rustproof.

meirgeach [mer'ig'əch] *adj* rusty.

meirgich [mɛr'ig'ich'] *v* rust.

mèirle [mērlɪ] *f* theft.

mèirleach [mērləch] *m* thief.

meomhair [myɔ.ɛr'] *f* (*faculty*) memory.

meòmhraich [myōrich'] *v* recollect; muse.

meud [miad] *m* size; amount; extent.

meudachd [miadəchg] *f* magnitude.

meudaich [miadɪch'] *v* increase; enlarge.

m' eudail! [mēdal] *excl* love! darling!

meur [miar] *f* finger; branch; (*piano, etc*) key.

meuran [miaran] *m* thimble.

meur-chlàr [miarchLār] *m* keyboard.

meur-lorg [miarLɔrəg] *f* fingerprint.

mi [mi] *pron* I, me.

mì- [mī] *prefix* un-, dis-, in-, mis-, un-, -less.

mial [miaL] *f* (*parasite*) tick.

miamhail [miaval] *f* mewing, miauling.

mial-chaorach [mialchūrəch] *f* sheep-tick.

miann [miaN] *m* wish; longing; (sexual) desire.

miannaich [miaNɪch'] *v* wish for; lust after.

mias [miəs] *f* platter; basin.

mias-ionnlaid [miəsiūNLɪd'] *f* wash-basin.

mì-bhlasta [mī vLasdə] *adj* tasteless.

mì-cheartas [mī ch'aršdəs] *m* injustice.

mì-dhileas [mī dh'īləs] *adj* disloyal.

mì-earbsa [mī ɛrəbsə] *m* mistrust.

mì-fhoighidinn [mī oid'ɪN'] *f* impatience.

mì-fhoighidneach [mī oid'ıN'əch]
adj impatient.

mì-ghnàthach [mī ghrāhəch] *adj*
abnormal; unusual.

mil [mil] *f* honey.

mìle [mīlı] *m* thousand; mile.

milis [milıš] *adj* sweet.

mill [mīL'] *v* damage; spoil; destroy.

millean [miL'an] *m* million.

millte [mīL't'ı] *adj* damaged; spoilt;
destroyed.

millteach [mīL't'əch] *adj* destructive.

milseachd [mīlšəchg] *f* sweetness.

milsean [milšan] *m* dessert, pudding.

mì-mhodhail [mī voghal] *adj* rude,
ill-mannered.

mìn[1] [mīn] *adj* smooth; soft.

mìn[2] [mīn] *f* (*ground*) meal; **minchoirce** [min chɔr'k'ı] *f* oatmeal.

mì-nàdarra [mī nādəRə] *adj* unnatural.

mìneachadh [mīnəchəgh] *m* explanation; interpretation.

mìneachail [mīnəchal] *adj* explanatory.

min-flùir [minflūr'] *f* flour.

min-iarainn [miniərıN'] *f* iron filings.

mìnich[1] [mīnıch'] *v* explain, illustrate; interpret; mean.

mìnich[2] [mīnıch'] *v* smoothe.

minig [minıg'] *adj* frequent.

ministear [minišdɛr] *m* (*church,
govt*) minister.

ministrealachd [minišd'r'əLəchg] *f*
(*church, govt*) ministry.

min-sàibh [minsāiv] *f* sawdust.

miodal [midaL] *m* flattery, fawning.

mìog [mıəg] *f* smirk.

mìogadaich [migadıch'] *f* bleat,
bleating.

mìolchu [mıəLchū] *m* greyhound.

mion [min] *adj* small; minute; detailed; punctilious.

mionach [minəch] *m* entrails, guts;
(*fam*) belly.

mionaid [minad'] *f* minute.

mionaideach [minıd'əch] *adj* thorough; detailed.

mion-aoiseach [minūšəch] *adj* minor.

mion-bhraide [minvraid'ı] *f* pilfering.

mion-chànan [minchānan] *m* minority language.

mion-cheasnaich [minch'esnıch'] *v*
question minutely, grill.

mion-chuid [minchud'] *f* (*proportion*) minority.

mion-chùiseach [minchūšəch] *adj*
meticulous.

mion-eòlas [miN'ɔ̄Ləs] *m* detailed
knowledge.

mion-fhacal [minaʰkəL] *m* (*gram*)
particle.

mion-gheàrr [mingh'āR] *v* cut up
finely.

mionnaich [miuNıch'] *v* curse,
swear.

mionnan [miuNan] *m* curse, swearword.

mion-phuing [minfuing'] *f* detail.

mìorbhail [mıərval] *f* marvel; miracle.

mìorbhaileach [mıərvaləch] *adj*
marvellous; miraculous.

mìos [mıəs] *m* month; **mìos nam
pòg** [mıəs nəm pōg] honeymoon.

mìosach [mıəsəch] *adj* monthly.

mìosachan [miəsəchan] *m* calendar.

miotag [miʰtag] *f* glove; mitten.

mìr [mir'] *m* bit, particle; scrap.

mire [mir'ɪ] *f* mirth; light-heartedness.

mì-rùn [mĩ rūn] *m* malice, ill-will.

misde *see* **miste**

mise [mišɪ] *pron emphatic form of* **mi**.

misg [mišg'] *f* drunkenness, intoxication.

misgear [mišg'ɛr] *m* drunkard, boozer.

mì-shealbhach [mĩ hɛLavəch] *adv* unlucky, unfortunate.

misneachadh [mišnəchəgh] *m* encouragement.

misneachail [mišnəchal] *adj* courageous; spirited; in good heart; encouraging.

misneachd [mišnəchg] *f* courage.

misnich [mišnɪch'] *v* encourage; inspire courage in.

miste [mišd'ɪ] *adj* the worse for; **cha bu mhisde mi X** [cha bə višd'ɪ mi] I'd be none the worse for X.

mithich [mi.ɪch'] *adj* timely.

mo [mɔ] *poss pron* my.

moch [mɔch] *adj* early; **bho mhoch gu dubh** [vɔ vɔch gu du] from morning till night.

mòd [mɔ̃d] *m* (*with art*) **am Mòd (Nàiseanta)** [əm mɔ̃d Nãšəndə] the (National) Mod.

modh [mɔgh] *f* manner, mode; manners; (*gram*) mood.

modhail [mɔghal] *adj* polite, well-bred.

Moslamach [mɔsLəməch] *m/adj* Mohammedan, Muslim.

mòine [mɔ̃N'ɪ] *f* (*collective*) peat; **dèan/buain mòine** [d'ian/buəN' mɔ̃N'ɪ] *v* cut peat.

mòinteach [mɔ̃N'd'əch] *f* moor, moorland.

moit [mɔʰt'] *f* pride.

moiteil [mɔʰt'ɛl] *adj* proud.

mol[1] [mɔL] *v* praise; recommend.

mol[2] [mɔL] *m* shingle; shingly beach.

molach [mɔLəch] *adj* hairy; rough.

moladh [mɔLəgh] *m* praise; recommendation.

moll [mɔuL] *m* chaff.

molldair [mɔuLdɛr'] *m* (*jelly, etc*) mould.

molt [mɔLt] *m* wether.

mòmaid [mɔ̃mɪd'] *f* moment, second.

monadail [mɔnədal] *adj* hilly, mountainous.

monadh [mɔnəgh] *m* moor, moorland; common hill grazing.

mòr [mɔr] *adj* big; great; **mòr aig a chèile** [mɔr ɛg' ə ch'ēlɪ] great friends/pals.

mòrachd [mɔrəchg] *f* greatness, grandeur.

morair [mɔrɛr'] *m* lord.

mòran [mɔ̃ran] *m* many, a lot of; much.

mòrchuis [mɔrchūš] *f* pride, conceit.

mòr-chuid [mɔrchud'] *f* (*with art*) **a' mhòr-chuid** the majority; most people.

morghan [mɔrəghan] *m* gravel, shingle.

mòr-inbhe [mɔr inivɪ] *f* eminence; high rank.

mòr iongnadh [mɔr iūnəgh] *m* astonishment, stupefaction.

mòr-roinn [mɔr rəiN'] *f* continent.

mòr-shluagh [mōr Luəgh] *m* multitude.

murt [muršd] *v* murder, assassinate. • *m* murder, assassination, manslaughter.

murtair [muršdɛr'] *m* murderer, assassin.

mòr-uasal [mōr uəsəL] *m* nobleman, aristocrat.

mosach [mɔsəch] *adj* nasty; scruffy; niggardly.

mosg [mɔsg] *m* mosque.

mosgail [mɔsgal] *v* (*from sleep*) wake, waken, rouse.

mo sgrios! [mə sgr'is] *excl* woe is me!

motair [mɔʰtɛr'] *m* motor.

motair-rothar [mɔʰtɛr'rɔhər] *m* motorbike.

motha [mo.ə] *adj* bigger, greater.

mothachail [mɔhəchal] *adj* aware; observant; sensitive; conscious.

mothaich [mɔhɪch'] *v* notice; feel; experience.

mo thruaighe! [mə ruəi.ɪ] *excl* woe is me!

mo thruaighe ort! [mə ruə.ɪ ɔršt] *excl* woe unto you!

mu [mə] *prep* around, about; concerning.

muc [muʰk] *f* pig; sow.

mu choinneimh [mə chəiN'əv] *prep* opposite.

mucfheoil [muʰk'ɔl] *f* pork.

mùch [mūch] *v* extinguish, quench; smother; strangle; repress.

muc-mhara [muʰkvarə] *f* whale.

mu dheas [mə gh'es] *adv* to/in the South.

mu dhèidhinn [mə dh'ē.ɪN'] *prep* about, concerning.

mu dheireadh [mə dh'er'əgh] *adj* last. • *adv* at last; **mu dheireadh thall** [mə gh'er'əgh hauL] at long last.

muga [mugə] *f* (*drinking*) mug.

mùgach [mūgəch] *adj* morose, surly.

muidhe [mui.ɪ] *m* churn.

mùig [mūg'] *f* frown, scowl.

muinichill [munɪchiL'] *m* sleeve.

Muileach [Muləch] *m*/*adj* Mull person, from Mull.

muileann [muləN] *m* mill.

muileann-gaoithe [muləNgui.ɪ] *m* windmill.

muile-mhàg [mulɪvāg] *f* toad.

muilinn *see* **muileann**

muillean *see* **milleann**

muillear [muL'ɛr] *m* miller.

muilt-fheoil [mult'ɔl] *f* mutton.

muime [muimɪ] *f* stepmother.

muin [muN'] *f* (*esp of animal*) back; top.

muineal [muN'aL] *m* neck.

muing [muing'] *f* mane.

muilcheann *see* **muinichill**

muinntir [muiN'd'ɪr'] *f* people; followers.

muir [mur'] *m*&*f* sea.

muir-làn [mur'Lān] *m* high tide.

mulad [muLad] *f* grief, sadness.

muladach [muLadəch] *adj* sad.

m' ulaidh! [muLɪ] my darling!, my love!.

mullach [muLəch] *m* top; summit; roof.

mult *see* **molt**

mun [mən], **mus** [məs] *conj* before.

mùn [mūn] *m* urine, piss.

muncaidh [munkɪ] *m* monkey.

mun cuairt [mun kuəršd'] *adv* around, about.

mun cuairt air [mun kuəršd' ɛr'] *prep* around, about.

mùr [mūr] *m* bulwark, rampart.

mura [murə] *conj* if not.

mus [mus] *conj same as* **mun**.

mu seach [mə šach] *adv* in turn, one by one.

mùth [mū] *v* change, alter; mutate; deteriorate.

mùthadh [mū.əgh] *m* change, alteration; mutation; deterioration.

mu thimcheall [mə himichəL] *adv* around.

mu thràth [mə rā] [mər hā] *adv* already.

mu thuath [mə huə] *adv* to/in the North.

N

na[1] [nə] *imper part* do not, don't.

na[2] [na] *conj* than.

na[3] [nə] *rel pron* what, that which, those which.

na[4] [nə] *art (f sing)* of the; *(pl)* the.

nàbachas [Nābəchəs] *m* neighbourliness.

nàbaidh [Nābɪ] *m* neighbour.

nàbaidheachd [Nābɪ.əchg] *f* neighbourhood.

nàbaidheil [Nābɪ.ɛl] *adj* neighbourly.

nach [nach] *neg rel pron* that not.

nach math a rinn thu! [nach ma ə rəiN' u] *excl* well done!

'na chrùbagan [nə chrūbagən] *adv* crouched down.

'na chrùban [nə chrūbən] *adv* crouching, squatting.

nàdar [Nādər] *m* nature; temperament.

nàdarrach [NādəRəch] *adj* natural.

'na dhùisg [nə dhūšg'] *adv* awake.

'na dhùsgadh [nə dhūsgəgh] *adv* awake.

nàdur *see* **nàdar**

na h-uile [nə chulɪ] *pron* everybody, everyone.

naidheachd [Nɛ.əchg] *f* piece of news; anecdote; *(pl TV, etc)* **na naidheachdan** [nə nɛ.əchgən] the news.

nàidhlean [Nailən] *m* nylon. [nə nār'ɪ ɔršt] *f* shame, ignominy; bashfulness. • *excls* **mo nàire!** [mə nār'ɪ] for shame! **mo nàire ort!** **nàire** [Nār'ɪ] shame on you!

nàisean [Nāšən] *m* nation.

nàiseanta [Nāšəndə] *adj* national.

nàiseantach [Nāšəndəch] *m* nationalist.

nàiseantachd [Nāšəndəchg] *f* nationalism; nationhood.

naisgear [Našg'ɛr] *m (gram)* conjunction.

nàimhdeas [Naid'əs] *m* enmity, hostility.

nàimhdeil [Naid'ɛl] *adj* inimical, hostile.

nàireach [Nār'əch] *adj* shamefaced; bashful; diffident.

'na laighe [nə Laɪ.ɪ] *adv* lying, reclining.

nam *see* **nan**.

'nam aonar [nəm ūnər] *adv* on my own.

'nam bheachd-sa [nəm vyachgsə] in my opinion.

'nam chomain [nəm chomɛN'] *adj* obliged to me.

nàmhaid [Nā.ıd'] *m* enemy.

nan[1] [nən] (**nam** [nəm] *before b, f, m, p*) *conj* if.

nan[2] [nən/nəN/nəN'] (**nam** [nəm] *before b, f, m, p*) *pl art* of the.

naoi [Nuy] *m/adj* nine.

naoidhean [Nui.an] *m* baby; infant.

naoinear [NūN'ɛr] *m* nine (people).

naomh [Nūv] *m* saint. • *adj* holy, sacred; saintly.

naomhachd [Nūvəchg] *f* holiness; saintliness.

nàr [Nār] *adj* shameful; disgraceful.

nàrach *see* **nàireach**.

nàraich [Nār'ıch'] *v* put to shame; disgrace.

'na ruith [nə ruy] *adj* running.

nas motha [nəs mo.ə] *adv* either, (*with neg v*) neither.

'na stad [nə sdad] *adj* stationary; in abeyance.

'na shuidhe [nə hui.ı] *adv* seated, sitting.

nathair [Nahɛr'] *f* adder; serpent, snake.

'na thràill do [nə rāL' də] addicted to.

'na thrasg [nə rasg] *adv* fasting.

neach [Nɛch] *m* person; one, someone.

neach-ceàirde [fɛrk'ārd'ı] *m* craftsman.

neach-chungaidhean [N'ɛchchungı.ən] *m* chemist, pharmacist.

neach-faire [N'ɛchfar'ı] *m* guard.

neach-fòirneart [N'ɛchfōrN'ɛršd] *m* oppressor.

neach-fuadain [N'ɛchfuadɛN'] *m* wanderer; exile.

neach-giùlain [N'ɛchg'ūLɛN'] *m* carrier, bearer.

neach-ionnsaigh [N'ɛchíuNsı] *m* assailant, attacker.

neach-labhairt [N'ɛchLavıršd'] *m* speaker; spokesman.

neach-lagha [N'ɛchLoghə] *m* lawyer, solicitor.

neach-naidheachd [N'ɛchNɛ.əchg] *m* journalist.

neach-poileis [N'ɛchpolıš] *m* policeman.

neach-siubhail [N'ɛchšu.al] *m* traveller.

neach-taice [N'ɛchtaiʰk'ı] *m* supporter; patron, backer.

neach-teagaisg [N'ɛcht'ɛgıšg'] *m* teacher.

neach-tomhais [N'ɛchto.ıš] *m* surveyor.

neachtair [N'ɛchtɛr'] *m* nectar.

nead [N'ed] *m* nest.

nèamh [N'ɛv] *m* heaven(s).

nèamhaidh [N'ɛvı] *adj* heavenly, celestial.

neapaigear [N'ɛʰpıg'ɛr] *m* handkerchief.

neapaigin [N'ɛʰpəg'ın] *f* napkin.

nearbhach [N'ɛrvəch] *adj* nervous; nervy.

neart [N'aršd] *m* strength; might; vigour; **an trèine a neirt** [ən tr'ēnı ə nɛršd'] in his prime.

neartaich [N'aršdıch'] *v* strengthen; invigorate.

neartmhor [N'aršdvər] *adj* strong; mighty.

neas [N'es] f weasel; ferret; **neas mhòr** [N'es võr] stoat.

neasgaid [N'esgɪd'] f boil; ulcer, abscess.

neimh [N'ɛv] m poison; malice.

Neaptùn [Nɛʰptūn] m Neptune.

neo [N'ɔ] conj same as **no**

neo- [N'ɔ] prefix un-, in-, non-.

neo-chrìochnach [N'ɔch'r'iəchnəch] adj infinite.

neo-eisimeileach [N'ɔ ešɪmɛləch] adj independent.

neo-eisimeileachd [N'ɔ ešɪmɛləchg] f independence.

neòinean [N'ɔ̃N'an] m daisy.

neòinean-grèine [N'ɔ̃N'angr'ēnɪ] m sunflower.

neo-làthaireachd [N'ɔ Lā.ɪr'əchg] f absence.

neo-mhisgeach [N'ɔ višg'əch] adj sober.

neònach [N'ɔ̃nəch] adj strange, curious.

neo-sheachanta [N'ɔ hɛchəndə] adj unavoidable, inevitable.

neul [N'ial] m cloud; complexion; faint.

neulach [N'iaLəch] adj cloudy.

neulaich [N'iaLɪch'] v cloud over; obscure.

nì[1] [N'ī]
[ən N'ī ma] m thing; matter; circumstance; **an Nì Math** God.

nì[2] [N'ī] future tense of v **dèan**.

Nic [N'iʰk'] (in surnames) daughter of.

nigh [N'ī] v wash.

nigheadair [N'i.ədər'] m washer, washing machine.

nigheadaireachd [N'i.ədər'əchg] f washing.

nigheadair-shoithichean [N'i.ədər'ho.ɪch'ən] m dishwasher.

nighean [N'i.an] f girl; young woman; daughter; **nighean bràthar** [N'i.an brāhar]/**peathar** [N'i.an pɛhar] niece.

nimh see **neimh**

nimheil [N'ívɛl] adj poisonous; malicious.

Nirribhidh [N'iRɪvɪ] f Norway.

nitheil [N'i.ɛl] adj concrete, actual.

no [nɔ], **neo** [N'ɔ] conj or.

nobhail [Nɔval] f novel.

nochd [Nɔchg] v show; appear; **nochd an clò** [Nɔchg ən kLɔ̄] be printed/published.

Nollaig [NɔLɛg'] f Christmas.

norrag [NɔRag] f nap, snooze; **norrag cadail** [NɔRag kadal] a wink of sleep.

nòs [Nɔ̄s] m way; custom; style.

nota [Nɔʰtə] f note; (money) pound.

nuadh [Nuə] adj new.

nuadhaich [Nuə.ɪch'] v renovate.

nuallaich [NuəLɪch'] v howl; roar; bellow.

nurs [Nors] f nurse.

O

o [vɔ] [ə] *prep* from; since.

o àm gu àm [vɔ aum gə aum] *adv* from time to time.

òb [ɔ̃b] *m* bay.

obair [obɪr'] *f* work; job, employment.

obair-ghrèise [obɪr'*gh'r'ẽ*ʃɪ] *f* (*the product of*) embroidery, needlework.

obair-làimhe [obɪr'*Laivɪ*] *f* handiwork.

obair-lannsa [obɪr'*LauNsə*] *f* (*med*) operation.

obair-taighe [obɪr'*tɛhɪ*] *f* housework.

obann [obəN] *adj* sudden.

obh! obh! [ovɔ.əv] *excl* dear oh dear! good heavens!

obraich [obrɪch'] *v* work, function; operate.

oibrich *see* **obraich**

och (nan och)! [ɔch nə Nɔch] *excl* alas! woe is me!

ochd [ɔchg] *m/adj* eight.

ochdad [ɔchgəd] *m* eighty.

ochdamh [ɔchgəv] *adj* eighth.

ochd deug [ɔchg d'iag] *m/adj* eighteen.

ochdnar [ɔchgnər] *m* eight (people).

o chionn [ɔ ch'uN] *prep* ago; since; **o chionn ghoirid** [ɔ ch'uN ghor'ɪd'] recently; **o chionn fhada** [ɔ ch'uN adə] long ago.

odhar [o.ər] *adj* dun(-coloured); sallow.

òg [ɔ̃g] *adj* young.

ògan [ɔ̃gan] *m* shoot, tendril.

òganach [ɔ̃ganəch] *m* young man; adolescent.

ogha [o.ə] *m* grandchild.

Òg-mhìos [ɔ̃gviəs] *m* (*with art*) **an t-Òg-mhìos** [ən tɔ̃gviəs] June.

ogsaigin [oʰgsəg'ɪn] *m* oxygen.

obraiche [obrɪch'ə] *m* worker, workman.

oide [od'ɪ] *m* stepfather.

oideachas [od'əchəs] *m* education; learning.

oidhche [oi.ch'ɪ] *f* night; **oidhche mhath leat/leibh!** [oi.ch'ɪ va laʰt/leiv] goodnight! **Oidhche Challainn** [oi.ch'ɪ*chaLɪN'*] Hogmanay, New Year's Eve; **Oidhche Shamhna** [oi.ch'ɪ*haunə*] Halloween.

oidhirp [o.ɪrp] *f* attempt, try; effort.

oifig *see* **oifis**

oifigeach [əfɪgəch] *m* official.

oifigear [əfɪg'ɛr] *m* officer.

oifigeil [əfɪg'ɛl] *adj* official.

oifis [əfiʃ] *f* office; position; **oifis a' phuist** [əfiʃ ə fuʃd']post office; **Oifis na h-Alba** [əfiʃ nə haLabə] the Scottish Office Now Scotland Office or Scottish Parliament.

òige [ɔ̃g'ɪ] *f* youth.

òigear [ɔ̃g'ɛr] *m* youngster, adolescent.

òigh [ɔ̃y] *f* virgin; young woman.

òigheil [ɔ̃i.ɛl] *adj* virginal.

oighre [oi.r'ɪ] *m* heir, inheritor.

oighreachd [oir'əchg] *f* (*land*) estate; inheritance.

òigridh [ōg'r'ɪ] f (*collective*) young people.

oilbheum [ɔlvēm] m offence.

oilbheumach [ɔlvēmǎch] adj offensive.

oileanach [ɔlanǎch] m student.

oileanaich [ɔlanɪch'] v train; instruct.

oillt [əiL't'] f terror; horror.

oillteil [əiL't'təl] adj frightful, dreadful; horrible.

oilltich [əiL't'ɪch'] v terrify.

oilthigh [ɔlhoy] m university.

òinseach [ŏN'šǎch] f (*female*) fool, (*female*) idiot.

oir [ɔr'] f edge, margin; rim; **oir an rathaid** [ɔr' ən Ra.ɪd']verge; **oir a' chabhsair** [ɔr' ə chausɛr'] kerb.

oir [ɔr'] conj for.

oirbh [ɔr'iv] prep pron on you (*pl*).

òirdheirc [ŏr'gh'erk'] adj magnificent; illustrious.

òirleach [ŏrlǎch] m inch.

oirnn [ɔr'N'] prep pron on us.

oirre [ɔRɪ] prep pron on her, on it (*f*).

oirthir [ɔrhir] f coast, seaboard.

oisean [ɔšan], **oisinn** [ɔšiN'] m corner.

oiteag [ɔʰt'ag] f breeze; breath of wind.

òl [ɔL] v drink.

ola [ɔlə] f oil.

olann [ɔləN] f wool.

olc [ɔlk] m evil, wickedness. • adj evil, wicked.

olla [ɔlə] adj woollen.

ollamh [ɔLəv] m learned man; (*academic*) doctor.

òmar [ŏmər] m amber.

on a [vɔn ə] conj since, as.

onair [ɔnɛr'] f honour; honesty; esteem. • *excl* **air mo onair!** [ɛr' mɔnɛr'] honestly!

onorach [ɔnərǎch] adj honourable; honest; honorary.

onoraich [ɔnərɪch'] v honour.

on taigh [vɔn toy] adv out; away from home.

òr [ŏr] m gold.

òraid [ŏrɪd'] f speech, address; lecture.

òraidiche [ŏrɪd'ɪch'ə] m speaker.

orains [ɔrɛnš] adj orange.

orainsear [ɔrɛnšər] m orange.

òran [ŏran] m song; **òrain luaidh** [ŏran Luay]waulking songs; **na h-òrain mhòra** [nə hŏrɛN' vŏrə] the great ballads.

òr-chèard [ŏrch'ērd] m goldsmith.

òrd [ŏrd] m hammer.

òrdag [ŏrdag] f thumb.

òrdag-coise [ŏrdagkɔši] f toe.

òrdaich [ŏrdɪch'] v order, command; organise, tidy.

òrdaighean [ŏrdɪ.ən] mpl (*with art*) **na h-òrdaighean** [nə hŏrdɪ.ən] (*relig*) communion.

òrdail [ŏrdal] adj orderly; ordinal.

òrdugh [ŏrdu] m order, sequence; command.

òrgan [ŏrgan] m organ.

orm [ɔrɔm] prep pron on me.

orra [ɔRə] prep pron on them.

òrraiseach [ŏRɪšǎch] adj squeamish.

ort [ɔršd] prep pron on you (*sing*).

ortha [ɔRə] f spell, charm.

osan [ɔsan] m stocking, hose.

osann [ɔsəN] m same as **osna**

os cionn [ɔs k'ūN] prep above, over.

òstair [ŏsdɛr'] m hotelier, landlord, licensee.

o shean [vɔ hɛn] *adv* of old, long ago.

os ìseal [ɔs ĩʃal] *adv* quietly; secretly.

osna [ɔsnə] *m*, **osann** *m* sigh; breeze.

osnaich [ɔsnɪch'] *v* sigh.

ospadal [ɔspədaL] *m* hospital.

ospag [ɔspag] *f* sigh; breath of wind.

Ostair [ɔsdɛr'] *f* (*with art*) **an Ostair** [ə Nɔsdɛr'] Austria.

Ostaireach [ɔsdɛr'əch] *m/adj* Austrian.

othail [ɔhal] *f* hubbub, uproar.

othaisg [ɔhɪšg'] *f* hogg, ewe-lamb.

o thùs [vɔ hũs] *adv* originally.

òtrach [ɔ̃ʰtrəch] *m* dunghill, midden.

P

paca [paʰkə] *m* pack.

pacaid [paʰkɪd'] *f* packet.

pàganach [pāganəch] *m/adj* pagan, heathen.

paidh [pay] *m* pie.

paidhir [pai.ɪr'] *f* pair.

paidir [pad'ɪr'] *f* Lord's Prayer.

paidirean [pad'ɪr'an] *m* rosary.

pàigh [pāy] *v* pay (for); atone (for).

pàigh [pāy], **pàigheadh** [pāi.əgh] *m* pay, remuneration.

pàillean [pāLan] *m* pavilion; large tent.

pailt [palt'] *adj* plentiful.

pailteas [palt'əs] *m* plenty.

pàipear [pēʰpɛr] *m* paper.

pàipear-balla [pēʰpɛrbaLə] *m* wallpaper.

pàipear-gainmhich [pēʰpɛrgɛnavɪch'] *m* sandpaper.

pàipear-naidheachd [pēʰpɛrNɛ.əchg] *m* newspaper.

pàirc [pār'k'] *f* field; park.

paireafain [parəfɛN'] *m* paraffin.

pàirt [pāršd'] *m* part.

pàirt-càraidh [pāršd'kāri] *m* spare, spare part.

pàirtich [pāršd'ɪch'] *v* share out; divide up.

pàiste [pāšd'ɪ] *m* baby; infant; small child.

paisg [pašg'] *v* wrap (up); fold (up).

pàiteach [pāʰt'əch] *adj* thirsty.

pana [panə] *m* pan.

pannal [paNaL] *m* panel.

Pàpa [pāʰpə] *m* Pope.

pàpanach [pāʰpanəch] *m/adj* papist, popish.

pàrant [pārand] *m* parent.

pàrlamaid [pārLəmɪd'] *f* parliament.

pàrlamaideach [pārLəmɪd'əch] *adj* parliamentary.

parsail [parsal] *m* parcel, package.

pàrtaidh [pāršdɪ] *m* party.

partan [paršdan] *m* (*edible*) crab.

pasgadh [pasgəgh] *m* packing.

pasgan [pasgan] *m* bundle; package.

pastraidh [pasdrɪ] *f* pastry.

pathadh [pa.əgh] *m* thirst.

pàtran [pāʰtran] *m* pattern.

peacach [pɛʰkəch] *m* sinner. • *adj* sinful.

peacadh [pɛʰkəgh] *m* sin.

peacadh-bàis [pɛʰkəghbā̆š] *m* mortal sin.

peacadh-gine [pɛʰkəghg'íɪnɪ] *m* original sin.

peacaich [pɛʰkɪch'] *v* sin.

peanas [pɛnas] *m* punishment; penalty.

peanasaich [pɛnasɪch'] *v* punish.

peann [pyauN] *m* pen.

peansail [pɛnsal] *m* pencil.

peantaich [pɛntɪch'] *v* paint.

peanta [pɛntə] *m* paint.

peantair [pɛntɛr'] *m* painter.

pearraid [pɛRɪd'] *f* parrot.

pearsa [pɛrsə] *m* person; (*play, etc*) character.

pearsanta [pɛrsəntə] *adj* personal.

pearsantachd [pɛrsəntachg] *f* personality.

peasair [pɛsɛr'] *f* pea.

peata [pɛʰtə] *m* pet.

peatroil [pɛʰtrəl] *m* petrol.

peighinn [pe.ɪN'] *f* penny.

peile [pelɪ] *m* pail.

pèileag [pēlag] *f* porpoise.

peilear [pelɛr] *m* bullet; pellet.

peile-frasaidh [pelɪfrasɪ] *m* watering can.

peinnsean [peiN'šan] *m* pension.

peirceall [per'k'əL] *m* jaw, jawbone.

peitean [pɛʰt'an] *m* vest; waistcoat.

pèitseag [pēʰt'šag] *f* peach.

peur [piar] *f* pear.

pian [pian] *v* pain, distress; torture. • *f* pain.

piàna [pyānə] *m* piano.

pianail [pianal] *adj* painful.

pic [piʰk'] *m* (*tool*) pick.

picil [piʰk'ɪl] *f* pickle.

pile [pilɪ] *f* pill.

pileat [pīlat] *m* pilot.

pillean [piL'an] *m* cushion; pillion.

pinc [pink'] *adj* pink.

pinnt [pīN'd'] *m* pint.

pìob [pīb] *f* pipe; tube.

pìobaire [pībər'ə] *m* piper.

pìobaireachd [pībər'achg] *f* (bag-) piping; pibroch.

pìobar [pibər] *m* pepper.

pìob mhòr [pīb vōr] *f* Highland bagpipes.

pìobraich [pibrɪch'] *v* add pepper to; pep up.

pìob-thombaca [pībhombaʰkə] *f* (tobacco) pipe.

pìob-uilne [pībulinɪ] *f* uileann pipes.

pìoc [piʰk] *v* peck; nibble.

pìos [pīs] *m* piece, bit; packed lunch.

piseach [pišəch] *m* progress, improvement.

piseag [pišag] *f* kitten.

pit [piʰt'] *f* vulva.

piuthar [pyu.ər] *f* sister.

piuthar-chèile [pyu.ərch'ēlɪ] *f* sister-in-law.

plaide [pLad'ɪ] *f* blanket.

plàigh [pLāy] *f* plague; infestation; nuisance.

plàigheil [pLāi.ɛl] *adj* pestilential.

plana [pLanə] *m* plan.

planaid [pLanɪd'] *f* planet.

planaig [pLanɪg'] *v* plan.

plangaid [pLangɪd'] *f* blanket.

plap [pLaʰp] *v* flutter. • *m* fluttering.

plaoisg [pLūšg'] *v* shell; peel; skin.

plaosg [pLūsg] *m* shell; peel; skin; husk.

plàsd [pLāsd] *m* sticking plaster.

plastaig [pLasdɪg'] *f/adj* plastic.

plathadh [pLahəgh] *m* glance; glimpse; instant.

pleadhag [pLɛ.ag] *f (canoe, etc)* paddle.

pleadhagaich [pLɛ.əgɪch'] *v* paddle.

plèana [pLēnə] *f* (aero)plane.

ploc [pLɔhk] *m* clod; turf; block; lump.

ploc-prìne [pLɔhkpr'īnɪ] *m* pinhead.

plosg [pLɔsg] *v* gasp, pant; palpitate, throb. • *m* gasp; palpitation; throb.

plub [pLub], **plubraich** [pLubrɪch'] *m* splash, plop. • *v* splash, plop, slosh.

plucan [pLuhkan] *m* pimple; *(sink, etc)* plug.

pluic [pLuihk'] *f* (plump) cheek.

plumair [pLumɛr'] *m* plumber.

Plùta [pLūhtə] *m* Pluto.

poball [pobəL] *m* people.

poballach [pobəLəch], **poblach** [pobLəch *adj* public.

poblachd [pobLəchg] *f* republic.

poca [pohkə] *m* bag; sack.

pòca [pɔ̄hkə] *m*, **pòcaid** [pɔ̄hkɪd'] *f* pocket.

poca-cadail [pohkəkadal] *m* sleeping-bag.

pòcaid *see* **pòca**.

pòg [pōg] *v* kiss. • *f* kiss.

poidsear [pod'šɛr] *m* poacher.

poileas [poləs] *m* police; policeman.

poileataigeach [polətɪg'əch] *adj* political.

poileataigeachd [polətɪg'əchg] *f* politics.

poileataigear [polətɪgɛr] *m* politicians.

poit [pɔht'] *f* pot.

poit-dhubh [pɔht'dhu] *f* (whisky) still.

pòitear [pɔ̄ht'ɛr] *m* drinker, boozer.

pòitearachd [pɔ̄ht'ɛrəchg] *f* boozing, tippling.

poit-fhlùran [pɔht'lūrən] *f* flowerpot.

poit-mhùin [pɔht'vūN'] *f* chamberpot.

poit-teatha [pɔht'ɛ.ə] *f* teapot.

pòla [pɔ̄Lə] *m* pole; **am Pòla a Tuath/a Deas** [əm pɔ̄Lə ə tuə/ə d'es] the North/South Pole.

Pòlach [pɔ̄Ləch] *m/adj* Pole; Polish.

Pòlainn [pɔ̄LɪN'] *f* (with art) **a' Phòlainn** [ə fɔ̄LɪN'] Poland.

polas *see* **poileas**

poileasman *see* **neach-poileis**

poll [pouL] *m* mud; bog.

poll-mòna [pouLmɔ̄nə], **poll-mònach** [pouLmɔ̄nəch] *m* peat bog.

pònaidh [pɔ̄nɪ] *m* pony.

pònair [pɔ̄nɛr'] *f* bean(s); **pònair leathann** [pɔ̄nɛr' lɛhəN] broad bean(s); **pònair Fhrangach** [pɔ̄nɛr' rangəch] French bean(s).

pong [pong] *m (mus)* note.

pongail [pongal] *adj* concise; punctual; punctilious.

pòr [pɔ̄r] *m* seed; crops; growth.

port[1] [poršd] *[m* port, harbour; **port-adhair** [poršda.ɪr'] airport.

port[2] [poršd] *m* tune; **port-a-beul** [poršd a biaL] mouth music.

Portagail [poršdagal] *f (with art)* **a' Phortagail** [ə foršdagal] Portugal.

Portagaileach [poršdagaləch] *m/adj* Portuguese.

portair [poršdɛr'] *m* porter; doorman.

pòs [pōs] *v* marry.

pòsadh [pōsəgh] *m* marriage.

pòsda [pōsdə] *adj* married; **pòsda aig** [pōsdə ɛg']married to; **nuadh-phòsda** [Nuə fōsdə] newly married.

post [posd] *m* post, stake; post, mail; postman; **post-adhair** [posdə.ır'] air mail.

posta [posdə] *m* postman.

post-dealain [posd'ɛLɛN'] (*abbrev* **post-d**) *m* electronic mail, email.

prabar [prabər] *m* rabble, mob.

prab-shùileach [prabhūləch] *adj* bleary-eyed.

prais [praš] *f* cooking pot.

pràis [prāš] *f* brass.

pràiseach [prāšəch] *adj* brass.

preantas [pr'ɛndəs] *m* apprentice.

preas[1] [pr'es] *v* crease; corrugate; crush.

preas[2] [pr'es] *m* bush, shrub.

preas[3] [pr'es], **preasa** [pr'esə] *m* cupboard.

preasach [pr'esəch] *adj* wrinkly, wrinkled.

preasadh [pr'esəgh] *m* wrinkle.

preasag [pr'esag] *f* wrinkle, crease.

preas-aodaich [pr'esūdıch'] *m* wardrobe.

preas-leabhraichean [pr'esL'orıchən] *m* bookcase.

prìne [pr'īnı] *m* pin.

prìne-banaltraim [pr'īnıbanaLtrım] *m* safety pin.

priob [pr'ib] *v* wink; blink.

priobadh [pr'ibəgh] *m* wink; blink; instant.

prìobhaideach [pr'īvıd'əch] *adj* private.

prìomh [pr'iəv] *adj* main, head.

prìomhaire [pr'iəvər'ə] *m* prime minister.

prionnsa [pr'iuNsə] *m* prince.

prionnsabal [pr'iuNsəbaL] *m* principle.

prìosan [pr'īsan] *m* prison.

prìosanach [pr'īsanəch] *m* prisoner.

prìs [pr'īš] *f* price, cost.

prìseil [pr'īšɛl] *adj* precious; valuable.

prògram [prōgram] *m* programme; (*comput*) program.

proifeasair [profɛsır'] *m* professor.

proifeiseanta [profɛšəndə] *adj* professional.

pròis [prōš] *f* pride.

pròiseact [prōšɛkt] *f* project.

pròiseil [prōšɛl] *adj* proud.

pronn [prouN] *v* mash, pulverise; (*fam*) bash, beat up. • *adj* mashed, pulverised.

pronnasg [prəNəsg] *m* sulphur; brimstone.

prosbaig [prəsbıg'] *f* binoculars; telescope.

Pròstanach [prōsdanəch] *m/adj* Protestant.

prothaid [prohıd'] *f* (*fin*) profit; gain, benefit.

puball [pubaL] *m* marquee.

pùdar [pūdər] *m* powder.

pùdaraich [pūdərıch'] *v* powder.

puing [puing'] *f* point (in scale, etc); (*orthog*) stop, mark; **stad-phuing** [sdadfuing']full stop; **clisg-phuing** [klišg'fuing']exclamation mark; **dà-phuing** [dāfuing'] colon.

puinnsean [puiN'šan] *m* poison.

puinnseanach [puiN'šanəch] *adj* poisonous.

puinnseanaich [puiN'šanıch'] v poison.

pumpa [pūmpə] m pump.

punnd [pūNd] m (weight and money) pound; **punnd Èireannach** [pūNd ēr'əNəch] punt (now replaced by the euro); **punnd**

Sasannach [pūNd sasəNəch] pound sterling.

purpaidh [purpı] adj purple.

purpar [purpər] m purple.

put¹ [puʰt] v push, jostle.

put² [puʰt] m buoy.

putan [puʰtan] m button.

R

rabaid [Rabıd'] f rabbit.

rabhadh [Ravəgh] m warning; alarm.

rabhd [Raud] m idle talk; obscene talk.

ràc¹ [Rāʰk] v rake.

ràc² [Rāʰk] m drake.

racaid [Raʰkıd'] f (sports) racket.

ràcan [Rāʰkan] m rake.

rach [Rach] v go.

rach à bith [Rach a bi] v cease to be.

rach a cadal [Rach a kadəL] v go to bed.

rach à cuimhne [Rach a kuiN'ı] v be forgotten.

rach a dhìth [Rach a gh'ī] v go short.

rach air dìochuimhne [Rach ɛr' d'iəchəN'ı] v be forgotten.

rach air iomrall [Rach ɛr' imrəL] v wander; go astray, err.

rach air iteig [Rach ɛr' iʰt'ɛg'] v fly.

rach air muin [Rach ɛr' muN'] v have sex with; (animals) serve.

rach air seachran [Rach ɛr' šɛcharan] v wander; go astray.

rach am fad [Rach əm fad] v get/ grow longer.

rach am feabhas [Rach əm fyɔ.əs] v improve, get better.

rach am meud [Rach əm miad] v get bigger.

rach an geall gu [Rach ən g'auL gu] v bet that.

rach an laigse [Rach ən Lag'šı] v faint.

rach an neul [Rach ən N'iaL] v faint, pass out.

rach an sàs ann an [Rach ən sās auN ən] v get involved in.

rach an urras (air) [Rach ən uRəs ɛr'] v guarantee, vouch (for).

rach an urras gu [Rach ən uRəs gu] v guarantee that.

rach à sealladh [Rach a šɛLəgh] v disappear, go out of sight.

rach às mo chuimhne [Rach as mə chuiN'ı] v be forgotten.

rach às mo leth [Rach as mə le] v side with me.

rach bhuaithe [Rach vuəi.ı] v deteriorate.

rach car mu char [Rach kar mə char] v roll over and over.

rach fodha [Rach fo.ə] v sink; (firm, etc) fail.

rach 'na laighe [Rach nə Lai.ı] v lie down; go to bed.

rach 'na lasair [Rach nə Lasır'] v go up in flames.

rach 'na shaighdear [Rach nə səid'ɛr] *v* become a soldier.

rach ri taobh X [Rach r'i tūv] *v* take after X.

rach seachad (air) [Rach šɛchəd ɛr'] *v* pass by, go past.

rach thar a chèile [Rach har ə ch'ēlɪ] *v* fall out, quarrel.

radan [Radan] *m* rat.

ràdh [Rā] *m* saying, proverb.

radharc [Ro.ərk] *m* eyesight; sight, view.

rag [Rag] *adj* stiff; stubborn.

ragaich [Ragɪch'] *v* stiffen.

rag-mhuinealach [RagvuN'əLəch] *adj* pig-headed.

raineach [Ranəch] *f* bracken, fern(s).

ràinig [rānɪg'] *past tense of v* ruig

ràith [Rāy] *f* season; quarter (of year); while.

ràitheachan [Rāi.əchan] *m* (*magazine*) quarterly, periodical.

ràmh [Rāv] *m* oar.

ràn [Rān] *v* roar, yell; weep. • *m* roar, yell; weeping.

rann [RauN] *f* poetry; a verse.

rannsaich [RauNsɪch'] *v* search; rummage; research..

raon [Rūn] *m* field.

raon-adhair [Rūna.ɪr'] *m* airfield.

raon-cluiche [RūnkLuch'ɪ] *m* playing field.

rapach [Raʰpəch] *adj* slovenly, scruffy.

rathad [Ra.əd] *m* road; way, route.

rathad mòr [Ra.əd mōr] *m* main road.

Ratharsach [Ra.ərsəch] *m/adj* Raasay person, from Raasay.

Ratharsair [Ra.ərsɛr'] Raasay.

rè [Rē] *f* time, period.

rè [Rē] *prep* during, throughout.

reachd [Rɛchg] *m* rule; command; law.

reamhar [Rɛu.ər] *adj* fat.

reamhraich [Rɛurɪch'] *v* fatten.

reic [Reʰk'] *v* sell. • *m* sale; selling.

reiceadair [Reʰk'ədər'] *m* vendor; salesman; auctioneer.

rèidh [Rē] *adj* level; smooth; cleared; **rèidh ri** [Rē r'i] on good terms with.

rèidhlean [Rēlan] *m* (a) green.# (not colour, but level surface covered in grass, e.g. bowling green)

rèidio [Rēd'io] *m* radio.

rèile [Rēlɪ] *f* rail, railing.

rèilig [Rēlɪg'] *f* kirkyard.

rèis [Rēš] *f* (*sport, etc*) race.

rèiseamaid [Rēšəmɪd'] *f* regiment.

rèite [Rēʰt'ɪ] *f* agreement; reconciliation; betrothal; atonement.

rèiteach [Rēʰtəch], **rèiteachadh** [Rēʰtəchəgh] *m* betrothal.

rèitear [Rēʰtɛr] *m* referee.

reithe [Re.ɪ] *m* tup, ram.

rèitich [Rēʰt'ɪch'] *v* reconcile; appease; arbitrate; settle; adjust.

reòdh *see* **reòth**

reòiteag [Ryōʰt'ag] *f* ice cream.

reòta [Ryōʰtə] *adj* frozen.

reòth [Ryō] *v* freeze.

reòthadair [Ryō.ədər'] *m* freezer, deep freeze.

reòthadh [Ryō.əgh] *m* frost.

reothairt [Ryo.ɪršt'] *f* spring-tide.

reub [Riab] *v* tear; lacerate; mangle.

reubadh [Riabəgh] *m* rip, rent.

reubalach [RēbəLəch] *m* rebel.

reudan [Rēdan] *m* wood-louse.

reul [Rēl] *f* star.

reuladair [RēLədər'] *m* astronomer.

reul-bhad [RēLvad] *m* constellation.

reul-eòlas [RēlyōLəs] *m* astronomy.

reul-iùil [Rēlyūl] *f* pole star.

reusan [Rēsan] *m* reason; sanity.

reusanta [Rēsandə] *adj* reasonable; sensible; fair.

ri [r'i] *prep* to; against; during.

riabhach [Riəvəch] *adj* brindled; grizzled; drab; dun.

riadh [Riəgh] (*fin*) interest.

riaghail [Rī.al] *v* rule (over), govern; regulate; manage.

riaghailt [Rī.alt'] *f* rule, regulation; system, order.

riaghailteach [Rī.alt'əch] *adj* regular; systematical.

riaghailteachd [Rī.alt'əchg] *f* orderliness; regularity.

riaghailtich [Rī.alt'ıch'] *v* regularise; regulate.

riaghaltas [Rī.aLtəs] *m* government.

riaghladair [RiəLədər'] *m* ruler, governor.

riaghladh [RiəLəgh] *m* governing; management.

rianachd [Rianəchg] *f* administration.

rian [Rian] *m* orderliness; system; reason; (*mus*) arrangement.

rianadair [Rianədər'] *m* (*mus*) arranger; administrator.

rianail [Rianal] *adj* methodical.

riaraich [Riərıch'] *v* please; satisfy; distribute; (*cards*) deal.

riatanach [Riəʰtənəch] *adj* essential.

rib [Rib] *v* trap, ensnare.

ribe [Ribı] *f* trap, snare.

ribean-tomhais [Ribanto.ış] *m* tape measure.

ruibh [Raiv] *prep pron* to you (*pl*).

ribheid [Rivɛd'] *f* (*mus*) reed.

ribhinn [RīvıN'] *f* (*songs*) maiden, girl.

ridhil [Ri.ıl] *m* (*dance*) reel; **ridhil-ochdnar** [Ri.ıl ɔchgnər] eightsome reel.

ridire [Rid'ır'ə] *m* knight.

rìgh [Rī] *m* king.

Rìgh nan Dùl [Rī nən dūL] *m* Lord of the Universe, God.

righinn [Ri.ıN'] *adj* (*material, etc*) tough.

ri mo bheò [r'im vyō] *adv* all my life; in my lifetime.

rinn[1] [rəiN'] *past tense of v* **dèan**.

rinn[2] [RĪN'] *m* point, promontory.

ruinn [rəiN'] *prep pron* to us.

rioban [Riban] *m* ribbon.

riochd [Richg] *m* likeness, form; appearance.

riochdaich [Richgıch'] *v* represent; portray; impersonate.

riochdair [Richgɛr'] *m* (*gram*) pronoun.

riochdaire [Richgər'ə] *m* representative.

rìoghachadh [Rī.əchəgh] *m* reign; reigning.

rìoghachd [Rī.əchg] *f* kingdom.

rìoghaich [Rī.ıch'] *v* reign.

rìoghail [Rī.al] *adj* royal; kingly; regal.

rìomhach [Riəvəch] *adj* beautiful; splendid.

rionnach [RuNəch] *m* mackerel.

rionnag [RuNag] *f* star.

rionnag-earbaill [RuNagɛrabıL'] *f* meteor.

ris[1] [r'iš] *prep pron* to him, to it (*m*).

ris[2] [r'iš] *adv* showing, exposed.

ris a' bhruthaich [r'iš ə vru.ıch'] *adv* against the slope.

ris a' ghaoith [r'iš ə ghȳy] *adv* against the wind.

ris an t-sruth [r'iš ən tru] *adv* against the current.

ri taobh [r'i tūv] *prep* beside, alongside.

ri taobh a chèile [r'i tūv ə ch'ēlı] *adv* abreast.

ri teachd [r'i t'ɛchg] *adv* future, to come.

rithe [r'i.ı] *prep pron* to her, to it (*f*).

ri tìde [r'i t'īd'ı] *adv* in time, eventually.

ri uchd bàis [r'i uchg bāš] *adv* at the point of death.

rium [r'ium] *prep pron* to me.

riut [r'iuʰt] *prep pron* to you (*sing*).

riutha [r'iu.ə] *prep pron* to them.

ro [Rɔ] *prep* (*time and space*) before; in front of.

ro [rɔ] *adv* too; very, extremely.

ro- [Rɔ] *prefix* fore-, pre-.

robach [Robəch] *adj* hairy, shaggy; slovenly.

robh [rou] *past tense, neg and interrog, of v* **bith**

roc [Rɔʰk] *f* wrinkle.

rocaid [Rɔʰkıd'] *f* rocket.

ròcail [Rɔ̄ʰkal] *f* croak(ing), caw(ing).

ròcais [Rɔ̄kıš] *f* rook.

ro-chraiceann [Rɔchraʰk'əN] *m* foreskin.

roghainn [Ro.ıN'] *m* choice; preference.

roghnaich [Rɔ̄nıch'] *v* choose.

roilig [Rɔlıg'] *v* roll.

roimhe [Rɔi.ı] *prep pron* before him, before it (*m*).

roimhe [Rɔi.ı] *adv* before.

roimhear [Rɔi.ɛr] *m* preposition.

ro-innleachd [RɔıN'L'əchg] *f* strategy.

roimhpe [Rɔiʰpı] *prep pron* before her, before it (*f*).

ròineag [Rɔ̄N'ag] *f* (*single*) hair.

roinn [RəıN'] *v* divide (up); distribute; (*cards*) deal; (*arith*) divide.

roinn [RəıN'] *f* division; share; department; (*govt*) region; continent.

ròsdaich [Rɔ̄sdıch'] *v* roast; fry.

ro làimh [Rɔ Laiv] *adv* beforehand.

ròlaist [Rɔ̄Lašd'] *m* romance, romantic novel.

ro-leasachan [Rɔlesəchan] *m* (*gram*) prefix.

ròmach [Rɔ̄məch] *adj* woolly, hairy, shaggy; bearded.

Romàinia [RomāN'a] *f* Romania.

Romàineach [RomāN'əch] *m/adj* Romanian.

romhad [Ro.əd] *prep pron* before you (*sing*).

romhaibh [Ro.ıv] *prep pron* before you (*pl*).

romhainn [Ro.ıN'] *prep pron* before us.

romham [Ro.əm] *prep pron* before me.

romhpa [Rɔʰpə] *prep pron* before them.

ròn [Rɔ̄n] *m* (*animal*) seal.

rong[1] [Rɔng] *f* rung; spar; hoop.

rong² [Rɔng] *m* vital spark.

ron mhithich [Rɔn vi.ɪch'] *adv* premature(ly).

ronn [RɔuN] *m* mucus, phlegm.

ro-nochd [rɔ Nɔchg] *v* overexpose.

ro-òrdachadh [Rɔ ɔ̄rdəchəgh] *m* predestination.

ro-òrdaich [Rɔ ɔ̄rdɪch'] *v* predestine, predetermine.

ròpa [Rɔ̄ʰpə] *m* rope.

ròpa-aodaich [Rɔ̄ʰpūdɪch'] *m* clothes-line.

ro-ràdh [Rɔ rā] *m* foreword, preamble.

ròs [Rɔ̄s] *m* rose.

ròsda [Rɔ̄sdə] *adj* roast(ed); fried.

rosg¹ [Rɔsg] *m* eyelash.

rosg² [Rɔsg] *m* prose.

rosgrann [RɔsgrəN] *f* sentence.

roth [Rɔ] *m* wheel.

rothach [Rɔhəch] *adj* wheeled.

rothar [Rɔhər] *m* bicycle.

ro-throm [rɔ rom] *adj* overweight.

ruadh [Ruəgh] *adj* red; red-haired, ginger.

ruaig [Ruəg'] *v* chase; put to flight, (*milit*) rout. • *f* chase, pursuit; flight; rout; hunt.

ruamhair [Ruə.ɪr] *v* dig; rummage.

rubair [Rubər'] *m* rubber.

rubha [Ru.ə] *m* point, promontory.

rùchd [Rūchg] *v* grunt; belch; retch. • *m* grunt; belch; retching.

rud [Rud] *m* thing; fact.

rùda [Rūdə] *m* ram, tup.

rudail [Rudal] *adj* concrete, actual, real.

rùdan [Rūdan] *m* knuckle, finger-joint.

rud beag [Rud beg] *adv* a ḃit, somewhat.

rudeigin [Rudeg'ɪn] *pron* something, anything. • *adv* somewhat.

ruadhadh [Ruəghəgh] *m* blush(ing), flush(ing).

rud sam bith [Rud səm bi] *m* anything at all.

rug [rug] *past tense of v* beir.

rugadh mi [rugəgh mi] *v* I was born.

ruidhle [Ruilɪ] *m same as* ridhil

ruig [Ruig'] *v* arrive (at), reach.

ruig air [Ruig' ɛr'] *v* reach for; take, seize;.

ruighe [Rui.ɪ] *f* forearm; hillslope.

rùilear [Rūlɛr] *m* (*measuring*) rule, ruler.

Ruis [Ruš] *f* (*with art*) **an Ruis** [ən Ruš] Russia.

ruisean [Rušan] *m* (*with art*) **an ruisean** [ən Rušan] the midday meal.

Ruiseach [Rušəch] *m/adj* Russian.

rùisg [Rūšg'] *v* bare, strip; shear, fleece; peel; chafe.

rùisgte [Rūšg't'ɪ] *adj* stripped; shorn; peeled.

ruiteach [Ruʰt'əch] *adj* ruddy; blushing, flushed.

ruith [Rui] *v* run; flow; chase. • *f* run, running; pursuit; rout; rate, pace.

rùm [Rūm] *m* room; space.

Rumach [Ruməch] *m/adj* from Rum.

rùm-bìdh [Rūmbī] *m* dining-room.

rùm-ionnlaid [RūmíūNLɪd'] *m* bathroom.

rùn [Rūn] *m* secret; love, affection; wish, purpose; ambition.

rùnaich [Rūnɪch'] *v* wish, desire; resolve.

rùnaire [Rūnər'ə] *m* secretary;

Rùnaire na Stàite [Rūnər'ə nə sdãʰt'ɪ] the Secretary of State.

rùraich [Rūrɪch'] v rummage, grope; explore.

rìs [Rĩš] m rice.

rùsg [Rūsg] m fleece; peel, skin, husk; (*tree*) bark.

S

's [s] (*for* **agus, is**) *conj* and.

-sa [sə] *suffix* this.

sabaid [sabɪd'] v fight, scrap, brawl.
  • f fight(ing), scrap(ping), brawl-(ing).

sàbaid [sābɪd'] f sabbath.

sàbh [sāv] v saw. • m saw.

sàbhail [sāval] v save, rescue; economise.

sàbhailte [sāvalt'ɪ] *adj* safe.

sabhal [sɔ.əL] m barn.

sàbhaladh [sāvaLəgh] m rescuing; (*relig*) salvation; savings.

sabhs [saus] m sauce.

sac [saʰk] m sack.

sad [sad] v throw, toss, chuck.

sagart [sagəršt] m priest.

saibhear [saivɛr] m culvert; sewer.

saideal [sad'ɛL] m satellite.

saidhbhir [saivɪr'] *adj* wealthy, af-fluent.

saidhbhreas [saivr'əs] m wealth, affluence.

saighdear [səid'ɛr] m soldier.

saighead [sai.əd] f arrow.

sail [sal] f beam, joist.

sàil [sāl] f heel.

sailead [saləd] m salad.

saill[1] [saiL'] v salt; season (*with salt*).

saill[2] [saiL'] f fat, grease.

saillear [saiL'ɛr] f salt-cellar.

saillte [saiL't'ɪ] *adj* salt, salted; salty.

sal [saL] m filth; dross; stain.

sàl [sāL] m salt water, brine; (*with art*) **an sàl** [ən sāL] (*songs, etc*) the sea, the briny.

salach [saLəch] *adj* dirty, filthy; foul.

salaich [saLɪch'] v dirty, soil; defile, sully.

salann [saLəN] m salt.

salachar [saLəchar] m dirt, filth.

salm [saLam] m psalm.

saltair [saLtɛr'] v tread, trample.

sàmhach [sāvəch] *adj* quiet, peace-ful, tranquil; silent.

samhail [sau.al] m likeness; match; the like(s) of.

Samhain [sau.ɪN'] f Hallowtide; All Saints'/Souls' Day; **Oidhche Shamhna** [oi.ch'ɪ haunə] f Hal-loween; (*with art*) **an t-Samhain** [ən tau.ɪN'] November.

sàmhchair [sāvchɪr'] f quiet(ness), tranquility; silence.

samhladh [sauLəgh] m resem-blance; sign; (*lit*) symbol, simile, comparison, allegory; parable.

samhlaich (ri) [sauLɪch' r'i] v resem-ble; compare, liken (to).

samhradh [saurəgh] m summer.

sanas [sanəs] m announcement; notice; hint.

sanas-reic [sanəsReʰk'] m adver-tisement.

san fharsaingeachd [sə NarsɪN'əchg] *adv* generally, broadly speaking.

san radharc [sən Ro.ərk] *adv* in sight.

sannt [sauNd] *m* avarice, covetousness.

sanntach [sauNdəch] *adj* greedy, avaricious.

sanntaich [sauNdich'] *v* covet.

saobh [sūv] *adj* foolish, wrongheaded.

saobhaidh [sūvɪ] *f* den, lair.

saobh-chràbhadh [sūvchrāvəgh] *m* superstition.

saobh-shruth [sūvru] *m* eddy, counter-current.

saobh-smuain [sūvsmuəN'] *m* whim.

saoghal [sū.əL] *m* world; life; lifetime.

saoghalta [sū.əLtə] *adj* wordly; materialistic.

saoil [sūl] *v* think, believe; suppose.

saor¹ [sūr] *v* free; (*relig*) save, redeem. • *adj* free (of charge); cheap; free, at liberty.

saor² [sūr] *m* joiner, carpenter.

saoradh [sūrəgh] *m* liberation; absolution; salvation.

saor-àirneis [sūrārnɪš] *m* cabinet maker.

saor-làithean [sūrLai.ən] *mpl* holiday(s).

saor bho [sūr və] *adv* free from, untroubled by.

saorsa [sūrsə] *f* freedom; (*relig*) redemption.

saor an asgaidh [sūr ə Nasgɪ] *adv* free of charge.

saor-thoileach [sūr hətəch] *adj* voluntary.

saothair [sūhɪr'] *f* labour, toil.

saothraich [sūrɪch'] *v* labour, toil.

sàr [sār] *adv* very, extremely; through and through.

sàraich [sārich'] *v* oppress; distress; vex; weary.

sàr mhath [sār va] *adj* excellent.

sàr obair [sār obɪr'] *f* masterpiece.

sàsaich [sāsich'] *v* content, satisfy; satiate.

sàsaichte [sāsich'tɪ] *adj* contented, satisfied; sated.

Sasainn [sasɪN'] *f* England.

Sasannach [sasəNəch] *m/adj* Englishman; English.

sàsar [sāsər] *m* saucer.

sàth [sā] *v* stab; push, shove.

seabhag [šɛvag] *f* hawk, falcon.

seacaid [šɛʰɪd'] *f* jacket.

seac àraidh [šɛʰk ārɪ] *adv* especially, particularly.

seach¹ [šɛch] *prep* instead of; rather than; in comparison to.

seach² [šɛch] *adv/prep* past, by.

seachad¹ [šɛchəd] *adj* over, finished; (*space and time*) past.

seachad² [šɛchəd] *adv* past, by.

seachad air [šɛchəd ɛr'] *prep* past, by.

seachainn [šɛchɪN'] *v* avoid; shun, abstain from.

seachanta [šɛchəntə] *adj* avoidable.

seachd [šɛchg] *n/adj* seven.

seachdad [šɛchgəd] *m* seventy.

seachdainn [šɛchgɪN'] *f* week.

seachdamh [šɛchgəv] *adj* seventh.

seachdnar [šɛchgnər] *m* (*people*) seven.

seachd searbh sgìth (de) [šɛʰk šɛrav sgī d'e] sick and tired (of).

seachran [šɛcharan] *m* wandering; going astray.

seada [šedə] *m* shed.

seadag [šedag] *f* grapefruit.

seadh [šogh] *adv* (*non-affirmative*) yes, uh-uh.

seagal [šegəL] *m* rye.

seagh [šogh] *m* sense, meaning.

sealbh [šɛLav] *m* luck; fortune, providence; heaven. • *excl* **sealbh ort!** [šɛLav oršd] good luck! **aig Sealbh tha brath** [ɛgʹ šɛLav ha bra] Heaven knows.

sealbh [šɛLav] *f* property; possession.

sealbhach [šɛLavəch] *adj* lucky; possessive.

sealbhadair [šɛLavədərʹ] *m* owner, proprietor.

sealbhaich [šɛLavıchʹ] *v* own, possess.

sealg [šɛLag] *v* hunt.

sealg [šɛLag] *f* hunt, hunting.

sealgair [šɛLagɛrʹ] *m* hunter, huntsman; **an Sealgair Mòr** [ən šɛLagɛrʹ mōr] Orion.

seall [šauL] *v* see; look; show; watch over.

seall air [šauL ɛrʹ] *v* look at.

sealladh [šɛLəgh] *m* sight; view, prospect; eyesight; look; **an dà shealladh** [ən dā hɛLəgh] second sight.

sealladh-taoibhe [šɛLəghtuivı] *m* sideways look/glance.

Sealtainn [šɛLtıNʹ] *m* Shetland.

Sealtainneach [šɛLtıNʹəch] *m/adj* Shetlander; from Shetland.

seamrag [šɛmarag] *f* shamrock; clover.

sean [šɛn] *adj* old; former.

seana-ghille [šɛna ghʹiLʹı] *m* old batchelor.

seanair [šɛnırʹ] *m* grandfather; ancestor, forebear.

seanalair [šɛnaLɛrʹ] *m* general.

seana-mhaighdeann [šɛna vəidʹəN] *f* old maid.

seanchaidh [šɛnachı] *m* shenachie, tradition-bearer; story-teller.

seanchas [šɛnachəs] *m* traditional lore; chat, gossip; news.

seanfhacal [šɛnaʰkəL] *m* proverb, saying, adage.

sean-fhasanta [šɛnasəndə] *adj* old-fashioned.

sean-fhleasgach [šɛnlesgəch] *m* old bachelor.

seang [šɛng] *adj* thin; slim; lank, skinny.

seangan [šɛngan] *m* ant.

seanmhair [šɛnavırʹ] *m* grandmother.

seann [šauN] *adj* same as **sean** (used before d, n, t, l, s, r).

seann-phàrant [šauNfãrand] *m* grandparent.

sinn-seanair [šīNʹšɛnırʹ] *m* great grandfather.

sinn-seanmhair [šīNʹšɛnavırʹ] *f* great grandmother.

Seapan [šɛʰpan] *f* (*with art*) **an t-Seapan** [ən tʹɛʰpan] Japan.

Seapanach [šɛʰpanəch] *m/adj* Japanese.

sear [šɛr] *adj/adv* east, eastern.

sear air [šɛr ɛrʹ] *adv* east of.

searbh [šɛrav] *adj* bitter; sour, acrid; pungent; harsh; disagreeable; sharp, sarcastic.

searbhadair [šɛravədərʹ] *m* towel.

searbhanta [šɛravantə] *f* servant, maid.

searg [šɛrag] *v* wither, shrivel, dry up; fade away; pine away; blight.

seargach [šɛragəch] *adj* (*tree*) deciduous.

searmon [šɛramən] *f* sermon.

searmonaich [šɛramənich'] *v* preach.

searrach [šɛRəch] *m* colt, foal.

searrag [šɛRag] *f* flask; bottle.

seas [šes] *v* stand up; stand by, support; last.

seasamh [šesəv] *m* standing position; **'na sheasamh** [nə hesəv] standing.

seasamh-chas [šesəv chas] *m* footing.

seasg [šesg] *adj* barren, sterile; (*cattle, etc*) dry.

seasgad [šesgəd] *m* sixty.

seasgair [šesgɪr'] *adj* cosy, snug; comfortably off.

seasmhach [šesvəch] *adj* firm, stable; reliable; enduring; durable.

seathar [šɛ.ər] *m* chair.

seathar-tulgaidh [šɛ.ərtuLugɪ] *m* rocking-chair.

's e do bheatha! [še də vɛhə] *excl* you're welcome!

seic [šeʰk'] *f* cheque.

Seic [šeʰk'] *f* (*with art*) **an t-Seic** [ən t'eʰk'] the Czech Republic.

Seiceach [šeʰkəch] *m/adj* Czech.

seiche [šechʼɪ] *f* skin, pelt, hide.

seic-leabhar [šeʰk'lɔ.ər] *m* chequebook.

sèid [šēd'] *v* blow; swell, puff up.

seilbh, seilbheach, seilbheadair, seilbhich *same as* **sealbh, sealbhach, sealbhadair, sealbhaich.**

seilcheag [šelch'ag] *f* snail; slug.

seile [šelɪ] *m* saliva, spittle.

seileach [šeləch] *m* willow.

seillean [šeL'an] *m* bee.

seillean mòr [šeL'an mōr] *m* bumble-bee.

sèimh [šēv] *adj* calm, mild, gentle.

sèimhe [šēvɪ] *f* calm(ness), mildness, gentleness.

seinn [šeiN'] *v* sing; (*instrument, etc*) play, sound.

seinn [šeiN'] *m* singing; sounding.

seinneadair [šeiN'ədər'] *m* singer.

seirbheis [šer'ivɪš] *f* service; favour.

seirbheiseach [šer'ivɪšəch] *m* servant.

seirc [šer'k'] *f* love, affection; (Christian) charity.

seirm [šerim] *v* ring (out), sound.

sèisd [šēšd'] *m* siege.

seis [šeš] *m* like(s) of; equal, match.

seisean [šešan] *m* (*meeting, etc*) session; kirk session.

's e sin a'cheist! [še šin ə ch'ešd'] that's the question/point!

's e sin a' chùis! [še šin ə chūš] that's the point!

sèist [šēšd'] *m* refrain, chorus.

seo [šɔ] *adj/pron* this.

seòbhrach [šɔvrəch] *f* primrose.

seòclaid [šɔ̄ʰkLɪd'] *f* chocolate.

seòd [šɔ̄d'] *m* hero.

seòl [šɔ̄L] *v* sail; steer; navigate; guide, direct; manage; govern. • *m* sail; course; method; means.

seòladair [šɔ̄Lədər'] *m* sailor, seaman.

seòladh [šɔ̄Ləgh] *m* sailing; (*house, etc*) address.

seòl-beatha [šɔ̄Lbɛhə] *m* way of life.

seòl-mara [šɔ̄Lmarə] *m* (high) tide.

seòlta [šɔ̄Ltə] *adj* cunning; resourceful; shrewd.

seòmar [šɔ̄mər] *m* room.

seòmar-cadail [šɔ̄mərkadal] *m* bedroom.

seòmar-ionnlaid [šɔ̄məriūNLɪd'] *m* bathroom.

seòmar-leapa [šɔ̄mərLɛʰpə] *m* bedroom.

seòmar-mullaich [šɔ̄mərmuLɪch'] *m* attic.

seòrsa [šɔ̄rsə] *m* sort, kind; genus, species; class.

seòrsaich [šɔ̄rsɪch'] *v* classify; sort.

seud [šēd] *m* jewel, gem.

seumarlan [šēmərLan] *m* factor, land-agent; chamberlain.

seun [šian] *m* spell; charm, amulet.

seunta [šiandə] *adj* enchanted, spellbound.

's e ur beatha! [šɛr bɛhə] *excl* (*polite*) you're welcome!

's fheàirrde mi X [šāRd'ɪ mi] *v* I'm better for X, X is good for me.

's fheàrr leam X [šāR ləm] *v* I prefer X.

's fheudar dhomh [šiadər ghə] *v* I must, I have to.

sgadan [sgadan] *m* herring.

sgàil [sgāl] *v* shade, darken, eclipse; veil, mask. • *f* shade, shadow; covering; (*occas*) ghost, spectre.

sgailc [sgalk'] *v* slap, smack. • *f* slap, sharp blow; sharp sound; (*liquid*) swig; baldness.

sgàilc *n same as* **sgailc**.

sgàilean-grèine [sgālangr'ēnɪ] *m* parasol.

sgàilean-uisge [sgālanušg'ɪ] *m* umbrella.

sgàil-lampa [sgāLaumbə] *f* lampshade.

sgàil-sùla [sgālsūLə] *f* eyelid.

sgàin [sgāN'] *v* burst, crack, split.

sgàineadh [sgāN'əgh] *m* split, crack.

sgàird [sgārd'] *f* (*with art*) **an sgàird** [ən sgārd'] diarrhoea.

sgairt¹ [sgaršd'] *f* diaphragm.

sgairt² [sgaršd'] *f* yell; gusto; vigour, activity.

sgairteil [sgaršd'ɛl] *adj* brisk; active, bustling; enthusiastic; (*weather*) blustery.

sgait [sgaʰt'] *f* (*fish*) skate.

sgal [sgaL] *v* yell, squeal. • *m* yell; outburst; squall.

sgàl [sgāL] *m* tray.

sgàla [sgāLə] *f* (*mus*) scale.

sgalag [sgaLag] *f* farm servant; skivvy.

sgalanta [sgaLəndə] *adj* shrill.

sgall [sgauL] *m* baldness; bald patch.

sgallach [sgaLəch] *adj* bald-headed.

Sgalpach [sgaLbəch] *m/adj* Scalpay person, from Scalpay.

Sgalpaigh [sgaLbay] *n* Scalpay.

sgamhan [sgavan] *m* lung.

sgaoil [sgūl] *v* spread (out); stretch out; disperse; release.

sgaoth [sgū] *m* mass, multitude, swarm.

sgaothaich [sgūhɪch'] *v* (*crowds, etc*) flock, mass, swarm.

sgap [sgaʰp] *v* scatter.

sgar [sgar] *v* separate; sever.

sgaradh [sgarəgh] *m* separation.

sgaradh-pòsaidh [sgarəghpɔ̄sɪ] *m* separation (legal separation from partner).#

sgarbh [sgarav] *m* cormorant.

sgarbh an sgumain [sgarav ən sgūmɛN'] *m* (*bird*) shag.

sgarfa [sgarfə] *m* scarf.

sgàrlaid [sgārLɪd'] *f*/*adj* scarlet.

sgath [sga] *v* cut off; prune.

sgàth [sgā] *m* shadow; protection; fear.

sgàthan [sgāhan] *m* mirror.

sgeadaich [sg'edɪch'] *v* adorn, embellish; dress up; (*lamp, fire, etc*) attend to, trim.

sgealb [sg'ɛLab] *v* split; shatter, smash; chip; carve. • *f* chip; splinter, fragment.

sgealbag [sg'ɛLabag] *f* index finger.

sgealp [sg'ɛLp] *f* slap, smack; sharp sound.

sgeap [sg'ɛʰp] *f* beehive.

sgeilb [sg'elib] *f* chisel.

sgeileid [sg'elɪd'] *f* skillet.

sgeilp [sg'elp] *f* shelf.

sgeir [sg'er'] *f* rock, skerry.

sgeith [sg'e] *v* vomit, throw up.

sgeul [sg'iaL] *m* story; (*of person*) news, sign.

sgeulach [sg'iaLəch] *adj* like a story; fond of stories.

sgeulachd [sg'iaLəchg] *f* story.

sgeulachd ghoirid [sg'iaLəchg ghor'ɪd'] *f* short story.

sgeulaiche [sg'iaLɪch'ə] *m* storyteller.

sgeumhach [sg'ēvəch] *adj* beautiful.

sgeumhaich [sg'ēvɪch'] *v* beautify; adorn, ornament.

sgeunach [sg'ianəch] *adj* timid, shy; skittish, mettlesome.

sgith [sg'i] *f* ski.

sgiamh [sg'iəv] *v* squeal, shriek. • *m* squeal, shriek.

sgian [sg'ian] *f* knife.

sgiath [sg'ia] *f* wing; shield; shelter.

sgiathaich [sg'iahɪch'] *v* fly.

Sgitheanach [sg'i.ənəch] *m*/*adj* Skye person, from Skye. • *m* **an t-Eilean Sgitheanach** [ən t'elan sg'i.ənəch] (the Isle of) Skye.

sgil [sg'il] *m* skill.

sgileil [sg'ilɛl] *adj* skilled; skilful.

sgillin [sg'iL'ɪn] *f* penny.

sgillinn ruadh [sg'iL'ɪn ruəgh] *f* brass farthing.

sgioba [sg'ibə] *m* crew; team.

sgiobair [sg'ibɛr'] *m* skipper, captain.

sgiobalta [sg'ibəLtə] *adj* neat, tidy; quick, active; handy.

sgioblaich [sg'ibLɪch'] *v* tidy; put right/straight.

sgiorradh [sg'iRəgh] *m* accident; stumble, slip.

sgiort [sg'irt] *f* skirt.

sgiths [sg'īs] *f* tiredness; weariness.

sgìre [sg'ir'ı] *f* (*local govt*) district; area, locality; parish.

sgìreachd [sg'ɪr'əchg] *f* parish.

sgìth [sg'ī] *adj* tired; weary.

sgitheach [sg'ihəch] *m* whitethorn, hawthorn.

Sgiathanach *see* **Sgitheanach**

sgìtheil [sg'īhɛl] *adj* tiring; wearisome.

sgìthich [sg'īhɪch'] *v* tire; weary.

sgithich [sg'i.ɪch'] *v* ski.

sgiùrs [sg'ūrs] *v* whip, scourge.

sgiùrsair [sg'ūrsɛr'] *m* whip, scourge.

sglàib [sgLāib] *f* (*building, etc*) plaster.

sglàibeadair [sgLāibədər'] *m* plasterer.

sglèat [sgliaʰt] *m* slate.

sglèatair [sgliaʰtɛr] *m* slater.

sgleog [sglɔg] *f* slap.

sgob [sgob] *v* snatch; sting; peck; sprain.

sgoil [sgɔl] *f* school; schooling.

sgoil-àraich [sgɔlārich'] *f* nursery school.

sgoilear [sgɔlɛr] *m* pupil; scholar.

sgoilearachd [sgɔlɛr'achg] *f* scholarship; bursary.

sgoilt [sgɔlt'] *v* split, cleave; slit.

sgoinneil [sgɔN'ɛl] *adj (fam)* great, smashing.

sgol [sgɔL] *v* rinse.

sgolt *see* **sgoilt**.

sgoltadh [sgɔLtəgh] *m* split, cleft; chink; slit.

sgona [sgɔnə] *f* scone.

sgonn [sgɔuN] *m* lump, hunk.

sgòr [sgɔ̄r] *m (games, etc)* score.

sgòrnan [sgɔ̄rnan] *m* throat; gullet, windpipe.

sgoth [sgɔ] *f* skiff, sailing boat.

sgòth [sgɔ̄h] *f* cloud.

sgòthach [sgɔ̄hach] *adj* cloudy.

sgoth-long [sgɔ Loung] *f* yacht.

sgraing [sgrang'] *f* frown, scowl.

sgreab [sgr'ɛb] *f* scab.

sgread [sgr'ed] *v* scream, shriek. • *m* scream, shriek.

sgreadhail [sgr'ɛ.al] *f* trowel.

sgrèamh [sgr'ɛ̄v] *m* loathing, disgust.

sgreamhail [sgr'ɛval] *adj* loathsome, disgusting.

sgreataidh [sgr'ɛʰti] *adj* loathsome, nauseating.

sgreuch [sgr'iach] *v* scream, screech. • *m* scream, screech.

sgrìob [sgr'īb] *v* scratch, scrape; furrow. • *f* scratch, scrape; furrow; trip, jaunt.

sgrìobach [sgr'ībəch] *adj* abrasive.

sgrioban [sgr'īban] *m* hoe.

sgrìobh [sgr'īv] *v* write.

sgrìobhadair [sgr'īvədər] *m* writer.

sgrìobhadh [sgr'īvəgh] *m* writing; handwriting.

sgrìobhaiche [sgr'īvichə] *m* writer.

sgriobtar [sgr'ibdər] *m* scripture.

sgrios [sgr'is] *v* destroy; ruin. • *m* destruction; ruin.

sgriosail [sgr'isal] *adj* destructive; pernicious; *(fam)* terrible, dreadful.

sgriubha [sgr'u.ə] *f* screw.

sgriubhaire [sgr'u.ər'ə] *m* screwdriver.

sgròb [sgrɔ̄b] *v* scratch; cross out.

sgrùd [sgrūd] *v* scrutinize; investigate; research; audit.

sgrùdadh [sgrūdəgh] *m* scrutiny; investigation; research; audit.

sguab¹ [sguəb] *v* sweep, brush. • *f* brush, broom.

sguab² [sguəb] *f* sheaf of corn.

sguabadair [sguəbədər'] *m* hoover, vacuum-cleaner.

sguab fhliuch [sguəb luch] *f* mop.

sgud [sgud] *v* chop.

sgudal [sgudaL] *m* rubbish, refuse; nonsense.

sguir [sgur'] *v* stop, cease; desist.

sguir de [sgur' d'e] *v* give up, stop.

sgur [sgur] *m* stopping, ceasing.

sgùrr [sgūR] *m* peak, pinnacle.

shìos [hiəs] *adv* down; below *(location)*.

shìos bhuam [hiəs vuəm] *adv* below me, down from me *(location)*.

shuas [huəs] *adv* up; above *(location)*.

shuas bhuam [huəs vuəm] *adv* above me, up from me (*location*).

sia n/ [šiə] *adj* six.

siab [šiab] *v* wipe, rub; (*snow*) drift.

siabann [šiabəN] *m* soap.

siach [šiəch] *v* sprain, strain.

sia deug [šia d'iag] *m*/*adj* sixteen.

sian¹ [šian] *f* storm; (*wind*) blast; *pl* (*with art*). **na siantan** [nə šiantən] the elements.

sian² [šian] *m* thing; anything, (*with neg v*) nothing.

sianar [šianər] *m* (*people*) six.

siar [šiər] *adj*/*adv* west, western. • **na h-Eileanan Siar** [nə helanən šiər] *mpl* the Western Isles. **an Cuan Siar** [ən kuən šiər] *m* the Atlantic Ocean. **an taobh siar** [ən tūv šiər] *m* the west.

siar air [šiər ɛr'] *prep* west of.

sibh [šiv] *pers pron pl* you.

side [šīd'ı] *f* weather. **side nan seachd sian** [šīd'ı nən šechg šian] appalling weather.

sil [šil] *v* (*liquids*) drip, drop, flow, rain.

silidh [šilı] *m* jam; jelly.

silteach [šilt'əch] *adj* (*liquids*) dripping, dropping, flowing.

similear [šimılɛr] *m* chimney.

simplidh [šīmplı] *adj* simple, uncomplicated; simple-minded.

sin [šin] *adj* that; those. • *pron* that.

sin [šīn] *v* stretch, extend; pass, hand.

sinc [šink'] *m* zinc.

since [sink'ı] *f* (*kitchen*) sink.

sine [šinı] *f* nipple, teat.

sineach [šinəch] *adj* mammal.

sineadh [šīnəgh] *m* stretching; recumbent position. • **'na shineadh** [nə hīnəgh] *adv* stretched out, lying down.

sineas [šīnəs] *m* dole.

singilte [šing'ıltə] *adj* single; (*gram*) singular.

sinn [šiN'] *pron* we.

sinnsear [šīN'šɛr] *m* ancestor, forefather.

sinn-sinn-seanair [šīN' šīN' šɛnır'] *m* great-great-grandfather.

sinn-sinn-seanmhair [šīN' šīN' šɛnavır'] *f* great-great-grandmother.

sinteag [šīnt'ag] *f* hop; stride.

sin thu! [šin u], **sin thu-fhèin!** [šin u hēn] *excl* well done! good for you!

siobhag [šifag] *f* wick.

siobhalta [šīvəLtə] *adj* civil, polite.

siobhaltair [šīvəLtɛr'] *m* civilian.

siochail [šiəchal] *adj* peaceful.

sioda [šiədə] *m* silk.

siol [šiəL] *m* seed; race; progeny.

siolachan [šiəLəchan] *m* strainer, filter.

siolaidh [šiəLı] *v* subside, settle; filter, strain.

siol-cuir [šiəLkur'] *m* seed corn.

siol-ghinidh [šiəLgh'ını] *m* semen.

sioman [šiəman] *m* straw rope.

sion *see* **sian**²

Sìn [šīn] *f* (*with art*) **an t-Sìn** [ən t'īn] China.

Sìneach [šīnəch] *m*/*adj* Chinaman; Chinese.

sionnach [šuNəch] *m* fox.

sionnsar [šūNsər] *m* (*bagpipe*) chanter.

sìor- *pre* [šiər] *fix* ever-.

sìor-mhaireannach [šiərvar'əNəch] *adj* everlasting; immortal.

siorrachd [šiRəchg] *f* sheriffdom; county, shire.

siorram [šiRəm] *m* sheriff.

sìorraidh [šiəRɪ] *adj* everlasting, eternal.

sìorraidheachd [šiəRɪəchg] *f* eternity.

siorramachd [šiRəməchg] *f same as* **siorrachd**.

sìor-uaine [šiəruəN'ɪ] *adj* evergreen.

sìos [šiəs] *adv* down (*motion*).

siosar [šisər] *f* scissors.

siosarnaich [šisərnɪch'] *f* hissing; whispering; rustling.

sìos 'na inntinn [šiəs nə īN'd'ɪN'] *adv* depressed.

sir [šir'] *v* seek, search for; require.

siris [šir'iš] *f* cherry.

siteag [ši^ht'ag] *f* dunghill, midden.

sìth[1] [šī] *f* peace; tranquility.

sìth[2] [šī] *adj* fairy.

sithean [šihan] *m* fairy hill.

sitheann [šihəN] *f* venison; game.

sitheil [šihɛl] *adj* peaceable; tranquil.

sìthich [šī.ich] *v* pacify.

sìthiche [šī.ichə] *m* fairy.

sitir [ši^ht'ir'] *f* braying, neighing, whinnying.

siubhail [šu.al] *v* travel; seek; die.

siubhal [šu.əL] *f* travel.

siùbhlach [šūLəch] *adj* speedy; fluent; fluid.

siùcar [šū^hkər] *m* sugar; *pl* **siùcairean** [šū^hkɪr'ən] sweets.

siud [šid] *pron* that, yonder.

siuga [šugə] *f* jug.

siuthad [šu.əd] (*sing*), **siuthadaibh** [su.ədɪv] (*pl*) *imper* on you go! get on with it!

slabhraidh [sLavrɪ] *f* chain.

slac [sLa^hk] *v* thrash, beat, thump; bruise, maul.

slàinte [sLāN'd'ɪ] *f* health. • *excls* **slàinte!** cheers! good health! **slàinte mhath/mhòr!** [sLāN'd'ɪ va/võr]good health! **air do dheagh shlàinte!** [ɛr' də gh'ō LāN'd'ɪ] your very good health!

slaman [sLaman] *m* curds, crowdie.

slàn [sLān] *adj* well, healthy; complete. • *excl* **slàn leat!** goodbye! farewell!

slànaich [sLāNɪch] *v* heal, cure; get better.

slànaighear [sLānɪ.ɛr] *m* (*with art*) **an Slànaighear** [ən sLānɪ.ɛr] the Saviour.

slàn is fallain [sLān ɪs faLɛN'] safe and sound.

slaod [sLūd] *v* drag, haul. • *m* sledge.

slaodach [sLūdəch] *adj* slow; long-drawn-out, boring.

slaodair [sLūdɛr'] *m* trailer.

slaod-uisge [sLūdušg'ɪ] *m* raft.

slaoightear [sLuit'ɛr] *m* rascal, rogue.

slapag [sLa^hpag] *f* slipper.

slat [sLa^ht] *f* (*length*) yard; twig; rod; (*vulg*) penis, cock; spear; javelin.

slat-iasgaich [sLa^htiasgɪch'] *f* fishing rod.

slat-rìoghail [sLa^htriə.al] *f* sceptre.

slat-thomhais [sLa^hto.ɪš] *f* yardstick.

sleamhainn [šleu.ɪN'] *adj* slippy, slippery.

sleamhnag [šlɛunag] *f* (*children's*) slide.

sleamhnaich [šlɛunıch'] *v* slip, slide.

's leisg dhomh. [sL'ešg' ghə] *v* I hesitate to.

sleuchd [šliachg] *v* bow down; prostate oneself.

sliabh [šliav] *m* moor, moorland; hill.

sliasaid [šliasıd'] *f* thigh.

slige [šlig'ı] *f* (*mollusc, military*) shell.

slighe [šli.ı] *f* path, road, track; way, route.

slinnean [šliN'an] *m* shoulder.

slìob [šliəb] *v* stroke.

sliochd [šlichg] *m* descendants, lineage.

slios [šlis] *m* side, flank.

slisinn [šlišıN'] *f* slice.

slisinn-èisg [šlišıN'ēšg'] *f* fish slice.

slisnich [šlišnıch'] *v* slice.

sloc [sLɔʰk] *m* hollow; pit.

sloinneadh [sLoN'əgh] *m* surname, family name.

sluagh [sLuagh] *m* people, populace; crowd; army.

sluagh-ghairm [sLuəghor'im] *m* war-cry; slogan.

sluaghmhor [sLuəghvər] *adj* populous.

sluasaid [sLuasıd'] *f* shovel.

slugadh [sLugəgh] *m* swallow, gulp; swallowing.

sluig [sLuig'] *v* swallow; devour.

smachd [smachg] *m* authority, discipline; control; rule.

smachdail [smachgal] *adj* commanding, authoritative.

smàil [smāl] *v* (*fire*) put out; quench.

smal [smaL] *m* spot, stain.

smàladair [smāLədər'] *m* candle snuffers.

smàladh [smāLəgh] *m* extinguishing.

smalan [smaLan] *m* gloom, melancholy.

smalanach [smaLanəch] *adj* gloomy, melancholy.

smaoin [smūN'] *f* thought, notion, idea.

smaoin(t)ich [smūN'(d')ıch] *v* think, reflect; consider.

smàrag [smārag] *f* emerald.

's mar sin air adhart [ıs mar šin ɛr' o.əršd] and so on.

's math leam X [sma ləm] *v* I find X good.

's math sin! [sma šin] *excl* smashing!

smèid (air) [smēd' ɛr'] *v* beckon (to); wave (to).

smeòrach [smyōrəch] *f* thrush.

smeur[1] [smiar] *v* smear, daub; grease.

smeur[2] [smiar] *f* blackberry, bramble.

's miann leam [smiəN ləm] *v* I wish.

smid [smid'] *f* (*with neg v*) word, syllable.

smig [smig'], **smiogaid** [smigıd'] *m* chin.

smior [smir] *m* marrow; courage, spirit, guts; manliness, strength, vigour; best/pick of.

smiorail [smiral] *adj* strong; spirited; plucky; manly, vigorous.

smiùr [smyūr] *v same as* **smeur**[1].

smoc [smɔʰk] *v* (*tobacco*) smoke.

smocadh [smɔʰkəgh] *m* smoking; **smocadh toirmisgte** [smɔkəgh torimıšg't'ı] no smoking.

's mòr am beud e! [smōr əm bēd ɛ] *excl* it's a great pity!

smuain [smuaN'] *f same as* **smaoin**.

smuain(t)ich [smuaN'(d')ıch'] *v same as* **smaoinich**.

smugaid [smugɪd'] *f* spit.

smùid [smūd'] *v* smoke; smash. • *f* smoke, steam, vapour, fumes; drunkenness.

smùr [smūr] *m* dust; dross.

snagan-daraich [snagandarıch] *m* woodpecker.

snaidhm [snaim] *m* knot.

snàig [snāg'] *v* crawl, creep; grovel.

snàigeach [snāg'əch] *m* reptile.

snaigh [snaich'] *v* hew; carve.

snàmh [snāv] *v* swim; float. • *m* swimming, floating.

snasail [snasal], **snasmhor** [snasvər] *adj* neat, trim; elegant.

snàth [snā] *m* (*coll*) thread.

snàthad [snāhad] *m* needle.

snàthainn [snāhıN'] *m* (*single*) thread.

sneachd [šN'ɛchg] *m* snow.

snèap [šNē̆ʰp] *f* turnip, swede.

snigh [šNi] *v* drip, seep.

snìomh [šN'iəv] *v* spin; twist; wring.

snìomhaire [šN'iəvər'ə] *m* (*tool*) drill.

snodha-gàire [snɔ.əgār'ı] *m* smile.

snog [snog] *adj* pretty; nice.

snuadh [sNuəgh] *m* appearance; complexion.

so- [sɔ] *prefix* -able, -ible.

sòbhrach [sōvrəch] *f same as* **seòbhrach**.

socair [sɔʰkɪr'] *adj* mild; tranquil, relaxed; at peace. • *f* comfort; ease, leisure. • *excl* **socair!** take it easy!

socais [sɔʰkɪš] *f* sock.

sochar [sɔchər] *f* bashfulness; weakness, compliance; indulgence.

socharach [sɔchərəch] *adj* bashful; weak; soft, over-indulgent.

socrach [sɔʰkrəch] *adj* at ease; sedate, leisurely.

socraich [sɔʰkrıch'] *v* abate; assuage; settle; set, fix.

sodal [sɔdəL] *m* adulation; fawning, flattery.

so-dhèanta [sɔ gh'iand'ə] *adj* possible, feasible.

sòfa [sōfa] *f* sofa.

seilearaidh [šelərı] *m* celery.

soilleir [soL'ɛr'] *adj* bright, clear; obvious.

soilleirich [soL'ɛr'ıch'] *v* brighten (up); clarify, explain.

soillse [soiL'ši] *m* light.

soillsich [soiL'šıch'] *v* shine; gleam.

soirbh [sor'iv] *adj* easy.

soirbheachail [sor'ivəchal] *adj* successful; prosperous.

soirbhich le [sor'ivıch'.le] *v* turn out well for.

sòisealach [sōšəLəch] *adj* socialist.

sòisealta [sōšəLtə] *adj* social. • *fpl* **seirbhisean sòisealta** [šer'ivıšən sōšəLtə] social services.

soisgeul [sošg'iaL] *m* gospel.

soisgeulach [sošg'iaLəch] *adj* evangelical.

soisgeulaiche [sošg'iaLıch'ə] *m* evangelist.

soitheach [so.əch] *m* (*sailing*) vessel; dish, container.

soitheamh [so.əv] *adj* gentle, good-natured.

sòlaimte [sōlımt'ə] *adj* solemn; ceremonious.

solair [soLɪr'] v supply, purvey.

solas [soLəs] m light.

sòlas [sōLəs] m solace, consolation; joy.

sòlasach [sōLəsəch] adj comforting, consoling; joyful.

solta [soLtə] adj meek, gentle.

so-lùbadh [so Lūbəgh] adj flexible, pliable.

sona [sonə] adj happy, content.

sònraich [sōnrɪch'] v distinguish; specify, single out.

sònraichte [sōnrɪch'tə] adj special, particular; specific.

sop [sohp] m wisp.

soraidh [sorɪ] f farewell; greeting. • excl **soraidh leat!** [sorɪ lah t] farewell!

so-ruigsinneach [so rug'šɪN'əch] adj attainable; accessible.

so-thuigsinneach [so hig'šɪN'əch] adj intelligible, comprehensible.

spàid [sbād'] f spade.

spaideil [sbad'ɛl] adj (esp dress) smart.

spaidirich [sbad'ɪr'ɪch'] v strut.

spàin [sbāN'] f spoon.

spàin-mhìlsein [sbāN'vīlšɛN'] f dessert spoon.

Spàinn [sbāN'] f (with art) **an Spàinn** [ən sbāN'] Spain.

Spàinn(t)each [sbāN'(d')əch] m/adj Spaniard; Spanish.

Spàinnis [sbāN'ɪš] f (language) Spanish.

spàirn [sbārN'] f exertion, effort; struggle.

spanair [sbanɛr'] m spanner.

spàrr[1] [sbāR] v drive, thrust.

spàrr[2] [sbāR] m joist, beam; roost.

speach [sbɛch] f wasp.

speal [sbɛL] f scythe.

spealg [sbɛLag] v smash, splinter. • f splinter, fragment.

spèil [sbēl] v skate. • f ice-skate.

spèis [sbēš] f love; affection; regard.

speuclairean [sbiah kLɪr'ən] mpl spectacles, glasses.

speuclairean-grèine [sbiah kLɪr'əngr'ēnɪ] mpl sunglasses.

speur [sbiar] m sky; space; pl **na speuran** [nə sbiarən] the heavens.

speur-sheòladh [sbiarhyōLəgh] m space travel.

speuradair [sbiarədər'] m spaceman, astronaut.

speuradaireachd [sbiarədər'əchg] f astrology.

speurair [sbiarɛr'] m astrologer.

spìc [sbīh k'] f spike.

spideag [sbid'ag] f nightingale.

spìocach [sbīh kəch] adj miserly, mean.

spìocaire [sbīh kər'ə] m miser.

spìon [spiən] v snatch, grab; pluck.

spionnadh [sbyuNəgh] m strength; energy.

spiorad [sbirəd] m spirit, ghost; **an Spiorad Naomh** [ən sbirəd Nūv] the Holy Spirit/Ghost.

spioradail [sbirədal] adj spiritual.

spiosrach [sbisrəch] m spice.

spìosraich [sbisrɪch'] v spice; embalm.

spiris [sbir'ɪš] f perch, roost.

spleuchd [sbliachg] v stare, gape; squint. • m stare; squint.

spliuchan [sbliuchan] m pouch.

spòg [sbōg] f paw; (of clock or watch) hand; spoke.

spong [sbɔng] *m* sponge.

sporan [sbɒran] *m* purse; sporran.

spòrs [sbɔ̄rs] *f* sport; fun.

spot [sbɔʰt] *m* spot, stain.

spoth [sbɔ] *v* castrate.

spreadh [sbr'ɛ] *v* burst; explode.

spreadhadh [sbr'ɛ.əgh] *m* explosion.

sprèidh [sbr'ē] *f* livestock.

sprèig [sbr'ēg'] *v* incite, urge.

sprùilleach [sbrūL'əch] *m* crumbs.

sprùilleag [sbrūL'ag] *f* crumb.

spùill [sbūL'] *v* plunder, despoil.

spùinneadair [sbūN'əd'ɛr'] *m* plunderer, brigand.

spùinneadair-mara [sbūN'əd'ɛr'marə] *m* pirate, buccaneer.

spur [sbur] *m* claw, talon.

spùt [sbūʰt] *v* spurt; squirt. • *m* spout; spurt, gush; waterfall.

sràbh [sdrāv] *m* drinking straw.

srac [sdraʰk] *v* rip, tear.

sradag [sdradag] *f* spark.

sràid [sdrād] *f* street.

sràidearaich [sdrād'ərɪch'] *v* stroll, saunter.

srainnsear [sdraN'šɛr] *m* stranger.

srann [sdrauN] *f* snore; snoring.

srannartaich [sdraNəršdɪch'] *f* snoring.

sreang [sdr'ɛng] *f* string.

sreath [sdr'ɛ] *m* row, line, rank; layer; series.

sreothart [sdr'ɔhəršd] *m* sneeze.

sreothartaich [sdr'ɔhəršdɪch'] *f* sneezing.

srian [sdrian] *f* bridle, rein(s); streak, stripe.

sròn [sdrōn] *f* nose; ridge; point, promontory.

sròn-adharcach [sdrōno.ərkəch] *m* rhinoceros.

srùb [sdrūb] *v* spout; spurt; slurp. • *m* (*pot, etc*) spout.

srùbag [sdrūbag] *f* sip; snack, stroupach.

srùban [sdrūban] *m* cockle.

sruth [sdru] *v* flow, stream, run. • *m* stream, burn; flow; current.

stàball [sdābəL] *m* stable.

stad [sdad] *v* stop, cease; halt, pause. • *m* stop, end; halt, pause.

stad-phuing [sdadfuing'] *f* (*orthog*) full stop.

staid [sdad] *f* state, condition.

staidhre [sdair'ɪ] *f* stair, staircase.

stailc [sdalk'] *f* (*industry, etc*) strike.

stàillinn [sdāL'ɪN] *f* steel.

staing [sdaing'] *f* difficulty, tight corner, fix.

stàirn [sdārN'] *f* crashing, clattering, rumbling.

stairsneach [sdaršNəch] *f* threshold.

stàit [sdāʰt] *f* (*nation*) state; (*pl*) **na Stàitean Aonaichte** [nə sdāʰt'ən ünɪch't'ə] the United States. • *m* **Rùnaire na Stàite** [Rūnər'ə nə sdāʰt'ɪ] the Secretary of State.

stàiteil [sdāʰt'ɛl] *adj* stately.

stalc [sdalk] *m* starch.

stalcaire [sdalkər'ə] *m* fool, blockhead.

stalcaireachd [sdalkər'əchg] *f* stupidity; stupid action.

stamag [sdamag] *f* stomach.

stamh [sdav] *m* (*seaweed*) tangle.

stampa [sdambə] *v* stamp. • *f* (*postage*) stamp.

staoig [sdūg'] *f* steak.

staoin [sdūN'] *f* (*the metal*) tin.

steall [šd'auL] *v* spout, squirt, spurt, gush. • *f* outpouring. spout, spurt; (*fam*) swig, slug.

steallaire [šd'aLɪr'ə] *m* syringe.

stèidh [šd'ē] *f* base, foundation, basis.

stèidhich [šd'ē.ɪch'] *v* found, establish.

stèidhichte [šd'ē.ɪch't'ə] *adj* founded, established. • *f* **an Eaglais Stèidhichte** [ə N'egLɪš šd'ē,ɪch't'ə] the Established Church.

stèisean [sdēšan] *m* station.

stiall [šd'iaL] *v* stripe, streak.

stiall [šd'iaL] *f* stripe; tape; (*of clothing*) stitch, scrap.

stìoball [šd'ībəL] *m* steeple.

stiùbhard [šd'ū.ərd] *m* steward.

stiùir [šd'ūr'] *v* steer, direct; run, manage. • *f* rudder, helm.

stiùireadair [šd'ūr'ədɛr'] *m* steersman, helmsman.

stiùireadh [šd'ūr'əgh] *m* steering, directing; managing.

stiùiriche [šd'ūr'ɪch'ə] *m* director.

stob [sdɔb] *m* fence post; stake; (*tree*) stump.

stòbha [sdɔvə] *f* stove.

stoc [sdɔʰk] *m* (*tree*) trunk, stump; livestock; scarf, cravat.

stocainn [sdɔʰkɪN'] *f* sock; stocking.

stoidhle [sdoilɪ] *f* style.

stòirich [sdɔrɪch'] *v* store.

stòiridh [sdɔr'ɪ] *m* story; humorous anecdote.

stoirm [sdor'im] *f* storm.

stòl [sdɔL] *m* stool.

stòlda [sdɔLdə] *adj* sedate, staid, serious; sober.

stòr[1] [sdōr] *m* store; riches, wealth.

stòras [sdōrəs] *m* riches, wealth.

stòr-dàta [sdɔrdāʰtə] *m* database.

stràc [sdrāʰk] *m* stroke, blow; (*orthog*) accent.

stràic [sdrāiʰk'] *m* (*school, formerly*) belt, tawse.

streap [sdr'ɛʰp] *v* climb.

streap mhonaidhean [sdr'ɛʰp vɔnɪ.ən] *f* hillwalking.

streap bheanntan [sdr'ɛʰp vyauNtən] *f* mountain climbing.

strì [sdr'ī] *v* struggle; compete. • *f* struggle, strife; contest.

strìochd [sdr'iəchg] *v* surrender, yield; cringe.

strìpeach [sdrīʰpəch] *f* prostitute.

's truagh e/sin! [struəgh ɛ/šin] *excl* it's/that's a pity.

structair [sdruʰktɛr'] *m* structure.

struidheil [sdrui.ɛl] *adj* extravagant, prodigal. • *m* **am mac struidheil** [əm maʰk sdrui.ɛl] the prodigal son.

struth [sdru] *m* ostrich.

stuadh [sduəgh] *f* (*sea*) wave; (*house*) gable.

stuaim [sduaim] *f* abstemiousness, moderation, temperance; sobriety.

stuama [sduəmə] *adj* abstemious, moderate, temperate; sober.

stuamachd [sduəməchg] *f* abstinence, sobriety.

stùiceach [sdūiʰk'əch] *adj* surly, morose.

stuig [sduig'] *v* incite, urge.

stùr [sdūr] *m* dust.

stuth [sdu] *m* material, stuff.

suaicheantas [suɛch'əntəs] *m* badge, emblem.

suaimhneach [suɛvnəch] *adj* calm, quiet.

suain[1] [suɛN'] *v* wrap, entwine.

suain[2] [suɛN'] *f* sleep, slumber.

Suain [suɛN'] *f* (*with art*) **an t-Suain** [ən tuɛN'] Sweden.

Suaineach [suɛN'əch] *m/adj* Swede; Swedish.

suairc [suɛrk'] *adj* kind; courteous; affable.

suarach [suərəch] *adj* insignificant; petty; despicable.

suarachas [suərəchəs] *m* insignificance; pettiness.

suas [suəs] *adv* up.

suath [suə] *v* rub, wipe.

suath ri [suə r'i] *v* brush against.

sùbailte [sūbalt'ı] *adj* supple, flexible.

sùbh-làir [sū Lār'] *m* strawberry.

sugan [sugan] *m* straw rope.

sùgh [sū] *v* absorb; suck (up).

sùgh [sū] *m* juice; sap.

sùghach [sū.əch] *adj* absorbent.

sùgh-measa [sū mesə] *m* fruit juice.

sùghmhor [sūvər] *adj* juicy; sappy.

sùgradh [sūgrəgh] *m* mirth, merry-making; lovemaking.

suidh [suy] *v* sit down; **dèan suidhe** [suy šiəs] sit down.

suidhe [sui.ı] *m* seat; sitting position. • *adv* **'na shuidhe** [nə hui.ı] *adv* sitting.

suidheachadh [sui.əchəgh] *m* setting, site; situation.

suidheachan [sui.əchan] *m* seat; stool; pew.

suidhich [sui.ıch'] *v* seat; place; decide/agree upon;.

suidhichte [sui.ıch't'ə] *adj* settled, arranged; resolute; sedate, grave.

suidse [suid'šı] *f* switch.

suigeart [suig'əršd] *m* cheerfulness.

sùil [sūl] *f* eye; look, glance.

suilbhir [sulivır'] *adj* cheerful.

sùil-chritheach [sūl chr'i.əch] *f* quagmire.

sùlleach [sūləch] *adj* forward-looking, far-sighted.

sùilich [sūlıch'] *v* expect.

suim[1] [suim] *f* regard; attention.

suim[2] [suim] *f* (*money*) amount, sum; (*arith*) sum.

suipear [suiʰpɛr] *f* supper.

suirghe [sur'i.ı] *f* courting, courtship.

sùith [sūi] *m* soot.

sùlaire [sūLər'ə] *m* solan goose.

sult [suLt] *m* fat, fatness;.

Sultain [suLtɛN'] *f* (*with art*) **an t-Sultain** [ən tuLtɛN'] September.

sultmhor [suLtvər] *adj* fat, plump; lusty, in rude health.

sumainn [sumıN'] *f* (*sea*) surge, swell.

sùnnd [sūNd] *m* cheerfulness; mood.

sùnndach [sūNdəch] *adj* cheerful, in good spirits.

Suomach [su.əmch] *m/adj* Finn; Finnish.

Suomaidh [su.əmı] *f* Finland.

sùrd [sūrd] *m* cheerfulness; alacrity.

sùrdag [sūrdag] *f* jump, skip; bounce; caper.

sùrdagaich [sūrdəgıch'] *v* jump, skip; bounce; caper.

's urrainn dhomh [suRıN' ghə] *v* I can.

suth [su] *m* embryo.

sutha [su.ə] *f* zoo.

T

tàbhachdach [tāvəchgəch] *adj* sound, substantial.

tabhartaiche [tavɪršdɪch'ə] *m* donor, benefactor.

tabhannaich [tahəNɪch'] *v* bark. • *f* barking.

tabhartach [tavəršdəch] *adj* generous, liberal; (*gram*) dative.

tabhartas [tavəršdəs] *m* donation; presentation; grant.

taca [taʰkə] *f* proximity.

tacaid [taʰkɪd'] *f* tack, tacket.

tacan [taʰkan] *m* little while.

tachair [tachɪr'] *v* happen.

tachair ri [tachɪr' r'i] *v* meet.

tachais [tachɪš] *v* scratch; itch, tickle.

tachartas [tachərštəs] *m* happening; incident.

tachas [tachəs] *m* scratching; itching, tickling.

tachd [tachg] *v* smother, choke, throttle.

tacsaidh [taʰksɪ] *m* taxi.

tadhail (air) [to.al ɛr'] *v* visit, call (on).

tadhal [to.aL] *m* visit; (*sport*) goal.

tagair [tagɪr'] *v* claim; (*legal*) plead, argue.

tagh [to] *v* choose; elect, vote in.

taghadh [to.əgh] *m* choosing, choice; election.

taghta [toghtə] *adj* chosen; elected; (*fam*) great! perfect!

tagradh [tagrəgh] *m* claim; (*legal*) plea.

taibhse [taivši] *f* ghost.

taibhsearachd [taivšɛrəchg] *f* second sight.

taic [taiʰk'] *f* contact; proximity; prop; (*moral and phys*) support; patronage

taic airgid [taiʰk' ɛr'ɛg'ɪd'] *f* (*fin*) support, backing.

taiceil [taiʰk'ɛl] *adj* supporting, supportive.

taidhir [tai.ɪr'] *f* tyre.

taifeid [tafɪd'] *m* bowstring.

taigeis [tag'ɪš] *f* haggis.

taigh [toy] *m* house. • *adv* **aig an taigh** [ɛg' ən toy]at home. • *m/f* **fear/bean an taighe** [fɛr/bɛn ən tɛhɪ] the landlord/lady.

taigh-beag [toibeg] *m* toilet.

taigh-bìdh [toibī] *m* café, restaurant.

taigh-cluiche [toikLuich'ɪ] *m* theatre.

taigh-comhairle [toikɔ.ɪrlə] *m* council house.

taigh-dhealbh [toigh'ɛLav] *m* cinema.

taigh-eiridinn [toier'ɪd'ɪN'] *m* hospital.

taigh-grùide [toigrūd'ɪ] *m* brewery.

taigh na galla do X! [toi nə gaLə də] *excl* damn X! sod X!

taigh-nighe [toiN'i.ɪ] *m* wash-house, laundry.

taigh-òsda [toiōsdə] *m* hotel; inn, pub.

taigh-tasgaidh [toitasgɪ] *m* museum.

tailceas [talk'əs] *m* contempt, disdain.

tailceasach [talk'əsəch] *adj* reproachful; contemptuous.

tàileasg [tāləsg] *m* chess; backgammon.

tàillear [tāL'ɛr] *m* tailor.

taing [taing'] *f* thanks, gratitude. • *excl* **mòran taing** [mōran taing'] thank you.

taingeil [taing'ɛl] *adj* thankful, grateful.

tàir[1] [tār'] *v* escape, make off.

tàir[2] [tār'] *f* contempt, disparagement.

tairbhe [tɛr'ivɪ] *f* advantage, benefit; profit.

tairbheach [tɛr'ivəch] *adj* advantageous, beneficial; profitable.

tairbhich [tɛr'ivɪch'] *v* benefit, profit, gain.

tàireil [tār'ɛl] *adj* contemptible.

tairg [tɛr'ig] *v* propose, offer; bid.

tairgse [tɛr'ig'ʃɪ] *f* offer, bid.

tàirneanach [tārN'anəch] *m* thunder.

tairsgeir [tar'sgɛr'] *f* peat iron.

tais [taš] *adj* damp, moist, humid.

taisbean [tašbən] *v* show, reveal; display, exhibit; demonstrate.

taisbeanach [tašbənəch] *adj* clear, distinct; (*gram*) indicative.

taisbeanadh [tašbənəgh] *m* display, exhibition; demonstration.

taisbeanlann [tašbənLaN] *f* art gallery; exhibition hall.

taise [tašɪ], **taiseachd** [tašəchg] *f* moisture, damp, dampness, humidity.

taisg [tašg'] *v* store; hoard.

taisich [tašɪch'] *v* dampen, moisten.

taitinn (ri) [taʰt'ɪN' r'i] *v* please.

taitneach [taʰt'N'əch] *adj* agreeable, pleasant.

taitneas [taʰt'N'əs] *m* pleasantness; pleasure.

tàladh [tāLəgh] *m* attraction; allurement; soothing, calming; lullaby.

talaich [taLɪch'] *v* complain, grumble.

tàlaidh [tāLɪ] *v* attract; allure; tempt; calm; sing/rock to sleep.

tàlaidheach [tāLɪ.əch] *adj* attractive.

talamh [taLəv] *m* earth, soil; land; (*with art*) **an Talamh** [ən taLəv] the Earth.

tàlann [tāLəN] *m* talent, gift.

tàlantach [tāLantəch] *adj* talented, gifted.

talla [taLə] *m* hall; **talla a' bhaile** [taLə ə valɪ] the village/town hall.

talmhaidh [taLavɪ] *adj* earthly.

tàmailt [tāmalt'] *f* disgrace, shame; insult.

tàmailteach [tāmalt'əch] *adj* scandalous, shameful; insulting.

tàmailtich [tāmalt'ɪch'] *v* insult.

tamall [taməL] *m* while, time.

tàmh[1] [tāv] *v* dwell, live.

tàmh[2] [tāv] *m* rest, peace; inactivity; idleness; leisure.

tana [tanə] *adj* thin, runny; shallow; sparse.

tanaich [tanɪch'] *v* thin.

tancair [tankɛr'] *m* tanker.

tannasg [taNasg] *m* ghost.

taobh [tūv] *m* side; way, direction.

taobh an teine [tūv ən t'enɪ] *m* fireside.

taobh-duilleige [tūvduL'ɛgɪ] *m* page; **taobh-duilleige a dhà** [tūvduL'ɛgɪ ə ghā] page two.

taobh ri taobh [tūv r'i tūv] *adv* side by side.

taois [tūš] *f* dough.

taom [tūm] *v* pour (out), flow (out); empty; bale.

tap [taʰp] *f* (*water*) tap.

tapadh [taʰpəgh] *m* handiness, smartness; willingness.

tapadh leat/leibh! [taʰpə laʰt/leiv] *excl* thank you!

tapag [taʰpag] *f* slip of the tongue.

tapaidh [taʰpɪ] *adj* clever, quick; sturdy, manly; active.

tarbh [tarav] *m* bull.

tarbh-nathrach [tarav Narəch] *m* dragonfly.

tarcais [tarkɪš] *m* contempt, disdain.

tarcaiseach [tarkɪšəch] *adj* reproachful; contemptuous.

targaid [taragɪd'] *f* target; shield.

tàrmaich [tārmɪch] *v* beget; breed; propagate; produce.

tàrr [tāR] *v* escape, make off.

tarrag [taRag] *f* (*joinery*) nail.

tarraing [taRɪng'] *v* draw; drag; pull; attract.

tarraing à [taRɪng' a] *v* tease, kid.

tarraingeach [taRɪN'əch] *adj* attractive.

tarraing gu [taRɪng' gu] *v* approach.

tarraing srann [taRɪng' sdrauN] *v* snore.

tarrang [taRang] *f same as* **tarrag**

tarsainn [tarsɪN'] *adv* across, over.

tarsainn air [tarsɪN' ɛr'] *prep* across, over.

tasgadh [tasgəgh] *m* storehouse; museum; investment.

tasgaidh [tasgɪ] *m* store, hoard.

tastan [tasdan] *m* shilling.

tàth [tā] *v* join together; glue; cement; weld; solder.

tathaich [tāhɪch'] *v* frequent, haunt; visit.

tathaich air [tāhɪch' ɛr'] *v* call on.

tàthan [tāhan] *m* hyphen.

tè [t'ē] *f* one (*f*); woman.

teachdaire [t'ɛchgər'ə] *m* messenger; missionary.

teachdaireachd [t'ɛchgər'əchg] *f* message; mission, commission.

teachd-an-tìr [t'ɛchg ən t'ir'] *m* living, livelihood.

teachd-a-steach [t'ɛchg əšd'ach] *m* entry, entrance; income.

teadhair [t'ɛ.ɪr'] *f* tether.

teagaisg [t'ɛgɪšg'] *v* teach, instruct.

teagamh [t'ɛgəv] *m* doubt, uncertainty.

teagmhach [t'ɛgvəch] *adj* doubtful, doubting; sceptical.

teagasg [t'ɛgəsg] *m* teaching.

teaghlach [t'ōLəch] *m* family.

teallach [t'ɛLəch] *m* hearth, fireside; fireplace.

teallach ceàrdaich [t'ɛLəch k'ārdɪch'] *m* forge.

teampall [t'ɛumbəL] *m* temple.

teanchair [t'anachɛr'] *m* clamp, vice; pincers; tongs.

teanga [t'ɛngə] *f* tongue; (*occas*) language.

teann¹ [t'auN] *v* move, go, proceed.

teann² [t'auN] *adj* tight, tense; firm, secure; strict, severe.

teannachair *see* **teanchair**

teannaich [t'aNɪch] *v* tighten, tense; constrict, squeeze.

teann air¹ [t'auN ɛr'] *v* approach; begin.

teann air² [t'auN ɛr'] *prep* close to.

teann ri [t'auN r'i] *v* begin (to), set about.

teanta [tɛndə] *f* tent.

tèarainte [t'iarɪn'də] *adj* safe, secure.

tèarainteachd [t'iarɪnd'əchg] *f* safety, security.

tearc [t'ɛrk] *adj* scant, scarce, few.

tèarmann [t'ērməN] *m* protection; refuge, sanctuary.

teàrr [t'āR] *f* tar, pitch.

teas [t'es] *m* heat.

teasach [t'esəch] *f* fever.

teasaich [t'esɪch'] *v* heat (up).

teasairg [t'esrɪg'] *v* save, rescue.

teas-mheadhan [t'es vi.an] *m* dead centre.

teas-mheidh [t'es vey] *f* thermometer.

teasraig [t'esrɪg'] *v same as* **teasairg**.

teatha [te.ə] *f* (*drink*) tea.

tè bheag [t'ē veg] *f* nip, dram.

teich [t'ech'] *v* flee, abscond; desert.

teicheadh [t'ech'əgh] *m* running away; desertion.

teicneolach [teʰk'N'ɔLəch] *adj* technical, technological.

teicneolaiche [teʰk'N'ɔLɪchə] *m* technician; technologist.

teicneolas [teʰk'N'ɔLəs] *m* technology.

teicneolas-fiosrachaidh, **TF** [teʰk'N'Ləsfisrəchɪ] *m* information technology, IT.

teicnigeach [teʰk'N'ɪg'əch] *adj* technical.

teine [t'enɪ] *m* fire.

teinntean [t'eiN'dan] *m* hearth, fireplace.

teip [teʰp] *f* tape; cassette.

teip-clàraidh [teʰpkLāri] *f* recording tape.

teip-tomhais [teʰptɔ.ɪš] *f* measuring tape.

tèarainn [t'ērɪN'] *v* come down; go down; climb down; dismount; alight, descend.

teisteanas [t'ešd'anəs] *m* testimony, evidence; certificate, diploma; testimonial.

teisteanas breithe [t'ešd'anəs brehɪ] *m* birth certificate.

telebhisean [tɛləvišan] *m* television.

teòclaid [t'ɔʰkLɪd'] *f/adj* chocolate.

teodhachd [t'ɔ.əchg] *f* temperature.

teòthaich [t'ɔ.ɪch'] *v* warm (up); warm to, take to.

teòma [t'ɔmə] *adj* expert, skilful; ingenious.

teòth ri [t'ɔ r'i] *v* take to.

teth [t'e] *adj* hot.

teud [t'ēd] *m* (*harp, etc*) string.

tha [hā] *present tense of v* **bith**.

tha amharas agam [ha avərəs agəm] *v* I suspect.

tha an t-eagal orm [ha ən t'egaL ɔrəm] I'm frightened.

tha dùil agam air X [ha dūl agəm ɛr'] *v* I expect X.

tha eagal orm [ha egaL ɔrəm] I'm afraid, I'm sorry to say.

tha mi a' cur fallas [ha mi ə kur faLəs] *v* I'm sweating.

tha feum agam air X [ha fēm agəm ɛr'] *v* I need X.

tha fios [ha fis] *adv* of course, naturally.

tha fios agam [ha fis agəm] *v* I know.

tha gràin agam air [ha grāN' agəm ɛr'] *v* I hate him/it.

thàinig [hānıg] *past tense of v* thig.

thairis [har'ıš] *prep pron* over him, over it (*m*). • *adv* across, over; beyond.

thairis air [har'ıš ɛr'] *prep* across, over; beyond.

thairte [haršd'ı] *prep pron* over her, over it (*f*).

thall [hauL] *adv* over there, over yonder.

thalla [haLə] (*sing*), **thallaibh** [haLıv] (*pl*) *Imper* go, off you go.

thall is a-bhos [hauL sə vɔs] *adv* here and there; hither and thither.

tha mi an dòchas [ha mi ən dɔchəs] *v* I hope.

tha mi an dùil [ha mi ən dūl] *v* I hope, I expect.

tha mi duilich! [ha mi dulıch'] I'm sorry!

tha mi gu dòigheil! [ha mi gu dōi.ɛl] I'm fine!

thar [har] *prep* across, over; beyond; more than.

thar a chèile [har ə ch'ēlı] *adv* in confusion; at loggerheads.

tharad [harəd] *prep pron* over you (*sing*).

tharaibh [harıv] *prep pron* over you (*pl*).

tharainn [harıN'] *prep pron* over us.

tharam [harəm] *prep pron* over me.

thar mo chomais [har mə chomıš] *adv* beyond my ability.

tharta [haršdə] *prep pron* over them.

tha smùid orm [ha smūd' ɔrəm] I'm drunk.

tha ùidh agam ann an [ha ūy agəm auN ən] *v* I'm interested in it.

theab [hɛb] *defective v* nearly; **theab mi tuiteam** [hɛb mi tuʰt'əm] I nearly fell.

theagamh [hegəv] *conj* perhaps, maybe.

thèid [hēd'] *future tense of v* rach.

thig [hig'] *v* come; approach; arrive.

thig air adhart [hig' ɛr' o.əršd] *v* make progress.

thig am bàrr [hig' əm bāR] *v* surface.

thig am follais [hig' əm fɔLıš] *v* come to light.

thig an uachdar [hig' ən uəchgər] *v* surface; manifest itself.

thig a-steach air [hig' əšd'ach ɛr'] *v* occur to.

thig còmhla [hig' kōLə] *v* congregate, unite.

thig do [hig' dɔ] *v* (*clothes, etc*) suit; please, suit.

thig gu inbhe [hig' gu inıvı] *v* grow up.

thig ri [hig' r'i] *v* suit.

thoir [hɔr'] *v* give; bring; take.

thoir aoradh [hɔr' ūrəgh] *v* worship.

thoir air [hɔr' ɛr'] *v* make, force.

thoir air èiginn [hɔr' ɛr' ēg'ıN'] *v* rape.

thoir air falbh [hɔr' ɛr' faLav] *v* abduct.

thoir air gabhail [hɔr' ɛr' gahal] *v* lease.

thoir am bith [hɔr' əm bi] *v* bring into being/existence.

thoir am follais [hɔr' əm fɔLıš] *v* bring to light.

thoir an aire [hɔr' ə Nar'ɪ] v pay attention; take care.

thoir an car à [hɔr' ən kar a] v cheat.

thoir an t-siteag ort! [hɔr' ən t'ihht'ag ɔršd] v get out! outside!

thoir bàrr air [hɔr' bāR ɛr'] v beat, cap, top.

thoir breith [hɔr' br'e] v pass judgement.

thoir buaidh air [hɔr' buay ɛr'] v defeat; influence, affect.

thoir creideas do [hɔr' kr'ed'əs dɔ] v trust; believe.

thoir cuireadh do [hɔr' kur'əgh dɔ] v invite.

thoir do chasan leat! [hɔr' də chasən laht] get the hell out of here!

thoir dùbhlan do [hɔr' dūLan dɔ] v challenge; defy.

thoir facal air [hɔr' fahkəL ɛr'] v swear to.

thoir fianais [hɔr' fiənıš] v give evidence, testify.

thoir fios air [hɔr' fis ɛr'] v send for.

thoir gealladh [hɔr' gyaLəgh] v promise; vow.

thoir gu buil [hɔr' gu bul] v achieve; see through.

thoir gu stad [hɔr' gu sdad] v bring to an end/a stop.

thoir guth air [hɔr' gu ɛr'] v mention.

thoir ionnsaigh air [hɔr' iūNsɪ ɛr'] v attack, assault; have a shot/an attempt at.

thoir na buinn asam [hɔr' nə buiN' asəm] v take to my heels.

thoir oidhirp (air) [hɔr' o.ırp] v make an attempt (at).

thoir rabhadh do [hɔr' ravəgh dɔ] v warn; alert.

thoir seachad [hɔr' šechəd] v give, give away.

thoir seachad òraid [hɔr' šechəd ōrɪd'] v give/deliver a speech.

thoir sùil air [hɔr' sūl ɛr'] v have a look at.

thoir tairgse (air) [hɔr' tɛrig'šɪ ɛr'] v make an offer/a bid (for).

thoir tarraing air [hɔr' taRɪng' ɛr'] v mention, refer to.

thoir tuaiream air [hɔr' tuər'əm ɛr'] v guess at.

thoir urram do [hɔr' uRəm dɔ] v respect.

thoir uspag [hɔr' usbag] v (horse, etc) start, shy.

thoir X orm [hɔr' ɔrəm] v take myself off to X.

thu [ū] pers pron sing you.

thuca [huhkə] prep pron to them.

thug [hug] past tense of v **thoir**.

thugad [hugəd] prep pron to you (sing).

thugaibh [hugɪv] prep pron to you (pl).

thugainn [hugɪN'] prep pron to us.

thugam [hugəm] prep pron to me.

thuice [huihk'ɪ] prep pron to her, to it (f).

thuige [huig'ɪ] prep pron to him, to it (m).

thun [chun] prep to, towards, up to.

thuirt [hūršd'] past tense of v **abair**.

tì [tī] f (drink) tea.

tiamhaidh [t'iavɪ] adj melancholy; plaintive.

tibhre [t'ivr'ɪ] m dimple.

tiocad [tikəd] f ticket.

tiodhlag [t'iəLag] f gift, present.

tìde [t'īd'ı] *f* time; weather; *(with art)* **an tìde** [ən t'īd'ı], **an tìde-mhara** [ən t'īd'ıvarə] the tide. • *excl* **bha a thìde aige!** [va hīd'ı εg'ı] he took his time!

tidsear [tid'šεr] *m* teacher.

tighearna [t'iərnə] *m* lord; laird, landowner; *(with art)* **an Tighearna** [ən t'iərnə]the Lord, God. • *excl* **a Thighearna!** [ə hiərnə] (Oh) Lord!

Tileach [t'īləch] *m/adj* Icelander; Icelandic.

tilg [t'ilig'] *v* throw; throw up; *(weapon)* fire.

tilg air [t'ilig' εr'] *v* accuse of, reproach with.

tilg smugaid [t'ilig' smugıd'] *v* spit.

till [t'īL'] *v* return, come/go back.

tilleadh [t'iL'əgh] *m* return; returning.

tìm [t'īm] *f* time.

timcheall[1] [t'imich'əL] *adv* round.

timcheall[2] [t'imich'əL] *adv/prep* round, around, about.

timcheall air [t'imich'əL εr'] *prep* round, around, about.

timcheallan [t'imich'əLan] *m* roundabout.

tinn [tīN'] *adj* ill, sick.

tinneas [t'iN'əs] *m* illness, disease.

tinneas cridhe [t'iN'əs kr'i.ı] *m* heart disease.

tinneas mara [t'iN'əs marə] *m* sea-sickness.

tinneas na dighe [t'iN'əs nə d'i.ı] *m* alcoholism.

tiodhlac [t'iəLag] *m* gift, present.

tiodhlacadh [t'iəLaʰkəgh] *m* burial, funeral.

tiodhlaic [t'iəLıʰk'] *v* give, donate; bury.

tiomnadh [t'umnəgh] *m* will, testament; bequest; **an Seann Tiomnadh** [ən sauN t'umnəgh] the Old Testament; **an Tiomnadh Nuadh** [ən t'umnəgh Nuə] the New Testament.

tiomnaich [t'umnıch'] *v* bequeathe, leave.

tiompan [t'umban] *m* cymbal.

tionail [t'unal] *v* assemble, congregate; *(stock)* gather.

tionndaidh [t'ūNdı] *v* turn.

tionnsgail [t'ūNsgal] *v* devise, invent.

tionnsgal [t'ūNsgəL] *m* inventiveness; invention.

tionnsgalach [t'ūNsgəLəch] *adj* inventive.

tionnsgalair [t'ūNsgəLεr'] *m* inventor.

tìoraidh! [t'īrı] *excl* cheerio!

tioram [t'irəm] *adj* dry; thirsty.

tiormachd [t'irəməchg] *f* dryness; drought.

tiormadair [t'irəmədεr'] *m* dryer.

tiormaich [t'irəmıch'] *v* dry; dry up.

tiota [t'iʰtə] *m* second, instant.

tiotag [t'iʰtag] *f* instant, tick.

tiotal [t'iʰtəL] *m* title.

tiotan [t'iʰtan] *m* second, instant.

tìr [t'ir'] *m&f* land; country; area, region; ground, landscape.

tìr-eòlas [t'īr'ōLəs] *m* geography.

tìr-mòr [t'ir'mōr] *m* mainland; continent.

tiugainn! [t'ugıN'] *imper* come along! let us go!

tiugh [t'u] *adj* thick, dense; slow-witted.

tighead [t'i.əd] *m* thickness; density.

tlachd [tLachg] *f* pleasure, enjoyment; affection, liking.

tlachdmhor [tLachgvər] *adj* pleasant; likeable.

tnù [trū] *m* envy; malice.

tobar [tobər] *m* spring, well.

tobhta [tɔʰtə] *m* ruin(s).

tocasaid [tɔʰkəsɪd'] *f* barrel, hogshead.

tòchd [tōchg] *m* stink.

tochradh [tɔchrəgh] *m* dowry.

todha [tɔ.ə] *m* hoe.

todhaig [tɔ.ɪg'] *v* hoe.

todhair [tɔ.ɪr'] *v* manure; bleach.

todhar [tɔ.ər] *m* manure, dung.

tog [tog] *v* raise, lift; pick up; build; (*family, etc*) bring up.

togair [togɪr'] *v* wish for; covet; **ma thogras tu** [ma hogrəs tu] if you like.

togalach [togəLach] *m* building.

tog dealbhan [tog d'ɛLavən] *v* take photos.

tog ort [tog ɔršd] *excl* stir your stumps! get a move on!

togradh [togrəgh] *m* wish, desire.

toilbheum [tolvēm] *m* blasphemy.

toil [tɔl] *adj* pleasing; **is toil leam X** [ɪs tɔl ləm] I like X.

toil [tɔl] *f* will.

toileach [tɔləch] *adj* willing; content; glad.

toileachas [tɔləchəs] *m* contentment; gladness.

toilich [tɔlɪch'] *v* please, content.

toilichte [tɔlɪch't'ə] *adj* happy; pleased, satisfied.

toil-inntinn [tɔlīN't'ɪN'] *f* (*mental*) pleasure; peace of mind.

toill [toiL'] *v* deserve.

toillteanach (air) [toiL'tanəch] *adj* worthy (of).

tòimhseachan [tɔ̄išəchan] *m* puzzle; riddle.

tòimhseachan-tarsainn [tɔ̄išəchantarsɪN'] *m* crossword puzzle.

toinisg [toN'ɪšg'] *f* common sense.

toinisgeil [toN'ɪšg'ɛl] *adj* sensible; intelligent.

toinn [toiN'] *v* twist, wind, twine.

tòir [tɔ̄r'] *f* pursuit.

toirm [tor'im] *f* noise, din.

toirmeasg [tor'imisg] *m* forbidding; prohibition.

toirmeasgach [tor'imisg'əch] *adj* prohibitive.

toirmisg [tor'imišg'] *v* forbid, prohibit.

toiseach [tɔšəch] *m* start, beginning; vanguard; (*vehicle, etc*) front.

tòiseachadh [tɔ̄šəchəgh] *m* beginning.

tòiseachadh ùr [tɔ̄šəchəgh ūr] *m* fresh start.

tòisich (air) [tɔ̄šɪch' ɛr'] *v* start (to).

tòisich as ùr [tɔ̄šɪch' as ūr] *v* start afresh.

toit [tɔʰt'] *f* steam; smoke.

toitean [tɔʰt'an] *m* cigarette.

toll [tɔuL] *v* bore, drill, perforate; dig a hole. • *m* hole, pit, hollow; (*vulg*) arsehole.

tolladh-chluasan [tɔLəghchLuəsən] *m* ear-piercing.

tolltach [tɔuLtəch] *adj* full of holes.

toll-tòine [tɔuLtɔ̄N'i] *m* anus.

tolman [tɔLəman] *m* knowe, knoll.

tom [tɔum] *m* hillock; thicket.

tomaltach [tɔməLtəch] *adj* sizeable, bulky; burly.

tombaca [tombaʰkə] *m* tobacco.

tomhais [tɔ.ɪš] *v* measure; calculate; guess; survey.

tomhas [tɔ.əs] *m* measuring; dimension; calculation; guess, guessing; surveying.

tòn [tɔn] *f* anus, rectum; (*fam*) arse, bum, backside; (*building, etc*) back.

tonn [tɔuN] *m* wave.

tonna [tɔNə] *m* ton, tonne.

tonn teasa [tɔuN t'esə] *m* heat wave.

torrach [tɔRəch] *adj* fruitful, productive; fertile, fecund; pregnant; (*egg, etc*) fertilised.

torrachadh [tɔRəchəgh] *m* fertilisation.

torrachas [tɔRəchəs] *m* fertility.

toradh [tɔrəgh] *m* produce, fruit(s); result, effect.

toraich [tɔrich'] *v* fertilise.

torc [tɔrk] *m* boar.

torman [tɔrəman] *m* murmur, drone, hum; rumble.

tòrr [tɔR] *m* heap, mound; hill; (*fam*) lots, loads.

tòrradh [tɔRəgh] *m* burial, funeral.

tosd [tɔsd] *m* silence.

tosdach [tɔsdəch] *adj* silent, quiet.

tosgaire [tɔsgər'ə] *m* ambassador; envoy.

tosgaireachd [tɔsgər'əchg] *f* embassy.

trafaig [trafɪg'] *f* traffic.

tragtar [traʰgdər] *m* tractor.

tràghadh [trã.əgh] *m* draining; subsiding; (*car*) exhaust.

tràigh[1] [trãy] *v* drain, empty; subside, settle; ebb.

tràigh[2] [trãy] *f* shore, beach; tide.

tràill [trãiL'] *f* slave; drudge; addict.

tràilleachd [trãiL'əchg] *f* slavery; addiction.

tràillich [trãiL'ɪch'] *v* enslave.

traisg [trašg'] *v* fast.

tràlair [trãLɛr'] *m* trawler.

trang [trang] *adj* busy.

trannsa [trauNsə] *f* corridor, passage.

trasg [trasg] *f* fast, fasting.

tràth[1] [trã] *adv* early.

tràth[2] [trã] *m* time, season; while, period; (*gram*) tense.

tràth bidh [trã bĩ] *m* mealtime.

tràthach [trãhəch] *m* hay.

treabh [tr'ɔ] *v* plough.

trealaich [tr'ɛLich'] *f* jumble; odds and ends, stuff, paraphernalia; trash, rubbish; (*pl*) **trealaichean** [tr'ɛLɪchən] luggage, baggage.

trèan [tr'ɛn] *v* train.

trèana [tr'ɛnə] *f* train.

treas [tr'es] *adj* third.

treas deug [tr'es d'iag] *adj* thirteenth.

trèig [tr'ɛg'] *v* leave; abandon; relinquish.

trèigte [tr'ɛg't'ɪ] *adj* abandoned, deserted.

treis [tr'eš] *f* while, time.

treiseag [tr'ešag] *f* short while.

treòrachadh [tr'ɔrəchəgh] *m* guiding, leading; guidance.

treòraich [tr'ɔrich'] *v* guide, lead.

treòraiche [tr'ɔrich'ə] *m* guide.

treubh [tr'iav] *f* tribe.

treud [tr'ēd] *m* flock, herd; group; (*derog*) crowd, gang.

treun [tr'ēn] *adj* strong, stout. • *f* **treun a neirt** [tr'ēn ə nɛršd'] his prime.

trì [tr'ī] *n/adj* three.

triall (do) [tr'iəL dɔ] *v* travel, journey (to).

trian [tr'ian] *m* third.

triath [tr'iə] *m* lord.

tric [tr'iʰk'] *adj/adv* frequent(ly).

triantan [tr'iandan] *f* triangle.

trìd-shoilleir [tr'īd' hoL'ɛr'] *adj* transparent.

trioblaid [tr'iblid'] *f* trouble.

trithead [tr'īhəd] *m* thirty.

triubhas [tr'u.əs] *m* trews, trousers.

triùir [tr'ūr'] *f* (*people*) three, threesome.

triuthach [tr'u.əch] *f* (*with art*) **an triuthach** whooping cough.

tro [trɔ] *prep* through.

trobhad [trɔ.əd] (*sing*), **trobhadaibh** [trɔ.ədɪv] (*pl*) *imper* come here, come to me; come along.

tròcair [trɔʰkɛr'] *f* mercy.

tròcaireach [trɔʰkɛr'əch] *adj* merciful.

trod [trɔd] *m* quarrel, row; quarreling.

troich [troich'] *f* dwarf.

troid [trɔd'] *v* quarrel, squabble, fight.

troigh [troy] *f* (*measure*) foot.

troighean [troi.an] *m* pedal.

troimh *see* **tro**

tro chèile [trɔ ch'ēlı] *adv* at loggerheads; in confusion; untidy.

troimhe [trɔi.ı] *prep pron* through him, through it (*m*).

troimhpe [trɔiʰpı] *prep pron* through her, through it (*f*).

trom [trɔum] *adj* heavy; serious; important; depressed; pregnant.

tromalach [trɔməLəch] *f* preponderance, majority.

trombaid [trɔumbid'] *f* trumpet.

tromhad [trɔ.əd] *prep pron* through you (*sing*).

tromhaibh [trɔ.ɪv] *prep pron* through you (*pl*).

tromhainn [trɔ.ɪN'] *prep pron* through us.

tromham [trɔ.əm] *prep pron* through me.

tromhpa [trɔʰpə] *prep pron* through them.

trom-laighe [trɔumLai.ı] *f* nightmare.

trosg [trɔsg] *m* cod.

trotan [trɔʰtan] *m* trot; trotting.

truacanta [truəʰkəndə] *adj* compassionate, humane.

truacantas [truəʰkəndəs] *m* compassion, pity.

truagh [truəgh] *adj* sad; poor, pitiable, abject.

truaghan [truəghan] *m* wretch. • *excl* **a thruaghain!** [ə ruəghɛN'] poor man/creature!

truaill [truaL'] *v* pollute; corrupt, pervert; defile, profane.

truaghas [tru.əs] *m* pity, compassion.

truileis [trulıš] *f* rubbish, junk.

truimead [truiməd] *m* heaviness.

truinnsear [truiN'šɛr] *m* plate.

truis [truš], **trus** [trus] *v* bundle, roll up; (*skirt, etc*) tuck up; (*stock*) gather.

trusgan [trusgan] *m* clothes, clothing.

tuagh [tuəgh] *f* axe.

tuagh-chatha [tuəghchahə] *f* battleaxe, Lochaber axe.

tuainealach [tuaN'əLəch] *adj* dizzy, giddy.

tuainealaich [tuaN'əLıch'] *f* dizziness, vertigo.

tuaiream [tuər'əm] *f* guess, conjecture.

tuaireamach [tuər'əməch] *adj* random, arbitrary.

tuairisgeul [tuar'ıšg'iaL] *m* description.

tuar [tuər] *m* complexion, hue; appearance.

tuarasdal [tuərəsdaL] *f* salary, wage(s); stipend; fee.

tuasaid [tuəsıd'] *f* quarrel; scrap, tussle.

tuath[1] [tuə] *adj/f* northern, north.

tuath[2] [tuə] *f* peasantry; tenantry.

tuath air [tuəh er'] *prep* north of.

tuathal [tuəhal] *adj* widdershins; anti-clockwise; awry, wrong.

tuathanach [tuəhanəch] *m* farmer.

tuathanachas [tuəhanəchəs] *m* farming.

tuathanas [tuəhanəs] *m* farm.

tubaiste [tubašd'ı] *f* accident; mishap.

tubhailt [tu.alt'] *f* towel.

tubhailt-shoithichean [tu.alt'*ho*.ıchən] *f* tea-towel.

tùch [tūch] *v* make hoarse; smother; extinguish.

tùchadh [tūchəgh] *m* hoarseness.

tùchanach [tūchanəch] *adj* hoarse.

tudan [tudan] *m* stack; turd.

tugh [tū] *v* thatch.

tughadh [tū.əgh] *m* thatch.

tuig [tig'] *v* understand.

tuigse [tig'šı] *f* comprehension; intelligence; sense, judgement.

tuigseach [tig'šəch] *adj* understanding; intelligent; sensible.

tuil [tul] *f* flood, deluge.

tuilleadh [tuL'əgh] *m* more, additional; **tuilleadh is a chòir** [tuL'əgh sə chōr'] more than enough.

tuinich [tunıch'] *v* settle; dwell.

tuiniche [tuN'ıchə] *m* settler.

Tuirc [Tur'k'] *m* (*with art*) **an Tuirc** [ən tur'k'] Turkey.

tuireadh [turəgh] *m* mourning; lament.

tùirse [tūrši] *f* sorrow.

tuiseal [tušaL] *m* (*gram*) case.

tuislich [tušlıch'] *v* stumble, slip, trip.

tuit [tuʰt'] *v* fall.

tuit do [tuʰt' do] *v* happen to, befall.

tuiteamach [tuʰt'əməch] *adj* accidental, chance.

tuiteamas [tuʰt'əməs] *m* occurence, event; incident; accident.

tulach [tuLəch] *m* hillock.

tulg [tuLug] *v* rock, lurch, swing, toss.

tulgach [tuLugəch] *adj* rocking, lurching, swinging, tossing; rocky, unsteady.

tulgadh [tuLugəgh] *m* rocking, lurching, swinging, tossing.

tum [tūm] *v* dip, immerse; steep.

tunnag [tuNag] *f* duck.

tur [tur] *adj* whole, complete. • *adv* **gu tur** [gu tur] completely, altogether.

tùr[1] [tūr] *m* understanding; sense.

tùr[2] [tūr] *m* tower.

turadh [turəgh] *m* dry weather/spell.

turraid [tuRıd'] *f* tower; turret.

tùrail [tūral] *adj* sensible.

turas [turəs] *m* journey; trip; tour, touring; time.

turasachd [turəsəchg] *f* tourism.

turas-mara [turəsmarə] *m* voyage.

turas-tillidh [turəst'íLı] *m* return journey.

Turcach [turkəch] *m/adj* Turk; Turkish.

tursa [tursə] *m* standing stone.

tùrsach [tūrsəch] *adj* sorrowful.

tùs [tūs] *m* beginning, origin.

tùsanach [tūsanəch] *adj* aborigene.

tùthag [tūhag] *f* patch.

U

uabhar [uavər] *m* pride, haughtiness, arrogance.

uachdar [uəchgər] *m* surface; top; cream; upland.

uachdarach [uəchgərəch] *adj* upper; superior; superficial.

uachdaran [uəchgəran] *m* superior; landowner, laird.

uachdar-fhiaclan [uəchgəriəʰkLən] *m* toothpaste.

uaibh [uəiv] *prep pron* from you (*pl*).

uaibhreach [uaivr'əch] *adj* proud; haughty, arrogant.

uaibhreas [uaivr'əs] *m* pride; haughtiness, arrogance.

uaigh [uay] *f* grave.

uaigneach [uaig'nəch] *adj* lonely, solitary; secluded; private, secret.

uaimh [uaiv] *f* cave.

uaine [uaN'ɪ] *adj* green.

uainn [uəN'] *prep pron* from us.

uaipe [uəiʰpɪ] *prep pron* from her, from it (*f*).

uaipear [uaiʰpɛr] *m* botcher, bungler.

uair [uər'] *f* hour; (*clock*) time; time, occasion. • *adv* once.

uaireadair [uər'ədɛr'] *m* timepiece, clock; watch.

uaireadair-gloinne [uər'ədɛr'gLoN'ɪ] *m* hour-glass.

uaireadair-grèine [uər'ədɛr'gr'ēnɪ] *m* sundial.

uaireannan [uər'əNən] *adv* sometimes.

uaireigin [uər'eg'ɪn] *adv* some time.

uair is uair [uər' ɪs uər'] *adv* time and time again.

uair no uaireigin [uər' nɔ uər'eg'ɪn] *adv* some time or other.

uair sam bith [uər' səm bi] *adv* any time.

uaisle [uəšlɪ] *f* nobility, gentility.

uaithe [uəi.ɪ] *prep pron* from him, from it (*m*).

uallach [uəLəch] *m* load, burden; onus, responsibility; stress, worry.

uam [uəm] *prep pron* from me.

uamhann [uəvəN] *m* dread, horror.

uamhas [uəvəs] *m* dread, horror, terror; atrocity.

uamhasach [uəvəsəch] *adj/adv* dreadful(ly), awful(ly), terrible, terribly.

uamhasach fhèin math [uəvəsəch hēn ma] *adv* (*fam*) wonderful, brilliant.

uan [uan] *m* lamb.

uapa [uəʰpə] *prep pron* from them.

uasal [uəsəL] *adj* noble, aristocratic; genteel. • *m* gentleman; (*pl with art*) **na h-uaislean** [nə huəšlən] the nobility, the aristocracy.

uat [uəʰt] *prep pron* from you (*sing*).

ubhal [u.əL] *m* apple.

ubhalghort [u.əLghəršd] *m* orchard.

uchd [uchg] *m* breast, bosom; lap.

uchd-leanabh [uchgL'ɛnav] *m* adopted child.

uchd-mhacaich [uchgvaʰkɪch'] *v* adopt.

ud [əd] *adj* that, yonder.

ud ud! [ədəd] *excl* tut tut! now now!

uèir [uēr'] *f* wire.

ugan [ugan] *m* chest area.

ugh [ū] *m* egg.

ughach [u.əch] *m* oval. • *adj* oval.

ughagan [u.agan] *m* custard.

ùghdar [ūdər] *m* author.

ùghdarras [ūdəRəs] *m* authority; (*govt*) **ùghdarras ionadail** [ūdəRəs inədal] local authority.

ughlann [ūLəN] *f* ovary.

uibhir [ui.ir'] *f* number; amount, quantity; **na h-uibhir de** [nə hui.ir' d'e] a certain amount of; such a lot of; **uibhir eile** [ui.ir' elɪ] as much again.

uibhir ri [ui.ir' r'i] *prep* as much as.

Uibhist [u.ɪšd'] *m* Uist.

Uibhisteach [u.ɪšd'əch] *m/adj* from Uist.

ùidh [ūy] *f* hope; fondness; interest.

uidh [uy] *f* step; gradation; journey; **uidh air n-uidh** [uy ɛr' nuy] step by step, gradually.

uidheam [ui.əm] *f* equipment, tackle, gear; furnishings, trappings; harness; rigging.

uidheamaich [ui.əmɪch'] *v* equip, fit out; get ready.

uile [ulɪ] *adj/adv* all, every; fully, completely; **a h-uile** [ə hulɪ] every. • *npl* **na h-uile** [nə hulɪ] everybody.

uileann [uləN] *f* angle; corner; elbow.

uilebheist [ulɪvešd'] *m* monster.

uile-chumhachdach [ulɪchu.əchgəch] *adj* all-powerful, omnipotent.

uile-fhiosrach [ulísrəch] *adj* all-knowing.

uile gu lèir [ulɪ gu L'ēr'] *adv* altogether, completely.

ùilleach [ūL'əch] *adj* oily.

uilleagan [uL'agan] *m* spoilt brat.

uillnich [uL'nɪch'] *v* jostle, elbow.

uime [uimɪ] *prep pron* about him, about it (*m*).

uimpe [uimpɪ] *prep pron* about her, about it (*f*).

ùine [ūN'ɪ] *f* time; while; (*pl fam*) **ùineachan (is ùineachan)** [ūN'əchən ɪs ūN'əchən] ages (and ages).

uinneag [uN'ag] *f* window.

uinnean [uN'an] *m* onion.

uinnsean [uiN'šan] *m* (*tree*) ash.

ùir [ūr'] *f* soil, earth.

uircean [ur'k'an] *m* piglet.

uiread [ur'əd] *f* a certain amount/ quantity; **na h-uiread** [nə hur'əd] such a lot; **uiread eile** [ur'əd elɪ] as much again; **uiread ri** [ur'əd r'i] as much as. • *adv* (*sums*) times, multiplied by.

uireasbhach [ur'əsəch] *adj* needy; lacking. • *m* needy person.

uireasbhaidh [ur'əsɪ] *f* indigence; lack, need; shortage.

uirsgeul [ur'šg'iaL] *m* fable, legend, myth; fiction.

uirsgeulach [ur'šg'iaLch] *adj* legendary; fictional.

uiseag [ušag] f skylark.

uisge [ušg'ı] m water; rain; **tha an t-uisge ann** [ha ən tušg'ı auN] it's raining.

uisge-beatha [ušg'ıbɛhə] m whisky.

uisge-dìonach [ušg'ıd'iənəch] adj waterproof, watertight.

uisge na stiùireach [ušg'ı nə št'ūr'əgh] m (of boat, etc) wake.

uisgich [ušg'ıch'] v water.

ulaidh [uLı] f treasure; precious object.

ulbhag [uLuvag] f large stone, boulder.

ulfhart [uLəršd] m howl, howling.

ullaich [uLıch'] v prepare; provide.

ullamh [uLəv] adj ready; handy; finished.

ultach [uLtəch] m load; armful; bundle.

umad [uməd] prep pron about you (sing).

umaibh [umıv] prep pron about you (pl).

ùmaidh [ūmı] m blockhead, dolt, fool.

umainn [umıN'] prep pron about us.

umam [uməm] prep pron about me.

umha [u.ə] m bronze.

umhail [u.al] adj humble; lowly; obedient; obsequious.

ùmhlachd [ūLəchg] f humbleness; lowliness; obedience; obsequiousness; bow.

ùmhlaich [ūLıch'] v humble; humiliate.

umpa [umpə] prep pron about them.

Ungair [ungır'] f (with art) **an Ungair** [ə Nungır'] Hungary.

Ungaireach [ungır'əch] m/adj Hungarian.

ùnnlagh [ūNLəgh] m fine.

ùnnsa [ūNsə] m ounce.

ùpag [ūʰpag] f jostle, jab.

ùpraid [ūprıd'] f uproar; confusion; dispute.

ùpraideach [ūprıd'əch] adj rowdy, unruly.

ùr [ūr] adj new; recent; fresh.

ur [ər] adj your (pl).

ùrachadh [ūrəchəgh] m renewal; renovation; change.

ùraich [ūrıch'] v renew; renovate; refresh.

urchair [uruchır'] f shot.

urchair gunna [uruchır' guNə] f gun-shot.

urchasg [urchasg] m antidote.

ùrlar [ūrLər] m floor.

ùrnaigh [ūrnı] f prayer; praying; **Ùrnaigh an Tighearna** [ūrnı ən t'i.ərnə] the Lord's Prayer.

ùr nodha [ūr no.ə] adj brand new; up-to-date.

urra [uRə] f person; authority; responsibility.

urrainn [uRıN'] f power, ability.

urram [uRəm] m respect; honour.

urramach [uRəməch] adj honourable; honorary; (with art) (minister) **an t-Urramach X** [ən tuRəməch] the Reverend X.

urras [uRəs] m guarantee, surety; bond; bail; insurance; (fund, etc) trust.

ursainn [ursıN'] f prop, support; jamb.

ursainn chatha [ursıN' chahə] f (warrior) champion.

usgar [usgər] m jewel.

uspag [usbag] f (horse, etc) start, shy.

ùth [ū] m udder.

English–Gaelic Dictionary

A

abandon *v* trèig.
abate *v* lùghdaich.
abbey *n* abaid *f*.
abbot *n* aba *m*.
abbreviate *v* giorraich.
abdicate *v* leig dhe.
abdication *n* leigeil dhe *m*.
abdomen *n* balg *m*.
abduct *v* thoir air falbh.
abet *v* cuidich.
abhor *v* is lugha air.
abhorrence *n* gràin.
abide *v* fuirich.
ability *n* comas *m*.
abject *adj* truagh; dìblidh.
able *adj* comasach.
able-bodied *adj* fallain; corp-làidir.
abnormal *adj* mì-ghnàthach.
abnormality *n* mì-ghnàthas *m*.
aboard *adv* air bòrd.
abode *n* àite-còmnaidh *m*.
abolish *v* cuir às do.
abolition *n* cur às *m*
abominable *adj* gràineil.
aborigine *n* prìomh neach-àiteach-aidh *m*.
abortion *n* breith an-abaich *f*.
abound *v* bi lìonmhor.
about *adv* (*around*) timcheall (air); (*surrounding*) mun cuairt (air). • *prep* (*around & concerning*) mu; mu dhèidhinn. • *pron* **about me** umam; **about you** (*sing*) umad; **about him, it** uime; **about her** uimpe; **about us** umainn; **about you** (*pl*) umaibh; **about them**.
above *adv* shuas; gu h-àrd. • *prep* os cionn.
abrade *v* sgrìobaich.
abridge *v* giorraich.
abridged *adj* giorraichte.
abroad *adv* thall thairis.
abrupt *adj* cas; aithghearr.
abruptness *n* caise *f*.
abscess *n* niosgaid *f*.
abscond *v* teich, teich air falbh.
absence *n* neo-làthaireachd *f*.
absent *adj* nach eil an làthair.
absent oneself *v* dìochuimhneach, cùm air falbh.
absent-minded *adj* cian-aireachal.
absolute *adj* iomlan; làn.
absolutely *adv* gu h-iomlan.
absolution *n* saoradh, fuasgladh *m*.
absolve *v* saor; sgaoil.
absorb *v* sùgh, deoghail.
absorbent *adj* sùghach.
abstain *v* na buin (ri).
abstemious *adj* stuama.
abstinence *n* stuamachd *f*.
abstract *n* às-tharraing *f*.
abstract *v* às-tharraing, tarraing à.
abstracted *adj* beachdail.
absurd *adj* gòrach.
absurdity *n* gòraiche *f*.
abundance *n* pailteas *m*.

abundant *adj* pailt.

abuse[1] *n* mì-ghnàthachadh *m*; (*verbal*) càineadh *f*.

abuse[2] *v* mì-ghnàthaich; (*verbally*) càin.

abysmal *adj* uabhasach.

abyss *n* àibheis *m*.

academic *adj* sgoileireach. • *n* oilthigheach *m*.

academy *n* àrd-sgoil *f*.

accelerate *v* luathaich, greas.

acceleration *n* luathachadh, greasad *m*.

accelerator *n* inneal-luathachaidh *m*.

accent *n* blas *m*.

accept *v* gabh.

acceptable *adj* furasda gabhail ris.

access *n* inntrigeadh *m*.

accessible *adj* so-ruigsinneach.

accident *n* tubaist *f*.

accidental *adj* tubaisteach.

accommodate *v* gabh.

accommodation *n* rùm *m*.

accompaniment *n* com-pàirt *f*.

accompanist *n* com-pàirtiche *m*.

accomplice *n* fear-cuideachaidh *m*.

accomplish *v* coimhlion, thoir gu buil.

accomplished *adj* coimhlionta, deas.

accord *n* aonta, co-chòrdadh *m*.

according to *adv* a-rèir.

accordingly *adv* mar sin.

accordion *n* bocsa-ciùil *m*.

account *n* cùnntas, tuairisgeul *m*. • *v* thoir cùnntas air.

accountancy *n* cùnntasachd *f*.

accountant *n* cùnntasair *m*.

accounts book *n* leabhar-cùnntais *m*.

accumulate *v* cruinnich.

accumulation *n* co-chruinneach-adh *m*.

accuracy *n* cruinneas *m*.

accurate *adj* cruinn, grinn.

accusation *n* casaid *f*.

accuse *v* dèan casaid.

accustom *v* gnàthaich.

accustomed *adj* gnàthach; àbhaist.

ace *n* an t-aon *m*.

acerbic *adj* geur.

acerbity *n* goirte *f*.

ache *n* goirteas, cràdh *m*.

achieve *v* coimhlion.

achievement *n* euchd *m*.

acid *adj* searbh; geur.

acidity *n* searbhachd *f*.

acknowledge *v* aidich.

acknowledgement *n* aideachadh *m*.

acoustic *adj* fuaimneach.

acoustics *n* fuaimearrachd *f*.

acquaintance *n* fear-eòlais *m*.

acquainted *adj* eòlach.

acquiesce *v* aontaich.

acquire *v* faigh, buannaich.

acquit *v* fuasgail.

acre *n* acaire *m*.

across *adv* tarsainn, thairis. • *prep* tarsainn air, thairis air, thar.

act *n* gnìomh *m*; (*play*) earran *f*; achd. • *v* obraich, dèan gnìomh; cluich.

action *n* gnìomh *m*.

active *adj* deas, èasgaidh; spreig-each.

activity *n* gnìomhachd *f*.

actor *n* cleasaiche, actair *m*.

actress *n* bana-chleasaiche, bana-actair *f*.

actual *adj* dearbh, fìor.

acute *adj* dian, geur.

adapt *v* fàs suas ri, dèan freagarr-ach.

adaptable *adj* so-fhreagarraichte.

add *v* cuir ri, meudaich, leasaich.

adder *n* nathair *f*.

addict *n* tràill *m/f*.

addicted *adj* fo bhuaidh.

addiction *n* tràilleachd *f*.

addition *n* meudachadh, leasach-adh *m*.

additional *adj* a bharrachd, a thuilleadh.

address *n* seòladh *m*; (*oration*) òraid *f*. • *v* cuir seòladh air; dèan òraid ri.

adequate *adj* iomchaidh.

adhere *v* lean.

adherent *n* fear leanmhainn *m*.

adhesive *n* stuth leanmhainn *m*.

adjacent *adj* dlùth.

adjective *n* buadhair *m*.

adjudication *n* breitheamhnas *m*.

adjust *v* ceartaich, rèitich.

adjustable *adj* so-rèitichte.

administer *v* riaghlaich.

administration *n* riaghladh *m*.

administrative *adj* riaghlach.

administrator *n* fear-riaghlaidh *m*.

admirable *adj* ionmholta.

admiration *n* meas *m*.

admire *v* tha meas air.

admissible *adj* ceadaichte.

admission *n* cead *m*; (*confession*) aideachadh *m*.

admit *v* leig a steach; (*confess*) aidich.

ado *n* othail *f*.

adolescence *n* òigeachd *f*.

adolescent *n* òigear *m*.

adopt *v* uchd-mhacaich.

adoption *n* uchd-mhacachd *f*.

adore *v* trom-ghràdhaich.

adorn *v* sgeadaich.

adrift *adj* leis an t-sruth.

adult *adj* inbheach. • *n* inbheach *m*.

adulterate *v* truaill.

adulteration *n* truailleadh *m*.

adulterer *n* adhaltraiche *m*.

adultery *n* adhaltranas *m*.

advance *n* dol air adhart *m*; (*financial*) eàrlas *m*. • *v* rach air thoiseach; (*financial*) thoir eàrlas.

advanced *adj* adhartach.

advancement *n* àrdachadh *m*.

advantage *n* tairbhe, buannachd *f*.

advantageous *adj* tairbheach.

adventure *n* tachartas *m*.

adventurous *adj* dàna.

adverb *n* co-ghnìomhair *m*.

adverse *adj* an aghaidh.

adversity *n* cruaidh-chas *f*.

advertise *v* thoir sanas.

advertisement *n* sanas, sanas-reic *m*.

advice *n* comhairle *f*.

advise *v* comhairlich.

adviser *n* comhairleach *m*.

advocacy *n* tagradh *m*.

advocate *n* fear-tagraidh *m*.

advocate *v* tagair.

aerial *n* aer-ghath *m*.

aeronaut *n* speur-sheòladair *m*.

aeroplane *n* plèana *f*, itealan *m*.

affable *adj* suairce.

affair *n* gnothach *m*.

affect *v* drùidh air; (*let on*) leig air.

affection *n* gaol *m*.

affectionate *adj* gaolach.

affinity *n* dàimh *m/f*.

affirm *v* dearbh, daingnich.

affirmative *adj* aontach.

afflict *v* goirtich, sàraich.

affliction *n* doilgheas *m*.

affluence *n* beairteas *m*.

affluent *adj* beairteach.

afford *v* ruig air.

affront v maslaich.
afloat adj air fleòdradh.
afoot adj air chois; air bhonn.
aforementioned adj ro-ainmichte.
afraid adj fo eagal, eagalach.
afresh adv às ùr, a-rithist.
Africa n Afraga f.
African adj Afraganach.
after adv an dèidh làimhe. • prep
  an dèidh. • pron **after me** 'nam
  dhèidh; **after you** (sing) 'nad
  dhèidh; **after him, it** 'na dhèidh;
  after her 'na dèidh; **after us** 'nar
  dèidh; **after you** (pl) 'nur dèidh;
  after them 'nan dèidh.
afternoon n feasgar m.
afterthought n ath-smuain f.
again adv a-rithist.
against prep an aghaidh. • prep an
  dèidh. • pron **against me** 'nam
  aghaidh; **against you** (sing) 'nad
  aghaidh; **against him, it** 'na
  aghaidh; **against her** 'na aghaidh;
  against us 'nar n-aghaidh;
  against you (pl) 'nur n-aghaidh;
  against them 'nan aghaidh.
age n aois f. • v fàs aosda.
aged adj sean, aosda.
agency n ionadachd f.
agent n neach-ionaid m; dòigh m.
aggravate v antromaich.
aggression n (phys) ionnsaigh m;
  (mental) miann m.
aggressive adj ionnsaigheach.
agile adj lùthmhor.
agitate v gluais.
agitation n gluasad m.
ago adv air ais.
agog adv air bhiod.
agonise v bi an ioma-chomhairle.
agony n dòrainn f.

agree v aontaich; còrd.
agreeable adj taitneach.
agreement n còrdadh m, rèite f.
agricultural adj àiteachail.
agriculture n àiteachd f, tuathanachas m.
aground adv an sàs.
ahead adv air thoiseach.
aid n cuideachadh m. • v cuidich.
ailing adj tinn.
ailment n tinneas, galar m.
aim n (missile) cuimse f; (intent)
  amas f. • v cuimsich; amais.
air n àile; (mus) fonn; (look) aogas.
  • v leig an àile gu.
airborne adj air sgèith.
airmail n post-adhair m.
airport n port-adhair m.
airwave n tonn-adhair m.
aisle n trannsa f.
ajar adv leth-fhosgailte.
akin adj (related) càirdeach.
alacrity n sùrd m.
alarm v cuir eagal air.
alarming adj eagalach.
album n leabhar-chuimhneachan m.
alcohol n alcol m.
alcoholic n alcolach m.
alcoholism n alcolachd f.
alder n feàrna f.
ale n leann m.
alert adj furachail.
algebra n ailgeabra f.
alias adv fo ainm eile.
alien adj coigreach. • n coigreach
  m; Gall m.
alienate v fuadaich.
alight v teirinn.
alike adj co-ionnan.
alimony n airgead sgaraidh m.
alive adj beò.

all *adj* uile, na h-uile, iomlan.

allay *v* caisg.

allegation *n* cur às leth *m*.

allegiance *n* ùmhlachd *f*.

allegory *n* samhla *m*.

alleviate *v* aotromaich, lùghdaich.

alleviation *n* aotromachadh *m*.

alliance *n* càirdeas *m*.

alliteration *n* uaim *f*.

allow *v* leig le, ceadaich.

allowance *n* cuibhreann *f*.

allusion *n* iomradh *m*.

ally *n* caraid *m*; co-chòmragaiche *m*.

almighty *adj* uile-chumhachdach.

Almighty *n* An t-Uile-chumhachd-ach *m*.

almost *adv* gu ìre bhig.

alms *npl* dèircean.

aloft *adv* gu h-àrd, shuas.

alone *adj* aonarach.

along *adv* air fad; **along with** còmhla ri.

alongside *adv* ri taobh. • *pron* **alongside me** ri mo thaobh; **alongside you** (*sing*) ri do thaobh; **alongside him, it** ri 'thaobh; **alongside her** ri 'taobh; **alongside us** ri ar taobh; **alongside you** (*pl*) ri ur taobh; **alongside them** ri an taobh.

aloud *adv* gu h-àrd ghuthach.

alphabet *n* aibidil *f*.

alphabetical *adj* aibidileach.

already *adv* mar thà.

also *adv* cuideachd.

altar *n* altair *f*.

alter *v* atharraich.

alteration *n* atharrachadh *m*.

alternative *adj* eile. • *n* roghainn eile *m*.

although *conj* ged a.

altitude *n* àirde *f*.

altogether *adv* gu lèir, uile gu lèir.

aluminium *n* almain *m*.

always *adv* an-còmhnaidh, daon-nan.

amalgamate *v* cuir le chèile.

amateur *adj* neo-dhreuchdail.

amaze *v* cuir iongnadh air.

amazement *n* iongantas *m*.

amazing *adj* iongantach.

ambassador *n* tosgaire *m*.

ambidextrous *adj* co-dheaslamh-ach.

ambiguity *n* dà-sheaghachas *m*.

ambiguous *adj* dà-sheaghach.

ambit *n* cuairt *f*.

ambition *n* glòir-mhiann *m*.

ambitious *adj* glòir-mhiannach.

ambulance *n* carbad-eiridinn *m*.

ambush *n* feallfhalach *m*.

ameliorate *v* dèan nas fheàrr.

amen *int* amen.

amenable *adj* fosgailte.

amend *v* leasaich.

amendment *n* leasachadh *m*.

amenity *n* goireas *m*.

America *n* Aimeireagaidh *f*.

American *adj* Aimeireaganach.

amiable *adj* càirdeil.

amid, amidst *prep* am measg.

amiss *adv* gu h-olc.

ammunition *n* connadh làmhaich *m*.

amnesty *n* mathanas na coit-cheann *m*.

among, amongst *prep* am measg, air feadh.

amorous *adj* gaolach.

amount *n* suim, uimhir *f*; meud *m*.

amphibian *n* muir-thìreach *m*.

amphibious *adj* dà-bhitheach.

ample *adj* mòr, tomadach.

amplification *n* meudachadh *m*.
amplify *v* meudaich.
amputate *v* geàrr air falbh.
amputation *n* gearradh air falbh *m*.
amuse *v* toilich.
amusement *n* greannmhorachd *f*.
amusing *adj* greanmhor.
anachronism *n* às-aimsireachd *f*.
anaemic *adj* cion-falach.
anaesthetic *n* pràmhaiche *m*.
analogy *n* co-fhreagarrachd *f*.
analyse *v* mion-sgrùdaich.
analysis *n* mion-sgrùdadh *m*.
analyst *n* mion-sgrùdaire *m*.
anarchist *n* ceannairceach *m*.
anatomical *adj* bodhaigeach.
anatomy *n* eòlas bodhaig *m*.
ancestor *n* sinnsear *m*.
ancestry *n* sinnsearachd *f*.
anchor *n* acair *f*.
ancient *adj* àrsaidh.
and *conj* agus, is, 's.
anecdote *n* naidheachd *f*.
anew *adv* às ùr.
angel *n* aingeal *m*.
angelic *adj* mar aingeal.
anger *n* fearg *f*.
angina *n* grèim chridhe *m*.
angle *n* uilinn *f*.
angler *n* iasgair *f*.
angling *n* iasgachd *m*.
angry *adj* feargach.
anguish *n* dòrainn *f*.
animal *n* ainmhidh *m*.
animate *v* beòthaich.
animated *adj* beòthail.
animation *n* beòthachadh *m*.
ankle *n* adhbrann *f*.
annex *n* ath-thaigh *m*.
annihilate *v* dìthich.
annihilation *n* lèirsgrios *m*.

anniversary *n* cuimhneachan, bliadhnail *m*.
annotate *v* notaich.
annotation *n* notachadh *m*.
announce *v* cuir an cèill.
annoy *v* cuir dragh air.
annoyance *n* dragh; buaireas *m*.
annoyed *adj* diombach.
annoying *adj* buaireil.
annual *adj* bliadhnail.
annually *adv* gach bhliadhna.
annul *v* cuir às.
anoint *v* ung.
anon *adv* a dh'aithghearr.
anonymous *adj* neo-ainmichte.
another *pron* fear eile. • *adj* eile.
answer *n* freagairt *f*.
answer *v* freagair.
ant *n* seangan *m*.
antagonist *n* nàmhaid *m*.
antediluvian *adj* ron Tuil.
anthem *n* laoidh *m*.
anthology *n* duanaire, cruinneachadh *m*.
anthropology *n* daonn-eòlas *m*.
anticipate *v* sùilich.
anticipation *n* sùileachadh *m*.
antidote *n* urchasg *m*.
antipathy *n* fuath *m*.
antiquary *n* àrsair *m*.
antique *adj* seann-saoghlach. • *n* seann-rud *m*.
antiseptic *n* loit-leigheas *m*.
antler *n* cabar fèidh *m*.
anvil *n* innean *m*.
anxiety *n* iomagain *m*.
anxious *adj* iomagaineach.
any *adj* sam bith, air bith, idir.
• *pron* aon sam bith; aon; gin.
anyone *pron* neach sam bith.
anything *n* càil, dad *m*.

apartheid *n* sgaradh-cinnidh *m*.

apartment *n* seòmar *m*; taigh *m*.

apathy *n* cion ùidhe *m*.

ape *n* apa *f*.

aperture *n* toll, fosgladh *m*.

apex *n* binnean *m*; bàrr *m*.

apiece *adv* an-t-aon.

apologise *v* dèan leisgeul.

apology *n* leisgeul *m*.

apostle *n* abstol *m*.

apostrophe *n* ascair *m*.

appal *v* cuir uabhas air.

apparatus *n* uidheam *m*.

apparent *adj* soilleir, faicsinneach.

apparition *n* taibhse *f*.

appeal *n* tarraing *f*; (*legal*) ath-agairt *m*. • *v* tarraing; ath-agair.

appear *v* nochd.

appearance *n* taisbeanadh *m*; teachd an làthair *m*.

appease *v* rèitich.

append *v* cuir ri.

appendage *n* sgòdan *m*.

appendix *n* (*anat*) aipeandaig *f*; (*book*) ath-sgrìobadh *m*.

appetite *n* càil *f*.

applaud *v* bas-bhuail.

apple *n* ubhal *m*.

apple-tree *n* craobh-ubhal *f*.

appliance *n* goireas *m*.

applicable *adj* freagarrach.

applicant *n* tagraiche *m*.

application *n* cur an sàs *m*; (*for a job*) tagradh *m*.

applications *npl* (*comput*) cleachd-aidhean *mpl*.

apply *v* cuir a-steach.

appoint *v* suidhich.

appointment *n* suidheachadh *m*.

apportion *v* dèan roinn air.

appraise *v* meas.

appreciate *v* cuir luach air, luachaich; (*grow*) àrdaich.

appreciation *n* luachachadh *m*.

apprehend *v* (*infer*) thoir fa-near; (*arrest*) glac.

approach *n* modh-gabhail *f*. • *v* dlùthaich.

appropriate *adj* cubhaidh. • *v* gabh seilbh air.

approval *n* deagh-bharail *f*.

approve *v* gabh beachd math air.

approximate *adj* dlùthach.

apricot *n* apracot *m*.

April *n* An Giblean *m*.

apron *n* aparan *m*.

apropos *adv* a thaobh.

apt *adj* deas; freagarrach.

aptitude *n* sgil *m*; buailteachd *f*.

Arab *n* Arabach *m*.

Arabic *adj* Arabach.

arable *adj* so-àiteachaidh.

arbitrate *v* rèitich.

arbitrator *n* neach-rèiteachaidh.

arch *n* stuagh *m*.

archaeologist *n* àrsair *m*.

archbishop *n* àrd-easbaig *m*.

archetype *n* prìomh-shamhla *m*.

architect *n* ailtire *m*.

architecture *n* ailtireachd *f*.

archive *n* tasglann *f*.

ardent *adj* dian, bras.

arduous *adj* deacair.

area *n* farsaingeachd, lann *f*.

argue *v* connsaich; dearbh.

argument *n* connsachadh *m*; argamaid *f*.

argumentative *adj* connsachail.

arid *adj* loisgte.

arise *v* èirich suas.

arithmetic *n* cùnntas *m*.

ark *n* àirc *f*.

arm *n* gàirdean *m*. • *v* armaich.
armchair *n* cathair-ghàirdeanach *f*.
armistice *n* fosadh *m*.
armour *n* armachd *f*.
armpit *n* achlais *f*.
army *n* arm, armailt *m*.
around *adv* mun cuairt. • *prep* timcheall, mu chuairt.
arouse *v* dùisg.
arrange *v* rèitich, còirich.
arrangement *n* rèiteachadh *m*; (*mus*) rian *m*.
array *v* cuir an òrdugh.
arrears *n* fiachan gun dìoladh *m*.
arrest *v* cuir an làimh.
arrival *n* teachd *m*.
arrive *v* ruig, thig.
arrogance *n* dànadas *m*.
arrogant *adj* dàna.
arrow *n* saighead *f*.
arsenal *n* arm-lann *f*.
art *n* ealain *f*; dòigh *f*; alt *m*; (*artifice*) seòltachd *f*.
artery *n* cuisle *f*.
artful *adj* innleachdach; seòlta.
arthritis *n* tinneas nan alt *m*.
article *n* alt *m*; (*clause*) bonn *m*.
articulate *adj* pongail.
artifice *n* seòltachd *f*.
artificial *adj* brèige.
artist *n* fear-ealain *m*.
as *adv* cho . . . ri, cho . . . is. • *conj* mar, ceart mar.
ascend *v* dìrich, streap.
ascent *n* dìreadh *m*.
ascertain *v* lorg; faigh fios.
ascribe *v* cuir às leth.
ash *n* uinnseann *m*.
ashamed *adj* nàraichte.
ashes *n* luaithre *f*.
ashore *adv* air tìr.

ashtray *n* soitheach-luaithre *f*.
Asia *n* An Aisia *f*.
Asiatic, Asian *adj* Aisianach.
aside *adv* a thaobh.
ask *v* (*request*) iarr; (*inquire after*) faighnich, feòraich.
askew *adv* cam; claon.
asleep *adj* an cadal.
asparagus *n* creamh na muice fiadhaich *m*.
aspect *n* snuadh *m*.
aspen *n* critheann *m*.
asperity *n* gairbhe *f*.
aspiration *n* dèidh *m*.
aspire *v* iarr, bi an dèidh air.
ass *n* asal *f*.
assail *v* thoir ionnsaigh air.
assailant *n* neach-ionnsaigh *m*.
assassin *n* mortair *m*.
assassinate *v* moirt, dèan mort.
assault *n* ionnsaigh *f*.
assemble *v* cruinnich.
assembly *n* mòrdhail *m*.
assent *n* aonta *m*.
assert *v* tagair.
assertion *n* tagradh *m*.
assertive *adj* tagrach.
assess *v* meas; (*for taxation*) meas a thaobh cìs.
assessment *n* meas *m*; meas a thaobh cìs *m*.
assessor *n* measadair *m*.
asset *n* taic *f*.
assiduity *n* dùrachd *f*.
assiduous *adj* leanmhainneach.
assign *v* cuir air leth.
assignation *n* cur air leth *m*; (*tryst*) coinneamh-leannan *f*.
assignment *n* obair shònraichte *f*.
assimilate *v* gabh a-steach.
assist *v* cuidich.

assistance n cuideachadh m.

assistant n cuidiche m.

associate v theirig am pàirt; cuir as leth.

association n comann m; ceangal m.

assonance n fuaimreagadh m.

assortment n measgachadh m.

assuage v caisg.

assume v gabh air.

assumption n gabhail m; (supposition) barail f.

assurance n dearbhachd f.

assure v dearbh.

assuredly adv gun teagamh.

asterisk n reul f.

astern adv an deireadh na luinge.

asthma n a' chuing f.

astonish v cuir iongnadh air.

astonishment n iongnadh m.

astray adv air seachran.

astride adv casa-gobhlach.

astringent adj ceangailteach; geur is tioram.

astrologer n speuradair m.

astrology n speuradaireachd f.

astronaut n speur-sheòladair m.

astronomer n reuladair m.

astronomical adj reul-eòlasach.

astronomy n reul-eòlas m.

asunder adv air leth.

asylum n àite-dìon m.

at prep aig. • pron **at me** agam; **at you** (sing) agad; **at him, it** aige; **at her** aice; **at us** againn; **at you** agaibh; **at them** aca.

atheism n neo-dhiadhachd f.

atheist n neo-dhiadhaire m.

athletic adj lùthmhor.

athletics n lùth-chleasachd f.

athwart adv trasd.

Atlantic Ocean n An Cuan Siar m.

atlas n atlas m.

atmosphere n àile m.

atom n dadam m.

atomic adj dadamach.

atone v dèan èirig.

atonement n rèite f.

atrocious adj uabhasach.

atrocity n buirbe f.

attach v ceangail.

attached adj ceangailte.

attachment n dàimh, gràdh m.

attack n ionnsaigh m. • v thoir ionnsaigh.

attain v ruig.

attainable adj so-ruigsinn.

attainment n ruigsinn m; (ability) sgil m.

attempt n oidhirp f. • v dèan oidhirp.

attend v fritheil; **attend to** thoir aire.

attendance n frithealadh m.

attendant n neach-fhrithealaidh m.

attentive adj furachail.

attenuate v tanaich.

attest v thoir fianais.

attestation n teisteas m.

attire n aodach, trusgan m. • v sgeadaich.

attitude n seasamh m.

attract v tarraing.

attraction n sùgadh m.

attractive adj tarraingeach.

attribute v cuir às leth.

attrition n bleith f.

attune v gleus.

attuned adj air ghleus.

auburn adj buidhe-ruadh.

auction n reic-tairgse f.

audible adj so-chlaistinneach.

audience n luchd-èisdeachd m.

audiovisual *adj* claistinn-léirsinneach.
audit *n* sgrùdadh *m*. • *v* sgrùd.
auditor *n* sgrùdaire *m*.
augment *v* meudaich.
augur *n* fiosaiche *m*.
augury *n* tuar *m*.
August *n* Lùnasdal *m*.
aunt *n* antaidh *f*.
aurora borealis *n* Na Fir Chlis.
auspicious *adj* fàbharach.
austere *adj* teann.
austerity *n* teanntachd *f*.
Australasia *n* Astrailàisia *f*.
Australia *n* Astràilia *f*.
Austria *n* An Ostair *f*.
authentic *adj* cinnteach.
author *n* ùghdar *m*.
authorise *v* thoir ùghdarras.
authority *n* ùghdarras, smachd *m*.
autobiography *n* fèin-eachdraich *f*.
automatic *adj* fèin-ghluasadach.
autumn *n* foghar *m*.

auxiliary *adj* taiceil.
avail *v* foghainn.
available *adj* ri fhaighinn.
avarice *n* sannt *m*.
avaricious *adj* sanntach.
avenge *v* dìol.
average *adj* gnàthach. • *n* meadhan *m*.
aversion *n* fuath *m*.
avid *adj* gionach.
avoid *v* seachainn.
await *v* fuirich ri.
awake *v* dùisg.
award *n* duais *f*. • *v* thoir duais.
aware *adj* fiosrach.
away *adv* air falbh.
awesome *adj* fuathasach.
awful *adj* eagalach, uabhasach.
awhile *adv* tacan.
awkward *adj* cearbach.
awry *adj* cam.
ax, axe *n* tuagh *f*.
axle *n* aiseil *f*.

B

babble *n* glagais *f*.
baby *n* leanabh *m*.
bachelor *n* fleasgach *m*.
back *adv* air ais. • *n* cùl *m*; (*person*) druim *m*. • *v* theirig air ais; (*support*) seas.
backbone *n* cnàmh-droma *m*.
backgammon *n* tàileasg *m*.
backside *n* tòn *f*.
backsliding *n* cùl-sleamhnachadh *m*.
backwards *adv* an coinneamh a chùil.
bacon *n* muic-fheòil *f*.
bacterial *adj* bacteridheach.

bad *adj* dona, olc.
badge *n* suaicheantas *m*.
badger *n* broc *m*.
badness *n* donas *m*.
bad-tempered *adj* greannach.
baffle *v* dèan a chùis air.
bag *n* pòca *m*.
baggage *n* treallaichean *f*.
bagpipe *n* pìob, a' phìob mhòr *f*.
bail *n* fuasgladh air urras *m*. • *v* thoir urras air.
bailiff *n* bàillidh *m*.
bait *n* maghar *m*. • *v* biadh.
bake *v* fuin; bruich ann an àmhainn.

baker *n* fuineadair, bèicear *m*.
bakery *n* taigh-fuine *m*.
balance *n* meidh *f*; (*mental*) cothrom *m*; (*fin*) còrr *m*. • *v* cuir air meidh; cothromaich.
balcony *n* for-uinneag *f*.
bald *adj* maol.
baldness *n* maoile *f*.
baleful *adj* millteach.
ball *n* ball *m*; (*dance*) bàl.
ballad *n* bailead *m*.
ballast *n* balaiste *f*.
balloon *n* bailiùn *m*.
ballot *n* bhòtadh *m*.
balm *n* ìocshlaint *f*.
bamboo *n* cuilc Ìnnseanach *f*.
bamboozle *v* cuir an imcheist.
ban *n* toirmeasg *f*. • *v* toirmisg.
banana *n* banana *m*.
band *n* bann *m*; còmhlan *m*; (*mus*) còmhlan-ciùil *m*.
bandage *n* stìom-cheangail *f*.
bandy-legged *adj* camachasach.
baneful *adj* nimheil.
bang *n* cnag *f*; bualadh *m*. • *v* cnag; buail.
banish *v* fògair.
banishment *n* fògradh *m*.
basking shark *n* cearban *m*.
battery *n* bataraidh *m*.
bawdy *adj* drabasda.
bead *n* grìogag *m*.
beak *n* gob *m*.
beans *npl* pònair *m*.
beard *n* feusag *m*.
beast *n* beathach *m*, biast *m*.
beat *v* thoir buille.
beautiful *adj* bòidheach.
beauty maise, bòidhchead *m*.
beckon *v* smèid air.
bed *n* leabaidh *m*.

bedroom *n* seòmar-leapa *m*.
bee *n* seillean *m*.
beef *n* mairtfheoil.
beer *n* leann *m*.
beetle *n* daolag *m*.
before *prep* ro. • *pron* **before me** romham; **before you** (*sing*) romhad; **before him, it** roimhe; **before her** roimhpe; **before us** romhainn; **before you** (*pl*) romhaibh; **before them** romhpa.
beg *v* iarr; dèan faoighe.
beggar *n* dèirceach *m*.
behave *v* giùlain.
behaviour *n* giùlan *m*; modh *m*.
behind *prep* air cùlaibh. • *pron* **behind me** air mo chùlaibh; **behind you** (*sing*) air do chùlaibh; **behind him, it** air a chùlaibh; **behind her** air a cùlaibh; **behind us** air ar cùlaibh; **behind you** (*pl*) air ur cùlaibh; **behind them** air an cùlaibh.
bell *n* clag *m*.
bellow *v* beucaich.
bellows *n* balg-sèididh *m*.
belly *n* brù, broinn *f*.
belong *v* buin.
beloved *adj* gràdhach.
below *adv* shìos.
belt *n* crios *m*.
bench *n* being *f*.
bend *n* lùb *m*. • *v* lùb.
beneath *prep* fo.
benediction *n* beannachadh *m*.
benefaction *n* tabhartas *m*.
benefactor *n* taibheartach *m*.
beneficent *adj* deagh-ghnìomhach.
beneficial *adj* tairbheach.
benefit *n* sochair *m*.
benevolence *n* deagh-ghean *m*.

benevolent *adj* coibhneil.
benign *adj* suairc.
bent *adj* lùbte.
benumb *v* meilich.
bequeath *v* tiomnaich.
bequest *n* dìleab *m*.
bereaved *adj* rùisgte.
berry *n* dearc *f*, subh *m*.
beseech *v* dèan guidhe.
beside *prep* ri taobh. • *pron* **beside me** ri mo thaobh; **beside you** (*sing*) ri do thaobh; **beside him, it** ri 'thaobh; **beside her** ri 'thaobh; **beside us** ri ar taobh; **beside you** (*pl*) ri ur taobh; **beside them** ri an taobh.
besides *adv* a bhàrr air.
besiege *v* dèan sèisd air.
best *adj* as fheàrr. • *n* rogha *m*. • *v* fairtlich air.
bestial *adj* brùideil.
bestow *v* builich.
bet *v* cuir geall.
betray *v* brath.
betrayal *n* brathadh *m*.
betrayer *n* brathadair *m*.
betroth *v* rèitich.
better *adj* nas fheàrr.
between *adv* eadar. • *prep* eadar. • *pron* **alongside us** eadarainn; **alongside you** (*pl*) eadaraibh; **alongside them** eatorra.
bewail *v* caoidh.
beware *v* thoir an aire.
bewitch *v* cuir fo gheasaibh.
beyond *prep* air taobh thall; seachad air.
bias *n* claonadh *m*.
bible *n* bìoball *m*.
biblical *adj* sgriobturail.
bicycle *n* bàidhseagal *m*.

bid *n* tairgse *f*. • *v* thoir tairgse.
bidding *n* (*invitation*) cuireadh *m*.
bide *v* fuirich.
biennial *adj* dà-bhliadhnach.
bier *n* carbad-adhlacaidh, giùlan *m*.
big *adj* mòr.
bigamy *n* dà-chèileachas *m*.
bigot *n* dalm-bheachdaiche *m*.
bigotry *n* dalm-bheachd *m*.
bilateral *adj* dà-thaobhach.
bile *n* domblas *m*.
bilingual *adj* dà-chànanach.
bill *n* gob *m*; (*account*) bileag.
billion *n* billean *m*.
bin *n* biona *f*.
binary *adj* càraideach.
bind *v* ceangail.
binding *n* ceangal *m*.
biochemist *n* bith-cheimicear *m*.
biochemistry *n* bith-cheimiceachd *f*.
biography *n* beath-eachdraidh *f*.
biological *adj* bith-eòlasach.
biology *n* bith-eòlas *m*.
biped *n* dà-chasach *m*.
birch *n* beithe *f*.
bird *n* eun *m*.
bird-song *n* ceilear *m/f*.
birth certificate *n* teisteanas-breith *m*.
birth *n* breith *f*.
birthday *n* ceann-bliadhna *m*.
birthright *n* còir-bhreith *f*.
biscuit *n* briosgaid *f*.
bisect *v* geàrr sa mheadhan.
bishop *n* easbaig *m*.
bit *n* mìr, bìdeag *m*; (*horse*) cabstair *m*.
bitch *n* galla *f*.
bite *v* bìd, thoir grèim à.
biting *adj* bìdeach.
bitter *adj* geur.
black *adj* dubh, dorch.
blackbird *n* lon-dubh *m*.

blackboard n bòrd-dubh m.

blacken v dubh, dèan dubh.

black-humoured adj gruamach.

blackness n duibhead m.

blacksmith n gobha m.

bladder n aotroman m.

blade n (of grass) bilean; (of weapon) lann.

blame n coire f. • v coirich.

blameless adj neo-choireach.

blanch v gealaich.

bland adj mìn.

blank adj bàn.

blanket n plaide, plangaid f.

blasphemy n toibheum m.

blast n sgal m. • v sgrios.

blaze n teine lasrach m. • v las.

bleach v todhair.

bleak adj lom, fuar.

bleat v dèan mèilich.

bleed v leig fuil.

blemish n gaoid f.

blend n coimeasgadh m. • v coimeasgaich.

bless v beannaich.

blessed adj beannaichte.

blessing n beannachd f.

blight n fuar-dhealt.

blind adj dall. • n sgàil m.

blind man n dallaran m.

blindness n doille f.

blink v caog.

bliss n aoibhneas m.

blissful adj aoibhneach.

blister n leus m. • v thoir leus air; thig leus air.

blithe adj aoibhinn.

block n ploc m. • v caisg.

blockhead n bumailear m.

blonde n te bhàn f.

blood feud n folachd f.

blood group n seòrsa fala m.

blood n fuil f.

blood pressure n bruthadh-fala m.

blood transfusion n leasachadh-fala m.

bloodshed n dòrtadh-fala m.

bloody adj fuileach.

bloom n blàth m.

blot n dubhadh m.

blotting paper n pàipear-sùghaidh m.

blouse n blobhsa f.

blow v sèid.

blubber n saill (muice-mara) f.

blue adj gorm.

blueness n guirme f.

bluff v meall.

blunder n iomrall m.

blunt adj. maol. • v maolaich.

blur v dèan doilleir.

blush n rudhadh m.

bluster v bagair.

boar n torc m.

board n bòrd m, dèile f. • v rach air bòrd.

boarding house n taigh-aoigheachd m.

boarding pass n cead-bòrdaidh m.

boast n bòsd. • v dèan bòsd.

boaster n bòsdair m.

boastful adj bòsdail.

boat n bàta m.

body n corp m; (person) neach, creutair m; (band) buidheann m.

bog n boglach, fèithe f.

bog-cotton n canach m.

boggle v bi an teagamh.

boil v goil; bruich.

boiled adj bruich.

boiler n goileadair m.

boisterous adj stoirmeil; iorghaileach.

bold adj dàna.
boldness n dànadas m.
bolster v misnich.
bolt n crann m. • v cuir crann air.
bomb n bom, boma m. • v leag bom air.
bond n ceangal m.
bondage n daorsa m.
bone n cnàmh m.
boneless adj gun chnàimh.
bonfire n tein-aighear m.
bonnet n bonaid f.
bonny adj maiseach.
bonus n còrr m.
bony adj cnàmhach.
book n leabhar m.
bookcase n preas-leabhraichean m.
bookish adj dèidheil air leughadh.
book-keeper n fear chumail leabhraichean m.
book-keeping n leabhar-chùnntas m.
bookseller n leabhar-reiceadair m.
bookshop n bùth-leabhraichean m.
boor n amhasg m.
boorish n amhasgail m.
boot n bròg m.
booty n cobhartach m/f.
booze n stuth òil m. • v òl.
border n crìoch f.
borderer n fear àiteach nan crìoch m.
bore n duine ràsanach m.
bore v cladaich.
boring adj fadalach.
borrow v faigh, gabh iasad.
borrower n fear gabhail iasaid m.
bosom n uchd m.
boss n ceann m.
botanise v cruinnich luibhean.
botanist n luibh-eòlaiche m.
botany n luibh-eòlas m.
both adj araon, le chèile, an dà; (people) an dithis.
bother n sàrachadh m. • v sàraich.
bottle n botal m.
bottom n lochdar m; grùnnd m; màs m.
bottomless adj gun ghrùnnd.
bough n geug f.
bound n sìnteag f. • v thoir leum.
bountiful adj fialaidh.
bourgeois adj bùirdeasach.
bow n bogha m; (ship) toiseach m; (head) ùmhlachd m.
bowels n innidh f.
bowl n cuach f, bobhla m.
bowsprit n crann-spreòid m.
bowstring n taifeid f.
box n bocsa, bucas m. • v (sport) dèan sabaid.
boxer n bocsair, dòrnadair m.
boxer shorts n briogais bocsair f.
boy n balach, gille m.
brace n (pair) dithis m.
braces npl galars.
bracken n raineach f.
bracket n camag f.
brae n bruthach f.
brag v dèan bòsd.
bragging n bòsd, spaglainn m.
brain n eanchainn f.
bramble n smeur f.
bramble-bush n dris f.
branch n meangan m, geug f. • v sgaoil.
brandish v beartaich.
brandy n branndaidh f.
brass n pràis f.
brat n isean m.
brave adj gaisgeil.
bravery n misneachd f.
brawl n stairirich m. • v dèan stairirich.

bray *v* dèan sitir.
breach *n* briseadh *m*. • *v* dèan briseadh.
bread *n* aran *m*.
breadcrumb *n* criomag arain *f*.
breadth *n* leud *m*.
break *v* bris; sgar.
breakfast *n* breacaist *m*.
breast *n* cìoch *f*.
breath *n* anail *f*.
breathe *v* (*out*) leig anail; (*in*) tarraing anail.
breathless *adj* plosgartach.
breed *n* seòrsa *m*. • *v* tarmaich.
breeding *n* oilean *m*.
breeze *n* tlàth-ghaoth *f*.
brevity *n* giorrad *m*.
brew *v* dèan grùdaireachd; tarraing.
brewer *n* grùdaire *m*.
bribe *n* brìb *f*. • *v* brìb.
bribery *n* brìbeireachd *f*.
brick *n* breice *f*.
bricklayer *n* breicire *m*.
bridal *adj* pòsda.
bride *n* bean-bainnse *f*.
bridegroom *n* fear-bainnse *m*.
bridesmaid *n* maighdean-phòsaidh *f*.
bridge *n* drochaid *f*.
brief *adj* geàrr.
brigand *n* spùinneadair *m*.
bright *adj* soilleir; (*mind*) tuigseach.
brighten *v* soillsich.
brightness *n* soilleireachd *f*.
brilliant *adj* boillsgeach; (*mind*) air leth geur.
brim *n* oir *m*.
brine *n* sàl *m*.
bring *v* thoir.
brink *n* oir *m*.

brisk *adj* beòthail.
briskness *n* beòthalachd *f*.
bristle *n* calg *m*. • *v* cuir calg air.
Britain *n* Breatainn *f*.
British *adj* Breatannach.
brittle *adj* brisg.
broach *v* (*open*) toll; (*introduce*) tog.
broad *adj* leathann.
broadcast *v* craoil.
broadcaster *n* craoladair *m*.
brochure *n* leabhran *m*.
brogue *n* bròg-èille *f*; (*language*) dualchainnt *f*.
broken *adj* briste.
broker *n* neach-gnothaich *m*.
brokerage *n* duais fir-ghnothaich *f*.
bronchial *adj* sgòrnanach.
bronchitis *n* at sgòrnain *m*.
bronze *n* umha *m*.
bronzed *adj* (*tanned*) donn, grian-loisgte.
brooch *n* bràiste *f*.
brood *n* àl *m*. • *v* àlaich.
brook *n* alltan *m*.
broom *n* bealaidh *m*; sguab *m*.
broth *n* eanraich *f*, brot *m*.
brothel *n* taigh-siùrsachd *m*.
brother *n* bràthair *m*.
brotherhood *n* bràithreachas *m*.
brotherly *adj* bràithreil.
brow *n* mala *f*; (*of hill*) maoilean *m*.
brown *adj* donn.
brownness *n* duinne *f*.
browse *v* criom; (*book*) thoir ruith air.
bruise *n* pronnadh *m*. • *v* pronn.
brunette *n* tè dhonn *f*.
brush *n* sguab *f*. • *v* sguab.
Brussels *n* A' Bhruiseal *f*.

brutal *adj* brùideil.

brutality *n* brùidealachd *f*.

brute *n* brùid *m*.

bubble *n* builgean *m*.

buck *n* boc *m*.

bucket *n* cuinneag *f*.

buckle *n* bucall *m*.

bud *n* gucag *f*.

budge *v* caraich.

budget *n* buidsead *f*.

buffet *n* beum *m*; (*food table*) clàr bìdh *m*.

bug *n* (*infection*) galar *m*.

bugle *n* dùdach *f*.

build *v* tog.

builder *n* togalaiche *m*.

building *n* togalach *m*.

building society *n* comann-togalaich *m*.

bulb *n* bolgan *m*.

bulk *n* meudachd *f*.

bulky *adj* tomadach.

bull *n* tarbh *m*.

bulldog *n* tarbh-chù *m*.

bulldozer *n* tarbh-chrann *m*.

bullet *n* peilear *m*.

bulletin *n* cùirt-iomradh *m*.

bullock *n* tarbh òg *m*.

bully *n* pulaidh *m*.

bum *n* màs *m*.

bump *n* meall; bualadh *m*.

bumper *n* bumpair *m*.

bun *n* buna *m*.

bunch *n* bagaid *f*.

bundle *n* pasgan *m*.

bung *n* tùc *m*.

bungle *v* dèan gu cearbach.

bungler *n* cearbaire *m*.

buoy *n* put *m*.

buoyancy *n* fleodradh *m*.

buoyant *adj* aotrom.

burden *n* eallach *m*. • *v* uallaich.

bureau *n* biùro *m*.

burgh *n* borgh *m*.

burglar *n* gadaiche-taighe *m*.

burglary *n* gadachd-taighe *f*.

burial *n* adhlacadh *m*.

burlesque *n* sgeigeireachd *f*.

burly *adj* tapaidh.

burn[1] *n* losgadh *m*. • *v* loisg.

burn[2] *n* (*stream*) alltan *m*.

burning *n* losgadh *m*.

burnish *v* lìomh.

burst *v* spreadh.

bury *v* adhlaic.

bus *n* bus *m*.

bush *n* preas *m*.

bushy *adj* preasach.

business *n* gnothach *m*, malairt *f*.

businessman *n* fear-gnothaich *m*.

bust *n* ceann is guaillean *m*.

bustle *n* othail *f*.

busy *adj* trang.

busybody *n* gobaire *m*.

but *conj*, *adv*, *prep* ach.

butcher *n* feòladair *m*. • *v* casgair.

Bute *n* Bòid.

butler *n* buidealair *m*.

butt[1] *n* cùis-bhùirt *m*; (*cask*) baraill *m*; (*target*) targaid *f*.

butt[2] *v* sàth.

butter *n* ìm *m*.

buttercup *n* buidheag-an-t-samraidh *f*.

butterfly *n* dealan-dè *m*.

buttery *adj* ìmeach.

buttock *n* màs *m*.

button *n* putan *m*. • *v* putanaich.

buxom *adj* tiugh.

buy *v* ceannaich.

buyer *n* ceannaiche *m*.

buzz *n* srann *f*. • *v* srann.

buzzard *n* clamhan *m*.
by *adv* seachad; (*aside*) an dara taobh. • *prep* fasg air; le; **by and by** *adv* a dh' aithghearr, dh' aithgearr.

by-election *n* frith-thaghadh *m*.
bypass *n* seach-rathad *m*.
byre *n* bàthach *f*.
bystander *n* fear-amhairc *m*.

C

cab *n* tagsaidh *m*.
cabbage *n* càl *m*.
caber *n* cabar *m*.
cabin *n* seòmar-luinge, cèaban *m*.
cadaverous *adj* cairbheach.
cadence *n* dùnadh *m*.
cadger *n* neach-faoighe *m*.
café *n* cafaidh *m*.
cage *n* cèidse *f*.
cairn *n* càrn *m*.
cajole *v* breug.
cake *n* breacag *f*.
calamitous *adj* dosgainneach.
calamity *n* dosgainn *f*.
calculate *v* tomhais.
calculation *n* tomhas *m*.
calculator *n* àireamhair *m*.
calculus *n* riaghailt-àireamh *f*.
Caledonia *n* Alba *f*.
calendar *n* mìosachan *m*.
calf *n* laogh *m*; (*leg*) calpa *m*.
calibre *n* meudachd *f*.
call *v* glaodh.
call-box *n* bocsa-fòn *m*.
calligraphy *n* làmh-sgrìobhaidh *f*.
calling *n* eughachd *f*; (*vocation*) dreuchd *f*.
calliper *n* cailpear *m*.
callous *adj* cruaidh-chridheach.
calm *adj* ciùin; fèathach.
calm *v* ciùinich.
calumniate *v* cùl-chàin.
calve *v* beir laogh.

camel *n* càmhal *m*.
camera *n* camara *m*.
camouflage *n* breug-riochd *m*.
camp *n* càmpa *m*.
camp *v* càmpaich.
campaign *n* còmhrag *f*.
can[1] *n* canastair *m*.
can[2] *v* (*may*) faod; (*be able*) is urrainn do.
Canadian *adj* Canadach.
canal *n* clais-uisge *f*.
cancel *v* dubh a-mach.
cancellation *n* dubhadh a-mach *m*.
cancer *n* aillse *f*.
cancerous *adj* aillseach.
candid *adj* neo-chealgach.
candidate *n* iarradair *m*.
candle *n* coinneal *f*.
candlestick *n* coinnlear *m*.
candour *n* fosgarrachd *f*.
canine *adj* conail.
cannibal *n* canabail *m*.
canny *adj* cùramach.
canonise *v* cuir an àireamh nan naomh.
canter *n* trotan *m*.
canvas *n* canabhas *m*.
canvass *v* beachd-rannsaich.
canvasser *n* sireadair *m*.
cap *n* bonaid *m/f*, ceap *m*.
cap *v* còmhdaich; (*fig*) thoir bàrr air.
capability *n* cumhachd *m*.

capable adj comasach.

capacious adj farsaing.

capacity n comas m.

cape n rubha m; cleòc m.

caper v leum.

capital n ceanna-bhaile m.

capital letter n corr-litir f.

capitalism n calpachas m.

capitalist n calpaire m.

capitulate v strìochd.

capitulation n strìochdadh m.

caprice n neònachas m.

capricious adj neònach.

capsule n capsal m.

captain n caiptean m.

caption n tiotal m; fo-thiotal m.

captive n ciomach m.

captivity n ciomachas m.

capture n glacadh m.

capture v glac.

car n càr, carbad m.

carbohydrate n gualaisg m.

carbon n gualan m.

carcass n cairbh m.

card n cairt f.

card v càrd.

cardboard n cairt-bhòrd m.

cardiac adj cridhe.

cardiac disease n tinneas cridhe m.

cardinal adj prìomh. • n càirdin-eal.

card index n clàr-amais cairt m.

care n cùram m. • v gabh cùram.

career n (rush) rèis f; (work) dreachd f.

careful adj cùramach.

careless adj mì-chùramach.

carelessness n mì-chùram m.

caress v cnèadaich.

caretaker n neach-aire m.

cargo n lùchd m.

caricature n dealbh-magaidh m.

carnage n àr m.

carnal adj feòlmhor.

carnival n fèill f.

carnivorous adj feòil-itheach.

carousal n fleadh m.

carpark n pàirc-chàraichean f.

carpenter n saor m

carpet n brat-ùrlair m.

carriage n carbad m; (gait) giùlan m.

carrier n neach-ghiùlain m.

carrion n ablach m.

carrot n curran m.

carry v giùlain, iomchair, thoir.

cart n cairt f. • v giùlain le cairt.

cartilage n maoth-chnàimh m.

cartoon n dealbh-èibhinn m/f.

cartridge n catraisde f.

carve v geàrr; snaigh.

carving n snaigheadh m.

cascade n eas m.

case n còmhdach m; ceus m; staid m; cùis m; tuiseal m.

cash n airgead ullamh m.

cash-book n leabhar-airgid m.

cashier n glèidheadair-airgid m.

cash machine n inneal-airgid m.

cash register n inneal-cùnntaidh airgid m.

cask n buideal m.

cassock n casag f.

cast v tilg, cuir; **cast loose** v sgaoil.

caste n dual-fhìne f.

castigate v cronaich.

castle n caisteal m.

castrate v spoth.

casual adj tuiteamach.

casualty n leòinteach m.

cat n cat m.

catalogue n ainm-chlàr m.

catalyse v cruth-atharraich.

catapult n tailm m.

cataract see cascade; (eye) n meamran sùla m.

catarrh n an galar smugaideach m.

catastrophe n droch thubaist f.

catch n glacadh m. • v glac, greimich.

catching adj gabhaltach.

catechism n leabhar-cheist m.

categorical adj làn-chinnteach.

category n gnè f.

cater v solair.

caterpillar n burras m.

caterpillar-tracked adj burrasach.

cathedral n cathair-eaglais f.

Catholic adj Caitligeach.

catholic adj coitcheann.

cattle n spreidh f.

cattle show n fèill a' chruidh f.

cauldron n coire mòr m.

cauliflower n colag f.

causal adj adhbharach.

causation n adhbharachadh m.

cause n adhbhar m; cùis m. • v dèan, thoir gu buil.

causeway n cabhsair m.

caustic adj loisgeach.

caution n cùram m. • v cuir air fhaicill.

cautious adj cùramach.

cavalry n marc-shluagh m.

cave n uamh f.

cavity n lag m/f, sloc f.

cease v stad.

cease-fire n stad-losgaidh m.

ceaseless adj gun stad.

cedar n seudar m.

cede v gèill.

ceilidh n cèilidh m/f.

ceiling n mullach m.

celebrate v glèidh; bi subhach.

celebrity n neach iomraiteach m.

celestial adj nèamhaidh.

celibacy n aontamhachd f.

celibate adj aontamhach.

cell n cealla; prìosan f.

cellar n seilear m.

cello n beus-fhidheall f.

cellular adj ceallach.

celluloid n ceallaloid m.

Celt n Ceilteach m.

Celtic adj Ceilteach.

cement n saimeant m. • v tàth.

cemetery n cladh m.

censor n caisgire m. • v caisg.

censorious adj cronachail.

censure n coire f. • v coirich.

census n cùnntas-sluaigh m.

centenary n ceud blianna m.

centennial adj ceud-bhliadhnach.

centimetre n ceudameatair m.

central adj anns a' mheadan.

central heating n teasachadh meadhanach m.

central processing unit n prìomhghnìomh-inneal m.

centre n meadhan m.

centrifugal adj meadhan-sheachnach.

centripetal adj meadhan-aomachail.

century n ceud bliadhna, linn m.

cereal n gràn m.

ceremony n deas-ghnàth m.

certain adj cinnteach.

certainly adv gu cinnteach.

certainty n cinnt f.

certificate n teisteanas m.

certify v teistich.

cesspool n poll-caca m.

chagrin n mìghean m.

chain n slabhraidh f. • v cuibhrich.

chain store n bùth-sreatha f.

chair n cathair f.

chairman n cathraiche m.

chalk n cailc f.

challenge n dùbhshlan m.

chamber n seòmar m.

chambered adj seòmrach.

champ v cagainn.

champion n gaisgeach m.

championship n urram gaisgeachd m.

chance n tuiteamas m.

change n caochladh m; (money) iomlaid f. • v mùth.

changeable adj caochlaideach.

channel n amar, caolas m.

chant v sianns.

chanter n feadan m.

chaos n eucruth m.

chapel n caibeal m.

chapter n caibideil m/f.

character n beus, mèinn f; (story) pearsa m.

characteristic adj coltach.

charcoal n gual-fiodha m.

charge n earbsa f; ionnsaigh f; prìs f. • v earb; thoir ionnsaigh; cuir.

charity n gràdh, coibhneas m.

charm n mealladh m; (spell) ortha f. • v meall; cuir fo dhraoidh-eachd.

chart n cairt-iùil f.

charter v fasdaidh.

chase n sealg. • v ruith.

chaste adj geanmnaidh.

chastity n geanmnachd f.

chat v dèan còmhradh.

chatter v dèan cabaireachd.

cheap adj saor; air bheag prìs.

cheapness n saoiread m.

cheat n mealltair m. • v dèan foill air.

check n casg m. • v caisg.

checkmate n tul-chasg m.

cheek n gruaidh f.

cheer v brosnaich.

cheese n càise m, càbag f.

chemical adj ceimiceach.

chemist n ceimicear m; neach-chungaidhean.

cheque n seic f.

cherry n sirist f.

chess n fidhcheall m.

chest n ciste f; cliabh f.

chew v cagainn.

chicken n isean m.

chief n ceann-feadhna m.

chilblain n cusp f.

child n leanabh m.

childhood n leanabas m.

childless adj gun sliochd.

children n clann f.

chill v fuaraich.

chilly adj fuar.

chimney n similear m.

chin n smig m.

China n An t-Sìn.

chocolate n teòclaid f.

choice n roghainn m.

choir n còisir-chiùil f.

choke v tachd.

choose v roghnaich.

chop n staoig. • v sgud.

chord n còrda f.

chorus n sèist f; co-sheirm f.

Christ n Crìosd m.

christen v baist.

Christmas n Nollaig f.

chronic adj leantalach.

chronicle n eachdhraidh f.

church n eaglais f.

churchyard n cladh m.

churlish adj mùgach.

cigarette n toitean m.

cinema n taigh-dhealbh m.

circle n cearcall; còmhlan m. • v cuairtich.

circuit n cuairt f.

circular adj cruinn.

circulate v cuir mun cuairt.

circumnavigate v seòl mun cuairt.

circumstance n cùis f.

circus n soircas m.

citizen n neach-àiteachaidh m.

city n cathair f.

civil adj sìobhalta.

civilian n sìobhaltair m.

civilisation n sìobhaltachd f.

civilise v sìobhail.

claim n tagairt f. • v tagair.

claimant n tagraiche m.

clan n fine f, cinneadh m.

clanship n cinneadas m.

clap n buille f. • v buail ri chèile.

claret n clàireat f.

clarify v soilleirich.

clash v dèan glagadaich.

clasp n dubhan m.

class n buidheann f, clas m. • v seòrsaich.

classical adj clasaigeach.

classify v seòrsaich.

claw n iongna f.

clay n crèadh f.

claymore n claideamh-mòr m.

clean adj glan. • v glan.

cleanness n gloinead m.

clear adj soilleir. • v soilleirich.

cleft n sgoltadh m.

cleg n crèithleag f.

clench v dùin.

clergy n clèir f.

clergyman n pears-eaglais m.

clever adj tapaidh.

click v cnag.

clientèle n luchd-dèilig m.

cliff n creag f, sgùrr m.

climate n clìomaid f.

climb v dìrich, streap.

climber n streapaiche m.

climbing n dìreadh m.

cling v slaod.

clinic n clìonaic f.

clink v thoir gliong.

clip v geàrr.

clipper n gearradair m.

clock n uaireadair, cleoc m.

clod n ploc m.

clog v tromaich.

cloister n clabhstair m.

clone n lethbhreac ginteil m. • v mac-samhlaich.

close[1] adj (near) faisg; (stuffy) dùmhail. • n (entry) clobhsa m.

close[2] v dùin. • n dùnadh m.

clot n meall m.

cloth n aodach m.

clothe v còmhdaich.

clothes npl aodach, trusgan m.

cloud n neul m.

cloudy adj neulach.

clout, n (cloth) clùd m.

clover n clòbhar m.

clown n amadan m.

cloy v sàsaich.

club n (stick) cuaille, caman m.

cluck v dèan gogail.

clump n tom m.

clumsy adj cearbach.

cluster n bagaid f.

clutch n grèim m; (car) put. • v greimich.

coagulate v binndich.

coal n gual m.

coalesce v aonaich.

coarse *adj* garbh.
coast *n* oirthir *f*.
coastguard *n* freiceadan-oirthire *m*.
coastline *n* iomall-fairge *f*.
coat *n* còta *m*. • *v* cuir brat air.
coax *v* tàlaidh.
cobweb *n* eige *f*.
cockle *n* coilleag *f*.
cocksure *adj* coccanta, spairisteach.
cock *n* coileach *m*.
cod *n* trosg *m*.
code *n* riaghailt *f*.
co-education *n* co-fhoghlam *m*.
coerce *v* ceannsaich.
coeval *adj* co-aimsireach.
co-exist *v* bi beò le.
coffee *n* cofaidh *m*.
coffin *n* ciste-laighe *f*.
cog *n* fiacaill *f*.
cogent *adj* làidir.
cohabitation *n* co-fhuireachd *f*.
cohere *v* lean.
coherent *adj* so-leantainn.
coil *n* cuibhleachadh *m*. • *v* cuibhlich.
coin *n* bonn airgid *m*.
coinage *n* cùinneadh *m*.
coincide *v* co-thuit.
coincidence *n* co-thuiteamas *m*.
cold *adj* fuar. • *n* fuachd *m*; cnatan *m*.
coldness *n* fuairead *m*.
collaborate *v* co-oibrich.
collapse *v* tuit am broinn a chèile.
collapsible *adj* so-thuiteamach.
collar *n* coilear *m*.
collarbone *n* ugan *m*.
colleague *n* co-oibriche *m*.
collect *v* cruinnich.
collective *adj* co-choitcheann.
college *n* colaisde *f*.

collision *n* co-bhualadh *m*.
collusion *n* co-rùn *m*.
colonel *n* còirneal *m*.
colony *n* tìr-imrich *f*.
colour *n* dath *m*. • *v* dath.
column *n* colbh *m*.
coma *n* trom-neul *m*.
comb *n* cìr *f*. • *v* cìr.
combination *n* co-aontachadh *m*.
combine *v* co-aontaich.
come *v* thig; (*imper*) trobhad!
comedian *n* cleasaiche *m*.
comedy *n* cleas-chluich *f*.
comet *n* reul-chearbach *f*.
comfort *n* cofhurtachd *f*.
comfortable *adj* cofhurtail.
comic *adj* àbhachdach.
coming *n* teachd *m*.
comma *n* cromag *f*.
command *n* òrdugh *m*.
commemorate *v* cuimhnich.
commend *v* mol.
commendable *adj* ri a mholadh.
comment *n* facal *m*. • *v* thoir tarraing.
commerce *n* malairt *f*.
commercial *adj* malairteach.
commiserate *v* co-bhàidhich.
commission *n* ùghdarras *m*.
commit *v* earb; (*crime, etc*) ciontaich.
committee *n* comataidh *f*.
commodious *adj* luchdmhor.
commodity *n* badhar *m*.
common *adj* coitcheann.
Commonwealth *n* Co-fhlaitheas *m*.
communicate *v* com-pàirtich.
communication *n* com-pàirteachadh *m*; **communications** *npl* eadar-cheangal *m*.
community *n* pobal *m*.
commute *v* malairtich; triall.

compact *adj* teann.
compact disc *n* meanbh-chlàr *m*.
companion *n* companach *m*.
company *n* cuideachd *f*; companaidh *f*.
compare *v* coimeas.
compass *n* combaist *f*; meud *m*.
compassion *n* truas *m*.
compatible *adj* co-chòrdail.
compatriot *n* co-thìreach *m*.
compel *v* co-èignich.
compensate *v* diol.
compete *v* strì.
competition *n* co-fharpais *f*.
competitor *n* farpaiseach *m*.
complacent *adj* somalta.
complain *v* gearain.
complaint *n* gearan *m*; (*illness*)
galar.
computer *n* coimpiutair *m*.
conjugate *v* co-naisg.
conjunction *n* naisgear *m*.
conjure *v* cuir impidh air.
connection *n* ceangal *m*.
connoisseur *n* neach-eòlach *m*.
conquer *v* ceannsaich.
conquest *n* buaidh *f*.
conscience *n* cogais *f*.
conscientious *adj* cogaisach.
conscious *adj* mothachail.
consciously *adv* le mothachadh.
consecrate *v* coisrig.
consecutive *adj* leanmhainneach.
consent *n* aonta *m*.
consent *v* aontaich.
consequence *n* toradh *m*.
consequently *adv* uime sin.
conservancy *n* glèidhteachas *m*.
conservation *n* glèidheadh *m*.
conserve *v* taisg.
consider *v* smaoinich.

considerable *adj* math, cudromach.
consideration *n* tuigse *f*.
consignment *n* lìbhrigeadh *m*.
consistency *n* seasmhachd *f*.
consolation *n* sòlas *m*.
console *v* furtaich.
consonant *n* co-fhoghar *m*.
consort *n* cèile *m*.
conspicuous *adj* faicsinneach.
conspire *v* dèan co-fheall.
constancy *n* neo-chaochlaideachd *f*.
constant *adj* daingeann.
constellation *n* reul-bhad *m*.
constipation *n* teannachadh-innidh
m.
constituency *n* roinn-taghaidh *f*.
constitution *n* dèanamh, nàdar *m*;
(*political*) bonn-stèidh.
constriction *n* teannachadh *m*.
construct *v* tog.
construction *n* togail *f*.
consult *v* gabh comhairle.
consume *v* caith.
consumer *n* caitheadair *m*.
consummate *v* crìochnaich.
contact *v* (*physical*) suath ann;
(*message*) cuir fios gu.
contain *v* cùm; caisg.
container *n* bocsa-stòraidh *m*.
contemplate *v* beachd-smuainich.
contemporary *adj* co-aoiseach.
contempt *n* tàir *f*.
contemptuous *adj* tarcaiseach.
content *adj* toilichte.
context *n* co-theacs *m*.
continent *n* mòr-thìr *f*.
contingent *adj* tuiteamach.
continual *adj* sìor.
continually *adv* gun sgur.
continue *v* lean air.
continuous *adj* leanailteach.

contour n (*map*) loidhne àirde f.

contraception n casg-gineamhainn m.

contract n cùnnradh. • v teannaich; rèitich.

contraction n teannachadh m.

contradict v cuir an aghaidh.

contradiction n breugnachadh m.

contrary adj an aghaidh.

contrast v eadar-dhealaich.

contravene v bris.

contribute v cuir ri.

contribution n cuideachadh m.

contrivance n innleachd f.

control n smachd m.

control v ceannsaich; stiùir.

controversial adj connsachail.

controversy n connspaid f.

convalescence n iar-shlànachadh m.

convalescent adj iar-shlànach.

convener n fear-gairm m.

convenient adj goireasach.

convent n clochar m.

converge v co-aom.

conversation n còmhradh m.

converse v dèan còmhradh.

conversion n iompachadh m.

convert v iompaich.

convex adj os-chearclach.

conveyance n còir-sgrìobhte f.

conveyancer n sgriobhadair-chòirichean m.

convict n ciomach m. • v dearbh.

conviction n dìteadh m.

convivial adj cuideachdail.

convulsion n criothnachadh m.

cook n còcaire m. • v deasaich, bruich.

cooker n cucair m.

cookery n còcaireachd f.

cool v fuaraich.

cooperate v co-oibrich.

cope v dèan an gnothach.

copious adj pailt.

copper n copar m.

copulate v cuplaich.

copy n lethbhreac m. • v ath-sgrìobh.

copyright n dlighe-sgrìobhaidh.

coral n corail m.

cord n còrd m.

cordial adj càirdeil.

core n cridhe m.

cork n àrc f. • v cuir àrc ann.

corkscrew n sgriubha àrc m.

corn n coirce m.

corner n oisean f.

cornice n bàrr-mhaise m.

coronary adj coronach.

coronation n crùnadh m.

corpse n corp m.

corpuscle n corpag f.

correct adj ceart. • v ceartaich.

correspond v co-fhreagair.

correspondence n (*mail*) co-sgrìobhadh m.

corridor n trannsa f.

corrie n coire m.

corrode v meirgnich.

corrosion n meirg f.

corrugated adj preasach.

corrupt adj grod.

cosmetic n cungaidh maise f.

cosmopolitan n os-nàiseanta m.

cost n cosgais f. • v cosg.

costly adj cosgail.

costume n culaidh f.

cosy adj seasgair.

cottage n bothan m.

cotton n cotan m.

couch n uirigh f.

cough n casd m. • v dèan casd.

council n comhairle f.

councillor n comhairliche m.

count v cùnnt.

countenance n gnùis f.

counter n cuntair m.

counteract v cuir bacadh air.

counter-clockwise adv tuathal.

counterfeit v feall-chùinneach.

countersign v cuir ainm ri.

counting n cùnntas m.

countless adj do-àireamh.

country n dùthaich, tìr m.

countryman n fear-dùthcha m.

county n siorrachd f.

couple n càraid f.

couplet n rann dà-shreathach f.

coupon n cùpon m.

courage n misneach f.

courageous adj misneachail.

courier n teachdaire m.

course n slighe m.

court n cùirt f. • v dèan suirghe.

courtesy n modh f.

courthouse n taigh-cùirte m.

cousin n co-ogha m.

cove n bàgh, camas m.

cover n còmhdach, brat m. • v còmhdaich.

cow n bò f.

coward n gealtaire m.

cowardice n geilt f.

cowherd n buachaille m.

coy adj nàrach.

crab n partan m, crùbag f.

crack n sgàinneadh m. • v sgàin.

cradle n creathail f.

craft n cèaird m; (cunning) seòltachd f; (vessel) bàta m.

craftsman n neach-ceàirde m.

crag n creag f.

cram v dìnn.

crane n crann m.

crannog n crannag f.

cranny n cùil f.

crash v co-bhuail.

craving n miann m/f.

crawl v snàig.

crazy adj às a chiall.

creak v dèan dìosgan.

cream n uachdar m.

crease n filleadh m.

create v cruthaich.

creation n cruthachadh m.

creature n creutair m.

credible adj creideasach.

crèche n ionad-latha leanaban m.

credit n creideas m. • v creid.

credit card n cairt-iasaid f.

creditor n creideasaiche m.

creed n creud f.

creel n cliabh m.

cremate v loisg.

crest n cìrean m.

crew n sgioba m/f.

crime n eucoir f.

criminal adj eucoireach. • n eucoir-each m.

crimson adj crò-dhearg.

cringe v crùb.

cripple n crioplach m.

crisis n gàbhadh m.

crisp adj brisg; fionnar.

criterion n slat-tomhais m.

critic n sgrùdair m.

critical adj breitheach.

criticise v dèan sgrùdadh.

criticism n breithneachadh m.

croak v dèan gràgail.

crockery npl soitheachan-crèadha.

croft n croit f.

crofter n croitear m.

crook n cromag f; (person) cruc m.

crooked adj cam, crom.

croon v crònaich.

crop n bàrr m. • v beàrr, buain.

cross adj crosta. • n crois f. • v rach tarsaing.

cross-breed n tar-sìolaich m.

cross-examine v ath-cheasnaich.

cross-roads n crois a' rathaid f.

crossword puzzle n tòimhseachan-tarsainn m.

crotch n gobhal m.

crotchet n (music) dubh-nota m.

crouch v crom.

crow n feannag f.

crowd n sluagh m. • v dòmhlaich.

crowdie n gruth m.

crown n crùn m. • v crùn.

crucible n soitheach-leaghaidh m.

cruciform adj crasgach.

crude adj amh.

cruel adj an-iochdmhor.

cruelty n an-iochdmhorachd m.

cruise n cùrsa mara m.

crumb n criomag f.

crumple v rocaich.

crush v pronn.

crust n plaosg m.

crutch n crasg f.

cry v èigh; guil.

cub n cuilean m.

cube n ciùb m.

cuckoo n cuach m.

cuff n bun-dùirn m.

culprit n ciontach m.

cultivate v àitich.

culture n saothrachadh m; (arts) cultur m.

cup n cupan m.

cupboard n preas m.

cupidity n sannt f.

curable adj so-leigheas.

curb v bac.

curdle v binndich.

cure n leigheas m. • v leigheis.

curious adj ceasnachail.

curl n bachlag f. • v bachlaich.

curlew n guilbneach m.

currency n sgaoileadh m; airgead m.

current adj gnàthaichte. • n sruth m.

curse n mallachd f. • v mallaich.

curtain n cùrtair m.

curvature n caime f.

curve v crom.

cushion n pillean m.

custody n cùram m.

custom n àbhaist m.

customary adj àbhaisteach.

cut n gearradh m. • v geàrr.

cutlery n uidheam-ithe f.

cynical adj searbhasach.

cyst n ùthan m.

D

dabble v crath uisge air.

dad n dadaidh m.

daffodil n lus a' chrom-chinn m.

dagger n biodag f.

daily adj làitheil. • adv gach latha.

dainty adj mìn.

dairy n taigh-bainne m.

daisy n neòinean m.

dale n dail f.

dam n dàm m.

damage n dochann m. • v dochainn.

damnable adj damaichte.

damnation n dìteadh m.

damp adj tais.

dampen v taisich.

dance n dannsa m. • v danns.

dandelion n beàrnan-brìde m.

dandle v luaisg.

danger n cunnart m.

dangerous adj cunnartach.

dappled adj ball-bhreac.

dare v gabh air.

daring adj neo-sgàthach.

dark adj dorch.

darken v dorchaich.

darkness n dorchadas m.

darling n annsachd, eudail f, luaidh m.

darn v càirich.

dash v spealg.

database n stòr-dàta m.

date n ceann-latha m; (fruit) deit f.

daub v smeur.

daughter n nighean f.

daughter-in-law n ban-chliamhainn f.

dawn n camhanach f.

day n latha m.

daylight n solas an latha m.

daze v cuir bho mhothachadh.

dazzle v deàrrs.

dead adj marbh.

deadlock n glasadh m.

deadly adj marbhtach.

deaf adj bodhar.

deafen v bodhair.

deafness n buidhre f

deal n cùnnradh m. • v dèilig.

dealer n malairtaiche m.

dealing n dèiligeadh m.

dear adj gaolach; (cost) daor.

dearness n (cost) daoire f.

dearth n gainne f.

death n bàs m.

debar v bac.

debase v truaill.

debate n deasbad m. • v deasbair.

debit n fiach-shuim f. • v cuir fiach-shuim.

debts npl fiachan.

decade n deichead m.

decadent adj air claonadh.

decant v taom.

decanter n searrag ghlainne f.

decay n crìonadh m. • v caith.

deceit n cealg f.

deceive v meall, breug.

December n An Dùbhlachd.

decency n beusachd f.

decent adj beusach.

deception n mealladh m.

decide v co-dhùin.

deciduous adj seargach.

decimal adj deicheach.

decision n breith f.

decisive adj cinnteach.

deck n bòrd-luinge m. • v sgiamhaich.

declaration n dearbhadh m.

declare v cuir an cèill.

decompose v lobh.

decorate v sgeadaich.

decoration n sgeadachadh m.

decorous adj cubhaidh.

decrease n lùghdachadh m. • v lùghdaich.

decrepit adj breòite.

decry v càin.

dedicate v coisrig.

deduce v tuig.

deduct v beagaich.

deduction n beagachadh m.

deed n gnìomh m; (legal) gnìomhas m.

deep adj domhainn.

deepen v doimhnich.

deer *n* fiadh *m*.
deer-forest *n* frìth *f*.
deface *v* mill.
defamation *n* tuaileas *m*.
defame *v* cùl-chàin.
default *n* dearmad *m*.
defeat *n* call *m*. • *v* gabh air, faigh buaidh.
defect *n* easbhaidh *f*.
defective *adj* easbhaidheach.
defence *n* dìon *m*; leisgeul *m*.
defenceless *adj* gun dìon.
defend *v* dìon.
defensive *adj* dìona.
defer *v* cuir air dàil.
deference *n* ùmhlachd *f*.
deferment *n* dàil *f*.
defiance *n* dùlan *m*.
deficiency *n* dìth *m*.
deficit *n* easbhaidh *f*.
definable *adj* sònrachail.
define *v* sònraich.
definite *adj* comharraichte.
definition *n* comharrachadh *m*.
deflect *v* aom.
deform *v* cuir à cumadh.
deformity *n* mì-dhealbh *m*.
defraud *v* feallaich.
deft *adj* ealamh.
defy *v* thoir dùlan do.
degenerate *v* meath. • *adj* meath-aichte.
degrade *v* ìslich.
degree *n* inbhe *f*; (*academic*) ceum *m*; (*temp*) puing *f*.
deign *v* deònaich.
deity *n* diadhachd *f*.
dejected *adj* fo bhròn.
delay *n* maille *f*. • *v* cuir maille air.
delegate *n* neach-ionaid *m*.
delegation *n* luchd-tagraidh *m*.

delete *v* dubh às.
deliberate *adj* mall. • *v* meòraich.
delicacy *n* mìlseachd *f*.
delicate *adj* fìnealta.
delicious *adj* ana-bhlasta.
delight *v* toilich.
delightful *adj* aoibhneach.
delinquency *n* ciontachd *f*.
delinquent *adj* ciontach.
delirium *n* breisleach *f*.
deliver *v* saor; (*baby*) asaidich.
delivery *n* teàrnadh *m*; post *m*; (*baby*) asaid *m*.
dell *n* lagan *m*.
deluge *n* tuile *f*.
demand *n* tagradh *m*. • *v* tagair.
demean *v* ìslich.
demented *adj* air bhoile.
dementia *n* seargadh-inntinn *m*.
demerit *n* lochd *m*.
democracy *n* sluagh-fhlaitheas *m*.
democrat *n* sluagh-fhlaithear *m*.
demolish *v* sgrios.
demon *n* deamhan *m*.
demonstrable *adj* so-dhearbhte.
demonstration *n* taisbeanadh *m*.
demote *v* thoir ceum a-nuas.
demur *v* cuir teagamh ann.
demure *adj* stuama.
den *n* saobhaidh *m*.
denial *n* àicheadh *m*.
denigrate *v* dèan dìmeas air.
dense *adj* tiugh; (*mind*) maol.
density *n* dlùths *m*.
dent *v* dèan lag ann.
dentist *n* fiaclaire *m*.
denture *n* deudach *m*.
denude *v* rùisg.
deny *v* àicheidh.
depart *v* imich.
department *n* roinn *f*.

departure n falbh m.

depend v (on) cuir earbsa ann.

dependence n eisimealachd f.

dependent adj eisimealach.

depict v dealbh.

deplorable adj truagh.

deplore v caoidh.

deportment n giùlan m.

depose v cuir às oifig.

deposit n tasgadh m. • v tasgaich.

depravity n truailleachd f.

depreciate v cuir an dìmeas.

depress v brùth sìos.

depressant n ìocshlaint-ìsleach-aidh f.

depression n ìsleachadh m.

deprive v toirt air falbh.

depth n doimhneachd f.

depute adj leas-. • v sònraich.

derelict adj trèigte.

deride v dèan fanaid air.

derision n fanaid f.

derivation n sìolachadh m.

derive v sìolaich.

descend v teirinn.

descent n teàrnadh m.

describe v thoir tuairisgeul air.

description n tuairisgeul m.

desert[1] n fàsach m/f.

desert[2] v trèig.

deserve v toill.

design n rùn m; (art) dealbh m.

design v rùnaich; deilbh.

designer n dealbhadair m.

desire n miann m. • v miannaich.

desist v stad.

desk n deasg m.

despair n eu-dòchas m. • v leig thairis dòchas.

desperate adj eu-dòchasach; damainnte.

despicable adj suarach.

despise v dèan tàir air.

despite prep a dh'aindeoin.

dessert n mìlsean m.

destiny n dàn m.

destitute adj falamh.

destroy v sgrios.

destruction n milleadh m.

detach v dealaich.

detail n mion-chùnntas m; mion-phuing f.

detain v cùm air ais.

detect v lorg.

detective n lorg-phoileas m.

determination n diongbhaltas m.

determine v cuir roimh.

determinism n cinnteachas m.

detest v fuathaich.

detestation n fuath m.

detonate v toirm-spreadh.

detour n bealach m.

detract v thoir air falbh.

detriment n dolaidh f.

devalue v di-luachaich.

devastate v lèirsgrios.

devastation n lèirsgrios m.

develop v leasaich; fàs.

development n leasachadh m.

deviate v claon.

device n innleachd f.

devil n diabhal m.

devious adj seachranach.

devise v innlich.

devolution n sgaoileadh-cumhachd m.

devolve v thig fo chùram; (political) sgaoil cumhachd.

devotion n cràbhadh m; teas-ghràdh m.

devour v sluig.

dew n dealt m.

dexterity n deisealachd f.

diagnose v breithnich.

diagnosis n breithneachadh m.

diagonal adj trasdanach.

dial n aodann m. • v comharraich àireamh.

diameter n meadhan-thrasdan m.

diarrhoea n a' bhuinneach f.

dice npl dìsnean.

dictate v deachd.

dictionary n faclair m.

die v bàsaich.

diesel n dìosail m.

diet n riaghailt bidhe f.

differ v eadar-dhealaich.

difference n eadar-dhealachadh m.

different adj air leth.

differentiate v diofaraich.

difficult adj duilich.

difficulty n duilgheadas m.

dig v cladhaich.

digest v cnàmh.

digestible adj so-chnàmhta.

digit n meur f; (number) meur-àireamh f.

digital adj meurach.

dignified adj urramaichte.

dilate v leudaich.

dilemma n imcheist f.

diligent adj dìcheallach.

dilute v tanaich.

dim adj doilleir; (person) mall 'na intinn.

dimension n tomhas m.

diminish v lùghdaich.

dimple n tibhre m.

din n toirm f.

dine v gabh dìnnear.

dining-room n seòmar-bidhe m.

dinner n dìnnear f.

dinner-time n tràth-dìnneireach m.

dip n tumadh m. • v tum, bog.

diplomacy n seòltachd f.

dipsomania n miann-daoraich m/f.

direct adj dìreach. • v seòl.

direction n seòladh m; àird f.

direction-finder n àird-lorgair m.

directly adv air ball; dìreach.

director n stiùiriche m.

dirk n biodag f.

dirt n salchar m.

dirty adj salach.

disability n neo-chomas m.

disadvantage n mì-leas m.

disagree v rach an aghaidh.

disagreement n eas-aonta f.

disappear v rach à sealladh.

disappoint v meall.

disapprove v coirich.

disaster n mòr-thubaist f.

disbelieve v dì-chreid.

disc n clàr m.

discard v cuir dhe.

discerning adj tuigseach.

discharge n di-luchdachadh m. • v di-luchdaich; cuir à dreuchd.

disclaim v àicheidh.

disclose v foillsich.

discomfort n anshocair f.

disconnect v sgaoil.

disconsolate adj brònach.

discontented adj mì-thoilichte.

discord n mì-chòrdadh m; (mus) dì-chòrda m.

discount n lasachadh m. • v lasaich.

discourage v mì-mhisnich.

discover v nochd; leig ris.

discovery n nochdadh m.

discrepancy n diofar m.

discretion n cùram m.

discriminate v (in favour of) gabh taobh f; (against) rach an aghaidh.

discuss v deasbair.

discussion n deasbaireachd f.

disease n euslaint f.

disembark v cuir air tìr.

disengage v dealaich.

disentangle v fuasgail.

disfavour n mì-fhàbhar m.

disgrace n masladh m. • v maslaich.

disgraceful adj maslach.

disguise n breug-riochd m. • v cuir breug-riochd air.

disgust n gràin f.

disgusting adj gràineil.

dish n soitheach m.

dish-cloth n tubhailt-shoithichean f.

dishearten v mì-mhisnich.

dishonest adj mì-onorach.

dishonesty n mì-onair f.

dishwasher n nigheadair-shoithich-ean m.

disillusion n briseadh-dùil m.

disinclined adj neo-thoileach.

disinherit v buin còir bhreith o.

disinterested adj neo-fhèin-chùiseach.

disjointed adj an-altaichte.

disk drive n clàr-inneal m.

disk n clàr m.

dislike v mì-thaitneamh.

dislodge v cuir à àite.

disloyal adj neo-dhìleas.

dismal adj dubhach.

dismay n uabhas m.

dismember v spion o chèile.

dismiss v cuir air falbh.

disobedience n eas-ùmhlachd f.

disobey v bi eas-umhail do.

disorder n mì-riaghailt f.

disown v na gabh ri.

disparity n neo-ionnanachd f.

dispel v fògair.

dispensation n riarachadh m.

dispense v riaraich.

dispersal n sgàpadh m.

displace v cuir à àite.

display n foillseachadh m. • v foills-ich.

displease v mì-thoilich.

dispose v suidhich.

disprove v breugnaich.

disputatious adj connsachail.

dispute v connsaich.

disqualification n neo-iomchaidh-eachd f.

disqualify v dèan neo-iomchaidh.

disregard v dèan dìmeas air.

disrepair n droch-chàradh m.

disrespect n eas-urram m.

disrupt v bris, reub.

disruption n briseadh m.

dissatisfaction n mì-thoileachadh m.

dissatisfied adj mì-riaraichte.

dissect v sgrùd; gèarr suas.

dissertation n tràchd f.

disservice n droch-chomain f.

dissimilar adj eu-coltach.

dissipate v sgap.

dissociate v eadar-sgar.

dissolute adj drùiseil.

dissolve v leagh; fuasgail.

dissuade v comhairlich an aghaidh.

distance n astar m, fad m.

distant adj cèin.

distaste n droch-bhlas m.

distasteful adj neo-bhlasta.

distil v tarraing.

distiller n grùdaire m.

distillery n taigh-staile m.

distinct adj soilleir.

distinction n eadar-dhealachadh m; (merit) cliù m.

distinctive adj so-aithnichte.

distinguish v eadar-dhealaich.

distort v fiaraich.

distract v buair.

distress n àmghar m. • v sàraich.

distribute v roinn, compàirtich.

district n ceàrn m.

district nurse n banaltram sgìre f.

distrust v an-earbsa.

disturb v cuir dragh air.

disturbance n aimhreit f.

disunite v eadar-sgar.

disunity n eadar-sgaradh m.

disuse n mì-chleachdeach m.

ditch n clais f.

ditto adv an nì ceudna.

ditty n luinneag f.

dive v daoìbhig.

diver n daoibhear m.

diverge v iomsgair.

diverse adj eugsamhail.

diversify v sgaoil.

diversion n claonadh m; (pastime) fearas-chuideachd f.

diversity n eugsamhlachd m.

divert v claon.

divide v roinn, pàirtich.

dividend n earrann f.

divination n fàistneachd f.

divine adj diadhaidh. • v dèan a-mach.

divisible adj so-roinnte.

division n roinn f.

divorce n dealachadh pòsaidh m. • v dealaich ri.

dizzy adj tuainealach.

do v dèan.

dock[1] n port m.

dock[2], **docken** n copag f.

dockyard n doca m.

doctor n lighiche, doctair m; (academic) ollamh m.

doctrine n teagasg m.

document n sgrìobhainn f.

documentary adj aithriseach.

dodge v seachainn.

doe n maoiseach f.

dog n cù m.

dogged adj doirbh, dùr.

dogmatic adj dìorrasach.

dole n dòil m.

dollar n dolair m.

domain n tighearnas m.

domestic adj teaghlachail.

domesticate v càllaich.

domicile n fàrdach f.

dominate v ceannsaich.

domineer v sàraich.

dominion n uachdranachd f.

donate v thoir tabhartas.

donor n tabhartaiche m.

doom n binn m. • v dìt.

doomsday n là-luain m.

door n doras m.

dope n druga, drugaichean f.

dose n tomhas m.

dot n puing f.

dotage n leanabachd na h-aoise f.

double adj dùbailte. • n dùbladh m. • v dùblaich.

double-bass n prò-bheus m.

doubt n teagamh m. • v cuir an teagamh.

doubtful adj teagmhach.

doubtless adv gun teagamh.

dough n taois f.

dour adj dùr.

down prep shìos, a-nuas.

downfall n tuiteam m.

downhill adv leis a' bruthach.

downright adv air fad.

downstairs adv shìos staidhre.

downward adj le bruthach.

downwards adv sìos.

dowry n tochradh m.

doze v rach an clò-chadal.

dozen n dusan m.

drag v slaod.

drain n drèana f. • v sìolaidh.

drake n dràc m.

dram n drama m.

dramatist n dràmaire m.

draught n (drink) tarraing f; (wind) gaoth troimh tholl. f

draughts n dàmais f.

draughtsman n neach-tarraing m.

draw v tarraing; (liquid) deoghail; (art) dèan dealbh.

drawer n drabhair m.

drawing n dealbh m/f.

drawing-pin n tacaid f.

dread n oillt f. • v oilltich.

dreadful adj eagalach.

dream n aisling f. • v bruadair, faic aisling.

dreamer n aislingiche m.

dredge v glan grùnnd.

dregs npl druaip f.

drench v dèan bog-fliuch.

dress v cuir aodach air.

dresser n dreasair m.

dressing n ìoc-chòmhdach m.

dribble v sil; (sport) drìoblaig.

drift v siab.

drill v drilich.

drilling platform n clàr-tollaidh m.

drink n deoch f. • v òl, gabh.

drinker n neach-òil m.

drip v snigh.

drive v greas; (car) stiùir.

drivel n briathran gòrach mpl, sgudal m.

driver n dràibhear m.

driving licence n cead-dràibhidh m.

drizzle n ciùthran m.

droll adj neònach; èibhinn.

drone n torman m; (pipes) dos m.

droop v searg.

drop n boinne f. • v leig às.

drought n turadh m.

drove n dròbh m.

drover n dròbhair m.

drown v bàth.

drowsy adj cadalach.

drudgery n dubh-chosnadh m.

drug addict n tràill-dhrugaichean m.

drug n droga f.

druggist n drugadair m.

druid n draoidh m.

druidism n draoidheachd f.

drum n druma f.

drum-major n màidseir-druma m.

drummer n drumair m.

drumstick n bioran-druma m.

drunk adj air misg.

drunkard n misgear m.

drunkenness n misg f.

dry adj tioram. • v tiormaich.

dub v dùblaich.

duck[1] n tunnag f.

duck[2] v tum; crùb.

dud n rud gun fheum m.

due adj dligheach.

duel n còmhrag-dithis f.

duet n òran-dithis m.

dull adj trom-inntinneach; tiugh.

dullness n truime m.

dulse n duileasg m.

duly adv gu riaghailteach.

dumb adj balbh.

dummy n fear-brèige m, breagag f.

dump n òcrach m. • v caith air falbh.

dumpling n turraisg f.

dunce n ùmaidh m.

dung *n* innear *f*.
dunghill *n* dùnan *m*.
duplicate *n* dùblachadh *m*.
duplicity *n* dùbailteachd *f*.
durable *adj* maireannach.
duration *n* fad *m*, rè *f*.
during *prep* rè.
dusk *n* duibhre *f*.
dusky *adj* ciar.
dust *n* dust, stùr *m*. • *v* glan stùrdhe.
dustbin *n* biona-stùir *m*.
Dutch *adj* Duitseach.
dutiful *adj* umhail.

duty *n* dleasdanas *m*; (*customs*) cìs-chusbainn *f*.
duty-free *adj* saor o chìs-chusbainn.
dwarf *n* troich *m*.
dwell *v* tuinich.
dwelling *n* fàrdach *f*.
dwindle *v* crìon.
dye *n* dath *m*. • *v* dath.
dyke *n* gàradh *m*.
dynamic *adj* fiùghantach.
dynamite *n* dineamait *m*.
dynasty *n* rìgh-shliochd *m*.
dyspepsia *n* an do-chnàmh *m*.

E

each *adj* gach, gach aon. • *pron* gach aon; an duine.
eager *adj* dealasach.
eagle *n* iolair *f*.
ear *n* cluas *f*.
earl *n* iarla *m*.
early *adj* tràth.
earn *v* coisinn.
earnest *adj* dùrachdach.
earphone *n* cluasan *m*.
earring *n* cluas-fhail *f*.
earth *n* talamh *f*.
earthenware *n* soitheach criadha *m*.
earthly *adj* talmhaidh.
earthworm *n* daolag *f*.
ease *n* fois *f*.
easel *n* dealbh-thaic *f*.
east *n* ear, an àirde an ear *f*.
Easter *n* Càisg *f*.
easterly *adj* an ear.
easy *adj* furasda.
eat *v* ith.
eatable *adj* so-ithte.

ebb *n* tràghadh *m*. • *v* tràigh.
eccentric *adj* iomrallach.
eccentricity *n* iomrallachd *f*.
echo *n* mac-talla *m*.
eclipse *n* dubhadh-grèine *m*; (*lunar*) dubhadh-gealaich *m*.
ecology *n* eag-eòlas *m*.
economics *n* eaconomachd *m*.
economise *v* caomhain.
economist *n* eaconomair *m*.
economy *n* eaconomaidh *f*; banas-taighe *m*.
ecstasy *n* àrd-èibhneas *m*.
ecstatic *adj* àrd-èibhneach.
ecumenical *adj* uil-eaglaiseil.
eddy *n* saobh-shruth *m*.
edge *n* oir, iomall *m*; faobhar *m*. • *v* dèan oir.
edgewise *adv* air oir.
edible *adj* so-ithte.
edict *n* reachd *m*.
edifice *n* aitreabh *m*.
edify *v* teagaisg.

Edinburgh n Dùn Èideann.
edit v deasaich.
edition n deasachadh m.
editor n deasaichear m.
educate v foghlaim.
education n foghlam m.
educational adj oideachail.
effect n buaidh f. • v thoir gu buil.
effective adj buadhach.
effeminate adj boireannta.
effervescent adj bruichneach.
efficacy n èifeachd f.
efficient adj èifeachdach.
effigy n ìomhaigh f.
effluent n sruthadh m.
effort n dìcheall m.
egg n ugh m.
egghead n eanchainn mhòr m.
egotism n fèin-spèis f.
Egypt n An Eiphit f.
eight n ochd.
eighteen n ochd deug.
eighth adj ochdamh.
eightsome n ochdnar m.
eightsome reel n ruidhle ochdnar m.
eighty n (old system) ceithir fichead; (new system) ochdad.
either conj either . . . or . . . an dara cuid . . . no . . . . • adv a bharrachd, nas motha.
ejaculate v cuir a-mach.
eject v tilg a-mach.
elaborate adj saothraichte.
elapse v rach seachad.
elastic adj sùbailte.
elate v tog suas.
elbow n uileann f.
elder n (church) eildear m; (tree) droman m. • adj nas sine.
elderly adj sean.
elect v tagh.

election n taghadh.
electioneering n taghadaireachd f.
elector n taghadair m.
electorate n luchd-taghaidh m.
electric adj dealain.
electricity n dealan m.
electrification n dealanachadh m.
electrocute v dealan-marbh.
electronic adj leactronach.
elegance n grinneas m.
elegant adj grinn.
elegiac adj caointeach.
elegy n tuireadh m.
element n dùil f.
elementary adj bun.
elephant n ailbhean m.
elevate v àrdaich.
eleven n aon deug.
eligible adj ion-roghnaidh.
eliminate v geàrr às.
elixir n ìocshlaint f.
elm n leamhan m.
elongate v fadaich.
elope v teich.
eloquence n deas-bhriathrachd f.
else adj/adv eile.
elude v seachainn.
elusive adj èalaidheach.
e-mail n post dealain m.
emancipate v saor.
embalm v spìosraich.
embargo n bacadh m.
embark v cuir air bòrd.
embarrass v cuir troimhe chèile.
embarrassment n beag-nàrachadh m.
embassy n tosgaireachd f.
ember n èibhleag f.
embezzle v dèan maoin-èalachadh.
emboss v gràbhail.
embrace v iath an glacaibh.

embroider *v* cuir obair-ghrèis air.
embryo *n* suth *m*.
emerald *n* smàrag *f*.
emerge *v* thig an uachdar.
emergency *n* bàlanaich *m*.
emigrant *n* eilthireach *m*.
emigrate *v* dèan eilthireachd.
eminent *adj* àrd.
emit *v* leig a-mach.
emotion *n* tòcadh *m*.
emotional *adj* tòcail.
emphasis *n* cudrom *m*.
emphatic *adj* làidir.
empire *n* ìompaireachd *f*.
empirical *adj* deuchainneach.
employ *v* fasdaich.
employee *n* neach-obrach *m*.
employer *n* fastaidhear *m*.
empty *adj* falamh.
emulation *n* strì *f*.
enable *v* dèan comasach.
enact *v* òrdaich.
enamel *n* cruan *m*.
enchant *v* cuir fo gheasaibh.
enchantment *n* draoidheachd *f*.
enclosure *n* crò *m*.
encourage *v* misnich.
encroach *v* thig a-steach.
encumbrance *n* uallach *m*.
end *n* deireadh *m*, crìoch *f*. • *v* cuir crìoch air.
endemic *adj* dùthchasach.
endless *adj* neo-chrìochnach.
endorse *v* cùl-sgrìobh.
endowment *n* bronnadh *m*.
enemy *n* nàmhaid *m*.
energetic *adj* brìoghmhor.
energy *n* brìogh *f*.
enforce *v* co-èignich.
engagement *n* gealladh-pòsaidh *m*.
engine *n* inneal *m*.

engineer *n* innleadair *m*. • *v* innlich.
England *n* Sasainn *f*.
English *n* Beurla *f*.
Englishman *n* Sasannach *m*.
enhance *v* meudaich.
enigma *n* dubhfhacal *m*.
enjoy *v* meal.
enlarge *v* meudaich.
enlighten *v* soillsich.
enlist *v* liostaig.
enormous *adj* uabhasach.
enough *adv* gu lèor.
enquire *v* feòraich.
enrage *v* feargaich.
ensue *v* lean.
ensure *v* dèan cinnteach.
enter *v* rach/thig a-steach.
enterprise *n* iomairt *f*.
enterprising *adj* ionnsaigheach.
entertainer *n* oirfideach *m*.
entertainment *n* aoigheachd *f*.
enthusiasm *n* dìoghras *m*.
entice *v* tàlaidh.
entire *adj* iomlan.
entirely *adv* gu lèir.
entitle *v* thoir còir.
entrance *n* dol a-steach *m*.
entreat *v* guidh.
entrepreneur *n* neach-tionnsgain *m*.
envelope *n* cèis *f*.
environment *n* comhearsnachd *f*; (*ecology*) àrainn-eachd *f*.
envy *n* farmad *m*.
ephemeral *adj* geàrr-shaoglach.
episode *n* tachartas *m*.
epitaph *n* leac-sgrìobhadh *m*.
epoch *n* tùs-aimsir *f*.
equal *adj* seise.
equalise *v* dèan co-ionann; (*game*) ruig an aon àireamh.
equation *n* co-ionannas *m*.

equator *n* meadhan-chearcall na talmhainn *m*.

equidistant *adj* co-fhad air falbh.

equinox *n* co-fhreagradh nan tràth *m*.

equip *v* uidheamaich.

equipment *n* uidheam *f*.

equipped *adj* uidheamaichte.

equity *n* ceartas *m*; (*fin*) stoc-roinn *f*.

equivalent *adj* co-ionann.

erase *v* dubh às.

erect *v* tog.

erection *n* togail *m*.

erode *v* meirg.

erotic *adj* drùis-mhiannach.

err *v* rach iomrall.

errand *n* gnothach *m*.

erratic *adj* iomrallach.

error *n* mearrachd *f*.

eruption *n* brùchdach *m*.

escalator *n* streapadan *m*.

escape *n* èaladh *m*. • *v* teich.

esoteric *adj* às an rathad.

essay *n* aiste *f*.

essence *n* gnè *f*.

essential *adj* riatanach.

establish *v* suidhich.

estate *n* oighreachd *f*.

esteem *n* meas *m*.

estimate *v* meas.

estrange *v* dèan fuathach.

estuary *n* inbhir *m*.

eternal *adj* bith-bhuan.

eternity *n* sìorraidheachd *f*.

ethical *adj* modhannach.

ethnic *adj* cinnidheach.

eunuch *n* caillteanach *m*.

Europe *n* An Roinn Eòrpa *f*.

European *adj* Eòrpach.

evaporate *v* deataich.

even *adj* rèidh. • *adv* eadhon; fhèin.

evening *n* feasgar *m*.

event *n* tuiteamas *m*.

ever *adv* aig àm sam bith, idir.

evergreen *adj* sìor-uaine.

everlasting *adj* sìorraidh.

evermore *adv* gu bràth.

every *adj* gach, na h-uile.

everyday *adj* làitheil.

everyone *pron* gach duine.

everything *pron* gach nì.

evict *v* fuadaich.

eviction *n* fuadachadh *m*.

evidence *n* fianais *f*.

evident *adj* soilleir.

evil *adj* olc. • *n* olc *m*.

ewe *n* othaisg *f*.

exact *adj* pongail.

exact *v* buin.

exactly *adv* dìreach.

exaggerate *v* cuir am meud.

examination *n* ceasnachadh *m*.

examine *v* ceasnaich.

example *n* eisimpleir *m*.

excavate *v* cladhaich.

excavation *n* cladhach *m*.

exceed *v* rach thairis air.

exceedingly *adv* glè.

excel *v* thoir bàrr.

excellence *n* feabhas *m*.

excellent *adj* barrail.

except *v* fàg a-mach. • *prep* ach a-mhàin; **except for** saor o.

exceptional *adj* sònraichte.

exchange rate *n* luach-iomlaid *m*.

exchange *v* malairtich.

exchequer *n* stàitchiste *f*.

exciseman *n* gàidsear *m*.

excite *v* gluais.

excitement *n* brosnachadh *m*.

exclaim *v* glaodh.

exclamation mark *n* clisg-phuing *f*.

exclamation *n* glaodh *m*.

exclusive *adj* dlùth.

excrement *n* cac *m*.

excrete *v* cac.

excuse *n* leisgeul *m*. • *v* gabh leisgeul, math.

executive *n* neach-gnìomha *m*.

executor *n* neach-cùraim tiomnaidh *m*.

exercise *n* eacarsaich *f*. • *v* obraich, cleachd.

exertion *n* spàirn *f*.

exhaust *v* falmhaich.

exhaustion *n* traoghadh *m*.

exile *n* fògarrach *m*.

exist *v* bi, bi beò.

existence *n* bith *f*.

exit *n* dol a-mach *m*.

exonerate *v* fìreanaich.

exorbitant *adj* ana-cuimseach.

exotic *adj* coimheach.

expand *v* sgaoil.

expatriate *adj* às-dhùthchach.

expect *v* bi dùil aig.

expedient *adj* coltach.

expedite *v* luathaich.

expedition *n* turas *m*.

expeditious *adj* cabhagach.

expend *v* caith.

expenditure *n* caiteachas *m*.

expensive *adj* cosgail.

experience *n* cleachdadh *m*. • *v* mothaich.

experiment *n* ɖeuchainn *f*.

expert *adj* ealanta. • *n* eòlaiche *m*.

expire *v* analaich; (*die*) bàsaich.

explain *v* mìnich.

explanation *n* mìneachadh *m*.

explicit *adj* fosgailte.

explode *v* spreadh.

exploit *n* euchd *m*. • *v* dèan feum de.

explore *v* rannsaich.

export *n* eas-tharraing *f*. • *v* cuir thairis.

expose *v* nochd.

exposure *n* nochdadh *m*.

express train *n* luath-thrèana.

express[1] *v* cuir an cèill.

express[2] *adj* luath.

expression *n* fiamh *m*.

exquisite *adj* òirdheirc.

extensive *adj* leathann.

exterior *n* taobh a-muigh *m*.

extinct *adj* bàthte.

extinguish *v* smàl.

extinguisher *n* smàladair *m*.

extra *adj* fìor, ro-. • *adv* a bharrachd.

extraordinary *adj* anabarrach.

extravagant *adj* ana-caiteach.

extreme *adj* fìor.

extricate *v* saor.

extrovert *n* duine fosgarra *m*.

exuberance *n* braise.

exuberant *adj* bras.

eye *n* sùil *f*. • *v* seall.

eyesight *n* fradharc *m*.

eyesore *n* cùis mhì-thlachd *f*.

eyrie *n* nead iolaire *m*.

F

fable n uirsgeul m.

fabric n aodach m; togalach m.

facade n aghaidh f.

face n aghaidh, gnùis f.

facet n taobh m.

facilitate v soirbhich.

facilities npl goireasan.

fact n beart m.

factor n seumarlan m.

factory n factaraidh m.

faculty n comas m; (university) dàmh m.

fad n àilleas m.

fade v searg.

fail v dìobair.

failure n fàilinn f.

faint adj fann. • v fannaich.

fair n fèill.

fairly adv an ìre mhath.

fairness n maisealachd f.

fairway n prìomh-raon m.

fairy adj sìdh. • n sìdhiche m.

faith n creideamh m.

faithful adj dìleas.

fake n rud brèige m.

fall n tuiteam m. • v tuit.

fallacy n saobh-chiall f.

fallow adj bàn.

false adj meallta.

falsehood n breug f.

falter v lagaich.

fame n cliù m.

familiar adj càirdeil.

familiarise v gnàthaich.

family n teaghlach m.

famine n goirt f.

famous adj ainmeil.

fanatic n eudmhoraiche m.

fancy adj guanach. • v smaoinich.

fank n faing f.

fantastic adj ro-iongantach.

fantasy n sgeul guaineis m.

far adj fada, fad às. • adv fada, fas às.

fare n faradh m; biadh m.

farewell n soraidh m.

farm n baile-fearainn, tuathanas m.

farmer n tuathanach m.

fart n (audible) braidhm m; (inaudible) tùd m.

farther adv nas fhaide.

fascinate v cuir fo gheasaibh.

fascination n geasachd f.

fascism n faisisteachas m.

fashion n fasan m. • v cum.

fashionable adj fasanta.

fast adj luath; daingeann.

fast food n grad-bhiadh m.

fasten v ceangail.

fastidious adj àilleasach.

fat adj reamhar. • n reamhrachd m.

fatal adj marbhtach.

fate n dàn m.

father n athair m. • v bi mar athair.

father-in-law n athair-cèile m.

fatherly adj athaireil.

fathom v ruig air.

fatigue n sgìos f. • v sgìthich.

fatuous adj baoth.

fault n coire f.

faultless adj neo-chiontach.

faulty adj easbhaidheach.

favour v bi fàbharach.

favourite n annsachd f.

fawn n mang f.

fax n facs m.

fear n eagal m. • v gabh eagal.

fearful adj eagalach.

fearless adj gun eagal.

feast n fèisd f, fleadh m.• v dèan fèist.

feat n euchd m.

feather n ite f.

February n An Gearran m.

federal adj feadarail.

fee n duais f.

feeble adj fann.

feed v biath.

feel v fairich.

feeling n faireachdainn f.

felicitous adj sona.

feline adj mar chat.

fellowship n companas m.

felon n slaoightear m.

female adj boireann, baineann.

feminine adj banail.

fence n lann. • v dùin.

fender n dìonadair m.

ferment n brachadh m. • v brach.

fermentation n brachadh m.

fern n raineach f.

ferret n feocallan m.

ferry n aiseag m. • v aisig.

ferry-boat n bàta-aiseig.

fertile adj torach.

fertilise v toraich.

fertility n torachas m.

fervent adj dian.

fervour n dèine f.

fester v at.

festive adj fleadhach.

fetch v faigh.

feu n gabhail m.

feud n falachd f.

fever n fiabhras m.

feverish adj fiabhrasach.

few adj beag, tearc. • n beagan m.

fibre n snàithleach m.

fibrous adj snàithlainneach.

fickle adj caochlaideach.

fiction n uirsgeul m.

fiddle n fidheall f. • v dèan fidhleireachd; foillich.

fiddler n fidhlear m.

fidelity n dìlseachd f.

field n achadh m.

field-glasses n prosbaig f.

field-mouse n luch-fheòir f.

fierce adj garg.

fierceness n gairge f.

fiery adj teinnteach.

fifteen n còig deug.

fifth adj còigeamh.

fiftieth adj leth-cheudamh; (old system) an dà fhiceadamh 's a deich; (new system) an caogadamh.

fifty n leth-cheud; (old system) dà fhichead 's a deich; (new system) caogad.

fig n fìogais f.

fight n còmhrag f. • v còmhraig.

figure n dealbh m; figear m.

file n eighe f; (documents) còmhlachadh m. • v lìomh; còmhlaich.

filial adj macail.

fill v lìon.

fillet v colpaich.

filly n loth f.

film-star n reul film m, reultag film f.

filter n sìolachan m. • v sìolaidh.

filth n salchar m.

filthy adj salach.

final adj deireannach.

finalise v thoir gu crìch.

finance *n* maoineachas *m.* • *v* maoinich.

financier *n* maoiniche *m.*

find *v* faigh, lorg.

fine[1] *adj* grinn.

fine[2] *n* ùnnlagh *m.* • *v* leag ùnnlagh.

finery *n* rìomhachas *m.*

finger *n* meur, corrag *f.*

fingernail *n* ìne *f.*

finish *n* crìoch *f.* • *v* crìochnaich.

fir *n* giuthas *m.*

fire *n* teine *m.* • *v* cuir 'na theine.

fire-arm *n* airm-theine *m.*

fire-escape *n* staidhre-èalaidh *f.*

fire-proof *adj* teine-dhìonach.

fireside *n* teallach *m.*

firewood *n* fiodh connaidh *m.*

firm[1] *adj* teann.

firm[2] *n* companaidh *f.*

first *adj* a' chiad. • *adv* (*time*) an toiseach; (*sequence*) air thoiseach.

first aid *n* ciad-fhuasgladh *m.*

first-born *n* ciad-ghin *m.*

firth *n* caol *m.*

fiscal *adj* fioscail.

fish *n* iasg *m.* • *v* iasgaich.

fisher *n* iasgair *m.*

fishing *n* iasgaireachd *f.*

fishing rod *n* slat-iasgaich *f.*

fishing-line *n* driamlach *m.*

fishy *adj* mar iasg; neònach.

fist *n* dòrn *m.*

fit[1] *adj* freagarrach.

fit[2] *n* taom *m.*

five *adj/n* còig.

fix *v* dèan teann; suidhich.

fixture *n* rud socraichte *m.*

fizz *n* copraich *f.*

flabby *adj* plamach.

flag *n* bratach *f.*

flagrant *adj* follaiseach.

flagstone *n* leac *f.*

flair *n* liut *m.*

flake *n* bleideag *f.*

flame *n* lasair *f.*

flannel *n* flannain *f.*

flap *n* cleiternach *m.* • *v* crath.

flare *n* lasair-bhoillsg *m.*

flash *n* lasair *f.* • *v* boillsg.

flask *n* searrag *f.*

flat[1] *adj* còmhnard; (*mus*) maol, flat.

flat[2] *n* còmhnard *m*; flat *m.*

flatten *v* laigh ri; (*mus*) maolaich.

flatter *v* dèan sodal.

flattery *n* sodal *m.*

flautist *n* cuisleannach *m.*

flavour *n* blas *m.* • *v* blasaich.

flea *n* deargann *f.*

fleece *n* rùsg *m.* • *v* rùisg.

fleecy *adj* rùsgach.

fleet *n* cabhlach *m.*

fleeting *adj* siùbhlach.

flesh *n* feòil *f.*

fleshy *adj* sultmhor.

flex *n* fleisg *f.*

flexible *adj* so-lùbaidh.

flicker *v* priob.

flight *n* itealadh *m.*

flimsy *adj* tana.

flinch *v* clisich.

flint *n* ailbhinn *f.*

flippant *adj* beadaidh.

flit *v* èalaidh; (*house*) dèan imrich.

float *v* snàmh.

flock *n* treud *m.*

flood *n* tuil *f.* • *v* còmhdaich le uisge.

floodlight *n* tuil-sholas *m.*

floor *n* ùrlar *m.* • *v* cuir ùrlar ann.

floppy disk *n* clàr sùbailte *m.*

floral *adj* flùranach.

flounder n leòbag f.

flour n flùr m.

flourish v fàs gu math; beartaich.

flow v ruith.

flower n blàth, flùr m.

fluctuate v atharraich.

fluency n fileantachd f.

fluent adj fileanta.

fluid adj silteach. • n lionn m.

flush v fàs dearg; (toilet) sruth-laich.

fluster v cuir gu cabhaig.

flute n cuisle chiùil f.

fly[1] n cuileag f; (fishing) maghar m.

fly[2] v theirig air iteig.

fly[3] adj carach.

foal n searrach m.

foam n cop m. • v cuir cop dhe.

focus n cruinn-ionad m; fòcas m. • v faigh cruinn-shealladh.

fodder n fodar m.

foetus n toircheas m.

fog n ceò m/f.

foggy adj ceòthach.

foil v cuir casg air.

fold n buaile f. • v cuir an crò.

folded adj fillte.

foliage n duilleach m.

folk n muinntir f.

folklore n beul-aithris f.

folk-song n mith-òran m.

folk-tale n mith-sgeul.

follow v lean.

folly n amaideachd m.

fond adj dèidheil.

fondle v cniadaich.

food n biadh m.

fool n amadan m. • v thoir an car à.

foolish adj gòrach.

foolproof adj do-mhillte.

foot n cas, troigh f.

footpath n frith-rathad m.

footwear n caisbheart f.

for prep (to) do • pron **for me** dhomh; **for you** (sing) dhut; **for him, it** dhà; **for us** dhuinn; **for you** (pl) dhuibh; **for them** dhaibh; (for the sake of) airson • pron **for me** air mo shon; **for you** (sing) air do shon; **for him, it** air a shon; **for her** air a son; **for us** air ar son; **for you** (pl) air ur son; **for them** air an son; (because) a chionn; (instead of) an àite; (on account of) do bhrìgh.

forage v solair.

forbid v toirmisg.

forbidding adj gruamach.

force n neart m. • v co-èignich.

forceps n teanchair m.

ford n àth m.

fore adj toisich.

forearm n ruighe f.

forecast n ro-aithris f. • v ro-aithris.

forefather n sinnsear m.

forefinger n sgealbag f.

forego v fàg.

foreground n ro-ionad m.

forehead n bathais m.

foreign adj gallda, coimheach.

foreigner n Gall, coigreach m.

foreknow v ro-aithnich.

foreknowledge n ro-aithne f.

foremost adj prìomh.

forerunner n ro-ruithear m.

foresail n seòl-toisich m.

foresee v faic ro làimh.

foresight n ro-shealladh m.

forest n coille f.

forester n forsair m.

forestry n forsaireachd f.

foretaste n ro-bhlasad m.

foretell v ro-innis.

forever adv a chaoidh.

forewarn v cuir air earalas.

foreword n ro-ràdh m.

forge v dèan goibhneachd.

forger n fallsaidhear m.

forget v dìochuimhnich.

forgetful adj dìochuimhneach.

forgetfulness n dìochuimhne f.

forgive v thoir mathanas.

forgotten adj air dìochuimhne.

fork n greimire, forc m. • v fàs gòbh-lach.

forlorn adj aonaranach.

form n cumadh m. • v dealbh, cum.

formal adj dòigheil, foirmeil.

formality n deas-ghnàth m.

format n cruth m.

formidable adj cumhachdach.

formula n foirmle f.

formulate v riaghailich.

fornicate v dèan strìopachas.

fornication n strìopachas f.

forsake v cuir cùl ri.

forsaken adj trèigte.

fort n daingneach f, dùn m.

forth adv a-mach.

forthwith adv gun dàil.

fortitude n cruadal m.

fortnight n cola-deug f.

fortuitous adj tuiteamach.

fortunate adj fortanach.

fortune n sealbh m.

fortuneteller n fiosaiche m.

forty adj/n (old system) dà fhichead; (new system) ceathrad.

forward adj iarrtach. • adv air adhart.

forwards adv air adhart.

fossil n fosail f.

foster v altrum.

foster-father n oide m.

foster-mother n muime f.

foster-sibling n co-dhalta m.

foul[1] adj breun.

foul[2] n fealladh m.

found v stèidhich.

foundation n stèidh f.

founder[1] n stèidhichear f.

founder[2] v theirig fodha.

foundling n faodalach m.

fountain n fuaran m.

four adj/n ceithir; (persons) ceathrar.

foursome n ceathrach f.

fourteen adj/n ceithir deug.

fourteenth adj ceathramh deug.

fourthly adv sa cheathramh àite.

fowl n eun m.

fox n sionnach m.

fraction n bloigh f.

fracture n bristeadh m.

fragile adj brisg.

fragment n fuigheall m.

fragrant adj cùbhraidh.

frail adj lag.

frailty n laige f.

frame n cèis f.

France n An Fhraing f.

frank adj faoilidh.

frank v (stamp) saor.

frantic adj air bhoile.

fraternal adj bràithreil.

fraud n foill f.

freak n tuiteamas m.

freckled adj breac-bhallach.

freckles npl breacadh-seunain m.

free adj saor; an-asgaidh.

free trade n saor-mhalairt f.

free will n saor-thoil f.

freedom n saorsa f.
freelance adj neo-cheangailte.
freemason n saor-chlachair m.
free-range adj saor-thogta.
freeze v reòth.
freezer n reòthadair m.
freight n luchd m.
French adj Frangach. • n Fraingis f.
frenzy n boile f.
frequency n tricead m.
frequent adj tric. • v tadhail.
fresh adj (air) fionnar; (food) ùr.
fret v luaisg.
fretful adj frionasach.
friar n bràthair-bochd m.
friction n suathadh m.
Friday n DihAoine m.
friend n caraid m, bana-charaid f.
friendliness n càirdeas m.
friendly adj càirdeil.
fright n eagal m.
frighten v cuir eagal air.
frightful adj oillteil.
frigid adj fuar.
frill n grinneas m.
frisky adj mireagach.
frivolity n faoineas m.
frivolous adj faoin.
fro adv air ais.
frock n froca m.
frog n losgann m.
from prep o • pron **from me** uam;
  from you (*sing*) uat; **from him, it**
  uaidhe; **from her** uaipe; **from us**
  uainn; **from you** (*pl*) uaibh; **from**
  them uapa; (*out of & from a*
  place) à • pron **from me** asam;
  from you (*sing*) asad; **from him, it**
  ás; **from her** aiste; **from us** asainn;
  from you (*pl*) asaibh; **from them**
  asta.

front n aghaidh f.
front-door n doras-mòr m.
frontier n crìoch f.
frost n reòthadh m.
frostbitten adj reo-sheargte.
frosty adj (*frozen*) reòta.
frown n gruaim f.
frugal adj glèidhteach.
frugality n glèidhteachd f.
fruit n meas m.
fruity adj measach.
frustrate v mill dùil.
fry v ròsd.
frying pan n aghann f.
fuck v rach air muin.
fuel n connadh m.
fugitive n fògarrach m.
fulfil v coilion.
fulfilment n coilionadh m.
full adj làn.
full stop n stad phuing f.
full-grown adj aig làn fhàs.
full-time adj làn-aimsireach.
fumble v làimhsich gu cearbach.
fun n spòrs f.
function key n (*comput*) iuchair-
  gnìomha f.
function n dreuchd f.
fundamental adj bunaiteach.
funeral n adhlacadh m.
funny adj sùgach, èibhinn.
fur n bian m.
furnish v uidheamaich.
furniture n àirneis f.
furrow n clais f.
furry adj molach.
further, furthermore adv rud eile, a
  bhàrr air sinn.
fury n cuthach m.
fuse n leagadh m.
fusty adj malcaidh.

futile *adj* dìomhain.
futility *n* dìomhanas *m*.

future *adj* ri teachd. • *n* àm ri teachd *m*.

G

gable *n* stuadh *f*.
gadget *n* uidheam *f*.
Gael *n* Gàidheal *m*.
Gaelic *adj/n* Gàidhlig.
gaiety *n* cridhealas *m*.
gaily *adv* gu cridheil.
gain *v* buannaich.
gale *n* gaoth mhòr *f*.
gallant *adj* basdalach.
gallery *n* lobhta *m*.
galley *n* birlinn *f*.
gallon *n* galan *m*.
gallop *v* luath-mharcaidh.
Galloway *n* A' Ghall-Ghàidhealtachd *f*.
gallows *n* croich *f*.
galore *adv* gu lèor.
gamble *v* iomair air gheall.
gambler *n* ceàrraiche *m*.
gambling *n* ceàrrachas *m*.
game *n* cluiche *f*; (*meat*) sitheann *f*.
gamekeeper *n* geamair *m*.
gander *n* gànradh *m*.
gang *n* buidheann *f*.
gannet *n* sùlaire *m*.
gaol *n* prìosan *m*.
gap *n* beàrn *m*.
gape *v* spleuchd.
garage *n* garaids *f*.
garbage *n* fuighleach *m*.
garble *v* cuir às a riochd.
garden *n* lios *m*.
gardener *n* gàirnealair *m*.
garland *n* blàth-fhleasg *f*.
garlic *n* creamh *m*.

garment *n* bad aodaich *m*.
garron *n* gearran *m*.
garrulity *n* goileam *m*.
garrulous *adj* cabach.
garter *n* gartan *m*.
gas fire *n* teine gas *m*.
gas-cooker *n* cucair-gas *m*.
gash *n* gearradh *m*.
gasp *v* plosg.
gastronomic *adj* sòghail.
gastronomy *n* sòghalachd *f*.
gate *n* geata *m*.
gather *v* cruinnich.
gathering *n* cruinneachadh *m*.
gaudy *adj* basdalach.
gauge *n* tomhas *m*.
gaunt *adj* lom.
gawky *adj* sgleòideach.
gay *adj* sùnndach; (*sexuality*) co-sheòrsach.
gaze *v* dùr-amharc.
gear *n* (*car*) gèar *m*.
gem *n* seud *m*.
gender *n* gnè *f*.
genealogical *adj* sloinnnteachail.
genealogist *n* sloinntear *m*.
genealogy *n* sloinntearachd *f*.
general *adj* coitcheann.
generalise *v* ginearalaich.
generally *adv* am bitheantas.
generation *n* àl *m*; linn *m*.
generator *n* gineadair *m*.
generic *adj* gnèitheach.
generosity *n* fialaidheachd *f*.
generous *adj* fial.

genetic *adj* ginteil.

genial *adj* coibhneil.

genitals *npl* buill gineamhainn.

genius *n* sàr-ghin *m*.

genteel *adj* suairce.

gentle *adj* ciùin.

gentleman *n* duine uasal *m*.

gentlewoman *n* bean uasal *f*.

gentry *npl* uaislean.

genuine *adj* fìor.

geography *n* cruinn-eòlas *m*.

geological *adj* geòlach.

geologist *n* geòlaiche *m*.

geology *n* geòlas *m*.

geometry *n* geoimeatras *m*.

germ *n* bitheag *f*.

German *n* Gearmailteach *m*. • *adj* Gearmailteach.

Germany *n* A' Ghearmailt *f*.

germinate *v* ginidich.

gestation *n* torrachas *m*.

gesture *n* gluasad *m*.

get *v* faigh, coisinn.

ghastly *adj* oillteil.

ghost *n* taibhse *m/f*, bòcan *m*.

ghostly *adj* taibhseil.

giant *adj* ana-mhòr. • *n* famhair *m*.

gibber *v* dèan goileam.

gibe *n* sgeig *f*.

giddy *adj* guanach.

gift *n* tiodhlac *m*.

gifted *adj* tàlantach.

gigantic *adj* fuamhaireil.

gild *v* òraich.

gill *n* giùran *m*.

gin *n* sine *f*; (*trap*) ribe *f*.

gingerbread *n* aran-crì *m*.

gipsy *n* giofag *f*.

giraffe *n* sioraf *m*.

girdle *n* greideal *f*.

girl *n* caileag, nighean *f*.

girth *n* giort *f*.

give *v* thoir.

glaciation *n* eighreachadh *m*.

glacier *n* eighre-shruth *m*.

glad *adj* toilichte.

glance *n* grad-shealladh *m*. • *v* grad-amhairc.

gland *n* fàireag *f*.

glare *n* deàrrsadh *m*.

Glasgow *n* Glaschu *f*.

glass *n* glainne *f*.

glassy *adj* glainneach.

gleam *v* soillsich.

glean *v* dìoghlam.

glee *n* mire *f*.

glen *n* gleann *m*.

glib *adj* cabanta.

glide *v* gluais.

glimmer *n* fann-sholas *m*.

glister *v* deàrrs.

glitter *n* lainnir *f*.

gloaming *n* fionnaraigh *f*.

global *adj* domhanta.

global warming *n* blàthachadh na cruinne *m*.

globe *n* cruinne *f*.

gloom *n* duibhre *f*.

gloomy *adj* doilleir.

glory *n* glòir *f*.

glossy *adj* lìomharra.

glove *n* miotag *f*.

glow *n* luisne *f*. • *v* luisnich.

glower *v* seall fo na mùgan.

glue *n* glaodh *m*.

glum *adj* gruamach.

glutton *n* craosaire *m*.

gluttony *n* craos *m*.

gnash *v* gìos.

gnaw *v* creim.

go *v* falbh, imich, theirich, rach, gabh.

goal n crìoch f; gòil m.
goalie n neach-bàire m.
goalpost n post-bàire m.
goat n gobhar m.
goblin n bòcan m.
god n dia m.
goddess n ban-dia f.
going n falbh m.
gold n òr m.
golden adj òir, òrach.
golf n goilf m.
good adj math, deagh.
goodbye interj mar sin leat; beannachd leat.
goodness n mathas m.
goods npl bathar m; (possessions) cuid f.
goodwill n gean math m.
goose n gèadh f.
gooseberry n gròiseid f.
gore v sàth.
gorge[1] n clais-mhòr f.
gorge[2] v lìon craos.
gorgeous adj greadhnach.
gorse n conasg m.
gory adj gaorrach.
gospel n soisgeul m.
gossip n goistidh m. • v bi a' gobaireachd.
govern v riaghail.
government n riaghaltas m.
gown n gùn m.
grab v gabh grèim air.
grace n gràs m; (prayer) altachadh m; (manner) loinn m. • v sgeadaich.
graceful adj maiseach.
grace-note n nota-altaidh m.
gracious adj gràsmhor.
grade n ceum m.
gradient n àrdachadh m.

gradual adj beag is beag.
gradually adv beag is beag.
graduate n ceumnaiche m.
graduation n ceumnachadh m.
graft n nòdachadh m. • v nòdaich; (toil) saothraich.
grain n gràinne f.
graip n gràpa m.
granary n sìol-lann f.
grand adj mòr, uasal.
grandchild n ogha m.
grandeur n mòrachd f.
grandfather n seanair m.
grandmother n seanmhair f.
granite n clach-ghràin f.
grant n tabhartas m.
granular adj cnapach.
grape n fìon-dearc f.
grapefruit n seadag f.
grapple v greimich.
grasp n grèim m. • v dèan grèim air, glac.
grass n feur m.
grassy adj feurach.
grate n cliath-theine f.
grate v sgrìob.
grateful adj taingeil.
grater n sgrìoban m.
gratitude n taingealachd f.
gratuity n tiodhlac m.
grave[1] adj stòlda.
grave[2] n uaigh f.
gravel n grinneal m.
gravestone n leac-uaghach f.
graveyard n cladh m.
gravity n iom-tharraing f.
graze[1] v (browse) feuraich.
graze[2] v (scrape) suath.
grease n saill f. • v crèisich.
greasy adj crèiseach.
great adj mòr; àrd.

greatness *n* mòrachd *f.*
Greece *n* A' Ghrèig *f.*
greed *n* sannt *m.*
greedy *adj* sanntach.
Greek *adj* Grèigeach. • *n* Grèigis *f.*
green *adj* uaine.
greenness *n* uainead *m.*
greet *v* fàiltich.
greeting *n* fàilte *f.*
gregarious *adj* greigheach.
grey *adj* glas, liath.
grey-haired *adj* liath.
grid *n* cliath *f.*
griddle *n* greideal *f.*
grief *n* mulad *m.*
grieve *v* cràidh.
grill *v* grìosaich.
grilse *n* bànag *f.*
grim *adj* gnù.
grimace *n* mùig *m.*
grin *n* braoisg *f.* • *v* cuir braosg air.
grind *v* meil.
gristle *n* maothan *m.*
grit *n* grian *m.*
grizzled *adj* grìsfhionn.
groan *n* cnead *m.* • *v* dèan cnead.
groceries *n* bathair grosaireach *m.*
groin *n* loch-bhlèin *f.*
groove *n* clais *f.*
grope *v* rùraich.
gross[1] *adj* dòmhail.
gross[2] *n* dà dhusan deug *m.*
grotesque *adj* mì-nàdurrach.
ground *n* grùnnd *m.* • *v* socraich.
group *n* còmhlan *m.*
grouse[1] *n* (*bird*) eun-fhraoich *m.*

grouse[2] *n* (*grumble*) gearan *m.*
grove *n* doire *m.*
grovel *v* snàig.
grow *v* fàs, meudaich.
growl *n* dranndan *m.* • *v* dèan dranndan.
growth *n* fàs *m.*
grudge *n* diomb *m.* • *v* talaich.
grumble *v* gearain.
grunt *n* gnòsail *f.* • *v* dèan gnòsail.
guarantee *n* barrantas *m.*
guard *n* faire *f*; (*individual*) freic-eadan *m.* • *v* dìon.
guardian *n* (*tutor*) taoitear *m.*
guess *n* tomhas *m.* • *v* tomhais.
guest *n* aoigh *m.*
guide *n* treòraiche *m.* • *v* treòr-aich.
guided missile *n* urchair thrèor-aichte *f.*
guillemot *n* eun dubh an sgadain *m.*
guilt *n* ciont *m.*
guilty *adj* ciontach.
gulf *n* camas *m.*
gully *n* gìl *f.*
gulp *n* slugadh *m.* • *v* sluig.
gum *n* càireas.
gumption *n* ciall *f.*
gun *n* gunna *m.*
gunwale *n* beul-mòr *m.*
gurgle *n* glugan *m.*
gust *n* oiteag *f.*
gusto *n* cridhealas *m.*
gusty *adj* stoirmeil.
gut *n* caolan *m.*

H

habit *n* cleachdadh *m*; (*monk*) earradh *m*.
habitual *adj* gnàthach.
hack *v* geàrr.
haddock *n* adag *f*.
haft *n* cas *m*.
hag *n* cailleach *f*.
haggis *n* taigeis *f*.
haggle *v* dèan còmhstri mu phrìs.
hailstones *npl* clachan-meallain.
hair *n* falt *m*.
hairy *adj* molach.
half *n* leth *m*.
half-bottle *n* leth-bhotal *m*.
half-way *adj* leathach-slighe.
hall *n* talla *m/f*.
Hallowe'en *n* Oidhche Shamhna *f*.
hallucination *n* mearachadh *m*.
halo *n* fàinne-solais *f*.
halt *v* stad.
halter *n* aghastar *m*.
halve *v* roinn 'na dhà leth.
ham *n* hama *m*.
hamlet *n* clachan *m*.
hammer *n* òrd *m*. • *v* buail le òrd.
hamper[1] *n* bascaid bìdh *f*.
hamper[2] *v* bac.
hand *n* làmh, cròg *f*. • *v* sìn.
handbag *n* poca làimhe *m*.
handful *n* dòrlach *m*.
handicap *n* bacadh *m*.
handkerchief *n* neapaigear *f*.
handle *n* làmh, cas *f*. • *v* làimhsich.
handshake *n* crathadh làimhe *m*.
handsome *adj* eireachdail.
handwoven *adj* làmh-fhighte.
handy *adj* deas.

hang *v* croch.
hangover *n* ceann daoraich *m*.
happen *v* tachair.
happening *n* tachartas *m*.
happiness *n* sonas *m*.
happy *adj* sona.
harass *v* sàraich.
harbour *n* cala, acarsaid *m*. • *v* gabh ri.
hard *adj* cruaidh.
hard disk *n* clàr cruaidh *m*.
harden *v* cruadhaich.
hardihood *n* cruadal *m*.
hardly *adv* gann.
hardship *n* cruaidh-chàs *m*.
hardware *n* cruaidh-bhathar *m*; (*comput*) bathar-cruaidh *m*.
hare *n* maigheach *f*.
hare-brained *adj* gaoitheanach.
harm *n* cron *m*. • *v* dèan cron air.
harmful *adj* cronail.
harmless *adj* neo-chronail.
harmonic *adj* co-cheòlach.
harmonious *adj* co-chòrdach.
harmonise *v* ceòl-rèim.
harmony *n* co-sheirm *m*.
harp *n* clàrsach *f*.
harper *n* clàrsair *m*.
Harris *n* Na Hearadh.
Harris tweed *n* clò na Hearadh *m*.
harrow *v* cliath.
harsh *adj* garg.
harshness *n* gairge *f*.
hart *n* damh-fèidh *m*.
harvest *n* buain *f*.
haste *n* cabhag *f*.
hasten *v* greas.

hasty *adj* cabhagach.
hat *n* ad *f*.
hatch *n* gur *m*; (*ship*) saidse *f*.
hatchet *n* làmh-thuagh *f*.
hate *n* fuath *m*. • *v* fuathaich.
hateful *adj* fuathach.
haughty *adj* àrdanach.
haul *v* tarraing.
haunch *n* leis *f*.
haunt *v* tathaich.
hauteur *n* àrdan *m*.
have *v* bi aig; seilbhich; (*eat, etc*) gabh; (*have to*) feum.
hawk *n* seabhag *m/f*.
hawser *n* taod *m*.
hawthorn *n* sgitheach *m*.
hay *n* feur, feur caoin *m*.
haystack *n* goc, tudan *m*.
haze *n* ceò *m*.
hazy *adj* ceòthach.
he *pron* e, (*emphatic*) esan.
head *n* ceann *m*.
headache *n* cràdh-cinn *m*.
header *n* buille-cinn *f*.
headland *n* rubha *m*.
headlight *n* solas-mòr *m*.
headmaster *n* maighstir-sgoile *m*.
headmistress *n* bana-mhaighstir-sgoile *f*.
headquarters *n* prìomh-àras *m*.
headstrong *adj* ceann-làidir.
headway *n* adhartas *m*.
heady *adj* bras.
heal *v* leighis.
healer *n* slànaighear *m*.
health *n* slàinte *f*.
healthy *adj* slàn.
heap *n* tòrr *m*. • *v* cruach.
hear *v* cluinn, èisd.
hearer *n* neach-èisdeachd *m*.
hearing *n* claisneachd *f*.

hearing-aid *n* inneal-claistinn *m*.
hearsay *n* iomradh *m*.
hearse *n* carbad-mharbh *m*.
heart *n* cridhe *m*.
hearten *v* misnich.
hearth *n* teinntean *m*.
hearty *adj* sùnndach.
heat *n* teas *m*. • *v* teasaich.
heater *n* uidheam teasachaidh *f*.
heathen *n* pàganach *m*. • *adj* pàganach.
heather *n* fraoch *m*.
heathery *adj* fraochach.
heave *n* togail *f*. • *v* tarraing.
heaven *n* nèamh *m*.
heavenly *adj* nèamhaidh.
heaviness *n* truime *f*.
heavy *adj* trom.
Hebrides *n* Innse Gall.
heckle *v* tras-cheusnaich.
hedge *n* callaid *f*.
hedgehog *n* gràineag *f*.
heed *n* aire *m*. • *v* thoir aire.
heedful *adj* faicilleach.
heedless *adj* neo-aireach.
heel *n* sàil *f*.
heifer *n* agh *f*.
height *n* àirde *f*.
heighten *v* àrdaich.
heir *n* oighre *m*.
heiress *n* ban-oighre *f*.
helicopter *n* heileacoptar *m*.
hell *n* ifrinn *f*.
help *n* cuideachadh *m*. • *v* cuidich.
helpful *adj* cobhaireach.
hem *n* faitheam *m*.
hemisphere *n* leth-chruinne *m*.
hen *n* cearc *f*.
hence *adv* às a seo.
henceforth *adv* o seo a-mach.
her *pron* i, ise. • *poss adj* (with *in-*

alienables) a; (with alienables)
. . . aice.
herald n teachdaire m.
herb n lus m.
herbal adj lusragach.
herd n treud, buar m. • v
buachaillich.
herdsman n buachaille m.
here adv (with a noun) seo;
(location) an-seo.
hereafter n an ath-shaogal m.
hereby adv le seo.
hereditary adj dùthchasach.
heredity n dùchas m.
heresy n saobh-chreideamh m.
heritage n oighreachd f.
hermit n aonaran m.
hero n curaidh, laoch m.
heroic adj gaisgeach.
heroine n bana-ghaisgeach f.
heron n corra-ghritheach f.
herring n sgadan m.
herring-gull n faoileag f.
herself pron ise, i fhèin.
hesitate v bi an imcheist.
hesitation n imcheist f.
hiccup n aileag f.
hide v ceil.
hideous adj gràineil.
hiding-place n àite-falaich m.
high adj àrd; mòr, urramach.
high tide n muir-làn m/f.
high-frequency adj àrd-tricead.
Highland adj Gàidhealach.
Highlander n Gàidheal m.
Highlands n A' Ghàidhealtachd f.
highlight v leig cudthrom air.
high-minded adj ard-intinneach.
high-powered adj mòr-chumhachd-
ach.
highway n rathad-mòr m.

hike v gabh cas.
hill n cnoc m.
hillock n cnocan, sìthean m.
hillside n leathan m.
hilly adj cnocach.
hilt n dòrn m.
himself pron e fhèin.
hind n eilid f.
hinder v bac.
hinge n bann m.
hint n sanas m.
hip n cruachann f.
hire purchase n cìs-cheannach m.
hire v fasdaidh.
his pron a. • poss adj (with inalienables) a; (with alienables) . . . aige.
hiss v siosarnaich.
historian n eachdraiche m.
historical adj eachdraidheil.
history n eachdraidh f.
hit n buille f. • v buail.
hither adv an-seo.
hive n sgeap f.
hoard n ulaidh f. • v taisg.
hoar-frost n liath-reòthadh m.
hoarse adj tùchanach.
hoarseness n tùchadh m.
hobby n cur-seachad m.
hobnail n tacaid f.
hoe n todha m. • v todhaig.
Hogmanay n Callain, Oidhche
Challain f.
hold v cùm.
hole n toll m.
holiday n saor-latha m.
hollow n còs m.
hollowness n falamhachd m.
holly n cuileann m.
holy adj naomh.
homage n ùmhlachd f.
home n dachaigh f. • adv dhachaigh.

home rule *n* fèin-riaghladh *m*.

homesick *adj* cianalach.

homesickness *n* cianalas *m*.

homespun *adj* dachaigheil.

homosexual *adj* co-sheòrsach.

honest *adj* onorach.

honesty *n* onair *f*.

honey *n* mil *f*.

honeymoon *n* mìos nam pòg *f*.

honeysuckle *n* lus na meala *m*.

honour *n* onair *f*; urram *m*. • *v* onar-aich.

hood *n* cochall *m*.

hoof *n* iongna *f*.

hook *n* dubhan *m*.

hooked *adj* crom.

hooligan *n* ùpraidiche *m*.

hoot *v* goir.

hop *n* sìnteag *f*. • *v* dèan sìnteag.

hope *n* dòchas *m*. • *v* tha dùil aig.

hopeful *adj* dòchasach.

hopeless *adj* eu-dòchasach.

horizon *n* fàire *f*.

horizontal *adj* còmhnard.

horn *n* adharc *f*; (*musical instrument, drink*) còrn *m*.

hornet *n* connspeach *f*.

horoscope *n* reul-shealladh *m*.

horrible *adj* oillteil.

horrid *adj* dèisinnneach.

horror *n* uamhann *m*.

horse *n* each *m*.

horseman *n* marcaiche *m*.

horseshoe *n* crudha *m*.

hose *n* (*sock*) osan *m*; (*pipe*) pìob *f*.

hospitable *adj* fialaidh.

hospital *n* taigh-eiridinn *m*.

hospitality *n* aoigheachd *f*.

host *n* fear-taighe *m*; sluagh *m*.

hostage *n* bràigh *m*.

hostess *n* bean-taighe *f*.

hostile *adj* nàimhdeil.

hostility *n* nàimhdeas *m*.

hot *adj* teth.

hotel *n* taigh-òsda *m*.

hour *n* uair *f*.

hourly *adv* gach uair.

house *n* taigh *m*. • *v* thoir taigh do.

household *n* teaghlach *m*.

hover *v* fo-luaimnich.

how *adv* ciamar?; dè cho?

however *adv* co-dhiù.

howl *n* donnal *m*. • *v* dèan donnal.

huddle *v* còmhlaich.

hug *v* glac teann.

hull *n* cochall *m*.

hum *n* srann *f*. • *v* dèan torman.

human *adj* daonna.

humane *adj* caomh.

humanity *n* daonnachd *f*.

humankind *n* an cinne daonna *m*.

humble *adj* umhal. • *v* ùmhlaich.

humid *adj* tais.

humorist *n* neach-àbhachdais *m*.

humorous *adj* àbhachdach.

humour[1] *n* àbhachd *f*.

humour[2] *v* toilich.

hump *n* croit *f*.

hundred *adj/n* ceud.

hundredth *adj* ceudamh.

hunger *n* acras *m*.

hungry *adj* acrach.

hunt *n* sealg *m*. • *v* sealg.

hunter *n* sealgair *m*.

hurricane *n* doinnean *f*.

hurry *n* cabhag *f*. • *v* luathaich.

hurt *n* dochann *m*. • *v* goirtich.

hurtful *adj* cronail.

husband *n* an duine aig . . . ; fear pòsda *m*.

hush *v* sàmhaich.

hut *n* bothan *m*.

hybrid *n* cros-chineal *m*.
hydro-electric *adj* dealan-uisgeach.
hydro-electricity *n* dealan-uisge *m*.
hygiene *n* slàinteachas *m*.
hymn *n* laoidh *m*.

hypocrisy *n* breug-chràbhadh *m*.
hypocrite *n* breug-chràbaiche *m*.
hysterical *adj* lethtaobhail.
hysterics *npl* lethtaobhachd *f*.

I

I *pron* mi; (*emphatic*) mise.
ice *n* deigh *f*.
iceberg *n* cnoc-eighre *m*.
ice-cream *n* reòiteag *f*.
icicle *n* caisean-reòta *m*.
icing *n* còmhdach-siùcair *m*.
icy *adj* reòta.
idea *n* beachd-smuain *f*.
ideal *adj* sàr. • *n* sàr-beachd *m*.
identical *adj* ionann.
identification *n* aithneachadh *m*.
identify *v* dearbh-aithnich.
identity *n* dearbh-aithne *f*.
idiom *n* gnathas-cainnt *m*.
idiot *n* amadan *m*.
idle *adj* dìomhain.
idleness *n* dìomhanas *m*.
idler *n* leisgean *m*.
idol *n* iodhal *m*.
if *conj* ma (+ *present/future*); nan,
   nam (+ *past conditional*).
if not *conj* mur.
ignite *v* cuir teine ri.
ignition *n* adhnadh *m*.
ignominious *adj* nàr.
ignorance *n* aineolas *m*.
ignorant *adj* aineolach.
ignore *v* leig le.
ill *adj* tinn.
illegal *adj* neo-laghail.
illegality *n* mì-laghalachd *f*.
illegible *adj* do-leughte.

illegitimate *adj* dìolain.
ill-health *n* euslainte *f*.
illiterate *adj* neo-litireach.
illness *n* tinneas *m*.
illogical *adj* mì-reusanta.
illuminate *v* soilleirich.
illumination *n* soillseachadh *m*.
illusion *n* mealladh *m*.
illusory *adj* meallach.
illustrate *v* dealbhaich.
illustrator *n* dealbhadair *m*.
ilustrious *adj* ainmeil.
image *n* ìomhaigh *f*.
imaginable *adj* so-smuainich.
imaginary *adj* mac-meanmnach.
imagination *n* mac-meanmna *m*.
imagine *v* smaoinich.
imbecile *n* lethchiallach *m*.
imbibe *v* òl.
imbue *v* lìon.
imitate *v* dèan atharrais air.
imitation *n* atharrais *f*.
immaculate *adj* fìorghlan.
immaterial *adj* neo-chorporra;
   coma.
immature *adj* an-abaich.
immaturity *n* an-abaichead *m*.
immediate *adj* ciad.
immediately *adv* gun dàil.
immense *adj* an-mhòr.
immerse *v* cuir fodha.
immigrant *n* inn-imriche *m*.

immigration n inn-imrich f.

imminent adj gus teachd.

immodest adj mì-nàrach.

immoral adj mì-bheusach.

immorality n mì-bheus f.

immortal adj neo-bhàsmhor.

immortality n neo-bhàsmhorachd f.

immunise v dìon o ghalar.

immunity n saorsa f; dìon m.

imp n spruis.

impair v mill.

impalpable adj do-fhaireachdainn.

impart v com-pàirtich.

impartial adj ceart-bhreitheach.

impassable adj do-shiubhal.

impassive adj socair.

impatience n mì-fhoighidinn f.

impatient adj mì-fhoighidneach.

impede v bac.

impediment n bacadh m.

impel v greas.

impenetrable adj do-inntrig.

imperative adj òrduigheach.

imperceptible adj do-mhothaichte.

impersonal adj neo-phearsanta.

impersonate v pearsonaich.

impertinence n mì-mhodh f.

impertinent adj mì-mhodhail.

impervious adj do-ruighinn.

impetuous adj cas, bras.

impetus n dèine f.

impinge v buail.

implacable adj gamhlasach.

implement n inneal m.

implement v thoir gu buil.

implicate v cuir an sàs.

implication n ribeadh m.

implicit adj fillte.

implore v aslaich.

imply v ciallaich.

impolitic adj neo-sheòlta.

import n brìgh f; (goods) bathar o chèin m. • v thoir a-steach bathar.

importance n cudrom m.

important adj cudromach.

impose v cuir air.

impossibility n nì do-dhèanta m.

impossible adj do-dhèanta.

impostor n mealltair m.

impotence n eu-comas m.

impotent adj eu-comasach.

impoverish v dèan bochd.

impracticable adj do-dhèanta.

impregnable adj do-ionnsaighe.

impressive adj drùidhteach.

imprison v cuir am prìosan.

improbability n mì-choltas m.

improbable adj mì-choltach.

improper adj neo-iomchaidh.

improve v leasaich.

improvement n leasachadh m.

improvident adj neo-fhreasdalach.

imprudent adj neo-chùramach.

impudence n dànachd f.

impulsive adj spreigearra.

impure adj neoghlan.

impute v cuir às leth.

in prep in, ann an. • pron **in me** annam; **in you** (sing) annad; **in him, it** ann; **in her** innte; **in us** annainn; **in you** (pl) annaibh; **in them** annta. • adv ann; (movement into) a-steach (inside location) a-staigh.

inability n neo-chomas.

inaccurate adj neo-chruinn.

inadequate adj uireasach.

inadvertent adj neo-aireach.

inane adj faoin.

inarticulate adj gagach.

inasmuch as conj aig a' mheud 's a.

incarnate adj san fheòil.

incense¹ n tùis f.

incense² v feargaich.

incest n col m.

incestuous adj colach.

inch n òirleach f.

inclement adj an-iochdmhor.

inclination n aomadh m.

incline v aom.

include v cuir san àireamh.

incognito adv gu dìomhair.

income n teachd a-steach m.

income tax n cìs cosnaidh f.

incomparable adj gun choimeas.

incompatible adj neo-fhreagarrach.

incomplete adj neo-choileanta.

incomprehensible adj do-thuigsinn-
each.

inconvenience n neo-ghoireasachd
f.

inconvenient adj mì-ghoireasach.

incorrect adj mearachdach.

increase n meudachadh m. • v
meudaich; rach am meud.

incredible adj do-chreidsinneach.

incredulous adj às-creideach.

incriminate v ciontaich.

incubate v guir.

incur v bi buailteach do.

incurable adj do-leigheasach.

indebted adj an comain.

indecent adj mì-chuibheasach.

indeed adv gu dearbh.

indelible adj do-sgriosta.

indemnify v theirig an urras air.

indent v eagaich.

independence n neo-eisimeileachd
f.

independent adj neo-eisimeileach.

index n clàr-amais m. • v clàraich.

indicate v comharraich.

indifferent adj coma.

indigestion n cion-meirbhidh m.

indignant adj diombach.

indignation n diomb m.

indiscreet adj neo-chrìonna.

indiscretion n neo-chrìonnachd f.

individual adj air leth.

individual n urra f.

indoor adj (location) a-staigh.

indulge v leig le.

indulgent adj bàigheil.

industrial adj tionnsgalach.

industrious adj gnìomhach.

industry n (abstract) saothair f;
gnìomhachas f.

inedible adj do-ithe.

inept adj baoth.

inequality n neo-ionnanachd f.

inert adj marbhanta.

inexcusable adj neo-leisgeulach.

inexpensive adj saor.

inexperienced adj neo-eòlach.

inexplicable adj do-mhìneachaidh.

inextricable adj do-fhuasglaidh.

infallible adj do-mhearachdach.

infant n naoidhean m.

infantile adj leanabail.

infantry n cois-shluagh m.

infect v cuir galar air.

infection n galar-gabhail m.

inferior adj ìochdarach.

infertile adj mì-thorrach.

infest v claoidh.

infinitesimal adj beag bìodach.

infirm adj anfhann.

inflammable adj so-losgaidh.

inflate v sèid.

inflation n (money) at cùinnidh m.

inflict v leag peanas air.

influence n buaidh f. • v treòraich.

influenza n fliù f.

inform v innis.

informal *adj* neo-fhoirmeil.

information *n* fiosrachadh *m*.

information technology *n* teicneol-as-fiosrachaidh *m*.

infrequent *adj* ainmig.

infringe *v* bris.

ingenious *adj* innleachdach.

ingenuous *adj* fosgarra.

ingot *n* uinge *f*.

ingredient *n* tàthchuid *f*.

inhabit *v* àitich.

inhabitable *adj* so-àiteachaidh.

inhabitant *n* neach-àiteachaidh *m*.

inhale *v* tarraing anail.

inherit *v* faigh mar oighreachd.

inhibit *v* cùm air ais.

inhibition *n* urchall *m*.

inhospitable *adj* neo-fhialaidh.

inhuman *adj* mì-dhaonna.

initial *adj* ciad. • *n* ciad litir *f*.

inject *v* ann-steallaich.

injection *n* ann-stealladh *m*.

injure *v* ciùrr.

injurious *adj* cronail.

injury *n* ciùrradh *m*.

ink *n* dubh *m*.

inland *adj* a-staigh san tìr.

inlet *n* caolas *m*.

inn *n* taigh-òsda *m*.

innate *adj* dualach.

inner *adj* an taobh a-staigh.

innkeeper *n* òsdair *m*.

innocent *adj* neo-chiontach.

innovate *v* ùr-ghnàthaich.

innovation *n* ùr-ghnàthachadh *m*.

innovator *n* ùr-ghnàthadair *m*.

innuendo *n* fiar-shanas *m*.

inoculate *v* cuir a' bhreac air.

inquire *v* feòraich.

inquiry *n* ceasnachadh *m*.

inquisitive *adj* faighneachail.

insane *adj* air chuthach.

insanitary *adj* mì-shlàinteil.

insanity *n* cuthach *m*.

insect *n* meanbh-fhrìde *f*.

insecure *adj* neo-thèarainte.

inseparable *adj* do-sgairte.

insert *v* cuir a-steach.

in-shore *adj* cladaich.

inside *prep* am broinn. • *adv* air an taobh a-staigh.

insincere *adj* neo-onorach.

insipid *adj* neo-bhlasda.

insist *v* cùm air.

insolvency *n* briseadh-creidis *m*.

insolvent *adj* ann am briseadh-creidis.

insomnia *n* bacadh cadail *m*.

inspect *v* sgrùd.

inspection *n* sgrùdadh *m*.

instal *v* cuir an dreuchd.

instalment *n* earrann *f*.

instance *n* eisimpleir *m*.

instant *adj* grad. • *n* tiota *m*.

instead *prep* an àite. • *adv* an àite sin.

instil *v* teagaisg.

instinct *n* dùchas *m*.

instinctive *adj* dùchasach.

institute *n* stèidheachadh *m*.

institution *n* stèidheachadh *m*.

instrument *n* inneal *m*, beart *f*.

insular *adj* eileanach.

insulate *v* dealaich.

insult *n* tàmailt *f*. • *v* tàmailtich.

insurance *n* urras *m*.

insurance policy *n* poileasaidh àrachais *m*.

insure *v* faigh àrachas air.

intact *adj* slàn.

integrity *n* ionracas *m*.

intellect *n* inntinn *f*.

intellectual *adj* inntleachdail.

intelligence *n* tuigse *f*.

intelligible *adj* so-thuigsinneach.

intend *v* cuir roimhe.

intense *adj* teann.

intensify *v* teinnich.

intensity *n* dèine *f*.

intention *n* rùn *m*.

intentional *adj* a dh'aon rùn.

intercede *v* dèan eadar-ghuidhe.

intercept *v* ceap.

intercourse *n* co-chomann *m*; (*sexual*) co-ghineadh *m*.

interest *n* ùidh *f*.

interesting *adj* ùidheil.

interfere *v* buin ri.

internal *adj* san leth a-staigh.

international *adj* eadar-nàiseanta.

internet *n* eadar-lìon *m*.

interpret *v* (*explain*) mìnich; (*translate*) eadar-theangaich còmradh.

interpreter *n* neach-mìneachaidh ; (*translator*) eadar-theangadair còmhraidh *m*.

interrupt *v* cuir casg air.

interruption *n* casgadh *m*.

intertwine *v* eadar-thoinn.

intervene *v* thig eadar.

intervention *n* eadar-ghabhail *m*.

interview *n* agallamh *m*. • *v* agallaich.

intestine *n* greallach *f*.

intimacy *n* dlù-chaidreamh *m*.

intimate *adj* dlù-chaidreach.

into *adv* a-steach do; ann an.

intonation *n* guth-cheòl *m*.

intricate *adj* eadar-fhighte.

intrigue *n* cluaineireachd *f*. • *v* dèan cluaineireachd.

intrinsic *adj* gnèitheach.

introduce *v* cuir an aithne.

introduction *n* cur an aithne.

intrude *v* brùth a-steach.

intruder *n* bruthaiche-steach *m*.

intuition *n* imfhios *m*.

invalid[1] *adj* neo-bhrìgheach.

invalid[2] *adj* (*ill*) tinn. • *n* euslainteach *m*.

invariable *adj* neo-chaochlaideach.

invent *v* innlich.

invention *n* innleachd *f*.

inventor *n* tionnsgalair *m*.

inventory *n* cùnntas *m*.

Inverness *n* Inbhir Nis.

invert *v* cuir bun os cionn.

invest *v* èid; (*money*) cuir an seilbh.

invisible *adj* do-fhaicsinneach.

invitation *n* cuireadh *m*.

invite *v* iarr.

invoice *n* maoin-chlàr *m*.

involuntary *adj* neo-shaor-thoileach.

involve *v* gabh a-steach.

inward *adv* a-staigh.

inwards *adv* a-steach.

Ireland *n* Èirinn *f*.

Irish *adj* Èireannach.

irksome *adj* buaireasach.

iron *n* iarann *m*. • *adj* iarrain. • *v* iarnaich.

ironic *adj* ìoronta.

irony *n* ìoronas *m*.

irrational *adj* eu-cèillidh.

irregular *adj* mì-riaghailteach.

irrelevant *adj* nach buin ri.

irreverent *adj* eas-urramach.

irrigate *v* uisgich.

irrigation *n* uisgeachadh *m*.

irritable *adj* crosda.

irritation *n* frionas *m*.

island *n* eilean *m*.

islander *n* eileanach *m*.

Islay n Ìle f.

isolated adj air leth.

issue n ceist f; (descendants) sliochd m.

isthmus n aoidh f.

it pron e, (emphatic) esan; i, (emphatic) ise.

Italian adj Eadailteach.

Italy n An Eadailt f.

itch n tachas m.

itchy adj tachasach.

itinerary n cùrsa m.

its pron aige, aice.

itself pron e fhèin, i fhèin.

ivory n ìbhri f.

J

jab n briogadh m. • v briog.

jacket n seacaid f.

jacobite adj seumasach.

jagged adj eagaich.

jail n carcair m.

jam n silidh m; (traffic) dòmhlachd m.

jamb n ursainn f.

jangle v dèan gleadhraich.

janitor n dorsair m.

jar n sileagan m.

jargon n goileam m.

jaundice n a' bhuidheach f.

jaunt n cuairt f.

jaunty adj sgeilmeil.

jaw n giall f.

jawbone n peirceall m.

jealous adj eudmhor.

jealousy n eud m.

jeans npl dìnichean.

jeer v mag.

jelly n slaman-milis m.

jellyfish n muir-tiachd m.

jerkin n còta-geàrr m.

jersey n geansaidh m.

jest n abhcaid f.

jester n cleasaiche m.

jet plane n diet-itealan m.

jettison v tilg a-mach.

jetty n cidhe m.

jewel n seud m.

jib¹ n dioba f.

jib² v cuir stailc ann.

jig n port-cruinn m.

jilt v trèig.

job n car-oibre m.

jockey n marcach m.

jog v put; (run) dèan dabhdail.

join v ceangail.

joiner n saor m.

joinery n saorsinneachd m.

joint adj co-; co-cheangail. • n alt m; (piece of meat) spòld m.

jointed adj altach.

jointly adv le chèile.

joke n fealla-dhà f.

jollity n cridhealas m.

jolly adj cridheil.

jolt n crathadh m. • v crath.

jostle v brùth.

jot n pong m.

journal n leabhar-latha; pàipear làitheil m.

journalism n naidheachdas m.

journalist n naidheachdair m.

journey n turas m, cuairt f.

jovial adj fonnmhor.

jowl n giall f.

joy n aoibhneas m.
joyful adj aoibhneach.
joyfully adv gu h-aoibhinn.
jubilant adj lùthghaireach.
jubilee n àrd-fhèill f.
judge n britheam m. • v thoir breith.
judgment n breitheanas m.
judicial adj dligheil.
judicious adj geur-chùiseach.
jug n siuga f.
juggle v dèan cleasachd.
jugular adj sgòrnanach.
juice n sùgh m.
juicy adj sùghmhor.
July n Iuchar m.
jump n leum m. • v leum.
jumper n leumadair m.

junction n ceangal m.
June n An t-Òg-mhìos m.
jungle n dlùth-fhàsach m.
junior adj às òige; (rank) iar-.
juniper n aiteann m.
junk n truilleis m.
junket, junketing n cuirm f.
juror n neach-diùraidh m/f.
just adj còir. • adv dìreach; (barely) air èiginn.
justice n còir f.
justifiable adj reusanta.
justification n fìrinneachadh m.
justify v fìrinnich.
jut v seas a-mach.
juvenile adj òganta.
juxtapose v chomhgharaich.

K

kail n càl m.
keel n druim m.
keen¹ adj geur.
keen² v caoin.
keenness n gèire f.
keep n daingneach f. • v cùm, glèidh.
keeping n glèidheadh m.
keepsake n cuimhneachan m.
kelp n ceilp f.
kennel n taigh-chon m.
kerb n cabhsair m.
kernel n eitean m.
kettle n coire m.
key n iuchair f; (mus) gleus f.
keyboard n meur-chlàr f.
keystone n clach-ghlasaidh f.
kick n breab m. • v breab.
kid n meann m.

kidnap v goid air falbh.
kidney n dubhag f.
kill v marbh.
killer n marbhaiche m.
kilogram n cileagram m.
kilometre n cileameatair m.
kilowatt n cileawatt m.
kilt n fèileadh, fèileadh beag m.
kin n cinneadh m.
kind¹ adj coibhneil.
kind² n gnè f.
kindle v las, fad.
kindly adj bàigheil.
kindred adj dàimheil.
kindred n muinntir f.
king n rìgh m.
kingdom n rìoghachd m.
kinsfolk npl luchd-dàimh.
kinsman n caraid m.

kinswoman *n* bana-charaid *f*.
kiosk *n* kiosk *f*.
kipper *n* ciopair *m*.
kiss *n* pòg *f*. • *v* pòg.
kit *n* trusgan *m*.
kitbag *n* màileid *f*.
kitchen *n* cidsin *m*.
kite *n* clamhan *m*; (*model*) iteileag *f*.
kitten *n* piseag *m*.
knack *n* liut *f*.
knapsack *n* aparsaig *f*.
knave *n* slaightear *m*.
knead *v* fuin.
knee *n* glùn *f*.
kneecap *n* failmean *m*.
kneel *v* sleuchd.
knickers *npl* drathars.

knife *n* sgian *f*.
knight *n* ridire *m*.
knighthood *n* ridireachd *m*.
knit *v* figh.
kniter *n* figheadair *m*.
knitting needle *n* bior-fighe *m*.
knob *n* cnap *m*.
knock *n* buille *f*. • *v* buail.
knoll *n* tolm *m*.
knot *n* snaidhm *m*. • *v* snaidhmich.
knotted, knotty *adj* snaidhmeach.
know *v* aithnich; tuig; bi eòlach air.
knowing *adj* eòlach.
knowingly *adv* gu h-eòlach.
knowledgeable *adj* fiosrach.
knuckle *n* rùdan *m*.
kyle *n* caol *m*.

L

label *n* bileag *f*.
labial *adj* liopach.
laboratory *n* deuchainn-lann *f*.
laborious *adj* deacair.
labour *v* saothraich.
labourer *n* oibriche *m*.
labyrinth *n* ioma-shlighe *f*.
lace[1] *n* lios *f*.
lace[2] *n* barrall *f*. • *v* (*shoe, etc*) dùin.
lacerate *v* reub.
laceration *n* reubadh *m*.
lack *n* easbhaidh *f*. • *v* bi a dh'easbhaidh.
lad, laddie *n* gille *m*.
ladder *n* fàradh *m*.
ladle *n* liagh *f*.
lady *n* bean-uasal *f*.
ladybird *n* an daolag dhearg-bhreac *f*.

ladylike *adj* bainndidh.
lair *n* saobhaidh *f*.
laird *n* tighearna *m*.
lake *n* linn *f*, loch *m*.
lamb *n* uan *m*; (*roast*) uainfheòil *m*.
lame *adj* bacach.
lameness *n* crùbaiche *f*.
lament *n* cumha *m*.
lament *v* caoidh.
lamentable *adj* tùrsach.
lamp *n* làmpa *m*.
lance *v* leig fuil.
lancet *n* lannsa *f*.
land *n* tìr, dùthaich *f*. • *v* rach air tìr.
landholder *n* neach-fearainn *m*.
landing *n* ceann staidhre *m*; (*of aeroplane*) laighe *m*.
landing strip *n* raon-laighe *m*.

landlady n bean an taighe f.
landlocked adj tìr-dhruidte.
landmark n comharradh m.
landscape n dealbh tìre m.
landslide n beum-slèibhe m.
landward adv gu tìr.
lane n lònaid f.
language n cànan m; (speech) cainnt f.
languish v fannaich.
lanky adj fada caol.
lantern n lanntair m.
lap[1] n uchd m.
lap[2] v sùgh.
lapel n liopaid f.
lapse n mearachd f. • v sleamhnaich.
lapwing n curracag f.
larceny n braide f.
larch n learag f.
lard n blonag f.
larder n preas-bìdh m.
large adj mòr.
lark n uiseag f.
lass, lassie n nighean f.
last[1] adj deireannach, mu dheireadh. • adv mu dheireadh.
last[2] v mair.
lasting adj maireannach.
late adj anmoch.
lately adv o chionn ghoirid.
lateness n fadalachd m.
latent adj dìomhair.
lather n cop m. • v dèan cop.
Latin n Laideann f.
latitude n leud m; (line) domhan-leud m.
latter adj deireannach.
laugh n gàire m. • v dèan gàire.
laughter n gàireachdaich f.
launch v cuir air bhog.

laurel n labhras m.
lavatory n taigh-failcidh, taigh-beag m.
lavish adj sgapach. • v sgap.
law n lagh, reachd m.
lawful adj laghail.
lawn n rèidhlean m.
law-suit n cùis lagha f.
lawyer n neach-lagha m.
laxative n purgaid f.
lay v càirich, cuir, leag sìos.
lay-by n far-rathad m.
layer n filleadh m.
layman n neo-chlèireach m.
laziness n leisge f.
lazy adj leisg.
lead[1] n luaidhe m/f.
lead[2] n (dog) iall f. • v treòraich.
leaden adj luaidhe.
leader n ceannard m.
leaf n duilleag f.
leafy adj duilleagach.
league n co-cheangal m; (sport) lìg m.
leak v leig a-steach.
leaky adj ao-dìonach.
lean[1] adj caol.
lean[2] v leig do thaic air.
leap v leum.
leap-year n bliadhna-leum f.
learn v ionnsaich.
learner n neach-ionnsachaidh m.
lease n lìos m.
least adj as lugha.
leather n leathar m.
leave n fòrladh m. • v fàg, trèig.
lecher n drùisire m.
lecherous adj drùiseil.
lecture n òraid f. • v teasgaig.
ledge n oir m.
ledger n leabhar-cùnntais m.

lee, lee-side n taobh an fhasgaidh m.

leech n deala f.

leek n cainneann m.

leet n (list) ciad-thaghadh m.

left hand n làmh chlì f.

left n an taobh ceàrr m.

left-handed adj ciotach.

leg n cas f.

legacy n dìleab f.

legalise v dèan laghail.

legend n fionnsgeul f.

legendary adj fionnsgeulach.

legibility n so-leughtachd f.

legible adj so-leughte.

legislate v dèan lagh.

legitimate adj dligheach.

leisure n suaimhneas m.

leisurely adj athaiseach.

lemon n liomaid f.

lend v thoir an iasad.

lender n iasadaiche m.

length n fad m.

lengthen v cuir am fad.

lengthwise adv air fhad.

lenient adj tròcaireach.

lenition n sèimheachadh m.

lens n lionsa f.

Lent n Carghas m.

leper n lobhar m.

leprechaun n luchraban m.

less adj nas lugha.

lessen v lùghdaich.

lesson n leasan m.

lest conj air eagal gu.

let[1] n bacadh m; (house) n gabhail f.

let[2] v leig; thoir air ghabhail.

lethal adj bàsmhor.

letter n litir f.

letter-box n bocsa-litrichean m.

lettuce n leiteis f.

level adj còmhnard.

level n còmhnard m. • v dèan còmhnard.

lever n luamhan m.

lewd adj draosda.

lewdness n draosdachd f.

Lewis n Leòdhas m.

liability n buailteachd f.

liable adj buailteach.

liar n breugaire m.

libel v dèan cliù-mhilleadh.

liberal adj pailt-làmhach.

Liberal n Libearaileach m.

librarian n leabharlannaiche m.

library n leabharlann f.

licence n cead m.

license v ceadaich.

lichen n crotal m.

lick v imlich.

lid n ceann m.

lie[1] n breug f. • v innis breug.

lie[2] v laigh.

life n beatha f.

lifeboat n bàta-teasairginn m.

lifeguard n freiceadan m.

lifestyle n seòl-beatha m.

lift n (elevator) àrdaichear m. • v tog.

light[1] adj aotrom; suarach; guanach;
soilleir.

light[2] n solas m. • v las.

lighten v deàlraich.

light-headed adj gog-cheannach.

lighthouse n taigh-solais m.

lightness n aotromachd m.

lightning n dealanach m.

like[1] adj coltach. • n samhail f.

like[2] v is toigh le.

liken v samhlaich.

likeness n coltas m.

likewise adv mar an ceudna.

limb n ball m.

lime n aol m; (fruit) n teile f.

lime tree *n* teile *f*.
limestone *n* aol-chlach *f*.
limit *n* crìoch *m*. • *v* cuir crìoch ri.
limited *adj* (*Ltd*) earranta (*Earr*).
limp[1] *adj* bog.
limp[2] *n* ceum *m*. • *v* bi crùbach.
limpet *n* bàirneach *f*.
linden tree *n* teile *f*.
line[1] *n* loidhne *f*; streath *f*.
line[2] *v* lìnig.
lineage *n* linn, sliochd *m*.
lineal *adj* dìreach.
linear *adj* streathach.
linen *n* anart *m*.
linger *v* gabh ùine.
linguist *n* cànanaich *m*.
link *n* tinne *f*. • *v* co-cheangail.
links *npl* machair goilf *f*.
linnet *n* gealbhonn-lìn *m*.
lion *n* leòmhann *m*.
lioness *n* ban-leòmhann *f*.
lip *n* bile *f*.
liquefy *v* leagh.
liquid *adj* lionnach. • *n* lionn *m*.
liquidate *v* glan air falbh.
lisp *n* liotachas *m*. • *v* bi liotach.
list *n* liosta *f*; (*items*) clàr-ainm *f*.
 • *v* liostaig; cuir sìos.
listen *v* èisd.
listener *n* neach-èisdeachd *m*.
listless *adj* coma; gun smior.
literacy *n* litireachd *f*.
literal *adj* litireil.
literate *adj* litir-foghlaimte.
literature *n* litreachas *m*.
litre *n* liotair *m*.
litter *n* treamsgal *m*; (*young*) cuain
 m. • *v* dèan treamsgal; beir.
little *adj* beag.
littoral *n* cladach *m*.
liturgy *n* ùrnaigh choitcheann *f*.

live[1] *adj* beò.
live[2] *v* bi beò.
livelihood *n* teachd-an-tìr *m*.
lively *adj* beòthail.
liver *n* adha *m*.
livid *adj* dùghorm.
lizard *n* laghairt *m*.
load *n* luchd *m*. • *v* luchdaich.
loaf *n* buileann *f*, lòf *m*.
loan *n* iasad *m*.
loath *adj* aindeonach.
loathe *v* fuathaich.
loathing *n* gràin *f*.
loathsome *adj* gràineil.
lobster *n* giomach *m*.
lobster-pot *n* cliabh-ghiomach *f*.
local *adj* ionadail.
locality *n* àite *m*.
locate *v* (*situate*) cuir 'na àite.
loch *n* loch *m*.
lock[1] *n* glas *f*. • *v* glais.
lock[2] *n* (*hair*) dual *m*.
locket *n* glasag-mhuineil *f*.
locksmith *n* gobha-ghlasan *m*.
lodge *n* taigh-gheata *m*. • *v* suidhich; gabh còmhnaidh.
lodger *n* lòisdear *m*.
loft *n* lobhta *m*.
log *n* sgonn *m*.
logic *n* loidig *f*.
logical *adj* loidigeach.
loiter *v* dèan màirneal.
loll *v* seas ri taic.
London *n* Lunnainn.
lone *adj* aonarach.
loneliness *n* aonaranachd *f*.
long ago *adv* o chionn fhada.
long[1] *adj* fada; buan.
long[2] *v* miannaich.
longevity *n* fad-shaoghalachd *f*.
longing *n* miann *m*.

longitude n domhan-fhad m.
long-suffering adj fad-fhulangach.
long-term adj fad-ùineach.
long-wave adj fad-thonnach.
long-winded adj fad-anaileach.
look n fiamh m; sùil f. • v seall, amhairc; **look for** sir.
looking-glass n sgàthan m.
loop n lùb f.
loophole n fosgladh m.
loose adj sgaoilte. • v fuasgail.
lop v sgath.
lop-sided adj leathoireach.
lord n tighearna, morair m.
lore n oilean m.
lorry n làraidh f.
lose v caill.
loser n neach a chaill m.
loss n call m.
lost adj air chall.
lotion n cungaidh f.
lottery n crannchur m.
loud adj labhar.
loudness n faram m.
loudspeaker n glaodhaire m.
lounge n seòmar-suidhe m. • v seàrr.
lour, lower v (face) bi an gruaim.
louse n mial f.
lousy adj mialach.
lout n burraidh m.
love n gaol, gràdh m.
lovely adj àlainn.
lover n leannan m.
lovesick adj tinn le gaol.
loving adj gràdhach.
low adj ìosal.
lower[1] v ìslich.

lower[2] see **lour**.
lowest adj as ìsle.
Lowland adj Gallda.
Lowlands n A' Ghalltachd f.
lowly adj iriosal.
loyal adj dìleas.
loyalty n dìlse f.
lubricate v lìomh.
lucid adj soilleir.
luck n fortan m.
lucky adj fortanach, buidhe.
lucrative adj buannachail.
ludicrous adj amaideach.
luggage n treallaich f.
lukewarm adj meadh-bhlàth.
lull v cuir a chadal.
lullaby n òran tàlaidh m.
luminous adj deàlrach.
lump n meall m.
lumpy adj meallanach.
lunacy n cuthach m.
lunar adj gealachail.
lunch n ruisean m.
lung n sgamhan m.
lurch[1] n sitheadh m.
lurch[2] v dèan sitheadh.
lure n mealladh m. • v meall, buair.
lurid adj cròn.
lurk v falaich.
luscious adj sòghmhor.
lust n ana-miann m.
lustre n deàlradh m.
lusty adj sultmhor.
luxuriant adj fàsmhor.
luxurious adj sòghail.
luxury n sògh m, n sòghalachd f.
lyre n cruit f.
lyric n liric f.

M

mace *n* cuaille-suaicheantais *m*.

machine *n* inneal *m*.

machinery *n* innealradh. *m*.

mackerel *n* rionnach *m*.

magazine *n* iris *f*.

magic *adj* draoidheil. • *n* draoidh-eachd *f*.

magician *n* draoidh *m*.

magistrate *n* bàillidh *m*.

magnet *n* clach-iùil *f*.

magnification *n* meudachadh *m*.

magnificence *n* greadhnachas *m*.

magnificent *adj* òirdheirc.

magnify *v* meudaich.

magnitude *n* meudachd *m*.

magpie *n* pioghaid *f*.

maid *n* maighdeann *f*.

mail *n* litrichean *pl*; post *m*. • *v* seòl.

mail order *n* òrdugh-puist *m*.

main *adj* prìomh.

mainland *n* tìr-mòr *m*.

mainly *adv* anns a' mhòrchuid.

maintain *v* glèidh.

maintenance *n* glèidheadh *m*.

majestic *adj* flathail.

majesty *n* mòrachd *f*.

major *adj* as motha. • *n* màidsear *m*.

make *v* dèan, dealbh; make to do thoir air; make towards dèan air. • *n* dèanamh *m*.

maker *n* dealbhadair *m*.

make-up *n* rìomhadh *m*.

making *n* dèanamh *m*.

male *adj* fireannach. • *n* fireannach *m*.

malevolence *n* gamhlas *m*.

malice *n* mì-rùn *m*.

malicious *adj* mì-rùnach.

malign *v* càin.

malignant *adj* millteach; (*med*) ailseach.

mallet *n* fairche *m*.

malt *n* braich *f*.

maltster *n* brachadair *m*.

maltreat *v* droch ghrèidh.

mam, mammy *n* mam, mamaidh *f*.

mammal *n* sineach *m*.

man *n* fear, duine *m*.

manage *v* stiùir.

manageable *adj* so-riaghlaidh.

management *n* riaghladh *m*.

manager *n* manaidsear *m*.

manageress *n* bana-mhanaidsear *f*.

mane *n* muing *f*.

manful *adj* duineil.

manger *n* prasach *f*.

mangle *v* reub.

manhood *n* fearalas *m*.

maniac *n* dearg amadan *m*.

manifest *v* taisbein.

manifestation *n* foillseachadh *m*.

manifesto *n* gairm-fhollaiseach *f*.

manipulate *v* oibrich.

mankind *n* cinne-daonna *m*.

manner *n* modh *m/f*.

mannerism *n* magaid *f*.

mannerly *adj* modhail.

manners *npl* modh *m*.

manse *n* mansa *m*.

mansion *n* taigh-mòr *m*.

mantelpiece *n* breus *m*.

manual *adj* làmhach. • *n* leabhar-tuairisgeil *m*.

manufacture v saothraich.

manure n mathachadh m. • v mathaich.

manuscript n làmh-sgrìobhainn m.

many adj mòran; iomadh. • n mòran, tòrr m.

map, n map m.

mar v mill.

marble n màrmor m.

March n Am Màrt m.

march n màrsail f. • v dèan màrsail.

mare n làir f.

marijuana n a' bhang f.

marine adj mara.

mariner n maraiche m.

maritime adj fairgeach.

mark n comharradh m.

market n fèill f, margadh m/f.

marketable adj margail.

maroon v cuir air eilean uaigneach.

marquee n puball m.

marriage n pòsadh m.

marriageable adj so-phòsaidh.

married adj pòsda.

marry v pòs.

marshy adj bog, fèitheach.

marten n taghan m.

martial adj gaisgeanta.

martyr n martarach m.

marvel n iongnadh m. • v gabh iongnadh.

marvellous adj iongantach.

mascot n suaichnean m.

masculine adj fireannta.

mash v pronn.

mask n aghaidh-choimheach f.

mason n clachair m.

masonry n clachaireachd m.

mass n tomad m; meall m; (church) aifreann m.

massacre n casgradh m. • v casgair.

massage n suathadh m.

massive adj tomadach.

mast n crann m.

master n maighstir m.

masterly n ealanta m.

masterpiece n euchd m.

masturbate v brod.

mat n brat m.

match n lasadair m; seise m. • v freagair.

matchless adj gun choimeas.

mate n cèile m; (ship) meite m; (chess) clos m. • v cuir clos air.

material n stuth m.

maternal adj màithreil.

maternity n màthaireachd f.

mathematics n matamataig.

matins npl maidnean.

matrimony n dàimh-pòsaidh m/f.

matter n stuth m; brìgh f; gnothach m.

mattress n bobhstair m.

mature adj abaich.

maul v pronn.

mavis n smeòrach m.

maw n goile f.

maximum n cuid as motha f.

May n An Cèitean m.

may v faod.

May Day n Là Bealltainn.

maze n ioma-shlighe f.

me pron mi, mise.

meadow n lòn m.

meagre adv gann.

meagreness n gainne f.

meal n min f; (repast) biadh f.

mealy adj mar mhin.

mean¹ adj suarach.

mean² n cuibheasachd f.

mean³ v ciallaich.
meaning n ciall f.
means npl comas m; seilbhean fpl.
meantime adv an dràsda.
measles n a' ghriùthlach f.
measurable adj so-thomhaiste.
measure v tomhais. • n tomhas m.
measurement n tomhas m.
meat n feòil f.
mechanic n meacanaig m.
mechanism n meadhan m.
medal n bonn m.
meddle v buin ri.
mediate v rèitich.
mediation n eadraiginn f.
mediator n eadar-mheadhanair m.
medical adj lèigh.
medicinal adj ìocshlainteach.
medicine n (science) eòlas-leighis;
  (medication) ìocshlaint m.
medieval adj meadhan-aoiseil.
mediocre adj meadhanach.
meditate v beachd-smuainich.
meditation n beachd-smuaineach-
  adh m.
medium n meadhan m.
medium-wave adj meadhan-
  thonnach.
meek adj macanta.
meekness n macantas m.
meet v coinnich.
meeting n coinneachadh m;
  (official) coinneamh f.
megalith n tursa m.
melancholy adj dubhach.
melancholy n leann-dubh m.
mellifluous adj mealach.
mellow adj tlàth.
melodious adj fonnmhor.
melody n binneas m; fonn m.
melon n meal-bhucan m.

melt v leagh.
member n ball m.
member of parliament n ball-
  pàrlamaid m.
membership n ballrachd f.
memento n cuimhneachan m.
memoir n tràchdas m; beatha-
  aisneis m.
memorable adj ainmeil.
memorise v cùm air mheomhair.
memory n cuimhne f.
mend v càraich.
menstrual adj mìosach.
menstruation n fuil-mìos f.
mental adj inntinneil.
mention v ainmich.
menu n cairt-bìdh f.
merchant n ceannaiche m.
mercy n tròcair m.
mere adj a-mhain.
merely adv a-mhain.
merge v rach an aon.
merit n luach m.
mermaid n maighdeann-mhara f.
merriment n aighear m.
mess n truidhleis f.
message n teachdaireachd f.
messenger n teachdaire m.
metal n meatailt f.
metallic adj meatailteach.
meteor n dreag f.
meter n inneal-tomhais m.
method n dòigh f.
metre n meatair m; (verse) rannaigh-
  eachd m.
mettle n smioralachd f.
microbe n bitheag f.
microwave oven n àmhainn
  mheanbh-thonn f.
mid adj eadar-mheadhanach.
middle n meadhan m.

middle-aged *adj* leth-shean.
midge *n* meanbh-chuileag *f*.
midnight *n* meadhan-oidhche *m*.
midwife *n* bean-ghlùine *f*.
might *n* cumhachd *m*.
migrate *v* dèan imrich.
mild *adj* ciùin.
mile *n* mìle *f*.
military *adj* cogail.
milk *n* bainne *m*. • *v* bleoghain.
milky *adj* bainneach.
mill *n* muileann *m/f*.
millennium *n* am mìle-bliadhna *m*.
miller *n* muillear *m*.
million *n* millean *m*.
mime *n* mìm *f*.
mimicry *n* atharrais *f*.
mince *n* mìons *m*.
Minch *n* An Cuan Sgìth.
mind *n* inntinn *f*.
mind *v* thoir an aire; cuimhnich.
mine[1] *n* mèinne *f*.
mine[2] *poss pron* (*with inalienables*) mo . . . -sa; (*with alienables*) an . . .agamsa.
mineral *adj* mèinneach. • *n* mèinn-earach *m*.
mingle *v* measgaich.
miniature *n* meanbh-dhealbh *m/f*.
minister *n* ministear *m*. • *v* fritheil.
minor *n* neach fo làn-aois *m*. • *adj* beag, as lugha.
minstrel *n* oirfideach *m*.
minus *prep* as aonais.
minute[1] *adj* meanbh.
minute[2] *n* mionaid *f*.
minx *n* aigeannach *f*.
miracle *n* mìorbhail *f*.
mirage *n* mearachadh-sùla *m*.
mirror *n* sgàthan *m*.
misapprehension *n* mì-thuigsinn *f*.

misbehaviour *n* droch-ghiùlan *m*.
miscarriage *n* asaid anabaich *f*.
mischief *n* aimhleas *m*.
mischievous *adj* aimhleasach.
misdeed *n* dò-bheart *f*.
miser *n* spìocaire *m*.
miserable *adj* truagh.
misinterpret *v* mì-bhreithnich.
misogyny *n* fuath-bhan *m*.
Miss *n* A' Maighdeann, A' Mh *f*.
miss *v* rach iomrall; ionndrainn.
missing *adj* a dhìth.
missionary *n* misionairidh *m*.
mist *n* ceò *m*.
mistake *v* mì-aithnich.
Mister *n* Maighstir, Mgr *m*.
mistletoe *n* uil-ìoc *m*.
mistress *n* bana-mhaighstir *f*; (*sexual*) coileapach *f*.
misty *adj* ceòthach.
misunderstand *v* mì-thuig.
mite *n* fineag *f*.
mix *v* measgaich.
mixture *n* measgachadh *m*.
moan *n* gearan *m*. • *v* gearain.
mob *n* gràisg *f*.
mobile phone *n* fòn-làimhe *f*.
mock *v* mag.
model *n* cumadh *m*. • *v* deilbh.
moderate *adj* stuama.
moderation *n* stuaim *m*.
modern *adj* ùr, nodha.
modernise *v* ùraich.
modest *adj* nàrach.
modesty *n* beusachd *f*.
moist *adj* tais, bog.
moisten *v* taisich.
mole[1] *n* famh *f*.
mole[2] (*spot*) ball-dòrain *m*.
molest *v* cuir dragh air.
mollify *v* maothaich.

mollusc *n* maorach *m*.

moment *n* tiota *m*.

momentary *adj* grad-ùineach.

momentous *adj* cudromach.

monarch *n* monarc *m*.

monastery *n* mannachain *f*.

Monday *n* DiLuain *m*.

money *n* airgead *m*.

monitor *n* foillsear *m*.

monk *n* manach *m*.

monkey *n* muncaidh *m*.

monopoly *n* lèir-shealbhachd *f*.

monotony *n* aon-ghuthachd *f*.

monster *n* uilebheist *m*.

month *n* mìos *m*.

monthly *adj* mìosach.

monument *n* carragh *f*.

mood *n* gleus *m*.

moody *adj* gruamach.

moon *n* gealach *f*.

moor[1] *n* mòinteach *f*.

moor[2] *v* tilg acair.

moral *n* beus *f*.

morale *n* misneach *f*.

morality *n* deagh bheusachd *f*.

more *adv* tuilleadh. • *n* tuilleadh *m*.

moreover *adv* a thuilleadh.

morning *n* madainn *f*.

mortal *adj* bàsmhor.

mosquito *n* còrr-mhial *m*.

moss *n* còinneach *f*.

most *adj* as motha. • *n* a' mhòr chuid *m*.

mostly *adv* mar as trice.

moth *n* leòman *m*.

mother *n* màthair *f*.

mother-in-law *n* màthair-chèile *f*.

motherly *adj* màithreil.

motion *n* gluasad *m*.

motive *n* adhbhar *m*.

motor *n* motair *m*.

motorist *n* motairiche *m*.

motto *n* facal-suaicheantais *m*.

mould *n* molldair *m*.

mouldy *adv* cloimh-liathach.

moult *v* tilg fionnadh.

mound *n* tom *m*.

mountain *n* beinn *f*, meall *m*.

mountaineer *n* streapaiche *m*.

mourn *v* caoidh.

mourning *n* bròn *m*.

mouse *n* luch *f*.

moustache *n* stais *f*.

mouth *n* beul *m*.

mouth-music *n* port-á-beul *m*.

mouthful *n* balgam *m*.

move *v* gluais; luaisg; imich.

mow *v* geàrr.

Mrs *n* A' Bhean, A' Bh *f*.

much *adv* mòran.

muck *n* salchar *m*.

mud *n* poll *m*.

muddle *n* troimhe-chèile *f*.

muddy *adj* eabarach.

mug *n* muga *f*.

Mull *n* Muile *f*.

multiple *adj* ioma-sheòrsach.

multiply *v* meudaich.

mumble *v* dèan brùnndail.

mumps *n* an tinneas-plocach *m*.

murder *n* mort *m*.

murderer *n* mortair *m*.

murmur *n* monmhor *m*.

muscle *n* fèith *f*.

museum *n* taigh-tasgaidh *m*.

mushroom *n* balgan-buachrach *m*.

music *n* ceòl *m*.

musical *adj* ceòlmhor.

musical instrument *n* inneal ciùil *m*.

mussel *n* feusgan *m*.

must *v* feum, 's èiginn, 's fheudar.

muster *n* cruinneachadh *m*.

mutation n mùthadh m.
mute adj balbh.
mutilate v ciorramaich.
mutiny n ceannairc f.
mutton n feòil caorach f.
mutual adj aontachail.
my pron (with inalienables) mo, m';
(with alienables) . . . agam.

myself pron mi fhìn.
mysterious adj dìomhair.
mystery n dìomhaireachd f.
mystical adj fàidheanta.
myth n miotas m.
mythical adj miotasach.
mythology n miotas-eòlas m.

N

nag v dèan dranndan.
nail n tarrag f.
naive adj soineannta.
naked adj lomnochd.
name n ainm m. • v ainmich.
nap n dùsal m.
narrate v aithris.
narrative n aithris m.
narrow adj cumhang.
nasal adj srònach.
nasty adj truaillidh.
nation n nàisean m.
national adj nàiseanta.
nationalism n nàiseantachd f.
nationalist n nàiseantach m.
nationality n nàiseantachd m.
native adj dùthchasach. • n
dùthchasach m.
natural adj nàdarrach.
nature n nàdar m.
naughty adj dona.
nausea n dèistinn f.
nauseous adj sgreamhail.
nautical adj seòlaidh.
navel n imleag f.
neap-tide n conntraigh f.
near adj faisg.
nearly adv faisg air. • adv (conj)
cha mhòr (nach).

near-sighted adj geàrr-fhradhar-
cach.
neat adj grinn.
necessary adj riatanach.
necessity n èiginn; aimbeart f.
neck n amhach f.
need n feum m. • v feum.
needle n snàthad f.
needy adj feumach.
negative adj àicheanach.
neglect v dèan dearmad.
negligent adj dearmadach.
negotiate v dèan gnothach ri.
neighbour n nàbaidh m.
neither adv/conj/pron cha mhò.
nephew n mac-peathar m.
nerve n fèith-mhothachaidh f;
(cheek) aghaidh f.
nest n nead m.
net n lìon m.
Netherlands n An Òlaind f.
nettle n deanntag f.
neutral adj neo-phàirteil.
never adv a chaoidh, gu bràth.
nevertheless adv gidheadh.
new adj ùr, nuadh.
New Year n A' Bhliadhna Ùr f.
news n naidheachd f.
next adj an ath . . . .

nice *adj* gasta.
niche *n* oisinn *f*.
nickname *n* farainm *m*.
niece *n* nighean-peathar *f*.
night *n* oidhche *f*.
nightingale *n* spideag *f*.
nil *n* neoni *m*.
nine *adj/n* naoi; (*persons*) naonar.
nineteen *adj* naoi deug.
ninety *adj* (*old system*) ceithir fichead 's a deich; (*new system*) naochad.
ninth *adj* naoidheamh.
nip *n* teumadh *m*; (*whisky*) tè bheag *m*.
nipple *n* sine *f*.
noble *adj* uasal, flathail.
nod *n* cromadh *m*.
noise *n* fuaim *m*.
noisy *adj* fuaimneach.
nominate *v* ainmich.
nonconformity *n* neo-aontachd *f*.
nonsense *n* amaideas *m*.
non-stop *adj* gun stad.
noon *n* meadhan-latha *m*.
nor *conj* no, nas mò.
normal *adj* gnàthach.
normally *adv* an cumantas.

north *adj* tuath. • *n* tuath *m*, an àirde tuath *f*.
northeast *n* ear-thuath *m*.
northern *adj* tuathach.
northwest *n* iar-thuath *m*.
nose *n* sròn *f*.
note *n* nota *f*. • *v* thoir fa-near.
notebook *n* leabhar-notaichean *m*.
nothing *n* neoni *m*.
notice *n* sanas, fios *m*. • *v* thoir fa-near.
notify *v* thoir fios do.
nuclear *adj* niuclasach.
nuclear waste *n* sgudal niuclasach *m*.
numb *adj* meilichte; (*cold*) air lathadh.
number *n* àireamh *f*; (*a lot*) mòran *f*. • *v* cùnnt, àireamhaich.
numeral *n* cùnntair *m*.
numerous *adj* lìonmhor.
nurse *n* banaltram *f*. • *v* altraim.
nursery *n* (*plants*) lios-àraich *m*; (*children*) sgoil-àraich *f*.
nursing home *n* taigh-altraim *m*.
nut *n* cnò *f*.
nutshell *n* plaosg-cnotha *m*.

O

oak *n* darach *m*.
oar *n* ràmh *m*.
oatcake *n* bonnach coirce *m*.
oath *n* bòid *f*.
oatmeal *n* min-choirce *f*.
obdurate *adj* rag-mhuinealach.
obedience *n* ùmhlachd *f*.
obey *v* gèill do.
object[1] *n* adhbhar *m*.

object[2] *v* cuir an aghaidh.
objection *n* gearan *m*.
oblige *v* cuir mar fhiachaibh air; (*help*) cuir fo chomain.
oblique *adj* siar.
oblivion *n* dìochuimhne *f*.
oboe *n* obo *m*.
obscene *adj* drabasda.
obscenity *n* drabasdachd *f*.

observant *adj* aireil.

observe *v* amhairc.

obsession *n* beò-ghlacadh *m*.

obsolete *adj* o fheum.

obstinacy *n* rag-mhuinealas *m*.

obstinate *adj* rag-mhuinealach.

obvious *adj* follaiseach.

occasion *n* fàth; cothrom *m*.

occasional *adj* corra.

occult *adj* dìomhair.

occupancy *n* seilbh *f*.

occupy *v* gabh sealbh.

ocean *n* cuan *m*, fairge *f*.

octagon *n* ochd-shliosach *f*.

octave *n* ochdad *m*.

October *n* An Dàmhair *m*.

octopus *n* ochd-chasach *m*.

ocular *adj* sùl, shùilean.

odd *adj* còrr.

ode *n* duanag *f*.

odour *n* boladh *m*.

of *prep* de. • *pron* **of me** dhìom; **of you** (*sing*) dhìot; **of him, it** dheth; **of her** dhith; **of us** dhinn; **of you** dhibh; **of them** dhiubh.

off *adv* dheth; (*away*) air falbh. • *prep* (*from*) o; bhàrr (+ *gen*).

offence *n* oilbheum *m*.

offend *v* dèan oilbheum do.

offer *n* tairgse *f*.

office *n* (*place*) oifis *f*; (*job*) dreuchd *f*.

officer *n* oifigeach *m*.

officious *adj* bleideil.

often *adv* tric; *adv* gu tric.

ogle *v* caog.

oil *n* ola *f*. • *v* olaich.

oil-field *n* ola-raon *m*.

oil-rig *n* crann-ola *m*.

oily *adj* uilleach.

ointment *n* ol-ungaidh *f*.

old *adj* aosda, sean.

old-fashioned *adj* sean-fhasanta.

omen *n* manadh *m*.

ominous *adj* droch-fhàistinneach.

omit *v* fàg às.

on *adv* air. • *prep* air. • *pron* **on me** orm; **on you** (*sing*) ort; **on him, it** air; **on her** oirre; **on us** oirnn; **on you** oirbh; **on them** orra.

once *adv* uair.

one *adj* aon. • *n* a h-aon *m*.

onion *n* uinnean *m*.

only *adj* aon. • *adv* a-mhàin. • *conj* ach.

onward *adv* air adhart.

ooze *v* drùidh.

open *adj* fosgailte. • *v* fosgail.

opening *n* fosgladh *m*.

operation *n* gnìomhachd *m*; (*surgical*) obair-lannsa *m*.

opinion *n* barail *f*.

opponent *n* nàmhaid *m*.

opportune *adj* tràthail.

opportunity *n* cothrom *m*.

oppose *v* cuir an aghaidh.

opposite *prep* fa chomhair.

oppress *v* claoidh.

oppressive *adj* fòirneartach.

optic *adj* fradharcach.

optimism *n* soirbh-dhùil *f*.

optimistic *adj* soirbh-dhùileach.

or *conj* no, air neo.

oral *adj* labhartha.

orange *adj* orainds.

orator *n* cainntear *m*.

orbit *n* reul-chuairt *f*.

orchard *n* ubhalghort *m*.

ordain *v* socraich.

order *n* òrdugh *m*. • *v* òrdaich.

ordinary *adj* gnàthaichte.

ore *n* mèinn *f*.

organ n ball m; orghan m.
organic adj innealach.
organise v eagraich.
organiser n eagraiche m.
orgasm n reachd f.
orgy n ruitearachd f.
oriental adj earach.
origin n tùs, bun m.
originality n bun-mhèinn f.
originate v tàrmaich.
Orkney n Arcaibh.
ornithology n eun-eòlas m.
orphan n dìlleachdan m.
osprey n iolair-uisge f.
ostensible adj a-rèir coltais.
ostrich n struth m.
other pron eile.
otherwise adv air modh eile.
otter n dòbhran m.
ought v bu chòir do.
ounce n ùnnsa m.
our pron (with inalienables) ar, (before vowel) ar n-; (with alienables) . . . againn.
ours pron (with inalienables) ar . . .-ne, (before vowels) ar n-. . .-ne; (with alienables) an . . . againne.
ourselves pron sinn fhìn.
out adv (location) a-muigh.
outdo v buadhaich air.
outlaw n neach-cùirn m.
out-of-date adj às an fhasan.
outrage n sàrachadh m.
outright adv gu buileach. • adj dearg.

outside adv (location) a-muigh.
outskirts n iomall m.
outspoken adj fosgarra.
outward adj faicsinneach.
outwit v thoir an car às.
oven n àmhainn f.
over prep (location) os cionn • pron **over me** os mo chionn; **over you** (sing) os do chionn; **over him, it** os a chionn; **over her** os a cionn; **over us** os ar cionn; **over you** os ur cionn; **over them** os an cionn; (motion) thairis air. • adv (here) a-null; (there) a-nall.
overall adv thar a chèile.
overboard adv thar bòrd.
overcharge v cuir tuilleadh 's a chòir.
overflow n cur thairis m. • v tar-shruth.
overnight adj ri linn oidhche.
overrrule v cuir fo smachd.
overseas adv thall thairis.
overtake v beir air.
overtime n seach-thìm f.
overturn v cuir bun os cionn.
overweight adj ro-throm.
owe v bi fo fhiachaibh.
owl n comhachag f.
own pron fhèin, (after forms of I and we) fhìn.
owner n seilbheadair m.
oxter n achlais f.
oyster n eisir m.

P

pace *n* ceum *m*. • *v* ceumnaich.
pacifism *n* sìochantas *m*.
pacifist *n* sìochantair *m*.
pack *v* paisg.
packet *n* pacaid *f*.
pact *n* cùmhnant *f*.
pad *n* pada *f*.
paddle *v* pleadhagaich.
paddling *n* plubraich *f*.
padlock *n* glas-chrochaidh *f*.
page *n* duilleag *f*; (*boy*) pèidse *m*.
pageant *n* taisbeanadh *m*.
pain *n* pian *f*.
painful *adj* piantach.
painless *adj* neo-phiantach.
paint *n* peant *m*. • *v* peant.
painting *n* dealbh *m*.
pair *n* càraid *f*.
palace *n* lùchairt *f*.
palate *n* bràighe-beòil *m*.
pale *adj* bàn. • *v* bànaich.
pallid *adj* bàn.
palm *n* bas *f*.
pamper *v* dèan peata de.
pan *n* pana *f*.
pancake *n* foileag *f*.
pane *n* gloinne *f*.
panic *n* clisgeadh *m*.
pant *v* plosg.
pantry *n* seòmar-bìdh *m*.
pants *npl* pantaichean.
papal *adj* pàpanach.
paper *n* pàipear *m*.
parable *n* cosamhlachd *f*.
paradise *n* pàrras *m*.
paradox *n* frith-chosamhlachd *f*.
paragraph *n* earran sgrìobhaidh *f*.

parallel *adj* co-shìnteach.
paralysis *n* pairilis *m*.
parapet *n* uchd-bhalla *m*.
parcel *n* parsail *m*.
pardon *n* mathanas *m*. • *v* math.
parent *n* pàrant *m*.
parish *n* sgìre *f*.
park *n* pàirc *f*.
Parliament *n* Pàrlamaid *f*.
parody *n* sgig-athrais *f*.
parrot *n* pearraid *f*.
parsimonious *adj* spìocach.
parsley *n* peirsill *f*.
part[1] *n* cuid *f*.
part[2] *v* dealaich.
partake *v* com-pàirtich.
participate *v* com-pàirtich.
particle *n* gràinean *m*.
particular *adj* àraidh.
parting *n* dealachadh *m*.
partition *n* roinneadh *m*; (*wall*) cailbhe *m*.
partly *adv* ann an cuid; gu ìre bhig.
partner *n* companach *m*.
partridge *n* cearc-thomain *m*.
party *n* (*company*) cuideachd *f*; (*political or gathering*) pàrtaidh *f*.
pass[1] *n* bealach *m*.
pass[2] *v* gabh seachad; (*sport*) pasaig.
passable *adj* cuibheasach.
passage *n* turas *m*; (*in building*) trannsa *f*.
passion *n* boile *f*.
passionate *adj* dìoghrasach.
passive resistance *n* aghaidheachd fhulangach *f*.

passivity n fulangachd m.
passport n cead-siubhail m.
past adj seachad. • n an t-àm a
dh'fhalbh m.
pastry n pastra f.
pasture n feurach m. • v feuraich.
pat v slìob.
patch n tùthag f.
paternal adj athaireil.
path n ceum m, slighe f.
pathetic adj tiamhaidh.
patience n foighidinn f.
patient n euslainteach m. • adj
foighidneach.
patrimony n dualchas m.
patronymic n ainm sinnsireil m.
pattern n pàtran m.
paunch n maodal f.
pause n stad m. • v fuirich.
paw n spòg f.
pawn[1] n pàn m.
pawn[2] v thoir an geall.
pay n pàigheadh m. • v pàigh.
pea n peasair f.
peace n sìth, fois f.
peaceful adj sìothchail.
peach n pèitseag f.
peak n stùc f, binnean m.
pear n peur f.
pearl n neamhnaid f.
peat n mòine f; (single) fad m.
peat-stack n cruach-mhònach f.
pebble n dèideag f.
peck v pioc.
pectoral adj uchdail.
peculiar adj àraid.
pedal n troighean m.
pedantry n rag-fhoglam m.
peddle v reic.
pedestrian n coisiche m.
pee v dèan mùn.

peel n rùsg m. • v ruisg.
peep n caogadh m. • v caog.
peevish adj dranndanach.
peewit n curracag f.
pelt v caith air.
pen n peann m.
penalty n peanas m.
penance n aithridh f.
pending adj ri thighinn.
penetrate v drùidh.
peninsula n leth-eilean m.
penis n bod m.
penny n peighinn f.
pension n peinnsean m.
pensioner n peinnseinear m.
people n sluagh, poball m.
pepper n piobair m.
per cent adv ... sa cheudad.
perceive v tuig, mothaich.
perch n spiris f. • v rach air spiris.
percolator n sìolachan m.
percussion n faram m.
perennial adj maireannach.
perfect adj foirfe. • v dèan foirfe.
perform v coimhlion.
perfume n cùbhrachd f.
perhaps adv is dòcha, ma
dh'fhaoite.
period n cuairt f.
perish v faigh bàs.
perishable adj neo-sheasmhach.
permanence n maireannachd f.
permanent adj buan.
permissive adj ceadachail.
permit n bileag-cead f. • v
ceadaich.
perpendicular adj dìreach.
perquisite n frith-bhuannachd f.
persecute v geur-lean.
persevere v lean air.
persistent adj leanailteach.

person n neach m.
personal adj pearsanta.
persuade v cuir ìmpidh air.
persuasion n ìmpidheachd f.
pertinent adj iomchaidh.
peruse v leugh.
perverse adj claon.
pervert n claonair m.
pessimist n neach gun dòchas m.
pest n plàigh f.
pestle n plocan m.
pet n peata m.
petition n iarrtas m. • v aslaich.
petrol n peatroil m.
petticoat n còta-bàn m.
pew n suidheachan m.
phantom n faileas m.
pheasant n easag f.
phenomenon n iongantas m.
philosopher n feallsanach m.
philosophy n feallsanachd f.
phlegmatic adj ronnach.
phone n fòn m. • v (cuir) fòn.
phosphorescence n teine-ghealan m.
photograph n dealbh m.
phrase n abairt m.
physical adj fisigeach; corporra.
pianist n cluicheadair piano m.
piano n piano m.
pibroch n ceòl-mòr f.
pick v tagh.
pickle v saill.
Pict n Cruithneach m.
picture n dealbh m.
picturesque adj àillidh.
pie n paidh m.
piece n pìos m.
pier n ceadha m.
pierce v toll.
pig n muc f.
pigeon n calman m.

pigsty n fail-mhuc f.
pile v cruach.
pilfer v dèan braide.
pilgrim n eilthireach m.
pill n pile f.
pillar n carragh f.
pillow n cluasag f.
pilot n pìleat m. • v treòraich.
pimple n plucan m.
pin n dealg f.
pinch v fàisg.
pine n giuthas m.
pink adj pinc.
pipe n pìob f.
piper n pìobaire m.
pirate n spùinneadair(-mara) m.
piss n mùn m. • v mùin.
pistol n daga m.
pitch n bìth f; (mus) àirde f; (field) raon-cluiche m.
pitiful adj truacanta.
pittance n suarachas m.
pity n truas m. • v gabh truas de.
place n àite m. • v suidhich.
placidity n ciùineachd f.
plague v plàighich.
plaice n lèabag-mhòr f.
plaid n breacan m.
plain adj còmhnard; soilleir.
plait n figheachan m.
plan n innleachd, plana f. • v innlich.
planet n planaid f.
plank n clàr m.
plant n luibh m. • v cuir.
plantation n planntachadh m.
plaster n sglàib f; plàsd m.
plastic adj plastaig; coineallach. • n plastaig f.
plate n truinnsear m.
plateau n àrd-chlàr m.

plausible *adj* beulach.

play *v* cluich.

player *n* cluicheadair *m*; cleasaiche *m*.

plead *v* tagair.

pleasant *adj* taitneach.

please *v* toilich, riaraich, taitinn, còrd.

pleasure *n* tlachd *f*.

pleat *n* pleat *f*.

plenty *adv* gu leòr.

plenty *n* pailteas *m*.

plight *n* cor *m*.

plod *v* saothraich.

plot *n* goirtean *m*; (*scheme*) cuil-bheart *f*.

plough *n* crann *m*. • *v* treabh.

plug *n* plucan *m*.

plum *n* plumas *m*.

plumb *v* feuch doimhneachd.

plump *adj* sultmhor.

plunder *n* cobhartach *m*. • *v* spùinn.

plunge *v* tum.

plural *adj* iolra.

plus *prep* agus.

poach *v* poidsig.

poacher *n* poidsear *m*.

pocket *n* pòcaid *f*.

poem *n* dàn *m*.

poet *n* bàrd *m*.

poetry *n* bàrdachd *f*.

point *v* comharraich.

poison *n* puinnsean *m*.

police *n* poileas *m*.

polish *n* lìomh *f*.

polite *adj* modhail.

pollute *v* truaill.

pompous *adj* mòr-chùiseach.

pond *n* linne *f*.

pony *n* pònaidh *m*.

pool *n* linne *f*.

poor *adj* bochd.

Pope *n* Pàpa *m*.

popular *adj* coiteanta.

population *n* sluagh *m*.

porch *n* sgàil-thaigh *m*.

porridge *n* lite *f*.

port *n* port *m*.

portable *adj* so-ghiùlan.

portion *n* earrann *f*.

Portugal *n* A' Phortagail *f*.

positive *adj* cinnteach.

possess *v* sealbhaich.

possible *adj* comasach.

possibly *adv* is dòcha.

post office *n* oifis a' phuist *f*.

post *v* cuir air falbh.

postal order *n* òrdugh-puist *m*.

postcard *n* cairt-phostachd *f*.

postcode *n* còd-puist *m*.

postman *n* posta *m*.

pot *n* poit *f*.

potato *n* buntàta *m*.

pottery *n* crèadhadaireachd *f*.

pound *n* pùnnd *m*.

pour *v* dòirt; (*rain*) sil.

powder *n* fùdar *m*.

power *n* cumhachd *f*.

power station *n* stèisean dealain *m*.

practicable *adj* so-dhèanamh.

practice *n* cleachdadh *m*.

practise *v* cleachd.

praise *n* moladh *m*. • *v* mol.

prank *n* cleas *m*.

prawn *n* muasgan-caol *m*.

pray *v* guidh.

prayer *n* guidhe *f*.

preach *v* searmonaich.

precarious *adj* cugallach.

precaution *n* ro-chùram *m*.

precentor *n* neach togail fuinn *m*.

precious *adj* prìseil.

precipitous *adj* cas.
precise *adj* pongail.
precocious *adj* ro-abaich.
predatory *adj* creachach.
predict *v* ro-innis.
predominant *adj* buadhach.
preface *n* ro-ràdh *m*.
prefer *v* is fheàrr le.
pregnant *adj* trom.
prehistoric *adj* ro-eachdraidheil.
prejudice *n* claon-bhàigh *f*.
preliminary *adj* tòiseachail.
premises *n* aitreabh *m*.
premonition *n* ro-fhiosrachadh *f*.
prepare *v* ullaich.
preposterous *adj* mì-reusanta.
prescription *n* òrdugh-cungaidh *f*.
presence *n* làthaireachd *f*.
present[1] *n* an t-àm tha làthair *m*
present[2] *n* (*gift*) tiodhlac *m*. • *v* thoir do.
presently *adv* an ceart uair.
president *n* ceann-suidhe *m*.
press release *n* aithris-naidheachd *f*.
pretence *n* leigeil air *m*.
pretend *v* leig air.
pretty *adj* brèagha.
prevailing *adj* buadhach.
previously *adv* ro làimh.
prey *n* creach *f*. • *v* creach.
price *n* prìs *f*.
prick *v* stuig.
prickly *adj* biorach.
pride *n* àrdan *m*.
priest *n* sagart *m*.
prim *adj* frionasach.
primary school *n* bunsgoil *f*.
primitive *adj* tùsach.
primrose *n* sòbhrach *f*.
prince *n* prionnsa *m*.

print *v* clò-bhuail.
printer *n* clò-bhualadair *m*.
print-out *n* lethbhreac clo-bhuailte *m*.
private *adj* uaigneach.
privilege *n* sochair *f*.
prize *n* duais *f*.
probable *adj* coltach.
probably *adv* is dòcha.
probity *n* treibhdhireas *m*.
problem *n* ceist *f*.
problematic *adj* ceisteach.
process *n* cùrsa *m*.
proclaim *v* èigh.
procurator fiscal *n* fioscail *m*.
prod *v* stob.
produce *n* toradh *m*. • *v* thoir gu cinneas.
producer *n* riochdaire *m*.
profession *n* dreuchd *f*.
professor *n* ollamh *m*.
profit *n* buannachd *f*. • *v* tairbhich.
profound *adj* domhainn.
profuse *adj* pailt.
program(me) *n* prògram *m*.
programming language *n* cànan-prògramaidh *m*.
progress *n* imeachd *f*; piseach *f*.
prohibit *v* toirmisg.
prolific *adj* torrach.
prominent *adj* faicsinneach.
promise *n* gealladh *m*. • *v* geall.
promontory *n* rubha *m*.
prompt *adj* deas.
pronoun *n* riochdair *m*.
pronounce *v* fuaimnich.
proof *n* dearbadh *m*.
prop *v* cùm suas.
proper *adj* iomchuidh.
property *n* seilbh *f*.
prophesy *v* fàisnich.

proportion *n* co-rèir *m*.
proprietor *n* sealbhadair *m*.
propulsion *n* sparradh *m*.
prose *n* rosg *m*.
prosecute *v* cùisich.
prosper *v* soirbhich.
prostitute *n* strìopach *f*.
prostrate *adj* sleuchdte.
protect *v* dìon.
protection *n* dìon *m*.
protest *v* tog casaid.
Protestant *adj* Pròsdanach.
proud *adj* uaibhreach.
prove *v* dearbh.
proverb *n* seanfhacal *m*.
provide *v* solair.
province *n* roinn *f*.
provocation *n* buaireadh *m*.
provoke *v* buair.
provost *n* pròbhaist *m*.
prow *n* toiseach *m*.
prowl *v* èalaidh.
prude *n* leòmag *f*.
prudent *adj* glic.
prune *v* sgath.
pry *v* lorgaich.
psalm *n* salm *m*.
psalter *n* salmadair *m*.
psychic *adj* anamanta.
ptarmigan *n* tàrmachan *m*.
pub *n* taigh-seinnse *m*.
public *adj* follaiscach.
public relations *n* dàimh phoblach *f*.
publicity *n* follaiseadh *m*.

publish *v* foillsich.
pudding *n* marag; mìlsean *f*.
puddle *n* lòn *m*.
puffin *n* buthaid *m*.
pull *v* tarraing.
pulpit *n* cùbaid *f*.
pulse *n* cuisle *f*.
pump *n* pumpa *m*; (*shoe*) bròg-dannsa *f*.
punctual *adj* pongail.
puncture *n* tolladh *m*.
punish *v* peanasaich.
punishment *n* peanasachadh *m*.
pupil *n* sgoilear *m*; (*eye*) dubh na sùla *m*.
puppy *n* cuilean *m*.
pure *adj* fìorghlan.
purge *v* glan.
purity *n* glaine *f*.
purple *adj* purpaidh.
purse *n* sporan *m*.
pursue *v* lean.
pursuer *n* neach-tòire *m*.
pursuit *n* tòir *f*.
push *n* bruthadh *m*. • *v* brùth.
pussy cat *n* piseag *f*.
put *v* cuir, suidhich.
putrid *adj* grod.
putt *v* amas.
puzzle *n* imcheist. • *v* cuir an imcheist, bi an imcheist.
pylon *n* paidhlean *m*.
pyramid *n* biorramaid *f*.

Q

quack n màgail f; (*sound*) mhàg mhàg! • v dèan màgail.

quaint adj neònach.

qualification n feart m.

qualify v ullaich.

quality n gnè f.

quantify v àirmhich.

quarrel n còmhstri m. • v connsaich.

quarrelsome adj connspaideach.

quarry n cuaraidh m; creach m. • v cladhaich.

quarter n ceathramh m; (*season*) n ràith f.

quartz n èiteag f.

quaver n crith f; (*mus*) n caman m.

queasy adj sleogach.

queen n ban-rìgh f.

quell v smachdaich.

quench v bàth.

quern n brà f.

question n ceist f. • v ceasnaich.

question-mark n comharradh ceiste m.

queue n ciudha f.

quibble v car-fhaclaich.

quick adj bras, luath.

quicksand n beò-ghainmheach f.

quiet adj sàmhach.

quiet n sàmhchair m.

quieten v sàmhaich.

quilt n cuibhrig m.

quirk n car m.

quit v fàg.

quite adv gu tur, gu lèir; gu math.

quiver[1] n balg-shaighead m.

quiver[2] v dèan ball-chrith.

quiz n ceasnachadh m.

quotation n luaidh m; (*price*) luach m.

quote v luaidh; thoir mar ùghdarras.

R

rabbit n coineanach m.

rabid adj cuthachail.

race n rèis f; (*human*) cinneadh f.

racism n cinneadachd f.

racket n gleadhraich f.

radiant adj lainnireach.

radiate v deàlraich.

radiator n rèididheatar m.

radical adj bunasach.

radio n rèidio m.

raffle n crannchur-gill m.

raft n ràth m.

rafter n taobhan m.

rag n luideag f.

rage n boile f.

raid n ruaig f.

railway n rathad-iarainn m.

rain n uisge m; frasachd f. • v sil, dòirt.

rainbow n bogha-frois m.

rainy adj frasach.

raise v àrdaich, tog.

rake v ràc.

ram n reithe m.

ram v spàrr.

rambler n neach-fàrsain m.

rampant adj sùrdagach.

rancid adj breun.

random adj tuaireamach.

range n sreath m. • v siubhail.

rank n (status) inbhe f; (line) sreath m.

rankle v feargaich.

ransom n èirig f. • v fuasgail.

rapacious adj gionach.

rape n toirt air èiginn f. • v èignich.

rapidity n braise f.

rare adj tearc.

rarity n annas m.

rash[1] n broth m.

rash[2] adj dàna.

raspberry n subh-craoibh m.

rat n radan m.

rate n ràta m.

rather adv rudeigin.

ravage v sgrios.

rave v bi air bhoile.

raven n fitheach m.

ravenous adj cìocrach.

raw adj amh.

razor n ealtainn f.

reach n ruigheachd f. • v ruig.

read v leugh.

reader n leughadair m.

readily adv gu rèidh.

readiness n ullamhachd f.

ready adj ullamh.

real adj fìor.

realise v tuig.

reality n fìrinn f.

really adv gu dearbh.

reap v buain.

rear n deireadh m.

reason n reusan m.

rebate n lùghdachadh m.

rebel n reubalach m. • v dèan ar-a-mach.

rebuff n diùltadh m.

rebuild v ath-thog.

recall v cuimhnich air.

recede v rach air ais.

receive v gabh.

recent adj ùr.

recently adv o chionn ghoirid.

reception n fàilteachadh m.

receptive adj so-ghabhail.

recession n ìsleachadh m.

recipe n modh m.

reciprocal adj malairteach.

recital n aithris; (mus) ceadal f.

reckless adj neo-chùramach.

reckon v cùnnt.

reclaim v ath-leasaich.

recline v sìn.

recognise v aithnich.

recommend v cliùthaich.

reconcile v rèitich.

reconnoitre v feuch.

record n cùnntas m; clàr m. • v sgrìobh; clàraich.

recover v (regain) faigh air ais; (improve) fàs nas fheàrr.

recovery n (regain) faighinn air ais f; (improve) fàs nas fheàrr m.

recreation n cur-seachad m.

rectify v ceartaich.

rector n ceannard m.

recur v tachair a-rithist.

red adj dearg; ruadh.

redeem v ath-cheannaich.

redirect v ath-sheòl.

redouble v dùblaich.

reduce v ìslich.

redundant adj anbharra.

reed n cuilc f; (mus) ribheid f.

reef n sgeir f.

reel n ruidhle m; (thread) piorna f.
refer v cuir gu.
referee n breitheamh, reaf m.
reference n iomradh m; teisteanas m.
refill v ath-lìon.
refit v ath-chàirich.
reflect v tilg air ais; (think) smaoinich.
reform n leasachadh m. • v ath-leasaich.
refrain n luinneag f.
refresh v ùraich.
refreshment n ùrachadh m; deoch f.
refuge n tèarmann m.
refund v ath-dhìol.
refusal n diùltadh m.
refuse v diùlt.
refute v breugnaich.
regard n suim f. • v gabh suim ann.
register n clàr m.
regret n duilchinn f. • v bi duilich.
regulate v riaghlaich.
rehearsal n ath-aithris f.
rehearse v ath-aithris.
reign v rìoghaich.
reimburse v ath-phàigh.
rein n srian f.
reinforce v ath-neartaich.
rejoice v dèan aoibhneas.
relate v innis.
related adj (akin) càirdeach.
relation n caraid m, bana-charaid f.
relative adj dàimheach.
relax v lasaich.
release v cuir ma sgaoil.
relent v taisich.
relentless adj neo-thruacanta.
relevant adj a' buntainn ri.
reliable adj earbsach.
relic n fuidheall m.

relief n furtachd f.
relieve v furtaich.
religion n diadhachd f.
relish n tlachd f. • v gabh tlachd de.
reluctant adj aindeonach.
rely v earb.
remain v fuirich.
remains npl fuidhleach m; (human) duslach m.
remark n facal m. • v thoir fa-near.
remarkable adj suaicheanta.
remedy n leigheas m.
remember v cuimhnich.
remind v cuimhnich do.
reminiscence n cuimhneachadh m.
remorse n agartas-cogais m.
remorseful adj cogaiseach.
remote adj iomallach.
renaissance n ath-bheòthachadh m.
rend v srac.
renew v nuadhaich.
rent n (tear) sracadh m; (fee) màl m. • v gabh air mhàl.
repair n càireadh m. • v càirich.
repay v ath-dhìol.
repeat v aithris.
repel v tilg air ais.
replace v cuir an àite.
replay v ath-chluich.
replete adj làn.
reply n freagairt f. • v freagair.
report v thoir iomradh.
representative n riochdaire m.
reprieve n stad-bhreith f.
reprimand n casaid f.
reprisal n èirig f.
reproach v cronaich.
reproduce v gin.
reproduction n gintinn m; (copy) macsamhlachadh m.
reptile n pèist f.

republic n poblachd f.
reputation n cliù m.
request n iarrtas m. • v iarr.
rescue n fuasgladh m. • v fuasgail.
research v rannsaich.
researcher n rannsaichear m.
resent v gabh tàmailt dhe.
resentment n doicheall m.
reserve n tasgadh m. • v caomhain.
reservoir n tasgadh-uisge m.
residence n ionad-còmhnaidh m.
resign v thoir suas, gèill.
resistance n strì f.
resolute adj gramail.
resonant adj glòrach.
resource n goireas m.
respect n urram m. • v thoir urram
do.
respectable adj measail.
respectful adj modhail.
respective adj àraidh.
respite n anail f.
responsibility n cùram m.
responsive adj freagairteach.
rest n fois f; (mus) clos m. • v gabh
fois.
restaurant n taigh-bìdh m.
restful adj sàmhach.
restless adj mì-fhoisneach.
restore v thoir air ais.
restrict v grab.
result n buil f.
retain v cùm.
reticent adj tosdach.
retire v rach air chluainidh, leig
dreuchd dhe.
retirement n cluaineas m.
retreat v teich.
retribution n ath-dhìoladh m.
return n tilleadh m. • v till.
reveal v nochd.

revelation n taisbeanadh m.
revenge n dìoghaltas m.
reverend adj urramach.
reverent adj iriosal.
review v ath-bheachdaich.
revise v ath-sgrùd.
revival n dùsgadh m.
revive v dùisg.
revolve v iom-chuartaich.
reward n duais f. • v dìol.
rheumatic adj lòinidheach.
rheumatism n an rumatas m.
rhubarb n rua-bhàrr m.
rhyme n comhardadh m. • v dèan
rann.
rib n aisean f.
ribbon n rioban m.
rice n rìs m.
rich adj beairteach.
riddle n tòimhseachan m.
ride v marcaich.
rider n marcaiche m.
ridge n druim m.
ridiculous adj amaideach.
right adj ceart; (hand) deas. • n
ceartas m; dlighe f. • v cuir ceart.
rigid adj rag.
rigour n cruas m.
rim n oir m.
rind n rùsg m.
ring n fàinne f; cearcall m. • v seirm.
rinse v sgol.
ripe adj abaich.
ripen v abaich.
ripple n luasgan m.
rise v èirich.
risk n cunnart m. • v feuch.
rival n co-dheuchainniche m. • adj
còmhstritheach.
rivalry n còmhstri f.
river n abhainn f.

rivulet *n* sruthan *m*.
road *n* rathad *m*, slighe *f*.
roam *v* rach air fàrsan.
roar *n* beuc *m*. • *v* beuc.
roast *v* ròist.
rob *v* spùinn, spùill.
robber *n* spùilleadair *m*.
robbery *n* goid *f*.
robe *n* fallaing *f*.
robin *n* brù-dhearg *m*.
rock[1] *n* carraig *f*.
rock[2] *v* luaisg.
rod *n* slat *f*.
roe *n* earba, ruadhag *f*; (*fish*) glasag *f*.
rogue *n* slaoightear *m*.
roll *n* rolla *f*. • *v* fill.
romance *n* romansachd *f*; (*tale*) ròlaist *m*.
romantic *adj* romansach.
roof *n* mullach *m*.
rook *n* ròcas *m*.
room *n* seòmar, rùm *m*.
roomy *adj* farsaing.
root *n* freumh *m*.
rope *n* ròpa, ball *m*.
rosary *n* paidirean *m*.
rose *n* ròs *m*.
rosy *adj* ruiteach.
rot *n* grodadh *m*.
rotten *adj* grod.

rough *adj* garbh, molach.
round *adj* cruinn. • *adv* mun cuairt.
rouse *v* dùisg.
rout *n* ruaig *f*.
routine *n* gnàth-chùrsa *m*.
row *n* (*rank*) sreath *m*; (*fight*) sabaid *f*.
rowan *n* caorann *f*.
rower *n* ràmhaiche *m*.
rub *v* suath.
rubbish *n* salchar, brusgar *m*.
rudder *n* stiùir *f*.
rude *adj* borb.
rue *v* crean.
rueful *adj* dubhach.
ruffian *n* brùid *f*.
rug *n* bràt-urlair *m*.
ruin *n* sgrios *m*; (*house*) làrach *m*.
rule *n* riaghailt *f*. • *v* riaghail.
rumble *v* dèan rùcail.
rummage *v* rannsaich.
rumour *n* fathann *m*.
run *v* ruith.
runnel *n* srùlag *f*.
rural *adj* dùthchail.
rush *v* brùchd.
rushes *npl* luachair *f*.
rust *n* meirg *f*.
rut *n* clais *f*; (*animal*) dàmhair *f*.
ruthless *adj* neo-thruacanta.

S

sabbath *n* sàbaid *f*.
sack[1] *n* poca *m*.
sack[2] *v* sgrios; cuir à obair.
sacrcastic *adj* searbh.
sacred *adj* naomh.
sacrifice *n* ìobairt *f*. • *v* ìobair.

sad *adj* brònach.
sadden *v* dèan brònach.
saddle *n* dìollaid *f*.
sadness *n* bròn, mulad *m*.
safe *adj* sàbhailte.
safety *n* tèarainteachd *f*.

saffron n cròch m.
sag v tuit.
sagacious adj geur-chùiseach.
sail n seòl m. • v seòl.
sailor n seòladair m.
saint n naomh m.
sake n sgàth m.
salad n sailead m.
sale n reic m.
saleable adj reiceach.
saliva n seile m.
sallow adj lachdann.
salmon n bradan m.
salmon trout n bànag f.
salt n salann m.
salt-cellar n saillear m.
salutary adj slàinteil.
salute v fàiltich.
salvage n tàrrsainn m.
same adj ionann, ceudna.
sameness n co-ionannachd.
sample n samhla m.
sanctify v naomhaich.
sanctuary n comraich f.
sand n gainmheach f.
sandstone n clach-ghainmhich f.
sandy adj gainmheil.
sane adj ciallach.
sapling n faillean m.
sapphire n gorm-leug f.
sarcasm n searbhas m.
satanic adj diabhlaidh.
satchel n màileid f.
satellite n saideal m.
satiate v sàsaich.
satin n sròl m.
satire n aoir f.
satirical adj aoireil.
satirist n èisg f.
satisfaction n sàsachadh m.
satisfied adj sàsaichte.

satisfy v sàsaich.
Saturday n DiSathairne m.
sauce n sabhs m.
saucepan n sgeileid f.
saucer n sàsar m.
sausage n isbean m.
save v sàbhail.
saved adj saorte.
savour v feuch blas.
savoury adj blasda.
saw n sàbh m. • v sàbh.
say v abair.
saying n ràdh, facal m.
scald v sgàld.
scale n cothrom m; (fish) lann m;
  (mus) sgàla m.
scalp n craiceann a' chinn m.
scaly adj lannach.
scan v sgrùd.
scandal n sgainneal m.
scandalise v sgainnealaich.
scandalous adj maslach.
scanty adj gann.
scar n leòn m.
scarce adj tearc.
scare v cuir eagal air.
scarecrow n bodach-ròcais m.
scarf n stoc m.
scatter v sgap.
scattering n sgapadh m.
scene n sealladh m.
scent n fàileadh m.
scented adj cùbhraidh.
sceptical adj às-creideach.
scheme n innleachd f.
school n sgoil f.
schoolmaster n maighstir-sgoile m.
schoolmistress n bana-mhaighstir-
  sgoile f.
science n saidheans m.
scientific adj saidheansail.

scissors *n* siosar *f*.
scold *v* troid.
scone *n* bonnach *m*, sgona *f*.
scorch *v* dadh.
score *v* cuir; sgrìob.
scorn *n* tàir *f*.
scornful *adj* tàireil.
Scotland *n* Alba *f*.
Scottish *adj* Albannach.
scour *v* nigh.
scourge *v* sgiùrs.
scout *n* beachdair *m*.
scowl *v* bi fo ghruaim.
scrape *v* sgrìob.
scratch *n* sgròbadh *m*. • *v* sgròb.
scream *n* sgreuch *m*. • *v* sgreuch.
scree *n* sgàirneach *f*.
script *n* sgrìobhadh *m*.
scroll *n* rolla *f*.
scrotum *n* clach-bhalg *m*.
scrub *v* nigh.
scruple *n* teagamh *m*.
scrupulous *adj* teagmhach.
scuffle *n* tuasaid *f*.
sculptor *n* deilbhear *m*.
sculpture *n* deilbheadh *m*.
scythe *n* speal *f*. • *v* speal.
sea level *n* àirde-mhara *f*.
sea *n* muir *m&f*.
seagull *n* faoileag *f*.
seal *n* ròn *m*; (*official*) seula *m*. • *v* seulaich.
seaport *n* longphort *m*.
sear *v* crannaich.
search *n* lorg *m*. • *v* lorg, rannsaich.
seashore *n* cladach *m*.
season *n* ràith *f*.
seasonable *adj* tràthail.
seaweed *n* feamainn *f*.
second *adj* dara.
secondary *adj* dàrnach.

secondary school *n* àrdsgoil *f*.
second-hand *adj* ath-dhìolta.
secondly *adv* anns an dara h-àite.
secrecy *n* cleith *f*.
secret *adj* dìomhair. • *n* rùn.
secretary *n* rùnaire *m*.
secretive *adj* ceilteach.
secretly *adv* gun fhiosda.
sect *n* dream *m*.
secular *adj* saoghalta.
secure *adj* seasgair. • *v* glais, glac.
security *n* dìon *m*.
seduce *v* truaill.
seduction *n* truailleadh *m*.
see *v* faic, seall, amhairc.
seed *n* sìol *m*. • *v* sìolaich.
seeing *n* lèirsinn *f*.
seek *v* iarr.
seer *n* fiosaiche *m*.
seize *v* glac, cuir làmh ann.
seldom *adv* gu tearc.
select *v* tagh.
self *pron*fhèin, (*after forms of I and we*) fhìn.
self-interest *n* fèin-bhuannachd *f*.
selfish *adj* fèineil.
sell *v* reic.
semiquaver *n* leth-chaman *m*.
semitone *n* leth-phong *m*.
senate *n* seanadh *m*.
send *v* cuir.
senile *adj* seantaidh.
senior *adj* as sine.
sensation *n* mothachadh *m*.
sense *n* ciall *f*.
senseless *adj* gun chiall.
sensible *adj* ciallach.
sensitive *adj* mothachail.
sensual *adj* feòlmhor.
sensuous *adj* ceudfaidheach.
sentence *n* rosgrann *m*; (*law*) binn *f*.

sentimental *adj* maoth-inntinneach.

separate *v* dealaich.

separation *n* dealachadh.

September *n* An t-Sultain *f.*

septic *adj* seaptaig.

sepulchral *adj* tuamach.

sequence *n* leanmhainn *m.*

serene *adj* soinneanta.

sergeant *n* sàirdeant *m.*

series *n* sreath *m.*

serious *adj* suidhichte.

serpent *n* nathair *f.*

serrated *adj* eagach.

servant *n* seirbheiseach *m.*

serve *v* fritheil.

service *n* seirbheis *f;* dleasnas *m.*

serviceable *adj* feumail.

session *n* seisean *m.*

set *v* suidhich, cuir.

setter *n* cù-luirg *m.*

settle *v* socraich.

settlement *n* suidheachadh; tuineachadh *m.*

seven *adj* seachd. • *n* (*people*) seachdnar.

seventeen *n* seachd deug.

seventh *adj* seachdamh.

seventy *n* (*old system*) trì fichead 's a deich; (*new system*) seachdad.

sever *v* sgar.

severe *adj* cruaidh.

severity *n* cruas *m.*

sew *v* fuaigh.

sewage *n* giodar *m.*

sewing *n* fuaigheal *m.*

sex *n* (*gender*) gnè *f;* (*act*) obairchraicinn *f,* feis *f.*

sextet *n* ceòl-sianar *m.*

sexual intercourse *n* cleamhnas *m.*

shade *n* sgàil *f.* • *v* sgàil.

shadow *n* faileas *m.*

shady *adj* dubharach.

shaggy *adj* molach.

shallow *adj* tana; faoin.

sham *adj* mealltach.

shame *n* nàire *f.* • *v* nàraich.

shameful *adj* nàr.

shape *n* cumadh *m.* • *v* cum, dealbh.

shapely *adj* cuimir.

share *n* roinn *f.* • *v* roinn, pàirtich.

shark *n* siorc *m.*

sharp *adj* geur.

sharpen *v* geuraich.

sharpness *n* gèire *f.*

shave *v* beàrr.

shawl *n* seàla *f.*

she *pron* i, (*emphatic*) ise.

shear *v* rùsg.

shearing *n* rùsgadh *m.*

sheath *n* truaill *f.*

shed[1] *n* bothan *m.*

shed[2] *v* dòirt.

sheep *n* caora *f.*

sheep-dog *n* cù-chaorach.

sheet *n* duilleag *f.*

sheiling *n* àirigh *f.*

shelf *n* sgeilp *f;* (*rock*) sgeir *f.*

shellfish *n* maorach *m.*

shelter *n* dìon *m.*

shepherd *n* cìobair *m.*

sheriff *n* siorraidh *m.*

Shetland *n* Sealtainn *m.*

shield *n* sgiath *f.* • *v* dìon.

shine *v* deàlraich.

shinty *n* iomain *f.*

shinty stick *n* caman *m.*

ship *n* long *f.*

shipwreck *n* long-bhriseadh *m.*

shire *n* siorrachd *f.*

shirt *n* lèine *f.*

shiver v crith.
shoal n bogha; sgaoth m.
shock n sgannradh m. • v criothnaich.
shoe n bròg f.
shoelace n barrall f.
shoemaker n greusaiche m.
shoot v tilg, loisg; (grow) fàs.
shop n bùth f.
shore n tràigh f.
short adj goirid.
shortage n dìth m.
shorten v giorraich.
shortly adv a dh'aithghearr.
shorts npl briogais ghoirid f.
short-sighted adj geàrr-sheallach.
short-wave n geàrr-thonnach m.
shot n urchair f.
shoulder n gualainn f.
shout n glaodh m.
shove n putadh m. • v put.
show v seall.
shower n fras f.
shred n mìr m.
shriek n sgread m.
shrimp n carran m.
shrink v seac.
shrub n preas m.
shudder v criothnaich.
shuffle v tarraing; (cards) measgaich.
shut v druid, dùin. • adj dùinte.
shy adj sochaireach.
sick adj tinn.
sickness n tinneas m.
side n taobh m.
sidelong adv air fhiaradh.
sideways adv an comhair a thaoibh.
siege n sèisd f.
sieve n criathar m.
sigh v leig osna.

sight n sealladh m; lèirsinn f.
sign n comharradh m.
signature n ainm m.
significant adj brìgheil.
signpost n post-seòlaidh m.
silence n sàmhchair f, tosd m.
silent adj tosdach.
silk n sìoda m.
sill n sòlla f.
silly adj gòrach.
silver n airgead m.
similar adj coltach.
simple adj sìmplidh.
simplify v sìmplich.
simultaneous adj còmhla.
sin n peacadh m. • v peacaich.
since conj a chionn 's gu. • prep o, o chionn.
sincere adj onorach.
sing v seinn, gabh òran.
singer n seinneadair m.
single adj singilte.
singular adj sònraichte.
sinister adj droch thuarach.
sink n since f. • v cuir fodha; rach fodha.
sip v gabh balgam.
sister n piuthar f.
sister-in-law n piuthar-chèile f.
sit v suidh.
sitting room n seòmar-suidhe m.
six adj sia. • n (people) sianar.
sixteen adj/n sia deug m.
sixty adj/n (old system) trì fichead; (new system) seasgad.
size n meud m.
skate[1] n bròg-spèilidh f. • v spèil.
skate[2] n (fish) sgait f.
skeleton n cnàimhneach m.
skerry n sgeir f.
sketch n tarraing f.

ski v sgithich.
skid v sleamhnaich.
ski-lift n àrdaichear-ski m.
skill n sgil m.
skim v thoir uachdar dhe.
skin n craiceann m. • v feann.
skinny adj caol.
skip v leum.
skirmish n arrabhaig f.
skirt n sgiort f.
skull n claigeann m.
sky n adhar m.
Skye n An t-Eilean Sgitheanach m.
skylark n uiseag f.
slam v thoir slàr do.
slander n sgainneal m.
slant n claonadh m. • v claon.
slap n sgailc f.
slash v geàrr.
slate n sglèat m.
slaughter n marbhadh m.
slave n tràill f.
sledge n càrn-slaoid m.
sleek adj slìom.
sleep n cadal m.
sleepy adj cadalach.
sleet n flin m.
sleeve n muinchill m.
slice n sliseag f.
slide v sleamhnaich.
slip n tuisleadh m. • v tuislich.
slipper n slapag f.
slippery adj sleamhainn.
slit n sgoltadh m.
slogan n sluagh-ghairm f.
slope n leathad m.
sloven n luid f.
slovenly adj luideach.
slow adj slaodach.
slowness n slaodachd f.
slur n tàir f; (speech) slugadh m.

sly adj carach.
smack n sglais f.
small adj beag.
smart adj tapaidh.
smattering n bloigh eòlais m.
smear v smiùr.
smell n fàileadh m. • v feuch fàileadh.
smile n snodha-gàire m. • v dèan snodha-gàire.
smith n gobha m.
smoke n ceò m. • v smocaig.
smoky adj ceòthach.
smooth adj mìn.
smoothe v mìnich.
smother v mùch.
smoulder v cnàmh-loisg.
smuggle v dèan cùl-mhùtaireachd.
smuggler n cùl-mhùtaire m.
snack n blasad bìdh m.
snake n nathair f.
snatch v glac.
sneak v snàig.
sneer v dèan fanaid.
sneeze v dèan sreothart.
sniff n boladh m. • v gabh boladh.
snipe n naosg m.
snivel v smùch.
snob n sodalan m.
snooze n norrag f.
snore v dèan srann.
snout n soc m.
snow n sneachd m. • v cuir sneachd.
snowdrift n cith m.
snug adj còsach.
snuggle v laigh dlùth ri.
so adv cho; mar seo; mar sin.
soak v drùidh.
soap n siabann m.
soapy adj làn siabainn.
sober adj stuama; sòbair.

sociable adj cuideachdail.

socialism n sòisealachas f.

society n comann m.

sock n socais f.

sod n fòid f.

soft adj bog.

soften v bogaich.

softness n buige f.

software n bathar bog m.

soil n ùir f. • v salaich.

solar adj na grèine.

soldier n saighdear m.

sole n bonn na coise m; (fish) lèabag m.

solemn adj sòlaimte.

solicit v aslaich.

solicitor n neach-lagha m.

solid adj teann.

solidarity n dlùthachd f.

solitude n uaigneas m.

solo n òran aon-neach m.

soloist n òranaiche m.

soluble adj so-sgaoilte.

solve v fuasgail.

solvent adj comasach air pàigh-eadh.

some pron cuid, feadhainn; pàirt.

somebody n cuideigin m.

somehow adv air dòigh air choreigin.

something n rudeigin m.

sometime adv uaireigin.

sometimes adv air uairibh.

somewhere adv an àiteigin.

son n mac m.

son-in-law n cliamhainn m.

soon adv a dh'aithghearr.

sophisticated adj ionnsaichte.

sordid adj suarach.

sore n creuchd m. • adj goirt.

sorrow n bròn m.

sorry adj duilich.

sort n seòrsa m. • v seòrsaich.

soul n anam m.

sound n fuaim m. • v seirm, seinn.

soup n eanraich f, n brot m.

sour adj geur.

south adj/n deas f.

southerly adj/adv deas, à deas.

sow n cràin f.

space n rùm m.

space probe n taisgealadh fànais m.

spacious adj farsaing.

Spain n An Spàinn f.

spaniel n cù-eunaich m.

Spanish n Spàinnis f.

spare v caomhainn.

spark n sradag f.

sparkle v lainnrich.

spawn v sìolaich.

speak v bruidhinn.

spear n sleagh f.

special adj àraidh.

species n seòrsa m.

spectacles npl speuclairean.

spectre n tannasg m.

speech n (language) cainnt f; òraid f.

speed n luas m.

speed v luathaich.

spell v litrich.

spend v caith.

spider n damhan-allaidh m.

spill v dòirt.

spin v snìomh.

spine n cnàimh-droma f.

spinning wheel n cuibhle-shnìomh f.

spirit n spiorad m.

spirited adj misneachail.

spit v tilg smugaid.

spite n gamhlas m.

splendid adj greadhnach.

split v sgoilt.

spoil v mill.

spoon n spàin f.

sporran n sporan m.

sport n spòrs f.

spot n ball m.

spouse n cèile m.

spreadsheet n duilleag-cleithe f.

spree n daorach f.

Spring n earrach m.

spring n fuaran m; leum m.

spume n cathadh-mara m.

spur v spor.

spy n beachdair m.

squalid adj sgreamhail.

squall n sgal m.

square adj ceithir-cheàrnach. • n ceàrnag f.

squash v brùth.

squat adj cutach.

squeak n bìog m.

squirrel n feòrag f.

squirt v steall.

stable[1] adj bunailteach.

stable[2] n stàball m.

stag n damh m.

stair n staidhre f.

stale adj cruaidh; goirt.

stalk n gas f.

stallion n àigeach m.

stammer v bruidhinn gagach.

stamp n stampa f; (embossing) stàmpa f.

stand v seas, stad.

standstill n stad m.

star n rionnag, reul f.

starboard n bòrd-beulaibh m.

stare v spleuchd.

starfish n crosgan m.

starry adj rionnagach.

start v clisg; (motor) cuir a dhol.

starvation n goirt f.

state[1] n staid f; (country) stàit f.

state[2] v cuir an cèill.

station n stèisean m.

statue n ìomhaigh f.

stature n àirde f.

stave n earran f; cliath f.

stay n stad m. • v fuirich.

steak n staoig f.

steal v goid.

steam n toit f.

steel n stàilinn f.

steep adj cas.

steer v stiùir.

step n ceum m.

sterile adj seasg.

stern[1] adj cruaidh.

stern[2] n deireadh m.

stick[1] n maide m.

stick[2] v sàth; (adhere) lean.

stiffen v ragaich.

still[1] adv fhathast; an dèidh sin.

still[2] n poit-dhubh f.

sting n gath m. • v guin.

stink n tòchd m.

stir v gluais.

stitch n grèim m.

stocking n stocainn f.

stomach n stamag f.

stone n clach f.

stool n stòl m.

stop v stad.

store v stòir.

storehouse n taigh-stòir m.

stork n corra bhàn f.

storm n doineann, stoirm f.

stormy adj stoirmeil.

story n sgeul m.

stove n stòbha f.

straight adj dìreach.

strain[1] n teannachadh m; (mental) uallach.

strain² *v* teannaich; (*filter*) sìolaidh.

strange *adj* iongantach.

stranger *n* coigreach *m*.

strath *n* srath *m*.

straw *n* connnlach *f*.

strawberry *n* subh-làir *m*.

streaky *adj* stiallach.

stream *n* sruth *m*.

street *n* sràid *f*.

strength *n* neart *m*.

stretch *v* sìn.

strict *adj* teann.

stride *n* sìnteag *f*.

strike *v* buail; (*work*) rach air stailc.

string *n* sreang *f*; teud *f*.

stringed *adj* teudaichte.

stroke *v* slìog.

stroll *v* siubhail.

strong *adj* làidir.

struggle *n* gleac *m*. • *v* gleac.

stubble *n* asbhuain *f*.

stubborn *adj* rag.

stuff *n* stuth *m*.

stupid *adj* baoghalta.

sturdy *adj* bunanta.

sty *n* fail-mhuc *f*.

stye *n* leamhnagan *m*.

style *n* modh *m*.

stylish *adj* baganta.

subject *adj* umhal, fo smachd. • *v* ceannsaich.

sublime *adj* òirdheirc.

submit *v* gèill.

subside *v* traogh.

subsidy *n* còmhnadh *m*.

substance *n* stuth *m*; brìgh *f*.

substitute *v* cuir an ionad.

subtle *adj* seòlta.

subtract *v* thoir o.

succeed *v* soirbhich; lean.

successful *adj* soirbheachail.

such *adj/pron* a leithid de, dhen t-seòrsa.

suck *v* deoghail.

suckle *v* thoir cìoch.

sudden *adj* grad.

suddenly *adv* gu h-obann.

sue *v* tagair.

suffer *v* fuiling.

sufferer *n* fulangaiche *m*.

sufficient *adj* leòr.

sugar *n* siùcar *m*.

suggest *v* mol, comhairlich.

suicide *n* fèin-mhort *m*.

suit *n* deise *f*. • *v* freagair.

suitable *adj* freagarrach.

sum *n* àireamh, suim *f*.

summer *n* samhradh *m*.

summit *n* mullach *m*.

summon *v* gairm.

sun *n* grian *f*.

sunbathe *v* blian.

Sunday *n* DiDòmhnaich *m*, Là na Sàbaid *m*.

sunny *adj* grianach.

sunrise *n* èirigh na grèine *f*.

sunset *n* laighe na grèine *m*.

supernatural *adj* os-nàdarrach.

superstition *n* saobh-chràbadh *m*.

supper *n* suipear *f*.

supple *adj* sùbailte.

supply *v* sòlaire ù.

support *v* cùm taic ri.

suppose *v* saoil.

suppress *v* cùm fodha.

supreme *adj* sàr.

sure *adj* cinnteach.

surely *adv* gun teagamh.

surface *n* uachdar *m*.

surge *v* brùchd.

surgeon *n* làmh-leigh *m*.

surgery *n* (*doctor's*) lèigh-lann *m*.

surly *adj* iargalta.
surname *n* sloinneadh *m*.
surplus *n* còrr *m*.
surprise *n* iongnadh *m*. • *v* cuir iongnadh air.
surprising *adj* neònach.
surrender *n* gèilleadh *m*.
surround *v* cuartaich.
survive *v* mair beò.
suspect *v* cuir an amharas.
suspend *v* croch.
suspense *n* teagamh *m*.
suspension bridge *n* drochaid crochaidh *f*.
suspicious *adj* amharasach.
swallow[1] *v* sluig.
swallow[2] *n* gòbhlan-gaoithe *m*.
swamp *n* fèith *f*.
swan *n* eala *f*.
swarm *v* sgaothaich.

swear *v* mionnaich.
sweat *n* fallas *m*. • *v* cuir fallas de.
swede *n* (*neep*) snèip *f*.
Sweden *n* An t-Suain *f*.
sweep *v* sguab.
sweet *adj* milis.
sweetheart *n* eudail *f*; leannan *f*.
sweeties *npl* siùcairean.
swim *v* snàmh.
swimming pool *n* amar-snàimh *m*.
swing *n* dreallag *f*.
switch *n* suidse *f*.
sword *n* claidheamh *m*.
symbol *n* samhla *m*.
symbolic *adj* samhlachail.
sympathetic *adj* co-mhothachail.
sympathise *v* co-mhothaich.
syringe *n* steallaire *m*.
syrup *n* siorap *f*.
system *n* siostam *m*.

T

table *n* bòrd; clàr *m*.
tablet *n* pile *f*; clàr *m*.
tacit *adj* gun bhruidhinn.
taciturn *adj* dùinte.
tack *n* tacaid *f*.
tacket *n* tacaid *f*.
tacksman *n* neach-baile *m*.
tadpole *n* ceann-pholan *m*.
tail *n* earball *m*.
taint *v* truaill.
take *v* gabh, thoir.
tale *n* sgeulachd *f*.
talent *n* tàlann *m*.
talk *v* bruidhinn.
tall *adj* àrd.
tame *adj* calla. • *v* callaich.
tangle *n* sàs *m*; (*seaweed*) stamh *m*.

tanker *n* tancair *m*.
tantalise *v* tog dòchas.
tap *n* goc *m*.
taper *v* dèan caol.
tapestry *n* grèis-bhrat *m*.
target *n* targaid *f*.
tart[1] *adj* searbh.
tart[2] *n* pithean *m*.
task *n* obair *f*.
taste *v* blais.
tasty *adj* blasta.
tawny *adj* lachdann.
tawse *n* stràic *m*.
tax *v* leag cìs.
tea *n* teatha, tì *f*.
teach *v* teasgaig.
teacher *n* teagasgar, tìdsear *m*.

teach-in *n* seisean connsachaidh *m*.

teacup *n* cupan teatha *m*.

team *n* sgioba *m*.

tear *n* deur *m*; (*rip*) sracadh *m*.

tease *v* farranaich.

tedious *adj* liosda.

teenager *n* deugaire *m*.

telephone *n* fòn *m*.

television *n* teilebhisean *m*.

tell *v* innis.

temper *n* nàdar *m*.

temperament *n* càil *f*.

temperature *n* teodhachd *f*.

tempest *n* doineann *f*.

temple *n* teampall *m*.

temporary *adj* sealach.

tempt *v* buair.

ten *adj/n* deich; (*persons*) deichnear.

tenacious *adj* leanailteach.

tenant *n* gabhaltach *m*.

tender *adj* maoth.

tennis *n* cluich-cneutaig *f*.

tent *n* teanta *f*.

tenth *n* an deicheamh earrann *f*.

term *n* (*time*) teirm *f*; (*word*) briathar *m*.

tern *n* steàrnan *m*.

terrier *n* abhag *f*.

terrorism *n* oillteachas *m*.

test *n* deuchainn *f*.

testament *n* tiomnadh *m*.

testicle *n* magairle *m*, clach *f*.

than *conj* na.

thank *v* thoir taing.

thankful *adj* taingeil.

thanks *npl* tapadh leat, tapadh leibh; taing *f*.

that *adj/pron* sin; (*distant*) siud, (*after noun*) ud. • *conj* gu(n). • *rel part* a. • *adv* a chionn, do brìgh.

thatch *n* tughadh *m*.

thaw *v* dèan aiteamh.

the *art* (*sing*) an, am, a', na (h-); (*plural*) nan, nam.

theft *n* meirle *m*.

their *pron* (*with inalienables*) an, am; (*with alienables*) ... aca.

them *pron* iad, (*emphatic*) iadsan.

themselves *pron* iad fhèin.

then *adv* an-sin; an dèidh sin; an uairsin.

thence *adv* às a sin.

theory *n* beachd *m*.

therapy *n* leigheas *m*.

there *adv* an-sin; (*distant*) an-siud.

thereby *adv* le sin.

therefore *adv* uime sin.

these *pron* iad seo.

they *pron* iad, (*emphatic*) iadsan.

thick *adj* tiugh.

thief *n* meirleach *m*.

thigh *n* sliasaid *f*.

thin *adj* tana.

thing *n* nì, rud *m*.

think *adj* smaoinich.

third *adj* treas.

thirst *n* pathadh *m*. • *v* bi pàiteach.

thirteen *adj/n* trì deug.

thirty *adj/n* (*old system*) deich ar fhichead; (*new system*) trithead.

this *pron* seo.

thistle *n* cluaran *m*.

thorny *adj* driseach.

those *pron* iad sin.

though *conj* ge, ged.

thought *n* smaoin *f*.

thousand *adj/n* mìle *f*.

thrash *v* slaic; (*corn*) buail.

threat *n* bagairt *f*.

threaten *v* bagair.

three *adj/n* trì; (*persons*) triùir.

thrilling *adj* gaoireil.

throat *n* amhach *f*.

through *prep* tro. • *pron* **through me** tromham; **through you** (*sing*) tromhad; **through him, it** troimhe; **through her** troimhpe; **through us** tromhainn; **through you** tromhaibh; **through them** tromhpa.

throw *v* tilg.

thrush *n* smeòrach *m*.

thumb *n* òrdag *f*.

thunder *n* tàirneanach *m*.

thunderous *adj* torranach.

Thursday *n* DiarDaoin *m*.

thus *adv* mar seo.

ticket *n* bileag *f*.

ticking *n* diogadaich *f*.

tide *n* seòl-mara *m*.

tidy *v* sgioblaich.

tiger *n* tìgeir *m*.

till *prep* gu; (*up until*) gu ruig.

tiller *n* ailm *f*.

time *n* àm *m*.

timely *adj* an deagh àm.

timeous *adj* an deagh àm.

tinker *n* ceàrd *m*.

tiny *adj* crìon.

tipsy *adj* froganach.

tired *adj* sgìth.

tiresome *adj* sgìtheachail.

title *n* tiotal *m*.

to *prep* (*to, for*) do • *pron* **to me** dhomh; **to you** (*sing*) dhut; **to him, it** dhà; **to her** dhi; **to us** dhuinn; **to you** dhuibh; **to them** dhaibh; (*towards*) gu • *pron* **to me** thugam; **to you** (*sing*) thugad; **to him, it** thuige; **to her** thuice; **to us** thugainn; **to you** thugaibh; **to them** thuca; (*with verbs of speaking and looking*) ri • *pron* **to me**

rium; **to you** (*sing*) riut; **to him, it** ris; **to her** rithe; **to us** ruinn; **to you** ruibh; **to them** riutha.

toad *n* muile-mhàg *f*.

toast *v* òl deoch-slàinte; tostaig.

tobacco *n* tombaca *m*.

today *adv* an-diugh.

together *adv* le chèile, còmhla.

toilet *n* taigh-beag *m*; (*preparation*) sgeadachadh *m*.

tomb *n* tuam *m*.

tomorrow *adv* a-màireach.

tone *n* fonn *m*; tòna *f*.

tongue *n* teanga *m*.

tonight *adv* a-nochd.

too *adv* cuideachd.

tool *n* inneal *m*.

tooth *n* fiacail *f*.

top *n* mullach, uachdar *m*.

torch *n* leus *m*.

torrent *n* bras-shruth *m*.

tortoise *n* sligeanach *m*.

Tory *n* Tòraidh *m*.

toss *v* luaisg.

total *adj* iomlan.

touch *v* bean do, suath ann.

tough *adj* righinn.

tour *n* turas *m*.

tourists *npl* luchd-turais.

towards *prep* a dh'ionnsaigh • *pron* **towards me** 'gam ionnsaigh; **towards you** (*sing*) 'gad ionnsaigh; **towards him, it** 'ga ionnsaigh; **towards her** 'ga h-ionnsaigh; **towards us** 'gar n-ionnsaigh; **towards you** 'gur n-ionnsaigh; **towards them** 'gan ionnsaigh.

tower *n* tùr *m*.

town *n* baile *m*.

toy *n* dèideag *f*.

trace v lorg.
track v lorg.
trade n malairt f.
tradition n tradisean m.
train n trèana f; (retinue) muinntir f. • v àraich.
traitor n brathadair m.
trance n neul m.
transfer v thoir thairis.
transient adj diombuan.
translate v eadar-theangaich.
transmitter n crann-sgaoilidh m.
transparent adj trìd-shoilleir.
trap n ribe f. • v rib.
travel n siubhal m. • v siubhail.
tray n sgàl m.
treasure n ionmhas m. • v taisg.
treat n cuirm f. • v riaraich.
tree n craobh f.
tremor n crith f.
trespass n (misdeed) peacadh m. • v inntrig gun chead.
trews npl triubhas m.
trial n deuchainn f.
tribe n treubh f, sliochd m.
tributary n leas-abhainn f.
trick n car m.
trim adj cuimir.
trip v tuislich.
triumph n gàirdeachas m.
triumph v thoir buaidh.
trivial adj suarach.
trot v dèan trotan.
trouble n dragh f. • v cuir dragh air.

trousers n briogais f.
trout n breac m.
true adj fìor.
trump card n buadh-chairt f.
trust n earbsa f. • v earb à.
truth n fìrinn f.
try v feuch; cuir gu deuchainn.
tub n balan m.
Tuesday n DiMàirt m.
tumble v tuit, leag.
tumult n iorghail f.
tune n fonn, port m. • v gleus.
tuneful adj fonnmhor.
tup n reithe m.
turf n sgrath, fòd f.
turn v tionndaidh; cuir air falbh.
turtle n turtur f.
tutor n (guardian) taoitear m.
tweak v teannaich.
tweed n clò m.
twelfth adj dara deug.
twelve adj/n dà dheug.
twentieth adj ficheadamh.
twenty adj/m fichead.
twice adv dà uair.
twilight n eadar-sholas m.
twin n leth-aon m.
twist v toinn.
two adj/n dà; (persons) dithis.
two-faced adj beulach.
typical adj dualach.
typography n clò-bhualadh m.
tyrant n aintighearna m.
tyro n foghlamaiche m.

U

udder *n* ùth *m.*

ugliness *n* grànndachd *f.*

ugly *adj* grànnda.

ulcer *n* neasgaid *f.*

ultimate *adj* deiridh.

umbrella *n* sgàilean *m.*

unable *adj* neo-chomasach.

unaccustomed *adj* neo-chleachdte.

unanimous *adj* aon-inntinneach.

unarmed *adj* neo-armaichte.

unavoidable *adj* do-sheachanta.

unaware *adj* gun fhios.

unbolt *v* thoir an crann de.

uncle *n* (*paternal*) bràthair-athar; (*maternal*) bràthair-màthar *m.*

uncomfortable *adj* anshocrach.

uncommon *adj* neo-gnàthach.

unconditional *adj* gun chùmh-nantan.

uncork *v* às-àrcaich.

unction *n* ungadh *m.*

undecided *adj* neo-chinnteach.

under *prep* fo • *pron* **under me** fodham; **under you** (*sing*) fodhad; **under him, it** fodha; **under her** foidhpe; **under us** fodhainn; **under you** fodhaibh; **under them** fodhpa.

undergo *v* fuiling.

underground *adj* fo thalamh.

underneath *adv* fodha. • *prep* fo.

understand *v* tuig.

underwear *n* fo-aodach *m.*

undeserved *adj* neo-thoillteanach.

undistinguished *adj* neo-chomharr-aichte.

undisturbed *adj* neo-bhuairte.

undo *v* fuasgail.

unemployed *adj* gun chosnadh.

unequal *adj* neo-ionnan.

uneven *adj* corrach.

unexpected *adj* gun dùil.

unfair *adj* mì-cheart.

unfinished *adj* neo-chrìochnaichte.

unfold *v* fosgail.

unfriendly *adj* neo-chàirdeil.

unfurl *v* sgaoil.

ungrateful *adj* mì-thaingeil.

uniform *n* culaidh *f.*

unimportant *adj* neo-chudromach.

uninhabited *adj* neo-àitichte.

union *n* aonadh *m.*

unique *adj* air leth.

unit *n* aonad *m.*

unity *n* aonachd *f.*

universal *adj* coitcheann.

universe *n* domhan *m.*

university *n* oilthigh *m.*

unless *conj* mur, mura.

unlike *adj* neo-choltach.

unload *v* thoir an luchd de.

unmask *v* leig ris.

unmusical *adj* neo-cheòlmhor.

unnecessary *adj* neo-fheumail.

unoccupied *adj* bàn.

unpack *v* fosgail.

unpardonable *adj* gun leisgeul.

unpleasant *adj* mì-thaitneach.

unpopular *adj* neo-ionmhainn.

unpremeditated *adj* gun ro-smuain.

unproductive *adj* neo-thorrach.

unreal *adj* neo-fhìor.

unreasonable *adj* mì-reusanta.

unrest *n* aimhreit *f.*

unripe *adj* an-abaich.
unsafe *adj* mì-shàbhailte.
unsatisfactory *adj* mì-shàsail.
unsightly *adj* duaichnidh.
unsuccessful *adj* mì-shealbhar.
unsuitable *adj* neo-iomchaidh.
untidy *adj* luideach.
untie *v* fuasgail.
until *adv* gu; (*up until*) gu ruig.
unto *prep* do, gu.
unused *adj* neo-chleachdte.
unusual *adj* neo-àbhaisteach.
unwanted *adj* gun iarraidh.
unwieldy *adj* trom.
unwise *adj* neo-ghlic.
unworthy *adj* neo-airidh.
unwrap *v* fuasgail.
up *prep* suas. • *adv* suas; a-nìos; shuas.
upbringing *n* togail *f*.
uphill *adv* ri bruthach.
uphold *v* cùm suas.
upland *n* aonach *f*.
upon *prep* air, air muin.
upper *adj* uachdrach.
upright *adj* dìreach; onorach.

uproar *n* gleadhar *m*.
upset *n* cur tro-chèile *m*.
upshot *n* co-dhùnadh *m*.
upside-down *adj/adv* bun os cionn.
upstairs *adv* (*loction*) shuas staidhre; (*motion*) suas staidhre.
upward *adv* suas.
urban *adj* cathaireil.
urge *v* spàrr.
urgency *n* (cùis-)èiginn *f*.
urgent *adj* dian.
urinal *n* ionad-mùin *m*.
us *pron* sinn, (*emphatic*) sinne.
usage *n* àbhaist *f*.
use *n* feum *m*. • *v* gnàthaich, dèan feum de.
useful *adj* feumail.
usefulness *n* feumalachd *f*.
useless *adj* gun fheum.
usual *adj* gnàthach.
usurp *v* glèidh gun chòir.
uterus *n* machlag *f*.
utmost *adj* as motha
utter[1] *v* abair, labhair.
utter[2] *adj* coilionta; dearg.
utterly *adv* gu tur.

V

vacancy *n* beàrn *m*.
vacant *adj* falamh.
vaccinate *v* cuir breac a' chruidh air.
vagabond *n* neach-fuadain *m*.
vagina *n* faighean *f*.
vague *adj* neo-dheimhinn.
vain *adj* dìomhain.
vale *n* srath *m*.
valid *adj* tàbhachdach.
valley *n* gleann, srath *m*.

valour *n* gaisge *f*.
valuable *adj* prìseil.
value *n* luach *m*.
value-added tax *n* cìs luach-leasaichte *f*.
valve *n* pìob-chòmhla *f*.
van *n* vana *f*.
vandal *n* creachadair, milltear *m*.
vanish *v* rach às an t-sealladh.
vapour *n* deatach *f*.
varied *adj* iomadh.

variegated *adj* breac.
variety *n* atharrachadh *m*.
various *adj* iomadh.
vary *v* caochail.
vase *n* vàsa *m*.
veal *n* laoigh-fheòil *f*.
vegetable *n* glasraich *f*.
vegetarian *n* feòil-sheachnair *m*.
vegetation *n* fàs *m*.
vehement *adj* dealasach.
vehicle *n* carbad *m*.
veil *n* sgàile *f*. • *v* còmhdaich.
vein *n* cuisle *f*.
velvet *n* meileabhaid *f*.
vengeance *n* dìoghaltas *m*.
venison *n* sitheann *m*.
venom *n* nimh *m*.
venture *n* tuaiream *m*.
venue *n* làthair *m*.
verdict *n* breith *f*.
verge *n* oir *f*.
verify *v* dearbh.
vermin *npl* mìolan *m*.
vernacular *n* cainnt na dùthcha *f*.
verse *n* dànachd *f*; (*stanza*) rann *m*.
version *n* innse *f*.
vertical *adj* dìreach.
vertigo *n* tuaineal *m*.
very *adv* glè; (*truly*) fìor.
vest *n* peitean *m*.
vestige *n* lorg *f*.
vet *n* veat *m*.
vex *v* buair.
viable *adj* so-obrachadh.
vibrate *v* crith, cuir air chrith.
vicarious *adj* ionadach.
vice *n* dubhailc *f*; (*tool*) teanchair *m*.
victim *n* ìobairteach *m*.
victor *n* buadhair *m*.
victory *n* buaidh *f*.

video recorder *n* chlàraichear bhidio *m*.
view *n* sealladh *m*; (*opinion*) beachd *m*. • *v* gabh sealladh; beachdaich.
viewpoint *n* àite-seallaidh *m*; ionad-beachd *m*.
vigil *n* faire *f*.
vigour *n* spionnadh *m*.
vile *adj* gràineil.
village *n* clachan *m*.
villain *n* slaoightear *m*.
vindicate *v* fìreanaich.
vine *n* crann-fìona *m*.
vintage *n* fìon-fhoghar *m*.
violence *n* fòirneart *m*.
violent *adj* fòirneartach.
violin *n* fidheall *f*.
violinist *n* fidhleir *m*.
viper *n* nathair-nimhe *f*.
virgin *n* maighdeann, òigh *f*.
virginity *n* maighdeannas *m*.
virile *adj* fearail.
virility *n* fearachas *m*.
virtual *adj* da-rìribh.
virtue *n* subhailc *f*.
virtuous *adj* beusach.
virus *n* bioras *m*.
visibility *n* lèireas *m*.
visible *adj* faicsinneach.
vision *n* fradharc *m*; (*mental*) bruadar *m*, taibhs *f*.
visit *v* tadhail.
visitor *n* aoigh *m*.
visual *adj* fradharcach.
vital *adj* riatanach; beò.
vitality *n* beathalachd *f*.
vivacious *adj* aigeannach.
vocal *adj* guthach.
vocalist *n* òranaiche, seinneadair *m*.
vocation *n* gairm *f*.

voice n guth m.
void adj fàs. • n fàsalachd f.
voluble adj deas-chainnteach.
voluntary adj toileach.
vomit n sgeith m. • v sgeith.
vote n bhòta f. • v thoir bhòta.

voucher n fianais f.
vow n bòid f. • v bòidich.
voyage n turas-mara m.
voyager n taisdealaich m.
vulgar adj gràisgeil.
vulnerable adj so-leònte.

W

wade v siubhail tro.
wafer n abhlan m.
wag v crath.
wager n geall m.
wagon n cairt f.
wagtail n breacan-buidhe m.
wail v dèan caoineadh.
waist n meadhan m.
wait v feith; fritheil.
waitress n caileag-fhrithealaidh f.
wake n taigh-fhaire m. • v dùisg.
waken v dùisg.
Wales n A' Chuimrigh f.
walk n cuairt f. • v coisich.
walking stick n bata m.
wall n balla m.
walrus n each-mara m.
wan adj glas-neulach.
wander v rach air seachran.
wanderer n seachranaiche m.
want n dìth m; bochdainn f. • v iarr;
thig geàrr.
war n cogadh m.
warble v ceileirich.
wardrobe n preas-aodaich m.
warehouse n tasglann m.
warlike adj coganta.
warm adj blàth.
warmth n blàths m.
warn v thoir rabhadh.
warren n broclach f.

warship n long-chogaidh f.
wart n foinne f.
wary adj faicilleach.
wash v nigh.
washing n nigheadaireachd f.
wasp n speach f.
waste n ana-caitheamh m. • v cosg,
caith.
watch n uaireadair; faire m. • v
dèan faire.
watchdog n cù-faire m.
water n uisge m. • v uisgich.
waterfall n eas m.
water-power n neart-uisge m.
waterproof adj uisge-dhìonach.
watershed n uisge-dhruim m.
watertight adj dìonach.
waulk v luaidh.
waulking n luadhadh m.
wave n tonn m. • v smèid; crath.
wax n cèir f.
way n slighe f.
waylay v dèan feall-fhalach.
we pron sinn, (emphatic) sinne.
weak adj lag.
weaken v lagaich.
weave v figh.
weaver n breabadair m.
web n eige, lìon f.
webbed adj eigeil.
wed v pòs.

wedding n banais f.
Wednesday n DiCiadain m.
weed n luibh m. • v priog.
week n seachdain f.
weep v guil.
weigh v cothromaich.
weight n cudthrom m.
weir n cairidh f.
welcome n fàilte f. • v fàiltich.
well[1] adj math; faillain. • adv gu
 math.
well[2] n tobar m.
west adj siar. • n an iar f. • adv an
 iar.
westerly adj on iar.
westward adv chun na h-àirde an
 iar.
wet adj fliuch.
whale n muc-mhara f.
what interr pron dè? (emphatic) gu
 dè? • rel pron na.
wheat n cruithneachd m.
wheel n cuibhle f.
wheeze v dèan pìochan.
whelk n faochag f.
when conj nuair. • interr pron
 cuine?
whence adv co às.
whenever adv gach uair.
where conj far. • interr pron càite?
whereas adv do bhrìgh gu.
whereby adv leis, leis a bheil.
whereupon adv leis sin.
wherever adv ge be ar bith càite.
whether adv co-dhiù. • pron cò aca.
which rel pron a, (neg) nach. • interr
 pron dè?, cò?
while conj fhad 's a. • n tacan m,
 greis f.
whin n conasg m.
whip n cuip f. • v sgiùrs.

whirlpool n cuairt-shlugan m.
whiskers npl feusag f.
whisky n uisge-beatha m.
whisper n cagar m. • v cagair.
whistle n feadag f. • v dèan fead.
white adj geal.
who rel pron a, (neg) nach. • interr
 pron cò?
whoever pron cò air bith.
whole adj slàn, iomlan.
wholefood adj slàn-bhiadh.
wholesale n mòr-reic m.
whoop n glaodh m.
whose interr pron cò leis?
why adv carson?
wick n siobhag f.
wicked adj olc.
wide adj leathann.
widow n banntrach f.
widower n banntrach m.
width n leud m.
wife n bean f.
wild adj fiadhaich.
wildcat n cat fiadhaich m.
wilderness n fàsach m.
will n toil f; (last) tiomnadh m.
willing adj toileach.
willow n seileach m.
willpower n neart toile m.
wily adj seòlta.
win v coisinn.
wind n gaoth f.
window n uinneag f.
windward n fuaradh m.
windy adj gaothach.
wine n fìon m.
wing n sgiath f.
wink v caog.
winter n geamhradh m. • v geamh-
 raich.
wintry adj geamhrachail.

wipe *v* suath.

wire *n* uèir *m*.

wiry *adj* seang.

wisdom *n* gliocas *m*.

wise *adj* glic.

wish *n* miann *m*. • *v* miannaich.

wit *n* toinisg *f*; eirmse *f*.

witch *n* bana-bhuidseach *f*.

with *prep* le fo • *pron* **with me** leam; **with you** (*sing*) leat; **with him, it** leis; **with her** leatha; **with us** leinn; **with you** leibh; **with them** leotha; (*together with*) còmhla ri.

wither *v* searg.

withered *adj* crìon.

within *adv* (*location*) a-staigh.

without *adv* (*location*) a-muigh. • *prep* (*with noun*) gun; (*with pronoun*) as aonais • *pron* **without me** as m' aonais; **without you** (*sing*) as d' aonais; **without him, it** as 'aonais; **without her** as a h-aonais; **without us** as ar n-aonais; **without you** (*pl*) as ur n-aonais; **without them** as an aonais;.

witness *n* fianais each*m*.

witty *adj* eirmseach.

wizard *n* draoidh *m*.

wolf *n* madadh-allaidh *m*.

woman *n* boireannach *f*.

womanly *adj* banail.

womb *n* machlag *f*.

wonder *n* iongnadh *m*; iongantas *m*. • *v* gabh iongantas.

woo *v* dèan suirghe.

wood *n* coille *f*; (*timber*) fiodh *f*.

woodland *n* fearann coillteach *m*.

woodlouse *n* reudan *m*.

woodwork *n* saoirsneachd *f*.

wool *n* clòimh *f*.

woollen *adj* de chlòimh.

word *n* facal *m*; (*bond*) gealladh *m*.

word processor *n* facladair *m*.

wordy *adj* briathrach.

work *n* obair *f*. • *v* oibrich.

worker *n* oibriche *m*.

workmanship *n* ealain *f*.

world *n* saoghal *m*.

worldly *adj* saoghalta.

world-wide web *n* lìonra domhanta *m*.

worm *n* cnuimh, durrag *f*.

worn *adj* caithte.

worry *n* dragh *m*. • *v* buair, dèan dragh do.

worse *adj* nas miosa.

worsen *v* fàs nas miosa.

worship *n* adhradh *m*.

worst *adj* as miosa.

worth *n* luach *m*. • *adj* fiù.

worthless *adj* gun fhiù.

worthy *adj* airidh.

wound *n* leòn *m*. • *v* leòn, lot.

wrangle *n* connsachadh *m*. • *v* connsaich.

wrap *v* paisg, fill.

wrapper *n* filleag *f*.

wrath *n* corraich *f*.

wrathful *adj* feargach.

wreath *n* blàth-fhleasg *f*.

wreck *n* long-bhriseadh *m*. • *v* sgrios.

wren *n* dreadhan-donn *m*.

wrench *v* spìon.

wrest *v* spìon.

wrestle *v* gleac.

wrestling *n* gleac *m*.

wring *v* fàisg.

wrinkle *n* preas *m*. • *v* preas.

wrist *n* caol an dùirn *m*.

wristwatch *n* uaireadair làimhe *m*.

write *v* sgrìobh.

writer *n* sgrìobhadair *m*.
writhe *v* snìomh.
writing *n* sgrìobhadh *m*.

wrong *adj* ceàrr; coireach. • *n* eucoir *f*.
wry *adj* cam.

XYZ

xenophobe *n* gall-gamhlasaiche *m*.
xenophobia *n* gall-gamhlas *m*.
X-ray *n* gath-x *m*.
yacht *n* iacht *f*.
yard *n* gàrradh *m*; (*length*) slat *f*.
yarn *n* sgeulachd *f*; (*thread*) snàth *f*.
yarrow *n* eàrr-thalmhainn *f*.
yawl *n* geòla *f*.
yawn *n* mèanan *m*. • *v* dèan mèananaich.
year *n* bliadhna *f*.
yearly *adj* gach bliadhna.
yearn *v* iarr gu làidir.
yearning *n* iarraidh *m*/*f*.
yeast *n* beirm *f*.
yellow *adj*/*n* buidhe *m*.
yelp *v* dèan tathann.
yes *adv* (*non-affirmative*) seadh (*affirmative replies repeat verb used in question*).
yesterday *adv* an-dè.
yet *adv* fhathast. • *conj* gidheadh, an dèidh sin, ach.
yew *n* iubhar *m*.
yield *v* gèill.
yoke *n* cuing *f*. • *v* beartaich.
yolk *n* buidheagan *m*.

yon *adv* thall, ud.
you *pron* (*sing*) thu, (*emphatic*) thusa; (*pl*) sibh, (*emphatic*) sibhse.
young *adj* òg.
youngster *n* òganach *m*.
your *pron* (*sing*) (*with inalienables*) do, (*before vowels*) d'; (*with alienables*) ... agad; (*pl*) (*with inalienables*) ur, (*before vowels*) ur n-; (*with alienables*) ... agaibh.
yourself *pron* thu fhèin.
yourselves *pron* sibh fhèin.
youth *n* òigear *m*; (*state*) òige *m*.
youthful *adj* ògail.
zeal *n* eud *m*.
zealous *adj* eudmhor.
zebra *n* asal-stiallach *f*.
zenith *n* bàrr *m*.
zero *n* neoni *f*.
zest *n* smior *m*.
zigzag *adj* lùbach.
zip *n* sip *f*.
zodiac *n* grian-chrios *m*.
zoo *n* sutha *f*.
zoology *n* ainmh-eòlas *m*.